THE ARMAGEDDON FACTOR

THE
ARMAGEDDON
FACTOR

THE RISE OF CHRISTIAN NATIONALISM IN CANADA

MARCI McDONALD

RANDOM HOUSE CANADA

www.randomhouse.ca

Random House Canada and colophon are registered trademarks.

Library and Archives Canada Cataloguing in Publication

McDonald, Marci
The Armageddon factor : the rise of Christian nationalism in Canada / Marci
McDonald.

Includes bibliographical references and index.

ISBN 978-0-307-35646-8

1. Christian conservatism—Canada. 2. Christianity and politics—
Canada. 3. Canada—Politics and government—2006–. I. Title.

FC640.M35 2010   322'.10971   C2009-905242-3

Design by Terri Nimmo

Printed in the United States of America

2 4 6 8 9 7 5 3 1

TO CLAIR

a saint in every sense of the word

CONTENTS

He shall have dominion also from sea to sea,
   And from the River to the ends of the earth.
Those who dwell in the wilderness will bow before Him,
   And His enemies will lick the dust.
                                    Psalm 72: 8–9

PREFACE

S he stared at me across the table as if I were out of my mind. A publisher had asked me to write a book on the rise of the Christian right in Canadian politics and, hearing the news, one of my closest friends was questioning my sanity for even contemplating such a task. "Why would you want to do that?" she asked. "Surely, you don't think that it can happen here. This is a profoundly different country than the United States."

To my surprise, she was hardly alone in that view. The book was to be an expansion of an article I'd written for the *Walrus* magazine shortly after Stephen Harper came to power, and in the course of researching it, I would hear the same argument from pundits and professors alike. As George W. Bush and his evangelical base lost their hold on power in the United States, swept into the annals of history on a wave of Obamamania that seemed to overwhelm the continent, commentators on both sides of the border offered up triumphal requiems for the religious right, the three-decade-old movement that had changed the fabric of American politics. In this country, where a new crop of evangelical leaders had begun to echo American rhetoric during the same-sex marriage debate, the elegies were riddled with even greater glee, underscored by an insistence that Canadians could never fall prey to such unseemly extremes of partisan piety.

For me, those dismissals had a familiar ring. During more than a decade in Washington, first as *Maclean's* bureau chief, later as a senior writer for *U.S. News & World Report*, I had repeatedly heard the same sort of assessments from academics and media analysts: the religious right was finished, kaput, a spent force at the ballot box, its leaders out of touch with the much more acceptable and tempered views of the masses. And each time, without exception, those assessments had been wrong.

When I had landed in the U.S. capital in the midst of Ronald Reagan's 1984 re-election campaign, I was intrigued by reports about Jerry Falwell's Moral Majority, which was credited with putting a television pitchman in the White House and seemed poised to repeat the feat. It struck me as a singularly exotic phenomenon, unlike anything that existed in Canada or Europe, my previous posting, and, determined to get a fix on it, I headed southwest to Lynchburg, Virginia, where Falwell presided over his twenty-thousand-member flock. Along U.S. Route 29, signs beckoned to storied Civil War battle sites, but it was only much later that I realized I was tracking the first skirmishes in a contemporary civil war unleashed by Falwell and his televangelical counterparts—a culture war that pitted Bible-believing fundamentalists against their mainline Christian brethren, liberal cities against the suburbs, and "values voters" against those who insisted on a strict separation between church and state.

Pulling up outside the massive white pillars of Falwell's Thomas Road Baptist Church, I was stunned to find a parking lot large enough for a mid-sized shopping mall jammed for a weeknight service. It was my first encounter with the role that megachurches had come to play in American life, doubling as de facto town squares for a sprawling exurban population adrift amid the alienating asphalt and strip malls that blanket the landscape.

It was also my introduction to a scriptural scenario I'd never heard back in Ontario's mainline Protestant pews. Slipping into a seat near the front of Falwell's immense blue-broadloomed sanctuary, I listened, enthralled, to the thunderous baritone he had honed to theatrical effect on the *Old-Time Gospel Hour* as he related his version of the Rapture— that mythic moment when some born-again Christians expect to be snatched up to salvation before the Battle of Armageddon. Only a single verse in St. Paul's first epistle to the Thessalonians hints at that apocalyptic plotline, but Falwell had no hesitation about fleshing it out in vivid, updated detail. The divine summons, he counselled, could ambush the faithful anytime, anywhere. No matter what believers were doing—even speeding along the highway at rush hour—they could find themselves suddenly wafting heavenward. Today, at the mere mention of the Rapture, Falwell's sermon flashes through my mind: driverless cars careening out of control in a cosmic expressway pileup.

As it turned out, I wasn't the only one captivated by his imagery. More than a decade later, San Diego pastor Timothy LaHaye and his writing partner, Jerry Jenkins, released *Left Behind*, the first of their best-selling potboilers depicting life on earth in the wake of the Rapture, which opens with exactly that scene of global traffic mayhem. A long-time pal of Falwell's, LaHaye had been one of the Republican strategists who devised the notion of tapping into evangelical discontent to expand the party's base, and then christened the resulting constituency the Moral Majority. But it was later in his *Left Behind* novels that he provided the rationale for the Christian right's sense of urgency about effecting political change—the conviction that, with Armageddon looming, the faithful have not a moment to lose in preparing the way for the Second Coming of Christ.

By the end of Reagan's presidency, some of America's star televangelists had been caught out in sex scandals that reduced them to the archetypes of hypocrisy once immortalized by Sinclair Lewis in *Elmer Gantry*. Falwell himself felt obliged to dissolve the Moral Majority and commentators lost no time in declaring the religious right history—an electoral flash in the pan ignited by Reagan's evil-empire rhetoric, which had finally run out of both enemies and credibility. But the ink was barely dry on those death notices when the media woke up to the news that Pat Robertson, the Christian Broadcasting Network mogul, had emerged as the wild card in the 1988 presidential race. As Robertson stormed the South, the panic within Republican circles was palpable: the *700 Club* host who claimed to receive personal commands from God stood only a few primaries away from becoming the party's nominee for the White House.

On a frigid February morning after the New Hampshire primary, I was among a gaggle of reporters who scrambled aboard Robertson's luxury jet for a flight to Florida, one of the states that would decide his electoral fate. In Miami, we were herded into the art-deco lobby of a chic South Beach hotel packed with Cuban Americans who had been bused in from across the city. Many of them appeared unable to understand more than a few words of English as they madly cheered "Go Pat, Go!" but what they did understand was Robertson's promise to mount another invasion of Cuba in the name of God and democracy, which he seemed to see as one and the same. In that improbable rally, two things became clear: the voters that Robertson could muster through his television empire outstripped the reach of any existing party apparatus, and his call for a return to traditional values included a no-holds-barred foreign policy that resonated far beyond the white-bread pews that had made up the bulk of Falwell's old following.

A decade after its inception, the American religious right had already metamorphosed into a vastly more complex and ideological mix, fuelled by immigrants with profoundly conservative worldviews. For them, the constitutional call for the separation of church and state carried no historical import. Many had fled brutal dictatorships and, like Reagan, they saw Big Government as the enemy and liberal causes, such as women's rights, as a threat to their precarious hold over restive modern families. When Pat Robertson and other televangelists preached the gospel of Christian nationalism, God and flag firmly entwined, that audience cheered the idea of a government run by conservative Christians according to the time-tested verities of the Bible, even if they didn't fully grasp its theocratic implications.

When Robertson's campaign flamed out, political analysts served up a new round of obituaries for the religious right, but once again, the reports of its death proved premature. Even as Robertson nursed a wounded ego, he was hatching his organizational revenge, hiring a fresh-faced young doctoral student named Ralph Reed to build a grass-roots evangelical network, focusing first on the takeover of school boards and town councils before ultimately commandeering the machinery of the Republican National Committee itself. That institutional coup took place almost entirely beneath the media's radar, and by the time it finally caught their attention, Reed's Christian Coalition controlled both houses of Congress and would later play a major role in putting George W. Bush in the White House, not once but twice.

In January 2009, as Bush left office with the economy and his scripturally inspired war on Iraq in tatters, the same pattern repeated itself: conventional wisdom once again pronounced the religious right on life support. But as the outrage over Barack Obama's pro-choice policies has shown, deeply held beliefs don't simply evaporate after a bad day at the ballot box. The conservative evangelical movement has so skillfully implanted itself in the American body politic that, regardless of its electoral fortunes, its most militant members are unlikely to be deterred from their mission to see the United States recreated as a Christian nation.

Even after California megapastor Rick Warren was anointed the new, more moderate voice of the religious right, hailed for shunning the old hot-button social issues in favour of fighting poverty and HIV/AIDS, the author behind the bestselling sensation *The Purpose Driven Life* failed to live up to his advance billing. At the very moment reporters were dispensing rosy predictions about the mellowing of the movement, Warren sent out a pastoral letter urging his twenty-thousand parishioners to vote for a 2008 California ballot initiative overturning the state's law permitting same-sex marriage. The new face of the religious right might be sporting a Hawaiian shirt and sermonizing in the laid-back language of self-help, but when it came to the core issues of the culture wars, it proved to be largely indistinguishable from the old.

For me, one of the shocks of returning to Canada in 2002 was the discovery that the rhetoric and militancy of that movement had spilled across the border. As tempers flared over gay rights and same-sex marriage, Canadian hotline shows sounded almost as inflammatory as those in the United States. Homegrown evangelical firebrands were emerging, spouting the same polarizing calls to the political barricades that I thought I had left behind in Washington. Astonishingly, they made no attempt to hide their ties to their American brethren, parading their coziness with Falwell and Robertson, and planting institutional bases in Ottawa just as their counterparts had done three decades earlier in the U.S. capital. When friends and colleagues waved off the suggestion that a religious right could take root in this country's famously centrist soil, I couldn't help but recall similar disclaimers during the 1980s in the *New York Times* and the *Washington Post*. The Canadian version might not yet resemble its American model, but it was bridging that thirty-year gap with alacrity.

One person who has betrayed no doubts about the potential of the movement is Stephen Harper, who has mined it to his political advantage. Drafting an electoral strategy to ensure the allegiance of his evangelical base, he has used social conservative policies to reach across faith and ethnic lines to broaden the appeal of his reconstituted Conservative Party. Just as Reagan once provided the access and regulatory openings that turned television preachers into political power-brokers in Washington, Harper has done the same in Ottawa, where a small band of conservative Christian activists with ties to his government has won a series of policy and personnel concessions destined to change the Canadian political landscape in ways that will be difficult to reverse.

Still, watching Harper court the country's burgeoning religious right—a coalition not limited to Christians—it seems no wonder that the media have failed to pick up the clues to its increasing influence. He has been determinedly secretive about his efforts to cultivate that constituency and, taking their cue from him, many Canadian evangelicals have learned to operate with a mixture of stealth and obfuscation.

As I tracked that emerging conservative Christian force, it soon became apparent that I was negotiating a parallel culture, one that gave new meaning to the old maxim of two national solitudes. Like novelist Hugh MacLennan, who portrayed two distinct societies separated by language, culture and geography, I realized I was grappling with two diametrically opposed worldviews. On one side are those who inhabit what is regarded as the mainstream—sophisticated, secular and urban, smugly assuming that everyone, given the facts, would share their reverence for tolerance and their taste in television shows. On the other is an increasingly self-sufficient conservative Christian cosmos, largely planted in Canada's suburbs and rural outposts, which believes the world is going to hell in a handbasket and is preparing for that divinely ordained eventuality. Many of those believers happily exist in a faith-based bubble they have helped create. Their children grow up attending private religious schools and revival-style youth rallies, with Christian rock programmed into their iPods and evangelical bestsellers on their bookshelves. Their entire experience is filtered through preachers either in the flesh or on the growing number of Christian media outlets, where the pronouncements of self-styled prophets can carry more weight than rulings from the Supreme Court. By the time they earn a college degree and land a job, perhaps in government, they might never have set foot in the public education system and have only a nodding acquaintance with the secular society they scorn.

That cultural apartheid wouldn't come as a surprise to anyone who has travelled this country's assorted Bible belts, from B.C.'s Fraser Valley and the expanses of southern Alberta to the verdant banks of New Brunswick's Saint John River. Here, in a land where 64 percent of Canadians profess a belief in God and 31 percent describe themselves as born-again, a vast parallel Christian subculture is thriving, its impact largely overlooked by the nation's pulse-takers. Far-flung and often fractious, not fitting neatly into strict denominational slots, this sub-culture may lack a central spokesperson or unifying structure, but its members find themselves increasingly linked through Christian school groups, prayer fellowships and social networks that the Internet is knitting together at warp speed.

That may be one reason the gathering strength of the evangelical movement routinely escapes the notice of outsiders. My cousin, a life-long resident of Calgary, had never heard of Centre Street Church, one of the country's largest congregations and a leading example of a U.S.-style megachurch. Then one Sunday, she accompanied me to the city's northeast quadrant where we stumbled on the imposing big-box struc-ture topped by a giant white cross amid a bleak industrial wasteland. Without a free space left in its mammoth parking lot, a cadre of vol-unteers waved traffic into adjacent auto-repair yards—confirmation that the church's 2,400-seat auditorium was already full for the second of three services. Inside, past a cavernous atrium that might have been mistaken for an airport terminal—complete with its own massive information counter, day care centre and Common Ground café—Senior Pastor Henry Schorr presided over a surprisingly traditional order of worship that featured a full choir and a small orchestra on a stage roomy enough to accommodate a Broadway extrvaganza.

But another reason for the invisibility of the evangelical community is its changing complexion. No longer do conservative Christians com-prise only descendants of those Anabaptists and Calvinists who once fled persecution in Europe. In his 2002 study, *Restless Gods*, University of Lethbridge sociologist Reginald Bibby reported that, contrary to common assumptions, fully one-third of new Canadian immigrants are Christians, many from Korea, the Philippines and Africa, where Pentecostalism is spreading on the winds of revival. Across the country, some Chinese congregations claim memberships in the thousands, their services held mainly in Cantonese and Mandarin. One of the largest, the Richmond Hill Chinese Community Church north of Toronto, has just completed its third expansion, its newest red brick incarnation welcoming more than four thousand worshippers a week. Only a few kilometres away stands the breathtaking sanctuary of the Scarborough Chinese Baptist Church, a soaring, stylized flying buttress that seats sixteen hundred and has won an architectural prize. So wealthy are some Chinese evangelical congregations that one came to the rescue of the National House of Prayer, anteing up the outstanding down payment for its Ottawa headquarters.

Researching these dispatches from the country's culture wars, I couldn't avoid the conclusion that the Canadian evangelical community defies every attempt to stereotype it. While much of the Christian right might be anchored in small-town Canada, it also boasts a handful of corporate titans who are quietly financing political expressions of their faith. On forty acres north of Surrey, B.C., Jimmy Pattison, the trumpet-playing billionaire ranked as the richest man in the province, has built a Pentecostal version of Upper Canada College called Pacific Academy, its fourteen hundred students eligible for an international baccalaureate degree and a telecommunications program centred on its own broadcasting studios. As proprietor of the country's largest billboard company, Pattison has also underwritten the national advertising campaign for the Alpha program, which teaches the fundamentals of Christianity in church basements and Bay Street boardrooms. Meanwhile, half an hour east of Pacific Academy stands Trinity Western University, Canada's largest private Christian institution of higher learning, which is sustained by the largesse of evangelical benefactors like Ontario trucking magnate Del Reimer, who bankrolled the multi-million-dollar student centre that bears his name. But it is the self-effacing Reg Petersen, a former nursing-home tycoon and Reform Party candidate from Cambridge, Ontario, who may wield the most political weight. Petersen's Bridgeway Foundation funds more than two dozen faith-based projects a year, doling out grants to the Christian Legal Fellowship and Preston Manning's Centre for Building Democracy, both dedicated to ensuring a greater role for Christians in government.

In this book, I have chosen to focus on those political activists whose goal is to attain the same political power that their counterparts have enjoyed in the United States. But while chronicling the forces shaping Canada's religious right, I have highlighted one faction I refer to as "Christian nationalists," a militant charismatic fringe with ties to Harper's Conservatives that has gained influence out of all proportion to its numerical heft. Not only is it helping to reshape foreign policy, the public service and the courts, it has thrown its weight behind a range of socially conservative policies that it regards as prerequisites to remaking Canada as a distinctly Christian nation.

Although those Christian nationalists deny any such agenda, they openly extol the idea of a government run by and for Bible believers according to scriptural principles that would trump the decisions of secular courts. If their rhetoric sounds harmless or even heartwarmingly patriotic—their rallies strewn with maple-leaf symbolism and tributes to national milestones—the vision of Canada they are promoting is both retrograde and exclusionary. On their watch, multiculturalism would be expunged from the policy books in favour of a unifying social-conservative ethos, and secularism, which they regard not as an instrument of interfaith neutrality but as a religion in its own right, would be replaced by the enshrinement of Christianity as the nation's official belief system.

For Quebecers of a certain age, that fundamentalist scenario offers a case of déjà vu: it bears a striking resemblance to the stifling two-decade reign of former Premier Maurice Duplessis, when the Roman Catholic church held sway over the province as a virtual instrument of government, its power so blatant that Duplessis could campaign on the slogan "A vote for the Union Nationale is a vote for your religion and your Catholic faith."

Such a radical theocratic vision is usually referred to as Dominionism—a belief system asserting the right of Christians to claim dominion over all forms of earthly life—or occasionally as Christian Reconstructionism, an even more extreme school that calls for the reconstruction of society according to a strict biblical mould. Instead, I have chosen to refer to both as forms of Christian nationalism, a term that embraces a much larger body of believers who parrot the same brand of hyperpatriotic religiosity and share many of the same aims, but have only the haziest grasp of any defining theology.

What drives that growing Christian nationalist movement is its adherents' conviction that the end times foretold in the book of Revelation are at hand. Braced for an impending apocalypse, they feel impelled to ensure that Canada assumes a unique, scripturally ordained role in the final days before the Second Coming—and little else. That preoccupation with final-days preparations may help explain why nearly a thousand young evangelicals could gather in Vancouver's Stanley Park, passionately calling for an end to abortion and premarital sex while ignoring the perils of global warming. For them, the essence of evangelism is saving souls for what they call the final "harvest," not staving off the tribulations of a doomed world.

It also informs their support for a foreign policy that empowers the most hawkish and expansionist forces in Israel at the expense of Middle East peace. Backed by a Christian Zionist lobby that is growing around the globe, they are convinced that the end times of biblical prophecy will only materialize after the Jewish homeland has been restored to its Old Testament might and the Battle of Armageddon against the forces of the Antichrist breaks out on the plains outside Jerusalem.

If that apocalyptic scenario seems to have been lifted straight from some thriller plot, it is, in fact, being promoted in Ottawa by an aggressive and organizationally savvy band of conservative Christians with increasing ties to the Conservative government. The degree to which they succeed in prevailing over policy may depend on whether Canadians wake up to the realization that slowly, covertly, the political process is being co-opted by an extremist vision of Christianity—one ultimately shaped by what I call "the Armageddon factor."

GOD'S DOMINION

I

On a sun-dappled Saturday in the summer of 2008, a thousand young people throng the lawns of the Parliament Buildings in a classic picture-postcard tableau. Against the iconic backdrop of the Peace Tower, toddlers race through the crowd trailing rainbow streamers and a fresh-faced blonde stretches out under an umbrella to breastfeed her plump newborn. As the compelling rhythms of an electronic keyboard pound over the loudspeakers and a dance troupe swoops across an impromptu stage twirling oversized maple-leaf parasols, an onlooker might be forgiven for assuming that Ottawa's tourist bureau orchestrated the idyllic scene. Then a young woman in a maple-leaf T-shirt shatters that perception with an anguished wail. "Father, save us!" she implores from the microphone, tears coursing down her cheeks. "Hear our cry!"

As her sobs erupt into the incantations of an old-time revival, it suddenly becomes clear that this is no occasion for celebration or national pride. For the conservative Christians who have flocked to Parliament Hill for this day-long fast and prayerfest called TheCRY, it is a concerted, eleventh-hour plea for the repentance and reformation of a nation they believe is headed straight to the hellfires of damnation for having betrayed its divinely appointed destiny—a destiny spelled out in the national motto, Psalm 72:8, chiselled around the neo-Gothic windows of the Peace Tower: "He shall have dominion also from sea to sea, and from the River to the ends of the earth."

Never mind that Old Testament scholars attribute that snatch of ancient Hebrew poetry to a desert patriarch whose entire cosmos was circumscribed by the Mediterranean and the Euphrates River. For Faytene Kryskow and a growing number of evangelicals whose faith is founded on the inerrancy of the Bible, the seventy-second psalm offers irrefutable proof that, thousands of years before Confederation and even before the birth of Jesus of Nazareth, God fingered Canada for a key role in the final days preceding the Battle of Armageddon and the Second Coming of Christ.

Now, as they chart the signs and portents that seem to signal the advent of those end times, as global warming thaws the polar ice caps and the global economy reels from another sort of meltdown, they are driven by an increasing imperative to reverse the moral impediments blocking the country from its scriptural fate. Despite decades of attempts to establish God's dominion north of the forty-ninth parallel, Canada remains one of the few countries in the developed world without an abortion law and was among the first to legalize same-sex marriage. But on the promotional video for TheCRY, Kryskow, the event's chief organizer, ticks off a longer list of transgressions—from "gross moral decay, family breakdown, immorality and perversion" to "general cultural demise"—all of which must be set right. At the microphone, her voice is hoarse with emotion, her thin frame wracked with grief. "Lord, we pray for the sins of this nation," she pleads. "Heal our land."

The only hope for national redemption, as she sees it, lies in the strategic prayers of born-again believers to prod the country back onto a righteous legislative track. Turning to face the Supreme Court down the street, then toward all three wings of the Parliament Buildings, she leads her followers in an hour-long anti-abortion rite, their arms outstretched like kung fu masters channelling spiritual vibes—"prayer bombs," she calls them—and their mouths plastered shut with scarlet duct tape inscribed with the word "life" to symbolize the stifled screams of an imperilled fetus.

But TheCRY is not merely another pro-life rally attempting to storm Parliament Hill. Its agenda is much broader and far more radical: nothing less than restructuring Canada as a devoutly Christian nation governed by biblical literalists according to principles selectively plucked from the Old and New Testaments. That theocratic vision provides the underpinnings for a new Christian nationalist movement emerging in the capital, where Kryskow has become its most public face, the winsome front for a handful of militant evangelical groups determined to infiltrate the political system and, as she puts it, "reclaim Canada for Christ."

Exactly what that phrase entails is as hard to pin down as Kryskow's sketchy explanations of the country's end-times role, but its implications for public policy are worthy of note. Establishing a Christian government in Ottawa—or re-establishing it, as Kryskow insists—would mean not only putting Bible believers in political office, but returning control of such services as education and social welfare to those institutions that Christian reconstructionists regard as the bedrock of a godly society: the family and the church.

While most of the teens and twenty-somethings in this crowd have been drawn to Kryskow's calls for a Christian revival in Canada, few realize that she is part of a charismatic renewal movement that aims to wipe out the distinctions between church and state around the globe. Even her hyperbolic brand of righteous patriotism has been lifted from an American template: TheCRY is patterned directly on TheCall, a daylong fast and prayer rally that drew fifty thousand Christian youth to the National Mall in Washington, D.C., only a week earlier. On TheCall's website, in fact, Kryskow's gathering is listed as the chief Canadian event sponsored by Missouri revivalist Lou Engle, the controversial pioneer of the red-duct-tape ritual that has become a staple of U.S. pro-life protests.

In Ottawa, Kryskow downplays those American ties, cultivating her reputation as a homegrown dynamo whose effervescence and impressive political connections have transformed her into one of the leading figures in this country's emerging Christian right. At a time when the press corps routinely gets the cold shoulder on Parliament Hill, she sails through the corridors of power with an official security pass, popping up in the House of Commons' gallery to cheer on the Conservative government's initiatives and huddling with members of Parliament in the privacy of their offices to tout traditional values while joining hands with them in prayer.

At the prophetic conferences Kryskow runs under the banner of her youth lobby, 4MYCanada, she seldom fails to snag a guest appearance from one of the evangelicals in Harper's caucus, and this edition of TheCRY is no exception to that rule: Conservative MP Bev Shipley has trekked back to Ottawa during the Commons' summer recess from his southwestern Ontario riding specifically to deliver greetings on behalf of his colleagues. A fellow Christian nationalist, Shipley has arrived fresh from a controversy of his own. Weeks earlier, he had been pilloried for handing out Canada Day bookmarks that asked constituents to pray for "godly" leaders who would govern "according to the Scriptural Foundation upon which our country was founded."

Still, his endorsement pales in comparison to Kryskow's chief public-relations coup: an effusive letter from the prime minister himself, which she reads to the crowd. In it, Harper lauds her youth movement for cultivating "thoughtful, faith-filled citizens" and praises its political activism. "Faith has shaped your perspective on the world and strengthened your resolve to make a political difference," he writes, signing off with a beneficent "God Bless."

What makes the letter noteworthy is that it arrived, unsolicited, from a politician who had spent years scrupulously avoiding any suggestion of coziness with the country's Christian right. All through the 2006 race that brought him to power, Harper had barred his evangelical candidates from airing their contentious views on same-sex marriage and deftly sidestepped the minefields of the culture wars. Yet here he was in the summer of 2008, about to call an unscheduled election, openly currying favour with that constituency.

Was he simply trying to energize a new cadre of Conservative foot soldiers for the upcoming campaign? Or had there been a more profound shift in his strategy? Was Harper now secure in the assumption that, after two years of muzzling the most rambunctious believers in his caucus, he could count on the mainstream media not to notice that the religious right was alive and well—indeed thriving—under his government, where it had already begun to change the nation in ways that are far-reaching and perhaps irreversible?

⹋

For most Canadians, the first clue that they had a born-again prime minister came on election night in January 2006 when Harper capped off his victory speech with a three-word closing, "God bless Canada," that sent commentators into conjectural overdrive. Some speculated that it was merely a case of rhetorical exuberance momentarily trumping his fabled cerebral cool. Others insisted it was yet another indication of his amply documented admiration for the American political system, a shameless imitation of every U.S. president within recent memory, no matter what their political stripes. Even among his intended audience, not everyone was thrilled. John Stackhouse, one of the country's leading evangelical scholars, decried the gesture as a "sop" that had managed to miff both non-believers and committed Christians like himself. "It remains so vague, it has no important political purchase," he argued. "It's done very little except to irritate people." In fact, Harper had used the phrase in some speeches as leader of the opposition, and for

Preston Manning, his old Reform Party boss, the fuss was infuriating. "It's just ridiculous to think that this is some novelty that was learned by watching Republicans on television," Manning bridled in a phone interview. "This is a country that used to end every public meeting by saying, 'God Save the Queen.'"

But as a *New York Times'* correspondent noted, Harper's benediction was an aberration "in a country where politicians do not customarily talk about God." Pierre Trudeau had been careful to cultivate his image as a playboy rather than betray his fervent Catholicism, and even Lester Pearson, the son of a Methodist minister, preferred to play up his identity as a baseball fanatic, not a wily coalition builder who occasionally prayed with Social Credit leader Robert Thompson, the devout evangelical whose votes kept his minority Liberals in power. As the first evangelical prime minister since John Diefenbaker, Harper didn't need any tutorials on the risks of mixing faith and politics: he had watched creationist sentiments sink the leadership career of his Canadian Alliance rival Stockwell Day. But when he proceeded to turn his election-night blessing into a trademark exit line—even commending the contents of his first throne speech to the will of "divine providence"—it raised an obvious question: why would a politician known for attempting to control every public utterance by his party choose to invoke what Liberal strategist Warren Kinsella dubbed "the G-word?"

One answer lay south of the border where George Bush was still in power, regularly seeding his speeches with coded scriptural allusions to reassure those evangelicals who had helped put him in office that he remained onside. In this country, where the evangelical community is a fraction of the size—10 to 12 percent of the population compared to more than 30 percent in the U.S.—any oratorical outreach was riskier, but there was no doubt that Harper, too, owed conservative Christians a debt for their support at the ballot box. After he took the same-sex-marriage issue off the table on the first day of the 2006 campaign, promising a free vote on whether to reopen the debate, evangelical leaders rallied their troops on the strength of that pledge. Taking over nomination meetings and often ousting more moderate candidates, they propelled their faithful to the polls and, as an Ipsos Reid survey revealed, those efforts translated into votes. Sixty-four percent of weekly Protestant churchgoers—most of them evangelicals— opted for the Conservatives, a 24 percent jump from the previous election. Even more significantly in a country where Roman Catholics make up the biggest slice of the spiritual pie, for the first time in the history of Canadian polling, a majority of the most devout Catholics had shifted their allegiance from the Liberals to the Conservatives. A religious right was taking shape in Canada, and Harper was determined to ensure that it was no fluke. For most conservative Christians tuning in to his victory speech, "God bless Canada" was the equivalent of a televised thank-you note.

Still, for many in the Ottawa press corps, it came as a shock. Invocations of the divine were not what they had come to expect from the buttoned-down policy wonk known to brighten at the mere mention of fiscal transfer payments. Although Harper had succeeded in remaining an enigma to all but a close circle of advisers, there had never been a hint that beneath his opaque mask lurked a covert Bible thumper. Even a four-hundred-page biography by his admiring Boswell, William Johnson, made no mention of his interest in a higher power.

Then, suddenly, just months before the election, Harper's cover was blown by an unlikely source. Lloyd Mackey, the veteran Ottawa editor of *B.C. Christian News*, published *The Pilgrimage of Stephen Harper*, a slim volume that chronicled Harper's spiritual odyssey from the stolid United Church pews of his Toronto boyhood to the rollicking guitar-and-drum-laced services of the evangelical church he sought out in the working-class obscurity of Ottawa's east end. It was there that Mackey found him one "Shoebox Sunday," beaming with paternal pride as his two children, Ben and Rachel, trooped to the front with their boxed mission gifts for the overseas relief agency, Samaritan's Purse.

Harper never accorded Mackey an interview and was furious that the book appeared on the eve of the 2006 vote, but he had little to fear. Because Mackey was an outsider in the capital, a bespectacled loner who seldom pursued the stories that obsessed political scribes, his revelations were largely ignored until after his subject was safely ensconced at 24 Sussex Drive. By then, Mackey's thesis was beyond dispute: as the former editor of the Reform Party's newspaper, he had known Harper during a period that Johnson's biography had glossed over—one that stood at odds with his reputation as a flinty control freak who brooked no ideological doubts. It was a period that a more confessional politician might have referred to as his dark night of the soul.

⁂

Until the 2006 election, Harper had publicly alluded to his faith on only two occasions, both of them interviews with small Christian media outlets where he was assured a sympathetic ear. In one, on JOY1250, a Toronto-area radio station, host Drew Marshall cued him for an apparently well-rehearsed confession. "Let's jump into the Jesus stuff here," Marshall announced. "Rumour has it that you actually are a genuine follower of Christ." In contrast to his usual impatience with the press, Harper seemed delighted by the query, acknowledging that he had become a Christian in his twenties but didn't like to talk about it much. Then he hastened to reassure secular listeners who might have tuned in with a deftly hedged declaration.: "I won't say I always keep my faith and politics separate," he conceded, "but I don't mix my advocacy of a political position with my advocacy of faith." Ten years earlier, in a profile for the now defunct *Ottawa Times*, he had admitted that as a teenager he thought of himself as "an agnostic central Canadian liberal," but "life experiences" led him to "other conclusions," and eventually to the pews of the Christian and Missionary Alliance church.

Mackey traced those experiences back to the late 1980s when Harper returned to Calgary after his first stint in Ottawa as an aide to Conservative MP Jim Hawkes—a postgraduate dream job that had turned into a nightmare year of disillusionment and self-doubt. Solitary and friendless in the foreign culture of the capital, his only confidante his backbencher boss, Harper watched, appalled, as his theoretical policy ideals smashed up against the compromises of parliamentary *realpolitik*. He fled back to Calgary only to face a traumatic breakup with his fiancée, then threw himself into studies for a master's degree in economics, determined to make his career in the loftier groves of academe. It was at the University of Calgary, sitting in on the "egghead lunches" convened by a group of political-science professors for the benefit of Preston Manning, that he was recruited to help draft the Reform Party's first platform.

In those days, Manning had not yet established himself as the voice of Western alienation and he carried the weight of a legacy that was not political alone: he was known chiefly as the charisma-challenged son of Ernest Manning, whose celebrity as Alberta's longest-serving premier was only outstripped by his career as a spellbinding radio preacher. "The premier's kid," as Manning called himself, grew up in the wings of his father's electronic pulpit, taking notes on his sermons and often running the kids' portion of the program while his mother played the organ and conducted the choir. Talking to Manning about the thorny path to personal faith was akin to signing up for Fundamental Christianity 101.

Today, Manning shrugs off his role as Harper's spiritual mentor. "Stephen does have deep spiritual convictions," he says warily, invoking Harper's penchant for privacy. But others are more forthright. Deborah Grey, the feisty Alberta high-school teacher who became Reform's first member of Parliament, and, briefly, Harper's boss, recalls his "very long, very involved discussions" with Manning over the course of several years: "Stephen saw Preston and a faith that was real, and how you could marry faith and politics."

Unlike George W. Bush, who claimed a life-changing epiphany on the booze-sodden road to perdition, Harper embarked on a spiritual journey that lacked a dramatic plot twist. Mackey describes him as a "cerebral" Christian who read and reasoned his way to faith. "When it came to his spiritual formation with Preston, he'd say, 'What are the classics?'" Mackey reports. "And Preston would say, 'Try C. S. Lewis,' or 'Try Muggeridge.'"

Both Malcolm Muggeridge, the acerbic British journalist who championed Mother Theresa, and Lewis, the celebrated author of *The Chronicles of Narnia*, came to their convictions late in life. In *Mere Christianity*, Lewis lays out core doctrines with wit and a relentless logic that speaks directly to rationalists like Harper who might be horrified by the unruly gusts of emotion that can ambush a convert. "Enemy-occupied territory—that is what this world is," Lewis wrote in a masterful metaphor sure to resonate with any student of politics. "Christianity is the story of how the rightful king has landed, you might say landed in disguise, and is calling us all to take part in a great campaign of sabotage."

Harper's quest coincided with a period when his father, the man he calls the most important influence on his life, was facing his own spiritual crossroads. On the *Drew Marshall Show*, he recounted how Joseph Harper, a gregarious accountant and lifelong teetotaller, became "quite an expert in theological matters" and suddenly, after years as a United Church elder, switched his allegiance to the Presbyterian camp. Harper sidestepped an explanation of why his father jumped ship, but pointedly noted that Marshall's audience would get his drift—a veiled allusion to the explosive 1988 decision by the United Church General Council to approve the ordination of homosexuals.

While his parents fled to the Presbyterian fold, Harper forged his own path, exploring the evangelical services that seemed to provide his Reform colleagues such enviable certainty. Diane Ablonczy, the party's newly widowed communications director, had found consolation at

Calgary's Centre Street Church, and she talked Harper into buying tickets for one of its fundraising galas, nudging him to invite a bubbly blonde graphic designer named Laureen Teskey on what would be their first date. In the end, Harper spurned Centre Street's bustle as well as the upscale reassurance of Manning's First Alliance Church, opting for an upstart branch of the same denomination near his home in the city's booming northwestern suburbs.

Founded in 1986 by a few dozen families who gathered in a school, Bow Valley Alliance had grown at such a heady rate that it was obliged to move to a shopping mall and a community college before taking over the Dutch Canadian Club hall, where Brent Trask, its ambitious young pastor, was turning Bow Valley into one of the high-energy experiments in conservative Protestantism that were erupting across the continent. Like Harper, Trask took his inspiration from the U.S., where two gurus of church growth, Rick Warren and Bill Hybels, were transforming contemporary worship, using Christian rock music and corporate marketing techniques to attract the enormous memberships that have made the evangelical movement a force to be reckoned with in American politics.

⁂

The view from the parking lot is the stuff of Alberta travel brochures. In the distance, the snow-slicked Rockies glisten white and magisterial beyond one of the rare expanses of untouched ranchland not yet ravaged by Calgary's relentless construction juggernaut. Here on a mesa just off Highway 1A on the northwest cusp of the city, Brent Trask's flock sits on a real-estate bonanza—twenty-three acres of pasture crowned by a mammoth cinder-block house of worship that could double as a Walmart, complete with wraparound space for a thousand cars. Acquired as part of a merger with a foundering Baptist congregation, the property serves as the headquarters of Trask's newly rebranded

RockPointe Church, a twenty-five-hundred-member, multi-site mega-church that counts the old Bow Valley sanctuary where Harper once worshipped as one of its three campuses.

In the lobby, volunteer greeters are on the watch for "seekers," those trepidatious drop-ins whose salvation has not yet been secured by a personal encounter with Christ. For them, the regular two-dollar fee at the espresso bar is waived, but anyone not up for a dose of high-test java can patronize the church's own Tim Hortons counter, where tables and chairs attempt to conjure up a café atmosphere. Inside the eight-hundred-seat auditorium, there are no pews, only rows of stackable metal chairs that gradually fill up with a well-heeled crowd in designer windbreakers, kids of all ages in tow. On the walls, no crosses or other symbols betray the fact that this is a sanctuary, nor is there a pulpit in sight. Onstage a five-piece band breaks into the infectious rhythms of a soft-rock anthem, paced by a mop-haired teen drummer who bobs ecstatically to his own beat, and two comely brunettes with the lungs of country-music divas appear with hand-held microphones, belting out upbeat lyrics projected onto three giant video screens. The congregation joins in, clapping and swaying, before a succession of speakers bound onstage with reports from African mission projects and a pitch for an upcoming fundraiser. "Mark it down," exhorts one excitable junior pastor. "We've got a gourmet caterer puttin' on an awesome spread. Here at RockPointe, we like to party. It's gonna be a good time."

Then the lights go down and video clips flash on the screens, all featuring men about to undertake hilariously ill-advised tasks, including one would-be handyman blithely poised on a metal ladder in a swimming pool, electric drill in hand. The congregation is still doubled over in laughter as another pastor on Trask's team strolls out in an open-necked sports shirt to serve up a sermon entitled "Foolish Wisdom." Pacing the stage like a seasoned nightclub emcee, a wireless microphone clamped to his head, he studs his patter with everyday anecdotes and self-deprecating jokes, occasionally calling on parishioners to turn to their Bibles. For those who haven't brought along a personal copy, there is no need for embarrassment: snappy summaries of the relevant passages pop up on the video screens. Despite the laid-back lingo and high-tech gloss, the sermon is an old-fashioned argument for adhering to the counsel of the Scriptures even when conventional wisdom counsels the opposite course. "Any number of Christian doctrines can seem like bunk," he concedes. "But a follower of Christ must not allow the source of their wisdom to be anything other than the wisdom of God. That is absolutely mission critical."

From its cappuccino bar and soft-rock band to its trendy repackaging of the gospel, RockPointe's service is based on a prototype pioneered in the suburbs of Chicago by Bill Hybels, the entrepreneurial founder of a 23,000-member megacongregation called Willow Creek Community Church. Starting out with 125 young people in a theatre, Hybels used live bands and a lounge-act format to pull in crowds, many of them upscale GenXers turned off by the formality or the fire-and-brimstone of their childhood worship. As Willow Creek grew into a colossus, other pastors clamoured for the secrets of its success. Now, for an annual fee of $249, more than 12,000 churches around the world—1,100 of them in Canada—are members of the Willow Creek Association, which entitles them to a monthly coaching tips from Hybels and entree to his annual leadership summits featuring corporate darlings such as Carly Fiorina. *Time* magazine anointed Hybels one of the twenty-five most influential evangelicals in America, but some critics scorn his "pastor-preneurial" approach for producing jammed pews and shallow believers, who are lulled by Christianity Lite.

Trask is one of hundreds of Alliance pastors who signed on with Hybels's franchise and, at a time when Calgary's population was exploding, the move paid off with soaring membership rolls. It isn't difficult to picture Harper sitting in on his super-caffeinated services, based on a corporate-inspired worship model profiled by the Stanford Business School magazine, but Trask makes clear that his most celebrated parishioner never presented himself as some unquestioning sheep. "He didn't just believe what he was told," the burly pastor told the *Vancouver Sun's* religion writer, Douglas Todd. "He had to rationalize what he was hearing about Christianity."

⁂

What Harper heard those Sunday mornings would hardly have come as a shock. Beneath the hip trappings, Trask's congregation is a member of a stoutly conservative denomination founded by a Prince Edward Island–born preacher named Albert B. Simpson who, in 1887, at the height of his career at a prestigious New York Presbyterian church, suddenly felt a more compelling call. Captivated by the prophetic end-times doctrines then sweeping the continent and a personal belief in faith healing, he launched soul-saving campaigns at home and abroad that eventually merged to form the Christian and Missionary Alliance.

For the straitlaced Presbyterians of his day, Simpson's emphasis on personal salvation and spiritual cures might have been considered outré. But he drew the line at charismatic practices such as speaking in tongues, parting ways with many early followers who bolted to the emotive Pentecostal camp. Now with nearly four million members in fourteen thousand congregations around the world, the Alliance is squarely in the evangelical mainstream. According to its Statement of Faith, adherents believe that the Bible is inerrant and the Second Coming "imminent," and that Christ's return will be both "personal and visible." Women are still not accepted for ordination, and a position paper on divorce does not mince words on a related matrimonial topic. "Homosexual unions are specifically forbidden," it decrees, "and are described in Scripture as manifestations of the basest form of sinful conduct."

Even the church's emphasis on overseas missions is rooted in a neo-conservative worldview. Trask's congregations have raised thousands of dollars for African communities struggling with HIV/ AIDS, and, like many Christian conservatives, he regards such charity toward the marginalized and impoverished as the business of the church, not the state. Although Trask recalls debates with Harper over Alliance doctrine, they never disagreed on that point: social welfare ought to be delivered by faith communities, not by the government. At a time when George Bush was funnelling millions for social programs through his White House Office of Faith-Based and Community Initiatives to foster that thesis, Harper carried the same conviction to Ottawa where, as the centrepiece of his first budget, he shelved plans for a national daycare scheme in favour of a monthly allowance doled out directly to families. The policy provoked howls of protest from child-care advocates, but Trask and a network of evangelical pastors signed on to promote it.

In 2003, when Harper had moved to the capital with his family, it was Trask who helped him find a new church: East Gate Alliance, where an elder named Laurie Throness, then an aide to British Columbia MP Chuck Strahl, could serve as a spiritual counsellor who was wise to the demands of political life. By any other measure, East Gate Alliance seemed an unlikely choice. Fifteen minutes east of the Parliament Buildings, around the corner from the faded storefronts and fast-food joints that line Montreal Road, it sits in the heart of a gritty blue-collar neighbourhood that seems light years from the neo-Gothic limestone of official Ottawa. A former elementary school with a row of white pillars across the front, its services are a tribute to working-class life in the capital, occasionally punctuated by the cries of a lost soul wandering in, dazed and dishevelled, after a hard night on the neighbouring streets. Capitalizing on its location, Pastor Bill Buitenwerf has tried to turn the church into a multicultural haven, sharing the sanctuary with Filipino, Hispanic and Arabic congregations. Aside from its live band, East Gate's services would never be mistaken for some slick Willow Creek spinoff.

Still, its very unfashionability and offbeat location were perfectly tailored for the next chapter in Harper's political life. He had arrived in Ottawa determined to cobble together a new conservative movement, and while it might have been unremarkable to attend an evangelical church in Calgary, that was certainly not the case in the capital. What better place to hide his evangelical ties than in this improbable sanctuary far from the prying eyes of the national press corps?

For nearly three years, Harper succeeded in keeping his attendance at East Gate Alliance under wraps, and when Lloyd Mackey finally broke the story, most of his press-gallery colleagues were stunned. Some speculated the Conservative leader must have been dragged there by his gregarious, motorcycle-riding spouse, but the opposite was true. Laureen Teskey had grown up in Alberta's Turner Valley watching her mother's growing obsession with a fundamentalist sect drive a wedge in her parents' marriage, and she now gave religion a wide berth. She seldom set foot in East Gate and Buitenwerf claimed never to have met her. "She's not interested in spiritual things," Deborah Grey confirms.

For Harper, it was yet another reason to keep his faith to himself. After all, some ultra-conservative evangelicals believe in "headship"—the notion that, as the biblically anointed head of his household, a husband has every right to march his helpmate straight to the pews, or anywhere else. Owning up to his solo attendance at East Gate Alliance might raise awkward questions with a constituency that already had suspicions about whether Harper was really one of their own.

⸙

"God is Alive!" trumpeted an April 1993 cover of *Maclean's*. Contradicting every news story in years, the magazine reported that the demise of the Almighty had been greatly exaggerated: a comprehensive national poll revealed that eight out of ten Canadians believed in a deity and two-thirds embraced the core Christian doctrine of the resurrection. Given such evidence of an "overwhelmingly Christian populace," *Maclean's* posed the obvious question: "Why is there a near total absence of religious discourse in Canadian politics?"

That question had long preoccupied Preston Manning, and six months later, when his fledgling Reform Party won fifty-two seats in Parliament, many of his new evangelical MPs were determined to fill the rhetorical void. Not since Social Credit's heyday had so many conservative Protestants found a home in a political party, but to most of Reform's born-again believers, Ottawa was hostile territory, a bastion of secular humanism, and they made clear that they had no intention of being co-opted by its highfalutin traditions or politically correct equivocations. Myron Thompson, the irrepressible member for the Alberta riding of Wild Rose, and his colleague Darrel Stinson, a former B.C. prospector, refused to doff their Stetsons in the Parliament Buildings or tone down their sentiments on gay rights. "I want the whole world to know that I do not condone homosexuals," Thompson famously told the House. "I do not condone their activity. I do not like what they do. I think it is wrong. I think it is unnatural and I think it is totally immoral. I will object to it forever whenever they attack the good, traditional Canadian family unit that built this country."

For Manning, who declined to campaign in churches or court the evangelical vote, social-conservative issues presented a tactical nightmare. He preferred to leave them to riding referendums but found himself under mounting pressure to take a moral stand on questions such as abortion and protecting homosexuals under the Canadian Human Rights Act. That put him at odds with Harper, who argued that such polarizing hot potatoes had no place in Reform's platform. Their conflict came to a head at the party's 1994 convention, when Manning presented a resolution to limit the definition of marriage to one man and one woman, especially when applied to federal spousal benefits, and Harper spoke out against it. "I think it's perfectly legitimate to have moral objections as well as moral approval of homosexuality," he told the assembled delegates, "but I don't think political parties should do that."

His fellow Reformers clearly disagreed—87 percent supported Manning's motion—but by then Harper was no longer the party's policy chief. He and Manning had parted ways after a power struggle over the direction of the 1993 campaign, and in Ottawa, Harper cemented that breach by publicly denouncing the Reform leader's expenses, a move that earned him a reputation for betrayal and the enduring distrust of Manning loyalists. Although their split had nothing to do with social issues, Harper's policy job went to Darrel Reid, an ardent evangelical who would later become Manning's chief of staff before heading the Canadian branch of Focus on the Family. Increasingly, Manning surrounded himself with social conservatives, and in a party with a family-values caucus, Harper had never been considered a member of that Christian-right tribe. When he finally left Reform in 1997 to run the National Citizens Coalition, some evangelical members of that organization quit in protest. "The so-cons did not like Harper one bit," recalls his former deputy Gerry Nicholls. "They thought he was too moderate."

Soon, they would have a standard bearer of their own.

⸙

In Bentley, a hamlet west of Red Deer, Alberta, Stockwell Day is still regarded as an iconic figure, the rightfully anointed leader of Canadian conservatism who was martyred by the media and scheming secularists. Although that sentiment is shared by many evangelicals across the country, nowhere has it found more fertile ground than in the town where Day's political career began, which has been dubbed "the buckle in Alberta's Bible Belt." Arriving there after years of false career starts in Edmonton and British Columbia, Day landed a job as youth pastor at Bentley Christian Centre, a renegade Pentecostal congregation known for its rousing services, where attendees regularly spoke in tongues. As the administrator of its private Christian school, he found himself in a fight with the provincial education ministry over the right to use curriculum guides published by Accelerated Christian Education (ACE), an American fundamentalist outfit whose science texts are based on biblical literalism, featuring lyrical expositions of creationism and no mention of evolution. A commission investigating Alberta's schools at the time found ACE materials disturbing for other reasons. Its social-studies lessons were deemed insensitive to blacks, Muslims and Jews, and appeared to promote the merits of a theocracy: one workbook dismissed the concept of a democratically elected government as "the ultimate deification of man, which is the very essence of humanism and totally alien to God's word." Defiant, Day emerged as the chief spokesperson for a coalition of the province's Christian schools, taking to the media spotlight like a duck discovering his first pond. "God's law is clear," he proclaimed. "Standards of education are not set by government, but by God, the Bible, the home and the school."

Within months of that declaration, he was elected to the Alberta legislature as the member for Red Deer North, launching a fifteen-year career in provincial politics that saw him rise to treasurer and what his official website calls "acting premier." Occasionally, the actual premier, Ralph Klein, moved to rein him in, notably when Day tried to eliminate abortion from health-care funding and exempt homosexuals from pro-tection under the provincial human rights code. But his embrace of a flat tax and his talent for glad-handing made him so popular that, when mutterings of discontent about Manning's leadership grew to a din, a group of dissidents persuaded Day to throw his hat into the leadership ring and then ensured his victory as head of the newly rebranded ver-sion of Reform, the Canadian Alliance.

Day had been leader of the opposition for only a month when a surprise federal election call shattered the image he had attempted to cultivate when he roared into his debut press conference in a wetsuit astride a Sea-doo. Midway through the election campaign, the CBC unearthed reports of a 1997 speech he had made at a Red Deer Christian school, asserting that the earth was only six thousand years old and that Adam and Eve had strolled in the Garden of Eden with dinosaurs. As the story turned into a media sensation, Liberal campaign wizard Warren Kinsella appeared on a *Canada AM* panel brandishing a purple Barney doll. "I just want to say to Mr. Day," Kinsella quipped, "that *The Flintstones* were not a documentary—and the only dinosaur that walked with human beings recently was this one right here."

Overnight, Day became a national laughingstock, dubbed by one columnist "Jump-for-Jesus Day." He would actually increase the Alliance seat count and its share of the popular vote, but all anybody seemed to remember about the 2000 campaign was that he had been outed as a creationist. Still, that was not his only problem. Gaffes dogged his tenure, provoking a constant turnover in his staff. He had been in the job just nine months when a caucus revolt, led by Manning loyalists Deborah Grey and Chuck Strahl, sparked a leadership challenge. As it turned out, a familiar face was waiting in the wings. A blue flyer suddenly appeared in Alliance mailboxes: "Draft Stephen Harper— True Reformer . . . True Conservative."

Technically, the leadership contest was a four-horse race in which all the contenders were conservative Christians—Diane Ablonczy was an evangelical and Grant Hill, a family doctor, was a Mormon convert— but only Day's faith became an issue in a battle that centred on whether he or Harper could sign up the most new party members. Across the country, Christian activists rallied to Day's side, many of them fellow Pentecostals, the fastest growing branch of the evangelical clan. In Calgary, a former Victory Church pastor named Roy Beyer revived a group called Families for Day, which had already helped overthrow Manning, and in Toronto, Beyer's pal, the Reverend Charles McVety organized a related recruitment blitz. Together, they claimed to have added ten thousand new names to the party lists, all in support of a candidate who, Beyer declared, would "properly advance and defend Christian principles."

But when Harper's backers discovered that Campaign Life Coalition, the national anti-abortion lobby, was illegally selling memberships for Day on its website, they launched a counterattack. Tom Flanagan, his campaign chief, sought out a *Globe and Mail* reporter to charge that Day was building "an unholy alliance" of evangelicals, right-wing Catholics and members of the Dutch Reformed Church in order to take over the party. On a visit to the *Ottawa Citizen*, Harper denounced Day for using churches as recruiting grounds, branding it both bad religion and bad politics. "My view is that the purpose of a Christian church is to promote the message and the life of Christ," he told the paper's editorial board. "It is not to promote a particular political party or candidacy."

Such jibes were a calculated reminder of the biblical baggage that Day would bring to 24 Sussex Drive. When the votes were finally tallied, Harper had triumphed and Day limped off into apparent political oblivion, reduced to a radio talk-show joke. Later, reflecting on the mistakes made in Harper's campaign, Flanagan confessed that although their scaremongering may have been excessive, "It kept alive concern among our supporters that Day might win the race, which was fine with us."

Certainly, Harper emerged from the contest as the determined voice of secularism. Watching him rebuke Day's Christian cohort for mixing piety and politics, Gerry Nicholls had no doubts about the course his old boss would chart as leader of the Canadian Alliance; months earlier, Harper had confided that, for anyone trying to build a conservative movement in Canada, cultivating the Christian right was a mistake. "He told me it was bad politics to court the social-conservative crowd," Nicholls recalled. "He said those ideas were no longer popular with the public and people who cared about them were a shrinking demographic." At the time, Nicholls chimed in with a dismissive riff about the religious right, but Harper cut him short. "He said, 'Make no mistake, Gerry: I am a Christian,'" Nicholls recounted years later. "But in terms of politics in those days, he didn't see [social conservatism] as winnable."

※

Nearly two years after taking over the Canadian Alliance, Harper stunned a ballroom of right-wing movers and shakers: speaking at the annual Civitas conference in June 2003, he laid out a blueprint for building a new conservative coalition that was tantamount to an ideological conversion. Suddenly, Harper, the unrepentant fiscal conservative and free marketeer, was calling on fellow economic libertarians to drop their preoccupation with tax cuts and deregulation. Instead, he argued, it was time to concentrate on those issues that mattered to what he called "theo-cons." In party circles, that group had always been referred to as "so-cons," but Harper had chosen his words with care. He borrowed the term from *Alberta Report* publisher Ted Byfield, one of the granddaddies of the Canadian Christian right. For his part, Byfield was delighted to hear about the Alliance leader's about-face, particularly when Harper made clear that he intended to wade into the social issues he had recoiled from under Manning's watch. Moral relativism, Harper told his audience, had replaced socialism as the new threat. "The truth of the matter is that the real agenda and the defining issues have shifted from economic issues to social values," he declared, "so conservatives must do the same."

That shift, Harper argued, would not limit the party to the usual social-conservative preoccupations such as abortion and gay rights. The key was to expand its concerns to a raft of issues once considered irrelevant by the family-values set: more muscular law-and-order measures and even defence and foreign affairs, where Alliance stands would leave no doubt about whose side the party was on. When Harper warned that taking a "moral" foreign policy position could entail backing up the country's traditional allies with "hard power," the implication was obvious: the Liberal government of Jean Chrétien had just declined Bush's invitation to join the Coalition of the Willing against Saddam Hussein, but a Harper regime would have regarded such a summons to war as a righteous call to arms. Still, he cautioned that the party would have to be judicious in picking its new political battlefronts. "The social conservative issues we choose should not be denominational," he said, "but should unite social conservatives of different denominations and even different faiths."

It was the first time Harper had laid out the Reaganesque strategy that would help bring him to power, championing policies that cut across faith and party lines to appeal not only to the evangelicals who had been the backbone of the Reform party, but also to those conservative Catholics, Jews and ethnic Canadians who had been considered the Liberals' electoral preserve. In a country with the world's highest immigration rate, he understood that most newcomers were as culturally conservative as prairie Bible believers, adamantly opposed to homosexuality and to the sort of permissiveness that threatened centuries of old-world patriarchy.

It was a strategy that risked alienating the very voters Harper appeared to be pursuing in his planned merger with Peter MacKay's Progressive Conservatives, but as he made clear to the Civitas crowd, he considered many of the players in that merger excess baggage. "We may lose some old 'conservatives,' Red Tories like the David Orchards or the Joe Clarks," he shrugged. "This is not all bad."

Under Civitas ground rules, his speech was off the record, but Harper made sure his turnabout reached its target audience: the full text was published in Byfield's magazine, displayed like a manifesto under the headline "Rediscovering the Right Agenda." One explanation for his astonishing change of course lay in the narrative then dominating American newscasts: the mounting evidence that George W. Bush owed his residency in the White House to the organizing efforts of Ralph Reed's Christian Coalition. But after more than a year of pondering the numerical odds, Harper had also concluded he had no choice. Although he had vanquished Day in the leadership race, he had taken over a party with a newly expanded and energized base of social conservatives. Darrel Reid, who was by then president of Focus on the Family Canada, underlined that dynamic shortly after Harper's victory in an article for the *Globe and Mail*: "You Better Get Used to Us, There Are a Lot More Social Conservatives Around Than You Think."

In his piece, Reid exposed a reality that few reporters or even other federal politicians grasped: religious conservatives in Canada were no neatly corralled demographic with uniform inclinations at the voting booth. They were, he stressed, "a shifting group who come together on various issues at various times," and not all were evangelical Protestants. Many conservative Catholics and Anglicans had no intention of setting aside their opposition to same-sex marriage to vote for a party they had once called their political home. Considering that more than 60 percent of Canadians believe Jesus is their personal redeemer, Reid argued, the pool of Christians motivated by faith issues could swell far beyond the usual head count in Canadian pews—a flawed measure at best. Ever since the 1960s, church attendance in this country has declined, unlike that in the U.S., but the number of people who consider themselves Christians has remained high, inspiring one analyst to term Canadian Christians "believers not belongers."

Harper's overture to theo-conservatives also offered instant access to campaign networks for a newly constructed party whose fractious wings still regarded each other with suspicion. George Bush's battle for the White House had demonstrated how a parallel network of churches and religious lobbies could reshape the political landscape, springing logistical surprises at the ballot box long before the mainstream media caught on. "This is the one group that can get people out to a meeting," says Dennis Pilon, a political scientist at the

University of Victoria. "They have these interlocking networks that they can very quickly activate."

Just how effectively those networks could be activated would become evident over the next three years as Harper cobbled together his new Conservative Party. At the time of his Civitas speech, right-wing Christians claimed scant organizing expertise. A few groups boasted Ottawa redoubts, including the Christian Embassy, a spinoff of Campus Crusade for Christ, but it focused on cultivating the capital's power-brokers—politicians, diplomats and the military—not getting bodies out to the voting booth. For that, Harper would have Paul Martin to thank. By legalizing same-sex marriage, Martin galvanized the Christian right in a way that no evangelical barnburner could, even prompting America's star televangelists to turn their attention and campaign skills north of the border. When pollsters parsed Harper's 2006 victory, one conclusion was unavoidable: the overwhelming impulse that had driven evangelicals to the Conservative camp was their concern over such moral issues as gay marriage.

Once elected, Harper's challenge was to keep that burgeoning Christian right on his side in a way that would not jeopardize his chances of winning an eventual majority government. It was a strategy that would oblige him to walk an uneasy policy tightrope, never taking too extreme a step, but it would also require him to offer his theo-conservative constituency more than an occasional scriptural nod in his speeches. Exiting stage right muttering "God bless Canada" was not going to suffice.

⊹

In evangelical pulpits, electronic and otherwise, the mood after the 2006 election was initially upbeat. "We've got a born-again prime minister!" crowed David Mainse, the founding host of 100 Huntley Street, the country's longest-running Christian talk show. But others sounded a cautionary note. Brian Stiller, the former head of the Evangelical Fellowship—who had known Harper since he was Deborah Grey's legislative assistant and had never detected any apparent spiritual leanings on his part—warned that although the new prime minister was indeed a fellow evangelical he might not choose to govern like one. Some conservative Christians on the opposition benches were more skeptical, hinting that leaks about Harper's faith had come at an exceedingly convenient political time—and, curiously, never before. "Has he ever been at the weekly prayer breakfast or Bible study?" demanded a senior Liberal strategist. "I've never seen him there."

One key to Harper's strategy was that it allowed him to remain an enigma. While critics sent up alarms about the potential extremism of his evangelical agenda, Christian-right leaders worried that Harper was too inherently cautious to demonstrate the true colours of his faith. In his Civitas speech and countless times afterward, Harper warned that his party-building strategy would require patience and an appreciation of "incremental change." In that phrase lay a warning not to expect showy—or politically suicidal—measures such as an anti-abortion bill. Not that many did; to the frustration of the pro-life movement, he had already announced that he had no intention of introducing abortion legislation. "People of faith don't see Stephen Harper as their messiah," noted Derek Rogusky, the vice-president of Focus on the Family Canada. "They don't feel he's going to change everything they want."

Embarking on that strategic tightrope, Harper initially seemed sure-footed. Following the lead of Bush's White House, which had created a deputy for "Christian outreach," he installed a gatekeeper for the evangelical community in the prime minister's office: Kevin Lacey, a former aide to Nova Scotia Premier John Hamm, whose title was "director of stakeholder relations." Georganne Burke, the Conservative Party's community-relations manager—later a ministerial aide—became his chief liaison with Jewish groups, whom Harper was courting with a new, unequivocal defence of Israel.

Instead of sidelining his former rival Stockwell Day, Harper rewarded him with the plum post of foreign affairs critic, then, after the Conservatives came to office, the prestigious ministries of public security and international trade, before naming him president of the Treasury Board. Nor did he marginalize Day's loyalists, those scrappy, self-proclaimed "Stockaholics" who had turned their ongoing allegiance into a badge of honour. When Harper announced his first cabinet, some pundits marvelled that he had overlooked Jason Kenney, the boisterous Calgary bachelor who had served as Day's chief of staff. But Harper had actually entrusted Kenney with a weightier task, one on which the Conservatives' theo-conservative strategy turned. Naming him his own parliamentary secretary, he anointed Kenney as his unofficial point man with the religious right, a backstage power-broker who wielded more influence than most of Harper's strictly supervised ministers.

For Kenney, the assignment was a perfect fit. A charismatic Catholic who regularly appeared at pro-life confabs, he was on a first-name basis with the leading lights in the evangelical and Jewish right, and never found himself at a loss for a partisan riposte. But a key part of his assignment was to woo the conservative wings of those immigrant groups at the heart of Harper's theo-con game plan, a brief that only came to light when a leaked strategy paper revealed that Kenney was running an "ethnic outreach team" under the cover of the PMO. Using sophisticated voter-profiling software, he compiled a massive database of immigrants, targeting them with direct-mail appeals and the lure of one-on-one meetings with Harper or his cabinet ministers during lavishly publicized drop-ins at ethnic festivals. The Conservatives' goal, Kenney admitted, was to "replace the Liberals as the primary voice of new Canadians and ethnic minorities"—a prospect that already seemed a distinct possibility. As his leaked report concluded, the values of new Canadians are "more aligned with the values of the Conservative Party of Canada" than with those of the Liberals, who had just introduced same-sex marriage.

Over the next two years, Kenney racked up appearances at more than five hundred ethnic events, a travel schedule that earned him the nicknames "Curry in a Hurry" and the "Smiling Buddha." His initial stress on shared conservative values was bolstered with more concrete gestures, such as cutting landed immigrant fees. Harper himself issued an official apology to the country's largest ethnic population, Canada's 1.3 million Chinese, for the hated head tax that had been imposed on their ancestors at the turn of the century, and he expressed remorse for the 1914 tragedy that befell Sikh refugees aboard the *Komagata Maru*, when government officials refused to let them disembark in Vancouver. In the 2008 election, that courtship paid off: ethnic support for the Liberals plummeted by 19 percent, virtually all of it going to Harper's Conservative Party, with some of the Liberals' South Asian superstars like Ruby Dhalla and Ujjal Dosanjh barely squeaking to victory in their once-safe ethnic strongholds.

⯑

For years, Harper's opponents had warned of his hidden agenda, but after he took office that agenda turned out to be hidden in plain sight. In a calculated leak of his legislative program, insiders confided that he planned to raise the age of sexual consent from fourteen to sixteen. The Ottawa press corps greeted the news with a barely concealed yawn, but blocks away, the Evangelical Fellowship of Canada, which had been lobbying for years on the issue, saw the bill as a breakthrough. "We took it as a message that we were being heard," said Janet Epp Buckingham, then the group's chief lobbyist, who noted that being heard was a refreshing change. In the previous two elections, the EFC's eighty member organizations had winced at opposition ads ominously underlining Harper's "scary" connections with evangelicals. "The Liberals were doing quite a bit of fear-mongering," Buckingham pointed out. "It's such a relief to have a party that says, 'You guys are welcome here.'"

Others on the Christian right felt the same. At a time when Harper was openly snubbing the Liberal premier of Ontario in a federal-provincial standoff, he made room on his schedule for dozens of faith-based groups, including a five-woman delegation from the Catholic Women's League in Calgary that hadn't managed to wangle time with a prime minister in twenty-four years. "Smile if you're a so-con," ran a headline in the *Western Standard*. "Canada's traditional Christian groups can't say enough good things about the Tories' social policies so far."

Not everyone, however, was as enthusiastic. When the most outspoken evangelicals from the Defend Marriage campaign bragged to a *Globe and Mail* reporter that Harper had recruited them to promote his contentious child-care allowance, the resulting outcry lasted for weeks. But that measure illustrated the canniness of Harper's tightly choreographed strategy. Not only did it delight social conservatives by keeping the government out of child-rearing decisions, but it left the other key wing of the party—economic conservatives—equally ecstatic by quashing a costly state-run program they considered fiscal heresy. Better still, so consistent was the measure with Harper's usual economic libertarianism that, until the *Globe*'s scoop, few outsiders twigged to the fact it was aimed at pleasing the religious right.

While the media scanned legislative initiatives for more theo-conservative fingerprints, most of Harper's moves to placate that constituency neatly bypassed the House of Commons floor. As Donald Savoie, the country's premier public-service scholar, points out, ever since the consolidation of power by Pierre Trudeau, Canadian prime ministers command many of the same prerogatives that French mobs once stripped from Louis XIV. Their ability to issue orders-in-council and dole out an estimated five thousand appointments to federal regulatory bodies gives them the authority of monarchs presiding over what Savoie terms "court government." Harper himself was well aware of the extra-parliamentary levers at his disposal. Years later, caught on video at a closed-door student conference, he enumerated the perils of electing a Liberal government in those very terms. "Imagine how many left-wing ideologues they would be putting in the courts, federal institutions, agencies, the Senate," he warned, having just done the same with his own Conservative loyalists.

Some of Harper's appointments were traditional patronage plums— rewards to party faithful of the very sort that in opposition he had vowed to stamp out. But he raised eyebrows when Jason Kenney named Douglas Cryer, the former director of public policy for the Evangelical Fellowship, to the Immigration and Refugee Board, and high-profile evangelicals like Preston Manning began popping up on commissions that have a say in shaping science policy. When Harper named the first panel on reproductive technology, he did so four days before Christmas, when few reporters or critics were likely to take note. To the consternation of many in the medical community, not a single expert on fertility or stem-cell research from a recommended short list appeared on the final board. Four of its ten members were social conservatives who had taken stands against abortion or embryonic stem-cell research, and the chair, Dr. John Hamm, the former Conservative premier of Nova Scotia, had just been recruited as a prime-ministerial adviser.

In opposition, Harper had railed against the liberalism and judicial activism of the country's courts, so it hardly came as a surprise when he named a flock of Conservative activists as judges. But the Canadian Bar Association was shocked to discover that merely by making a bureaucratic adjustment to the country's judicial advisory panels, he had surreptitiously put in place a mechanism that allowed him to impose a long-term ideological stamp on at least a thousand federal appointments to the bench. Learning of his ability to change the nature of the courts without the sort of congressional oversight required in the U.S., Paul Weyrich, one of the founders of the Moral Majority, marvelled that, "a Canadian prime minister has more power than a United States president."

But appointments were not the only instruments of policy change that Harper had at his fingertips. His government had inherited a $13 billion surplus, but he announced a $10 million belt-tightening that scored a direct hit on two agencies long scorned by social conservatives as left-wing slush funds. Status of Women Canada was put on life support, its budget slashed by 40 percent, forcing it to shutter twelve of sixteen regional offices and shelve its mandate to lobby for gender equality, essentially eviscerating the chief voice for women in the federal government. Then, cancelling the $5.6 million Court Challenges Program, he wiped out an arm of the justice department that had allowed a range of minorities, including women and the disabled, to appeal injustices under the Charter of Rights and Freedoms. Not that its demise was entirely unexpected. Although set up to underwrite claims of discrimination by linguistic minorities, the program had financed most of the lawsuits by homosexuals that led to the legalization of same-sex marriage.

For many evangelical activists, however, these were minor victories on the road to realizing their overriding goal of overturning that legislation. But when Harper did fulfil his pledge to call a free vote on reopening the debate over gay matrimony, he did so with such brisk despatch—expending no political capital on ensuring the motion's passage—that it ended up boomeranging on him, infuriating the very constituency the move had been designed to placate.

Suddenly, Harper's theo-con strategy appeared to be foundering and across the country, Christian conservatives began muttering about his machinations, lamenting that they had been used as pawns. In Surrey, a long-time activist named Ted Hewlett, the former head of the Campaign Life Coalition in British Columbia, launched a withering online attack, charging that the prime minister was too clever a tactician not to have foreseen the negative outcome of the vote. "This kind of transparent cleverness has negative consequences," Hewlett warned. "He may see a large segment of his party lose their enthusiasm for supporting a government which fails to support what they stand for."

Increasingly, whenever Harper attempted to mollify his social-conservative constituency, he did so with a furtive mixture of awkwardness and calculation. Once he had been lauded as a genius at pitting competing camps against one another and keeping rivals off-balance, but his overtures to the party's theo-con base took on a frantic quality, as if he was constantly rushing to put out ideological brush fires that threatened to bring down the Conservative edifice he had built.

That impression only increased when he ignored his own fixed-date election legislation and forced a surprise federal vote in the fall of 2008. As the global economy imploded and the free-market theories on which he'd built his career fell into disrepute, it was, inexplicably, his commitment to his theo-conservative constituency that he chose to jettison. He disowned a private member's bill designed to give legal status to a fetus harmed in a crime—a measure he had once showily voted for—and after months of resisting pressures to withdraw a controversial tax provision for morally offensive films, he abruptly ditched it seven days before the election, when it turned out to be costing him support in Quebec.

Charles McVety, president of the Canada Family Action Coalition, was furious. He warned that Harper would pay a price at the polls for such crass political expediency, and when the Conservatives only managed to eke out another minority government, he boasted that it was a boycott by his disenchanted Christian supporters—not the market-shattering economic meltdown—that had delivered the comeuppance. "The base did not come out in 2008 as they did in 2006," McVety declared in his *Evangelical Christian* magazine. "History is littered with the bones of those who bow to this world."

Depite that disenchantment, the 2008 election results produced a far less damning picture for the chastened game theorist who had been returned to 24 Sussex Drive. Although overall voter turnout had dropped significantly, pollster Andrew Grenville discovered that 64 percent of churchgoing Protestants who did cast their ballots had once again declared their allegiance to Harper's party. Among the most conservative evangelical denominations, the level of enthusiasm had leaped to an astonishing 74 percent. Another trend was even more striking: 49 percent of Catholics outside Quebec who identified themselves as regulars at mass had traded in their long-standing loyalty to the Liberals for Harper's camp. To Grenville, the senior researcher at Angus Reid Strategies, those figures signalled that the 2006 election was no aberration: a discernible Christian right was emerging that was unique to this country—a new "status quo," as he called it, that was as dependent on devout Catholics as it was on Bible-believing Protestants. "It's a new re-alignment: evangelicals are standing up with the Conservatives, and Catholics have abandoned the Liberals," he said. "That to me is a big change in a short period of time."

But that change passed almost unnoticed in the Canadian press. In a country where the media had been on constant alert for signs of just such an emerging Christian coalition, the punditocracy was distracted by the riveting milestone of the U.S. presidential election, busily composing obituaries for the American religious right, while remaining largely oblivious to the movement's growing muscularity on this side of the border. For Harper, that was not an unwelcome development.

⁜

The emergence of a religious-right voting block vindicated Harper's theo-con strategy, but, as its leaders made clear, he also had fences to mend, and he wasted no time in doing just that. Shortly after the 2008 election, conservative Christians in his caucus who had once been forbidden to utter a peep found themselves with unprecedented freedom to air their beliefs. When Winnipeg's Rod Bruinooge took over the Parliamentary Pro-Life Caucus, he received not a word of rebuke for telling a Canadian Press reporter that he intended to reopen the abortion debate. Other conservative Christians won new committee chairmanships or elevated profiles in cabinet, and more than a dozen were named parliamentary secretaries. Jason Kenney was rewarded with a full-fledged ministry—citizenship, immigration and multicultural-ism—from which he could continue courting ethnic conservatives.

Not only was Harper busily patching the holes he had punched in his own party-building strategy, he was doing so with a new boldness. One reason may be that, by 2008, four of the top officials in the PMO were committed theo-conservatives, led by Harper's chief of staff Guy Giorno, an architect of Mike Harris's Common Sense Revolution in Ontario who is a devout Roman Catholic known for his pro-life convictions and hard-ball partisan tactics. Giorno's deputy, Darrel Reid, was the former head of Focus on the Family Canada, who, in turn, had recruited his long-time friend Paul Wilson, the founding director of an elite evangelical training program in the capital, to replace him as Harper's policy director. The fourth member of the quartet, Mark Cameron, an evangelical who had converted to Catholicism and would remain in the PMO until the summer of 2009, had once addressed a student group on how to carry out a Christian mandate in government.

Their fingerprints were apparent in a series of gestures both sub-stantive and symbolic. As Harper doled out millions in academic infrastructure funds under his economic stimulus package, veteran university administrators were astonished to discover that, for the first time in memory, the federal gravy train had stopped by at least fourteen private Christian colleges to distribute more than $26 million in grants, each one unveiled at a splashy press conference featuring a local Conservative member of Parliament. Atlantic Baptist University in New Brunswick's Bible belt lucked into $6 million, the largest handout by far, while Redeemer University College, located outside Hamilton in the riding of Conservative MP David Sweet, the former president of Promise Keepers Canada, received nearly $3 million. "The fact that this money is going to private institutions—and fundamental Christian ones at that—is something we haven't seen in this country before," said James Turk, executive director of the Canadian Association of University Teachers.

In a bid to refurbish Harper's image, Christian media outlets became vehicles for his charm offensive. During the election campaign, he had been the only party leader who declined to discuss his faith with Lorna Dueck, the host of a syndicated current affairs show called *Listen Up!*, carried on Crossroads Television. But six months after the election, the PMO phoned Dueck out of the blue, requesting air time for Harper to convey his Easter greetings. As Dueck hinted in her introduction, even she found the overture curious—almost as curious as the slick, three-minute video supplied by the PMO, which showed Harper impeccably suited and coiffed, poised between a bouquet of lilies and the flag, lauding the "indispensable contribution" of Christian believers to the nation. But his assertion "that God works out His purposes in our history" set off alarm bells in some moderate evangelical circles. That unusual phrase seemed to be a coded confirmation of the Christian-nationalist conviction that Canada has a unique prophetic role to play in the final days before the Second Coming.

Harper was well into his public-relations blitz when he dropped by a closed-door reception at Preston Manning's annual conservative networking conference in the spring of 2009. Although his appearance was unannounced, it was not unplanned. Before an audience of hard-core conservatives, many of them economic libertarians apoplectic about his stimulus spending and the country's mounting debt loads, he delivered a carefully reasoned update on his Civitas speech. While most of the address was an exercise in self-defence, he tossed a calculated bouquet to the bruised theo-cons in his party with a newly honed definition of conservatism. The movement, he declared, had three pillars, which he dubbed the "three Fs": faith, family and freedom—the first two clearly intended to melt skeptical conservative Christian hearts.

Nor was that rhetorical flourish his only gesture of conciliation. A month later, Harper sat down for an interview with *Prestige*, a

Quebec City magazine, attempting to repair his standing in a province where his popularity had plummeted after his anti-arts diatribes during the 2008 campaign. Stressing the importance of his family, he professed to care more about "God's verdict" on his life than the judgment of historians.

To some conservative Christians, however, those declarations were mere window dressing, not unlike his mass mailings of Rosh Hashanah cards to Jewish ridings or his highly publicized meeting with the pope. To others, they indicated just what a strategic straitjacket Harper had created for himself as he attempted to re-inspire his theo-con troops while reassuring moderates that he was merely a benign, piano-playing centrist. Never was that uneasy balancing act clearer than when Charles McVety exploded at the news that $400,000 in federal stimulus funds had gone to Toronto's 2009 Gay Pride parade. As insiders pointed out, the grant had been approved at the highest levels of government, but no sooner had the religious right raised an outcry than Harper backtracked; he unleashed Saskatchewan MP Brad Trost to protest that it had come as a shock to social conservatives in the caucus, and let it be known that the minister responsible, Harper's former confidante Diane Ablonczy, was being stripped of a portion of her porfolio.

Increasingly, Harper appeared to be a prisoner of the very theo-con strategy that had brought him to power, but now threatened to put a majority mandate beyond his grasp. After his disastrous gamesmanship almost provoked an opposition coalition takeover in the fall of 2008, discontent within Conservative ranks burst into the open with leaked hints that it was time for a leadership change. Among those named as potential successors were two of the party's most high-profile social conservatives, Jason Kenney and Harper's old foe Stockwell Day. To the mainstream media and much of the Canadian public, the idea of Day as a prime-ministerial contender might seem preposterous, but to many in the charismatic wing of the Christian right, he remains a prophetic figure whose finest hour is yet to come.

In the PMO, it did not pass unnoticed that, during the height of specu-lation over Harper's future, the *National Post* ran a laudatory feature on Day, rating him "in the best political shape of his life."

Only history can measure the extent to which Harper has furthered God's dominion in Ottawa, but there is no doubt that the religious right he has so openly fostered is here to stay as a political force. Its presence has been guaranteed by a four-year spree that saw conservative Christians establish a half-dozen new organizations in the capital. Almost all are modelled on the institutions that the religious right planted in Washington three decades ago, designed to ensure that theo-cons have a lasting voice in the national debate no matter who happens to be in power. As Darrel Reid explained shortly after Harper's first victory, "The fact that there's a government that's more sympathetic is good, but the government won't be there forever. That's why we need to be there for the long haul."

COAT OF MANY COLOURS

II

B rian Stiller remembers it as if it were yesterday: his sense of elation as Bill C-43 squeaked through the House of Commons and landed in the Senate, then the heart-stopping suspense as the vote began in the upper chamber, the tension so thick he could have cut it with a knife. There, finally, he heard the sudden, collective gasp of disbelief. The count was a tie: forty-three ayes to forty-three nays. A look of momentary bewilderment flashed across the acting speaker's face before a clerk whispered in his ear: in the Senate, unlike in the House, a tie meant automatic defeat. The compromise abortion bill that Stiller had crafted with a band of evangelicals in Brian Mulroney's government was dead. Three years after the Supreme Court had thrown out the previous law as unconstitutional, Canada remained one of the few countries in the developed world without any legislation against abortion. For Stiller, the executive director of the Evangelical Fellowship of Canada, that January 1991 vote was devastating—"a sad, sad day" that he ranks as the worst of his career—but it convinced him that the time had come for the EFC to plunge directly into the hurly-burly of politics with its own Ottawa office. "We realized that if we wanted to have a voice at the table," he says, "we had to be there early in the conversation."

It was no easy undertaking, least of all for an organization whose forty member denominations included faith groups that had long regarded politics as the devil's playground. "My father, who was a preacher, made it very clear that politics was a dirty business, and he wasn't going to have anything to do with it," says retired televangelist David Mainse. "And that was the attitude of most evangelicals at the time."

The Lutherans, the Calvinists, the Mennonites—every denomination and its countless breakaway sects had a different take on how Christians ought to interact with Caesar's realm—and, until the early 1960s, most even avoided interacting with each other. The wonder was that Stiller's mentor, Harry Faught, the pastor of Toronto's Danforth Gospel Temple, had been able to corral any of them into forming the fellowship at all. Initially, his objective was simply to forge a degree of camaraderie among ministers of different theological persuasions, but even that had not been an easy sell. When he first arrived in Toronto in 1954 from the Dallas Theological Seminary, Faught was dumbfounded when Oswald J. Smith, the flamboyant pastor of the People's Church, spurned an invitation to preach at his temple. "I don't speak to other churches in Toronto," he had snapped as if such a foray might threaten his own booming franchise.

Smith eventually came around, serving as the EFC's honorary president, but the fellowship spent its first two decades with no staff and almost no budget, careful to avoid taking public stands. That meekness was a major disappointment to Faught, who had modelled the EFC on the National Association of Evangelicals in the U.S. Formed during World War II by Bible believers determined to set themselves apart from the big mainline Protestant denominations on the left and more militant fundamentalists on the right—even accepting the Pentecostals with whom most fundamentalists of the day refused to consort—the association established a Washington office expressly to intercede with the Federal Communications Commission on behalf of the radio preachers in its ranks.

Clyde Taylor, the official in charge of that political arm, persuaded Faught to start a Canadian version, but none of Faught's members had an appetite for venturing into the moral issues of the day, which included the legalization of the birth-control pill and the decriminalization of sodomy. Even in the 1970s, when the siren songs of free love and cheap drugs were shaking the foundations of society, the EFC kept its objections largely to itself. For Faught and Stiller, that silence was doubly frustrating: in the U.S., where Jerry Falwell's Moral Majority was making its presence felt at the ballot box, critics threatened to block him by invoking the constitutional amendment mandating a separation between church and state, but in Canada, there was no such proscription. "It doesn't exist here," Stiller points out, "but people operate as if it does."

In fact, ever since the first Jesuit missionaries arrived on these shores, sent out to repatriate aboriginal souls from the "stronghold of Satan" while claiming more tangible real estate for the French crown, Canadians have tended to turn a resigned eye on the complex minuet between religion and government. In Quebec, the Roman Catholic hierarchy called the shots for centuries as the equivalent of a state church, controlling schools, hospitals and even library reading lists until the Quiet Revolution of the 1960s ushered in a backlash so pronounced that the province now ranks as Canada's most secular: its birth and marriage rates are the lowest and its abortion rates the highest in the country. In Ontario, where Anglicans held sway until the 1850s, presiding over a staggering two million acres in land grants from the Crown, mainline Protestants remained the chief powerbrokers in a WASP establishment that prevailed until the advent of another 1960s revolution, the secularization that arrived with the dawning of the Age of Aquarius.

On the Prairies, rival strains of the evangelical movement found more fertile ground, producing two competing brands of populism. Preaching to the dispossessed farmers and famished jobless of the

Great Depression, a pair of evangelical ministers, J. S. Woodsworth and Tommy Douglas, turned the call for compassion at the heart of the Social Gospel movement into the Co-operative Commonwealth Federation, the predecessor to today's New Democrats; under its banner, Douglas captured the Saskatchewan legislature and launched his national crusade for medicare. Next door in Alberta, a fundamentalist Baptist firebrand named William Aberhart was so appalled by the liberalism of the Social Gospel that he used his weekly radio sermons to promote the anti-bank tirades of Social Credit, a right-wing expression of populism that swept him to power in 1935. When he died eight years later, he was succeeded by his protégé Ernest Manning, who took over both the premiership and Aberhart's duties hosting *Canada's National Back to the Bible Hour*. For the next quarter century, as Manning juggled his job running the province with his weekly gig as a radio preacher, the electorate barely raised a bleat of protest over a situation that would have been unthinkable in the U.S.: churchmen controlling the government.

But if there were no constitutional niceties keeping the EFC out of politics in this country, vast doctrinal differences among its denominations often precluded finding common ground. From the deeply held pacifism embraced by many Mennonites to the Calvinist call for Old Testament-style retribution advocated by some Christian Reformed churches, the fellowship was made up of such diverse theological viewpoints that even today coaxing a consensus out of its membership has been compared to herding ornery house cats.

Still, by the early 1980s, when *Time* magazine proclaimed God dead and mainline Protestant churches reported emptying pews, Faught decided it was time for evangelicals to get their own story out: their numbers defied the prevailing trends with breakaway congregations constantly sprouting in school gyms and strip malls, and new Christian schools being planted across the country at a dizzying rate. To reflect that energy, he chose the perennially boyish Stiller, a long-time EFC board member who had spent eight years as the Canadian president of Youth for Christ.

Compact and super-charged, Stiller had the rhetorical skills befitting a Pentecostal preacher's son and no reticence about the spotlight. After years of rousing stadiums full of sullen students, he was tailor-made for the task of raising the fellowship's profile. He would revamp its magazine and launch a television show called *The Stiller Report*, later rechristened *Cross Current*s, but he was also acutely aware that, in a survey he had commissioned, most EFC members expressed as much worry about their public image as about political issues—an obvious reaction to the Moral Majority's antics south of the border. "On one side, we felt we were misunderstood and therefore misrepresented," he says. "On the other, you had these inflammatory voices that were un-Christ-like and politically reactionary."

Like Stiller, most Canadian evangelicals were mortified by Jerry Falwell's bellicose conflation of the cross and the flag. At the height of the Cold War, the Moral Majority ran a full-page ad in the *New York Times* fretting that America's defence spending might not be up to its prophetic role battling the Evil Empire. As the EFC's new public face, Stiller spent most of his time trying to convince politicians and reporters that Canadian evangelicals bore little resemblance to their rowdy American cousins. So frustrated did he become that when CBC radio host Peter Gzowski referred to him as a fundamentalist—which Jerry Falwell was, but Stiller, as a Pentecostal, most definitely was not—he exploded in a tirade he can still repeat verbatim. "I told him that to call me a fundamentalist is like calling a homosexual a faggot or an African-American a nigger," Stiller recalls. "I said, 'Why doesn't the CBC call us what we call ourselves instead of this buzzword out of the U.S.?'"

Beneath that outburst lay his fear that the Christian right's designs on the Republican Party were prompting Canadian politicians to cast a wary eye on this country's evangelicals. That wariness stiffened when a hot-headed Hamilton evangelist named Ken Campbell, the founder of Renaissance Canada, hosted Falwell at rallies in Toronto and Edmonton. "We looked at what was happening in America, and we thought they were creating an unholy alliance," Stiller says. "They were politicizing faith in a way that didn't sit well with us."

Commissioned to give Canadian evangelism an image better suited to the national psyche, he stumped the country with a PowerPoint seminar called "Understanding Our Times" designed to show evangelicals the necessity of becoming political players. His argument then was the same as it is today: "Spirituality isn't to be lived in a corner," he says. "Christ is concerned about what happens in the public square and policy decisions matter to us as Christians." At the same time, he argued for a more conciliatory strategy, one based not on confrontation but on coalition-building. "You can't just be angry," he says. "You've got to be smart."

As part of that public diplomacy, Stiller orchestrated legal interventions on a handful of cases headed to the Supreme Court after Pierre Trudeau's Charter of Rights and Freedoms came into effect in 1982. What few knew was that he had played a backstage role in crafting that document. As Trudeau wrestled with the wording of its preamble, a young Liberal MP named David Smith, the son and brother of Pentecostal preachers, joined Tory evangelicals in pressing the prime minister to include a reference to God. When other voices demurred, Smith asked Stiller to come up with statistics that would convince his boss. Stiller obliged, producing a barrage of charts and graphs that showed the growth of evangelical congregations across the country and soaring graduation rates at evangelical seminaries in the West. According to Smith, now a senator and the chair of Michael Ignatieff's campaign team, those numbers clinched Trudeau's decision to open the Charter with a rhetorical flourish that has captivated Christian nationalists ever since, acknowledging Canada as a nation "founded upon principles that recognize the supremacy of God."

At the time, Stiller, like other conservative Christians, had high hopes for the Charter with its guarantee of religious freedom. What he didn't foresee was that it would soon become the object of their wrath, and that he himself would be leading the charge against it.

⸭

In 1983, the same year that Stiller took over the Evangelical Fellowship, police raided a Toronto clinic run by Henry Morgentaler, the Montreal doctor who had already spent ten months in a Quebec jail for defying the country's abortion law. Hailed as a selfless hero by feminists, denounced by the pro-life camp as a mass murderer, Morgentaler opened his Harbord Street clinic with a provocative invitation to the city's police chief, but at first only evangelist Ken Campbell and local pro-life protestors showed up. Long before Toronto's finest stormed through the door, lawyers on both sides agreed that the Morgentaler case was a Charter challenge waiting to happen. It would take five years to make its way through appeals and counter-appeals before landing on the docket of the Supreme Court, where the hearings were so charged that metal detectors were installed inside its august foyer. In 1988, when the court struck down the Criminal Code provision against abortion on the grounds that it violated section seven of the Charter, guaranteeing a woman's right to "life, liberty and security of person," the outrage over the decision obscured the fact that the justices had also left the door open for Parliament to come up with alternative legislation that could survive a constitutional test.

That challenge was one Stiller was eager to take up. He saw it as his chance to prove that evangelicals in Canada could do politics differently than those in Washington, with cooler heads and a knack for compromise. For support, he looked not to traditional allies like the United Church but to the Canadian Conference of Catholic Bishops, with whom he had already forged a united front on an anti-pornography bill. Their partnership marked the beginning of a long-term alliance between evangelicals and Catholics that would shape the unique ecumenical makeup of this country's Christian right.

Still, his chief interlocutors in the abortion fight were the two dozen evangelicals and Catholics in the Conservative caucus that Prime Minister Brian Mulroney called his "God Squad," led by his health minister Jake Epp, the first Mennonite ever named to a cabinet post. Working with Stiller, Epp and an evangelical MP from B.C. named Benno Friesen hammered out a bill that would sentence doctors to a maximum of two years in prison for performing abortions under almost all circumstances, except when a woman's health was at risk. For Stiller, that half-measure was better than no law at all, but the bill managed to enrage both sides in the debate—above all, those in the pro-life camp who considered any sanction of abortion unacceptable. Epp was singled out for attacks that became so vicious Mulroney shifted him out of the health portfolio to the more placid waters of energy. "Here you had a minister of health who expends his political capital trying to move things forward," Stiller marvels, "and the very people he's trying to serve turn on him."

For Deborah Grey, the Reform Party's first and only MP, the bill was equally fraught. Landing in Ottawa in the midst of the abortion maelstrom, she faced an agonizing choice. On the one hand, Preston Manning had decreed that Reform members ought to heed their consciences on moral issues, and Grey had never hidden her pro-life views. On the other, he insisted that, as the first standard bearer for a new populist movement, she had to reflect the wishes of her constituents. Fresh from her upset by-election victory in the sprawling Alberta riding of Beaver River, Grey had no idea how its scattered citizenry felt about the issue and little time to find out. Finally, her legislative assistant—a master's student named Stephen Harper whom Manning had persuaded to shepherd her through her parliamentary debut—devised a way to take a modest sampling of public opinion, and Grey announced she would abide by the results. That vow plunged her into a private hell. Although the results from Harper's poll eventually allowed her to follow her pro-life convictions, her admission that she was willing to set them aside in the service of democracy unleashed a torrent of vitriol that left her reeling. "I got more hate mail from Christians than from anybody else," Grey recalls. "I had believers come to my office and say, 'You're no Christian. May you rot and burn in hell.'"

The fury of that religious backlash was not lost on her young legislative assistant—an experience often cited in explaining Harper's reluctance to table an abortion measure—but it was also an omen of the bill's fate. For the first time in thirty years, the Senate defeated a piece of legislation put forward by the government, and it did so in a chamber dominated by the ruling Conservatives. Although Mulroney had allowed a free vote on the bill, seven members of his own party, including his former trade minister, Pat Carney, opposed it, despite a warning that she would suffer the consequences. For Stiller, the message was clear: the EFC could not rely on the random goodwill of politicians, or even a government; it needed a presence in the capital to tune into the complex cross-currents swirling around the legislative agenda.

It would take another five years, but in March 1996, Stiller threw a dinner to mark the opening of the fellowship's first Ottawa office, now known as the Centre for Faith and Public Life. He made a point of keeping it low-key—"No big splash and no protests," he calculated—and as his front man in the capital, he chose Bruce Clemenger, a soft-spoken student of political philosophy who had served with Samaritan's Purse.

Now chancellor of Toronto's Tyndale University College and Seminary, once known as Ontario Bible College, Stiller looks back on that move as the first in a series of victories that have turned evangelicals into key players in Canadian politics and helped put a born-again Christian in 24 Sussex Drive. "You've got an evangelical as prime minister and Chicken Little isn't out warning that the sky is falling," he beams. "The spiritual activity that's going on now is unprecedented. The secular pendulum has gone as far as it can go, and there's a renaissance of faith that is bubbling up in the country."

Not all evangelicals, however, are equally upbeat. For them, the loss of the same-sex marriage battle was yet another blow in a long line of crushing political defeats, one even more troubling than the abortion debacle, and many were furious that the EFC had not taken a more aggressive stand. During that stormy two-year battle, in fact, it was not the EFC's Clemenger who carried the colours of the Christian right; a chorus of new voices emerged to snag the lion's share of the sound bites and rally the biggest crowds. Those voices were far more militant and demanding, and they showed no inclination to tone down their rhetoric out of deference to some historic Canadian distaste for excess. Unlike Stiller, they admired the stridency and showmanship of Jerry Falwell and the U.S. religious right, and some had hitched their fortunes to its bandwagons, inviting its leaders north to share tips on how to pull off a similar coup.

None were more adept at attracting headlines than Reverend Charles McVety, the flamboyant president of Canada Christian College, who led the 2005 Defend Marriage campaign. McVety made no attempt to hide his scorn for the evangelical "old guard," scoffing at the EFC's election guides which advised churches against taking overtly partisan stands that might cost them their tax status as religious charities. For him, such caution was tantamount to admitting that evangelicals had no voice in the political arena. "It's ridiculous to say Christians are not welcome in politics," he says. "It's regressive, it's oppressive. We may be Christians, but we are voting Canadians. Who relegated us to this status of second class citizens?"

The EFC did not take kindly to his critique. Don Hutchinson, the new director of its Ottawa office, later told a reporter for the *Ottawa Citizen* that "there's a broad spectrum on the evangelical meter. Charles may be the representative of one end, probably one extreme end, of that spectrum." But the EFC itself would soon adopt a more assertive stand. In the struggle over who would represent the country's three and a half million evangelicals in Ottawa, the battle was joined.

⁜

At times, he seems ubiquitous—popping up on the airwaves to denounce the licencing of a new homegrown pornography channel or convening a press conference on Parliament Hill to warn against the scourge of legalized polygamy. When he isn't making headlines in the morning papers, he can be heard firing off tirades against liberals and secular humanists on a Toronto radio station or hosting his own weekly talk show on Crossroads Television. No one would accuse Charles McVety of being media-shy, but on the morning I have an appointment to interview him, he is nowhere to be found. The main-floor receptionist at Canada Christian College informs me he is not on the premises, but that is not the only surprise at McVety's Toronto fiefdom where the Defend Marriage bus sits beached out back in the parking lot.

Tucked behind a Loblaws Superstore at Eglinton Avenue and Don Mills Road, the five-storey building looks more like the pension-fund headquarters it once was than a campus that claims more than a thousand students on its rolls, three hundred of them full time. In a salon off the foyer, a half-dozen teenagers play Ping-Pong outside the Christian bookstore, but much of the space is rented out to the Canadian operations of American evangelists, including Ravi Zacharias and Oral Roberts—one explanation for the $700,000 in yearly rental income that the college lists on its charitable tax return.

Its chief tenant is John Hagee, the Texas televangelist who has become the continent's leading Christian Zionist and, not incidentally, a multi-millionaire whom McVety calls his business partner. From his nineteen-thousand-member Cornerstone Church in San Antonio, Hagee has spent nearly three decades championing the right of Israel to reclaim the geography of its Old Testament heyday. In 2006, he organized the first major evangelical lobby on its behalf, Christians United for Israel, with McVety as his Canadian major-domo, but their partnership was sealed long before that political pact. On the college's fourth floor, a trio of women tend the phones for the Canadian branch of John Hagee Ministries, which McVety claims brings in a million dollars a year. Dutifully filling out order forms that include the question, "Have you been saved? Yes/No," they dispense Hagee's books and DVDs, all of which sound the same ominous theme: the end of the world is at hand.

In *Jerusalem Countdown*, his 2006 bestseller, Hagee offers more specific details on that prospect and makes a case for the Israeli military to bomb Iran, thus eliminating both its nuclear threat and the anti-Semitic slurs of its president, Mahmoud Ahmadinejad. "The coming nuclear showdown with Iran is a certainty," he writes, making clear that he has this on good authority from Israeli intelligence. If such an attack should trigger a third world war or nuclear holocaust, Hagee counsels born-again readers that they have nothing to fear: they will escape the final, fateful conflagration by being snatched heavenward before the Second Coming. "Rejoice and be exceedingly glad," he concludes cheerily. "The best is yet to come."

Despite the timeliness of Hagee's scenario, it is hardly new. The inspiration for his plot line can be traced back to a nineteenth-century Irish evangelist named John Nelson Darby who came up with the notion of dividing biblical history into seven eras or dispensations—the current one due to climax with the Battle of Armageddon—then added the twist of a secret exit plan for true believers that he christened the "Rapture of the Church." Although most mainstream theologians dismiss Darby's theory as an outrageous misreading of the Bible—Donald Wagner, an American evangelical scholar, denounces it as "a modern

heresy with cultish proportions"—the broad brushstrokes of his narrative have become a Hollywood staple, popularized by television preachers like Pat Robertson and thriller writers like Jerry Jenkins and Tim
LaHaye, whose *Left Behind* series has sold more than sixty-two million
copies and provoked countless spinoffs.

Still, it seems no coincidence that LaHaye, one of the architects of
the Moral Majority, has been at the forefront of spreading the gospel
of dispensationalism. Darby's feverish end-times vision has become
the driving force behind the continent's religious right, fuelling its
sense of urgency and obsession with biblical literalism while providing
the cornerstone for one of its key constituencies, the Christian Zionist
movement. In McVety's college bookstore, one of LaHaye's most recent
non-fiction works is on sale, *Mind Siege*, which calls for a society that
is based on biblical values, with harsh sentences for those performing
abortion or engaging in homosexual acts and a religious litmus test for
politicians: only Christians who believe that every word of the Bible is
divinely dictated, he argues, ought to be allowed to hold public office.

For McVety, who grew up steeped in Darby's apocalyptic worldview,
both LaHaye's and Hagee's end-times warnings sounded a familiar
theme. In 1970, his uncle John Wesley White, one of Billy Graham's
deputies, published *Re-entry: Striking Parallels Between Today's News
Events and Christ's Second Coming*, which offered a Cold War take on
Darby's script, nominating the Kremlin for the role of Antichrist. After
the collapse of the Soviet Union, White and other dispensationalists
were obliged to revise their prophetic enemies list, focusing on an evolv-
ing roster of candidates for the book of Daniel's "wicked king of the
north." For some, it was the secretary general of the United Nations
with what they consider to be its one-world mandate, for others it was
Iraqi dictator Saddam Hussein, who controlled the contemporary acreage of the biblical kingdom of Babylon. But after the U.S. invasion of
Iraq, McVety and most other evangelicals joined Hagee in placing
Ahmadinejad in the crosshairs of dispensationalist suspicion,

convinced that the signs and portents in each day's newscast signalled the world was on the fast track to the Apocalypse. "Make no mistake about it," he would tell me later. "We're three seconds before midnight."

McVety's ties to Hagee and other celebrity tenants have given him a prominence he might never have achieved on his own, and provided him with a direct pipeline to the panic that shot through the U.S. Christian right when courts in Ontario and B.C. handed down landmark rulings sanctioning same-sex marriage. Suddenly, a nation regarded as the epitome of boring moderation was preparing to establish a legislative precedent that American televangelists feared would spill over the border. "They'd all say, 'What's happened to you?'" McVety recounts. "You're legalizing gay marriage, you're legalizing marijuana, you're legalizing porn—you've become extremists."

They also let it be known that it was time for Canadian evangelicals to take some extreme measures of their own. As McVety mounted his Defend Marriage campaign, he signalled that a new style of conservative Christian advocacy had arrived on the national scene—brash, unapologetic and, to some, distinctly un-Canadian. But while he made no attempt to hide the fact that he had patterned his activism on an American model, he still bridles at charges that he was financed by the U.S. religious right. "We haven't seen one greenback!" he protests. "Frankly, I'd like to have seen a greater focus on defending marriage by American preachers coming across the border."

⁘

On the spring morning in 2006 when I finally meet McVety, he is exuberant. In his airy corner suite on the fourth floor of Canada Christian College, he has just finished a phone conversation with one of the dozens of evangelicals in Harper's caucus and is basking in that proximity to power. "A lot of our friends are in government now," he says, "so that makes a lot of things easier."

He rhymes off a list of high-placed pals including Stockwell Day, who was then Harper's newly minted minister of public safety. Those connections have been a boon to McVety and his controversial educational institution, which was founded in the 1960s by his evangelist father Elmer as Richmond College and has survived assorted incarnations and rental accommodations before emerging in its current form. McVety purchased the building more than a decade ago for $2.1 million dollars, but the college's reputation has often mirrored the mercurial career of its founder. In the 1970s, Elmer McVety ended up in an unwelcome spotlight when a disgruntled donor complained to the *Toronto Star* about financial irregularities at one of his overseas mission projects. Although never found guilty of legal wrongdoing, McVety was forced to resign as the local head of Bibles for the World, a U.S.-based mission society, and his television show was dropped. Ever resilient, he bounced back only to find himself on the *Star*'s front page again in 1982 when the Ontario government threatened to revoke his college's credentials as an alleged diploma mill. That accreditation battle raged on for more than a decade, well past his death in 1993.

For Charles McVety, his second son and successor, a career in academia seemed an unlikely fit. A gifted hockey player who had dropped out of the University of Toronto to work as a contractor, his only degrees were from the family college and an even more controversial institution in Los Angeles that offers correspondence courses and claims ties to an obscure seminary in Korea. Still, McVety threw himself into the fight against Ontario's educational authorities with no lack of confidence. Five years later, when the province ordered him to close Canada Christian College, he defied the instruction with characteristic brio. "I told them to take a long walk on a short pier and get lost," he says.

It was then that McVety discovered the merits of political activism. Targeting the nearby riding of Ontario's minister of education, he enlisted his students to plaster it with posters and overwhelmed the ministry's phone lines and fax machine. Popping up on local airwaves as a self-styled crusader against Christian persecution, he had no trouble grabbing the attention of the premier, Mike Harris. Within months, Frank Klees, another member of Harris's cabinet, introduced a bill expressly designed to give Canada Christian College full degree-granting rights.

McVety had met Klees, a former Baptist minister, at a Conservative party shindig—"I learned that you can have great access to ministers at fundraisers," he confides—and that encounter proved mutually beneficial. Months after Klees's bill went through the legislature, McVety made a one-thousand-dollar donation to the minister's re-election campaign, and has backed him ever since. In the Conservatives' 2009 provincial leadership contest, McVety helped organize a membership drive that signed up more than nine thousand new supporters for Klees, who finished a surprising second in the race.

Buoyed by his fling with provincial politics, McVety threw himself into the campaign to overthrow Preston Manning's leadership of the Canadian Alliance, claiming to have recruited five thousand new members for Stockwell Day—a feat he repeated when Day's leadership came under fire from Harper. To this day, McVety remains a Day loyalist, his television show logo featuring the minister's countenance next to that of Jerry Falwell, and during the 2006 superpower summit in Russia, he arranged for Day to receive an honorary degree from St. Petersburg State University, the source of his own honorary doctorate.

They originally met through one of Canada Christian College's correspondence students, an Alberta youth pastor named Roy Beyer who co-founded the Canada Family Action Coalition, a grassroots Christian lobby over which McVety now presides. According to CFAC's mission statement, the Calgary-based coalition was set up "to see Judeo-Christian moral principles restored in Canada," a goal with a distinctly Christian nationalist ring. Indeed, for most of its thirteen-year history, it has prodded conservative Christians to vote for candidates with CFAC-vetted views in the hopes of ensuring a government which, as one essay on its website delicately puts it, will not interfere with the country's "divine destiny."

That political activism is one reason the coalition has never registered as a religious charity, a decision that has been a godsend for McVety. Despite his scorn for the fiscal worrywarts at the Evangelical Fellowship, he was aware that his outspoken stands on social issues could put the charitable tax status of his college at risk. When he took over CFAC's presidency in 2003, he suddenly found himself with an alternate bully pulpit, free from Revenue Canada's scrutiny, and he didn't hesitate to use it. As head of the coalition, he forced the Royal Bank to cancel a gay-friendly workplace campaign and spoke out against a Supreme Court decision limiting a parent's right to spank obstreperous offspring. On the wall behind his desk, McVety displays a framed front page from the *National Post* which identifies him as a self-proclaimed "spanker"—a notoriety he treasures second only to that immortalized on an adjoining page under the headline "Faiths Unite Against Same Sex."

In his fight against same-sex marriage, McVety saw himself following in the footsteps of Jerry Falwell, who took a special interest in Canada's gay-rights legislation and unleashed regular diatribes against homosexuality on his *Old-Time Gospel Hour*. So unbridled was one tirade that Vision TV ordered its station directors to screen Falwell's shows for language that could imperil its multi-faith licence from the Canadian Radio-television and Telecommunications Commission (CRTC). While evangelicals like Brian Stiller might shudder at Falwell's blistering hyperbole, for McVety he was an unmitigated hero whose achievements as a pioneer of the religious right were only matched by those as the founder of a major educational institution: Liberty University in Lynchburg, Virginia, where McVety would later send his son, Ryan.

In February 2004, he invited Falwell to Canada Christian College for a conference on same-sex marriage that he billed as an "Emergency Pastor's Briefing." Despite a paralyzing snowstorm, Falwell made it to Toronto in his private jet, and exhorted the six hundred evangelicals whom McVety had assembled to defeat the "principalities of evil" that appeared to have taken possession of the nation's capital. In the early days of the Moral Majority, he pointed out, he had been only one of many generals in the emerging American Christian right; now it was up to Canadians to find their own broadly based command team. "He graded us on being the salt and the light," McVety says, "and on activism, he gave us an F. It was a wake-up call for the pastors we brought here." For McVety himself, it was also confirmation that if Canadian evangelicals were to seed their own Christian right, they would need a host of different voices. "On the left, there are hundreds of organizations," he says. "On the right, there is a great void."

⸸

On the second floor of a bleak strip mall in a benighted section of northeast Calgary, Brian Rushfeldt bends over his computer screen, putting the finishing touches on yet another e-mail alert. From this modest two-room office, the unlikely nerve centre of the Canada Family Action Coalition, Rushfeldt rallies its forty thousand members to the moral ramparts, urging them to write or call their MPs over the latest outrage in the values wars. Charles McVety may be the public face of CFAC, throwing press conferences and coining quotable zingers when reporters phone, but miles away in this unprepossessing Calgary walk-up, it is Rushfeldt, a self-styled "nuts and bolts guy," who keeps the organization's machinery humming and fires up its troops with regular calls to arms.

"Government endorsement of pornography!" howls one bulletin issued after the CRTC approved an Alberta-based adult entertainment channel called Northern Peaks: "CRTC approves of sexual degradation, Canadian-style." Another warns of the "massive" consequences if a fundamentalist Mormon sect in British Columbia succeeds in escaping polygamy charges. "Polygamy—the Road to Fiscal, Legal and Social Chaos," its headline shrieks.

Meeting the mild-mannered Rushfeldt, it seems hard to imagine such rhetoric spewing from this slight, intense figure, who spent fifteen years as an air-traffic controller before an ulcer forced him to retire. Rushfeldt loved that job, sitting for hours in a darkened room watching dots of light dart across his radar screen, the safety of thousands of passengers hinging on his vigilance. He sees it as not unlike his current duties at CFAC and treasures the bronze tribute to his service that hangs on one wall, even if it is signed by the man who unleashed much of the legislation against which he now fights: Pierre Elliott Trudeau, the prime minister who decriminalized sodomy and decreed that the state has no business in the nation's bedrooms.

Rushfeldt has spent at least a decade working against gay rights, and once warned that if same-sex marriage were legalized, parents could be "criminalized" for teaching their biblical views on sexuality. He has received death threats, been called a bigot "and worse," he says, but then he has never been drawn to stress-free occupations. When his nerves forced him out of the control tower, he became a social worker, counselling runaways and drug-addled teens. Rushfeldt is no stranger to tales of misery and human degradation, most of which he blames on the breakdown of the family and a lack of firm Christian beliefs.

While working in schools as a provincial addictions counsellor, he also became convinced there was a more organized plot afoot to undermine society. One day, dropping in on a Grade 8 class, he listened as a guest speaker billed as an expert on HIV/AIDS pulled out a banana and a condom. "He didn't mention AIDS," Rushfeldt says. "He was talking about how to have sex. He was from the gay and lesbian community and he was promoting the homosexual lifestyle."

Eventually, Rushfeldt joined the Victory Church and was named head of its first Bible college despite the fact he had never been to divinity school himself. He and his colleague Roy Beyer hoped to remedy their lack of credentials through correspondence courses with Canada Christian College, but a 1996 bill to include sexual orientation as grounds for discrimination in the federal human rights code convinced them to drop everything and build a grassroots political force to demand the restoration of biblical principles to government. At Victory headquarters, their boss arranged for them to fly to Washington for a tutorial from the reigning expert on evangelical organizing, Ralph Reed, the Georgia wunderkind whom Pat Robertson had chosen to build the Christian Coalition.

Years earlier, Reed had confided to a reporter that stealth was essential to his modus operandi. "I want to be invisible," he said. "I do guerrilla warfare. I paint my face and travel at night." Warming to the metaphor, he boasted, "You don't know it's over until you're in a body bag. You don't know until election night." Nobody had paid much attention until 1994 when Reed realized that scenario on a national scale. The mainstream media woke up on election night to discover that the Christian Coalition had been instrumental in engineering a Republican takeover of both houses of Congress for the first time in forty-two years.

Flying to Washington for a Christian Coalition conference two years later, Beyer and Rushfeldt found Reed only vaguely interested in a pair of Canadians seeking to start their own version of his operation. "It certainly wasn't, 'Let's jump on it,'" Rushfeldt recalls. Still, Reed gave them a pep talk and a video called *Citizen Action* with specific instructions on how to build a grassroots movement through churches, taking over one riding and school board at a time. Weeks after they had launched the Canada Family Action Coalition, Alberta premier Ralph Klein called an election.

They scrambled to put together a homegrown version of a tool that Reed had developed for churches, a political report card aimed at pinpointing acceptable social-conservative candidates without taking a partisan stand that would jeopardize their charitable tax status. Those voters' guides graded lawmakers on how they had cast their ballots on bills close to theo-con hearts. Beyer and Rushfeldt sent out their first edition to ninety thousand Alberta households in what turned out to be a dry run for the federal election that was called months later. In a burst of enthusiasm, they ordered half a million copies of their new national guides, confident that evangelical corporate leaders would leap at the opportunity to underwrite such an innovative scheme, but Beyer came back from his first fundraising tour empty-handed. "Up here," Rushfeldt says, "the Christian community had bought into this idea that politics and religion don't mix."

That realization was all the more distressing with a twelve-thousand-dollar printing bill due. They turned to their Victory Church network for support, but the night before Rushfeldt was to pick up the guides, they were still facing a shortfall. Then his home phone rang just before midnight. "A lady said, 'Brian, I felt God telling me you need some help,'" he recounts. The next morning, she was on his doorstep with a twelve-thousand-dollar cheque. Now those guides have become a standard item in CFAC's tactical arsenal, but between elections, Rushfeldt keeps up a steady tattoo, beating the drums for family-values legislation. Still, his focus seldom strays from deploring the gains he sees being scored by the gay-rights lobby—a threat that never fails to fire up the thousands of Bible-believers whose small donations now provide 90 percent of CFAC's operating budget.

After Beyer dropped out to work on Stockwell Day's 2000 leadership campaign, Rushfeldt ran the coalition solo, building it into the country's leading theo-con advocacy group. Today, he also serves as its official lobbyist, regularly pilgrimaging to Ottawa to push for legislation with ministers and MPs, many of whom happen to be old friends, from Day to B.C. MP Russ Hiebert, an evangelical lawyer who once served as CFAC's legal counsel. But Rushfeldt's most valuable contact in the capital is one whom most lobbyists would kill to have on their speed-dial: the prime minister himself.

In the late 1990s as Rushfeldt was building CFAC, Harper was back in Calgary re-establishing the National Citizens Coalition, and Rushfeldt often turned to him for advice. That friendship endured even after Harper won the 2006 election, and a photo of them huddled together in the prime minister's office now hangs in pride of place on Rushfeldt's wall. Their history, however, is not the only reason Rushfeldt has access to the PMO: CFAC was the prime mover behind the Defend Marriage Coalition, which played almost as much of a role in Harper's 2006 victory as the Christian Coalition did in putting George W. Bush in the White House.

Cobbled together in 2004 after an Ontario court legalized same-sex marriage, the coalition was made up of a dozen conservative Christian organizations, including the Catholic Civil Rights League and Campaign Life, but it was run by Rushfeldt's former partner Roy Beyer, and CFAC's president, Charles McVety, became its chief ringmaster. Other leaders in the group might have claimed an equal media profile, among them Gwen Landolt, the veteran leader of REAL Women of Canada and Tristan Emmanuel, a scrappy young pastor from the Niagara Peninsula who founded Equipping Christians for the Public Square, but Landolt was identified too closely with the abortion battle and Emmanuel was deemed too edgy. "Charles was much more in the public eye," Rushfeldt points out. "And he had the bus."

In his Defend Marriage bus emblazoned with stylized red-and-white maple leaves, McVety stormed the country with his wife and seven-year-old daughter, staging provocative prayer vigils outside MPs' offices and even dropping in on the Liberal Party convention—a visit he later immortalized on his website in an article entitled, "Daddy, Why Are They Spitting at Us?" It was just the sort of razzamatazz that McVety felt had been missing from the Canadian political landscape, and funding appeared to be no problem as he rallied his forces to swamp Paul Martin's office with twenty-two thousand letters and twenty-six thousand e-mails. Many were handwritten and some quoted passages on the punishment reserved for homosexuals in the book of Leviticus. Other groups such as the Knights of Columbus and Enshrine Marriage Canada, run by dissident Liberal MP Pat O'Brien, were also active, but none were as colourful or confrontational as McVety and his Defend Marriage troops.

While some critics in the evangelical community dismissed him for counter-productive grandstanding, they underestimated his strategic wiles and readiness to play hardball. More than a dozen prominent Liberals who supported the same-sex marriage bill discovered he had bought Internet domains under their names: websites such as Joevolpe.com and Rubydhalla.com suddenly appeared, featuring merciless critiques of their namesakes' performance—a move that McVety termed an "educational service."

Weeks before the Defend Marriage bus pulled into Montreal's Palais des congrès for the Conservative Party's first policy gathering, McVety demonstrated a knack for one-upmanship that rendered some of Harper's advisers speechless. The convention was the first policy gathering since Harper had taken over as Conservative leader, hitching his Canadian Alliance to the remnant of Peter MacKay's Progressive Conservative Party in a merger that left some on both sides less than enthralled. As members met to decide the party's first platform, the struggle for ideological control was underway when McVety caught wind of a move to dodge debate on same-sex marriage and abortion—the two issues that mattered most to his theo-con crowd. He was livid, charging that "the homosexual community was attempting to take over the Conservative policy platform."

The plot, McVety believed, was orchestrated by auto-parts heiress Belinda Stronach, who had helped consummate the party merger and had long backed the gay-rights cause. He and Rushfeldt sprang into action, launching a cross-country membership blitz with a flyer that announced, "How to Stop the Hijack of the Conservative Party." Urging "people of faith and good will" to demand their place as convention delegates, they claim to have added twenty-five thousand new social conservatives to the party lists. "We communicated with Stephen Harper," McVety recalls. "We said, 'We have the majority and we'll defeat the caucus' proposition. That will create a leadership crisis.'"

The next morning, party officials quietly announced they had removed the contentious proposition. According to insiders, the vote was called when Stronach stepped out for coffee, resulting in a tie, which Harper then broke. McVety lost no time in commending the Conservative leader for his about-face. "That shows a good man who listens to the people," he pointedly told reporters, "and can say, 'Yes, I erred.'"

When the motion enshrining the traditional definition of marriage passed with the support of 75 percent of delegates, Conservative moderates were faced with a disconcerting truth: McVety and his fellow theo-cons were no longer out on the sidewalk with placards demanding policy input; they were flexing their muscle in the party's backrooms, using their leverage to show they had no intention of being taken for granted.

McVety turned the convention into an ongoing attack on Stronach, dogging her through the Palais des congrès with video cameras and booing her speech, but she was not the only object of his attentions. Four other Conservative MPs who had declared their support for same-sex marriage—including Calgary's Jim Prentice and Stronach's then paramour Peter MacKay—found their offices swamped with mail, their phone and computer in-boxes jammed. "We believe that it is unconscionable for a Conservative MP to abandon the very core of conservatism, which is marriage," McVety warned.

Despite Harper's mixed signals, McVety believed he was onside. The Conservative leader had lambasted the same-sex marriage bill in the House of Commons and had promised fifteen thousand enthusiasts at an Ottawa rally that, as prime minister, he would bring in a measure defining marriage as the union of one man and one woman. Two months later, when the Liberals' bill was rushed through Parliament, McVety was doubly shaken—the defeat came on his wedding anniversary—but he had no intention of giving up the fight. He and his Defend Marriage allies prepared to throw themselves behind Harper in the next election campaign with even greater zeal.

Reflecting on their legislative setback, his coalition partner Gwen Landolt noted that conservative Christians actually owed the Liberals a debt of gratitude: the same-sex marriage bill had galvanized them into a flurry of organizing, swelling membership lists and sending donations soaring for the first time since the abortion fight. It had transformed social conservatives into a force to be reckoned with. This was not simply her opinion, Landolt told her REAL Women supporters; it was an assessment from behind enemy lines: an editorial in *Capital Xtra!*, the newspaper of Ottawa's gay community.

"Something changed in Canada during the national debate over same-sex marriage," the editorial concluded. "We now live in a new period of religious anger. Of extremist rhetoric. Of evangelical absolutism. Our community needs to get ready for US-style trench warfare as a new generation of religious Canadians start to flex their still weak, but growing muscles in the public square." *Capital Xtra!* had seen what few in the mainstream media had grasped: "A sleeping giant has been awoken," it warned: "the Christian right."

⁜

While Landolt found comfort in that backhanded tribute, Charles McVety took his inspiration from another headline. "Canada Needs a Ralph Reed," declared the *National Post*. The advice came from Edmonton columnist Lorne Gunter who argued that if this country's conservative Christians wanted the clout their American counterparts enjoyed, they ought to emulate the organizational genius who was credited with Bush's White House victories. Considering that one of Gunter's fishing buddies was Tom Flanagan, the Calgary academic then in charge of the Conservatives' war room, some readers might have leaped to the conclusion that his column reflected the thinking of the party's loftiest ranks. McVety took the hint: two months later, on November 30, 2005, he threw a gala dinner for the American king-maker, whom *Time* magazine had dubbed "God's Right Hand Man."

In the two years since Reed served as an adviser on Bush's re-election campaign, his reputation had lost some of its lustre. He was embroiled in a scandal with a casino lobbyist and his bid to become Georgia's lieutenant governor was foundering. Still, for the four hundred social conservatives who showed up at Canada Christian College to hear him, Reed remained a heroic figure, and before he had uttered a word, they accorded him a standing ovation. Among McVety's invitees were Senator Anne Cools—a social conservative who had filed a per-sonal brief against same-sex marriage at the Supreme Court—and Jim Flaherty, who had won a reputation as a hard-liner in Mike Harris's Ontario government, slashing social programs and musing about throwing the homeless in jail.

Reed's speech was a primer on grassroots organizing, which suddenly took on new relevance: only a day earlier, Paul Martin's government had fallen in a non-confidence vote, and an election was less than two months away. Waving a four-point action plan, Reed stressed that nothing replaced the grunt work of recruiting new members, knocking on doors and driving hot prospects to the polls, but in a country where the phrase "religious right" had already been fodder for one Liberal scare campaign, he had another message for conservative Christians: don't be afraid to show your beliefs. In 2004, Bush's forces had swept the country and improved their standing in every demographic, he argued, because they ran "unapologetically and boldly" on a theo-con platform. "If the people of the church don't get involved," Reed warned, "somebody else will."

That unexpected call for straightforwardness from the master of covert electoral action was music to his host's ears. "He said, 'Never run and hide,'" McVety recalls. "Never allow anyone to tell you that family values are a liability. They're only a liability in the media, never at the ballot box."

Ironically, only a day earlier, Stephen Harper had signalled that he would be following exactly the opposite game plan. Kicking off his campaign with a promise to hold a free vote on whether to reopen the marriage debate, he neatly sidestepped all further discussion of the subject until after the election and imposed such a strict rein on his caucus that Conservative candidates seemed to avoid most unscripted encounters with the media. Outspoken social conservatives like Renfrew MP Cheryl Gallant, who had once insisted that there was "absolutely no difference" between abortion and an al-Qaeda beheading, were suddenly found reading primly from prepared texts. But that vaunted party discipline had a paradoxical effect: by stifling the theo-con voices within his own ranks, Harper left McVety with a virtual media monopoly, his pronouncements amplified and his press coverage often out of all proportion to the crowds he attracted on the Defend Marriage bus route.

Across the country, Conservative candidates whom McVety deemed insufficiently vigorous in opposing same-sex marriage suddenly found themselves ousted by covert membership coups. As Reed had pointed out to his Toronto audience, democracy is often a game played by a motivated few: in the nitty-gritty of grassroots organizing, it can take only a handful of citizens to commandeer a nomination contest. McVety liked to remind his audiences that Harper had won the Conservative leadership by a relatively small margin. "We're talking about a hundred and fifty people per riding—tiny numbers!" he says. "This is the size of a small church."

One place he chose to test Reed's thesis was his own riding of Ajax-Whitby, east of Toronto. There, Conservative hopefuls discovered that McVety and his allies had stacked the membership lists, defeating two prominent contenders in favour of Rondo Thomas, a relative unknown who turned out to be the vice-president of Canada Christian College. The coup boomeranged when a videographer caught Thomas at one whistlestop depicting the election as an apocalyptic clash between the forces of immorality and righteousness, the footage becoming an Internet sensation that sent Harper's officials into frantic damage control. Barring Thomas from further appearances, they declared that his views in no way reflected the Conservative leader's. McVety did not take kindly to that disavowal, and still rails against the Conservative honcho who "locked down" his sidekick, ensuring Thomas's defeat. To him, it was yet another example of Harper's refusal to embrace evangelical principles with the boldness Reed had advised. "They're afraid of a hostile, vicious media that hates Christians," he fumed.

Refusing to be cowed, McVety turned his attentions to Thomas's Liberal rival, Mark Holland. A rookie MP, Holland had organized the pivotal caucus petition that convinced Paul Martin to push through the same-sex marriage vote before the Commons' summer recess, a move seen as critical to its success. For Holland, the bill had special resonance: his aunt, a retired community worker who had served as a consultant with the hate-crimes division of the Ottawa police, was a long-time activist in the capital's gay and lesbian community. Early in the campaign, he heard that McVety was trying to organize local clergy against him, but shrugged it off. Then Holland started receiving calls from McVety, and one in particular left him shaken. "How are your constituents going to feel about you not being married?" McVety inquired. Almost no one knew that, in the fourteen years Holland had lived with the mother of his three children, they had never made their relationship official. He was shocked. "For a complete stranger to rush out and find out these things would take a fair amount of work," he said later in an interview. "To me, it was a veiled threat."

⁜

McVety was not alone in operating from the shadows. Other religious groups made their presence felt under an array of mysterious identities. Flyers from a group called Concerned Canadian Parents surfaced on the doorsteps of those MPs like Holland who had supported same-sex marriage, calling it "a canker" that would destroy the country. No incorporation data existed for Concerned Canadian Parents whose address was a rented post office box in a 7-Eleven store on Toronto's Weston Road, but it turned out to be the unregistered front for a tiny but highly secretive fundamentalist sect called the Exclusive Brethren whose origins can be traced back to John Nelson Darby, the father of dispensationalism.

Headquartered in Australia with only an estimated forty thousand members around the world—no more than a few thousand of them in Canada—the Exclusive Brethren were a new and improbable addition to the increasingly crowded playing field of the country's religious right. Its members are forbidden to socialize with non-Brethren, watch television, attend university or consort with those in their own families who have fled the sect. They are even barred from voting, but in 2004, their newly installed leader, an Australian office-supplies mogul named Bruce Hales—whose proper title is Elect Vessel—was so outraged by the prospect of homosexual marriage that he poured millions into full-page newspaper ads in the U.S. and Australia, urging others to do what he and his members were forbidden to: vote Bush and Prime Minister John Howard back into office. One expelled member alleged that Hales had declared both victories essential to staving off the premature advent of the Apocalypse, but whatever his motivation, Brethren coffers, fed by a network of thriving global businesses, proved equal to underwriting those costly advertising campaigns. According to a Florida newspaper, the sect spent nearly half a million dollars cheerleading for Bush in that key electoral-college state.

A year later, when Hales's focus shifted to Canada's same-sex marriage debate, similar ads began appearing in the *Globe and Mail*, the

Toronto Sun and Ottawa's influential *Hill Times*. All had been commissioned by a Brethren member in Toronto whose graphic design business was around the corner from the mysterious 7-Eleven post-office box. Ron Heggie, the point man for Concerned Canadian Parents, insisted the initiative was entirely his own, but a trio of his dark-suited Brethren had already been spotted in the Commons visitors' gallery during the marriage debate. They also hired the services of a noted power-broker: Calgary attorney Gerald Chipeur, an expert on religious-freedom issues who acted as legal counsel for the Conservative Party and its predecessors, Reform and the Canadian Alliance.

Only weeks before the 2006 election, Chipeur had inadvertently made headlines for attempting to ensure Harper's victory with a pre-emptive strike. In an e-mail to Paul Weyrich, one of the godfathers of the Moral Majority, he asked U.S. conservatives to resist interview requests from Canadian reporters looking for quotes about Harper that might derail the campaign. Weyrich was happy to oblige, but after the election, he made clear that he did not hold out much hope for an ideological revolution north of the border. As he wrote on his website, with only a minority government, Harper would have little power to correct what Weyrich termed "some premises of Cultural Marxism" that now prevailed in Canada—same-sex marriage and abortion-on-demand. Still, he counselled American conservatives with an eye on the new prime minister's career to be patient on both fronts: "It will take time," he advised.

⊕

In the early days of Harper's government, the leaders of the country's burgeoning Christian right had every reason to be upbeat. For the first time in memory, evangelicals who had felt like pariahs in Ottawa found themselves welcomed as honoured guests. On the day of Harper's first throne speech, Charles McVety was among more than two dozen theo-cons invited to a prestigious luncheon in the parliamentary dining room convened by Senator Anne Cools. Both Stockwell Day and Jason Kenney popped in to pay their respects, but it wasn't until nearly two weeks later that word of the event leaked out. "Social conservatives to sell Tory daycare plan," announced a front-page headline in the *Globe and Mail*, revealing that McVety and other militants behind the Defend Marriage campaign had been enlisted to promote the government's controversial new child-care allowance. Although Harper's office denied any connection to Cools's luncheon, its efforts at spin control came too late: McVety and Gwen Landolt had already spilled details of the scheme, proudly pledging to do their part. Despite that indiscretion, when Jim Flaherty unveiled the child-care allowance as the centrepiece of his first budget, McVety was in the Commons visitors' gallery as his personal guest.

For those who had dismissed McVety and company as an electoral necessity—a group Harper could shrug off as soon as the vote was in—reports of their ongoing influence came as a shock. "You can't be serious," one veteran evangelical leader told a reporter. "If these are the kinds of people the government is listening to, then you've got a story."

But another, more significant development that emerged from Cools's summit went largely ignored. Not only were conservative Christians being feted by Harper's government, they were putting down roots, creating an ideological infrastructure to give them a voice in policy-making for years to come. More than a decade after the failed abortion bill had prompted Brian Stiller to plant the Evangelical Fellowship's flag in Ottawa, the same-sex marriage defeat had convinced a new crop of evangelical organizations that it was time to establish their own persence in the capital as well. "There's no doubt it was a major lightning rod for a lot of people," says Dave Quist, a former Harper aide who was pegged to head a new Ottawa think tank for Focus on the Family Canada. "There was an awakening. People said, 'Wow, how did we get here? And is it too late? Is it all set in stone?'"

With Harper's promise to reopen the marriage debate, most counted on a second chance to reverse the legislation, but their strategy was not centred on that issue alone. Following the lead of the religious right in Washington, they set out to establish a multitude of independent voices—a chorus of think tanks, lobbies and youth groups, some interconnected, some not, but all singing from the same songbook in an effort to keep theo-conservative concerns on the national agenda.

Although several groups already had plans for Ottawa offices in the works, McVety was first off the mark. His pre-election dinner for Ralph Reed, in fact, had served as the debut of his Institute for Canadian Values, an offshoot of Canada Christian College funded by a $250,000 grant from retired trucking tycoon Sid Harkema. The institute, as McVety described it, was intended to churn out polls and editorials, backing up Brian Rushfeldt's Canada Family Action Coalition with hard numbers and a dose of academic gravitas. For the position of executive director, McVety chose Joseph Ben-Ami, a burly Orthodox Jew who had never attended university and was best known as a former operations director for Stockwell Day. Indeed, Ben-Ami's political connections were as impressive as they were confounding: after two years as B'nai Brith's chief lobbyist in Ottawa, he had segued seamlessly into the evangelical fold, emerging as McVety's deputy in the Defend Marriage campaign. Still, that career move was not as startling as it might have seemed. In the complex universe of the religious right, his leap from one of the most conservative Jewish organizations to the service of its leading Christian Zionist ally was more like a casual saunter.

Ben-Ami's facility for straddling those competing faith camps can be traced back to a small town in the Ottawa Valley where he grew up as Joseph Jung, the son of a Catholic mother and a nominally Jewish father, in a household he describes as "spiritually eclectic." At seventeen, a year shy of his high-school graduation, he enlisted in the navy until his conversion to Orthodox Judaism made that career impractical, and he resurfaced in Ottawa as a communications consultant and defence-department trainer under his current name. As a key back-room player in the movement to unite the right, Ben-Ami was one of the few Day insiders whom Harper kept on when he took over the party. Along the way, he carved out a role for himself as a bridge between warring conservative factions, but few knew that his interest in family-values issues stemmed in part from a bitter custody battle he had waged for years with his ex-wife—a battle he had even testified about to a special parliamentary inquiry on the subject.

Like McVety, Ben-Ami modelled his activism on that of a major player in the U.S. religious right: in his case, Don Feder, a fellow Orthodox Jew who had become an adviser to Vision America, dedicated to wiping out the constitutional amendment separating church and state and, not incidentally, fostering Christian Zionism. In 2005, Feder made a splash by marshalling a handful of Republican rabbis to join him in forming Jews Against Anti-Christian Defamation, aimed at defending evangelicals from attacks by the secular humanist establish-ment. "The people who are probably subjected to the most discrimina-tion in our society are evangelical Christians," Feder asserted. "We recognize that Christians are the last remaining obstacle to the moral deconstruction of America."

Naming Ben-Ami as the only Canadian on his board, Feder handed him a high-profile slot at a Washington conference he helped organize under the title, "The War on Christians and the Values Voter in 2006." At a time when the religious right appeared to have taken over the Republican Party and claimed one of their own in the White House, the event was devoted to the curious notion that conservative Christians were under siege. That sense of persecution was hammered home by a who's who from the second wave of the U.S. evangelical right—a post-Falwell generation of Christian nationalist leaders that included Teen Mania founder Ron Luce, Ohio televangelist Rod Parsley and conference co-organizer Rick Scarborough, whose Patriot Pastors coali-tion had played a major role in the 2004 presidential race. United by the conviction that secularists were thwarting America's destiny as a truly Christian nation, they shrank from calling for an outright theocracy, but Parsley personified their approach to greater evangelical engagement in politics. "We are under spiritual invasion," he thundered to the crowd. "Man your battle stations! Ready your weapons! Lock and load!"

Appearing on a panel with Feder, Ben-Ami advanced the notion that in Canada, too, both evangelicals and Jews faced a threat from the implacable forces of secularism, or, as he preferred to call it, "neo-paganism." It was an assertion he would repeat later at Christian right conferences back home, arguing that the country ought to be governed according to biblical principles. "As a Jew, I feel safer in a country where Christians are in power," he told a Toronto evangelical audience in 2008, "because the essence of Christianity is tolerance."

The mission of the Institute for Canadian Values was to push for a greater religious role in policy-making, and to that end Ben-Ami ground out essays applauding Harper's support for Israel and offering a rationale for introducing abortion legislation. To a majority of social conservatives, the most pressing order of business was prodding Harper to keep his campaign promise for a rerun of the marriage vote, but Ben-Ami argued there was no hurry to reopen that hornet's nest. He urged avoiding another parliamentary showdown until religious-right groups had time to win over more support, proposing an archetypal Canadian vehicle for foot-dragging: a royal commission to study the status of the family. In the fall of 2006, his institute produced a poll reporting that 64 percent of respondents supported such a review. "I think they're saying to our politicians and parliamentarians, 'Look, go back to the drawing board and take another look at this,'" Ben-Ami told the *National Post*.

Instead, word came down from the prime minister's office that Harper intended to call the marriage vote before the end of his first year in power. Panic rippled through social conservative ranks as it seemed increasingly likely that the Defend Marriage camp was headed for defeat. Even Charles McVety was uncharacteristically glum. "You can only re-address things so many times," he worried.

Those fears appeared well-founded when he and Ben-Ami convened a National Marriage Caucus in Ottawa, and only a sparse crowd showed up. On a bleak day in October 2006, they gathered with a few dozen hard-core supporters on the steps of the Parliament Buildings—a small forlorn circle where, only a year earlier, they had welcomed a crowd of fifteen thousand, all madly cheering as Harper promised victory for their cause. In desperation, Brian Rushfeldt met with the prime minister, pleading with him not to rush ahead with the motion. "I said, 'Stephen, we can't have the vote now because we've got the same people sitting in Parliament,'" Rushfeldt recounts. "'You're setting us up for a loss.'"

But Harper remained unmoved. Rushfeldt blames his intransigence on the influence of Tory strategists who had always scorned the party's social-conservative base and wanted to get the vote out of the way before the next election call. That December, when the government's motion on reopening the marriage debate failed by a fifty-two vote margin, Harper left the distinct impression that he was relieved to have dispersed with the obligation so swiftly. "I don't see reopening this question in the future," he declared in tones so dismissive that Rushfeldt was deluged with irate calls from members of the Canada Family Action Coalition. "People are just so discouraged with politicians and politics, generally," he said. "I've had the odd person say, 'I don't even want to be a member of the party anymore—it's not a conservative party.'" In a carefully worded press release, Ben-Ami reminded Harper of the course he had charted back in 2003 with his theo-con strategy. "Either the new Conservative Party is a big tent with room at the table for all conservatives, including social conservatives, or it's not," he warned. "I hear lots of talk about how there's nowhere else for these voters to go come election time. The fact is that they can just stay home."

By then, fissures were already beginning to appear in the nascent religious right. Nearly a year after the Institute for Canadian Values had been unveiled with such fanfare, it remained essentially a one-man show that Ben-Ami ran out of his basement with the help of his journalist wife, Lynne Cohen. To his dismay, all the money he had raised for the institute was funnelled through McVety's college, which never seemed to have enough left over to rent him a proper Ottawa office or, at times, pay his salary. Furious and frustrated, he finally parted ways with McVety.

The split prompted speculation that the Christian right was collapsing, but in fact McVety tucked the Institute for Canadian Values back under his organizational wing, while Ben-Ami founded a new Ottawa think tank, the Canadian Centre for Policy Studies, and launched a blog he called "Reflections of an Unrepentant Conservative." His influence in the capital remained undiminished as he threw himself into the sort of strategizing that had bored McVety. "You can't simply keep saying to MPs, 'If you don't cooperate, we're going to vote you out of office,'" Ben-Ami points out. "That can't be the only weapon in your arsenal. At some point in time, you have to start winning the arguments."

⁜

Three blocks from the Parliament Buildings, another key player in the capital's evangelical infrastructure shared Ben-Ami's opinion but none of his financial constraints. Ensconced in the penthouse suite of an office tower that is home to Conservative Party headquarters, Dave Quist had more space than he could then use and a view that only the backing of a multi-million-dollar organization could buy. Not that such well-appointed digs are unexpected for the awkwardly named Institute of Marriage and Family Canada (IMFC), the largest and most lavishly funded of the new faith-based organizations that sprang up in the wake of the same-sex marriage debate. The think tank is part of the

Colorado-based empire of James Dobson, the parenting sage whose *Focus on the Family* broadcasts are heard by as many as ten million listeners a week, making him one of the most influential voices in the U.S. Christian right.

What was unexpected, during my quick tour of the institute's Ottawa offices, was a telling omission in its decor: no photos of the avuncular Dobson stared down from its walls and his countless books and publications were nowhere in sight. So eager is the IMFC to distance itself from Dobson's controversial political role in the U.S. that, shortly after its opening, Quist made a point of telling me that he had never met the Focus founder nor had he visited his Colorado Springs lair where nearly a thousand employees dispense Dobson's wares from an eighty-eight-acre compound with its own postal code. Quist underlined that his bosses were in Langley, B.C., where Focus on the Family's independent Canadian affiliate is based in more modest quarters: an upscale mall on the edge of town. But while his disclaimer of ties to Focus on the Family's U.S. operation may be legally accurate, his Canadian board includes two top officials from the American parent organization, including president and CEO Jim Daly, Dobson's chosen institutional heir. Indeed, when the *Montreal Gazette* examined the group's U.S. annual reports in 2005, it discovered contributions for computer, broadcast and technical support services to the Canadian branch valued at $1.6 million over four years.

The subject was clearly a sensitive one for a religious charity whose U.S. political activities were then under investigation by the Internal Revenue Service—and all the more so since Focus on the Family's Canadian office had taken a leading role in the same-sex marriage fight. Running full-page newspaper ads urging, "Traditional marriage—if you believe in it, protect it," the organization distributed a Marriage Action Kit that offered forms to e-mail politicians, along with a script for follow-up phone conversations that left nothing to chance ("Hello, my name is . . . ," the instructions began.) Dobson also threw his most valuable asset into the fight, his own well-burnished vocal cords. Buying advertising time on 130 Canadian radio stations, he broadcast a personal appeal, exhorting listeners to voice their objections directly to members of Parliament.

For Dobson, the advances of the gay-rights movement had become an obsession. "It's gay, gay, gay everywhere," he once raged, and his 2004 book, *Marriage Under Fire*, compares proponents of same-sex unions to Adolf Hitler. As early as 1998, he had his eye on this country as a hotbed of moral subversion. "Nowhere is the homosexual agenda more successful than in Canada," he announced in a newsletter. And when the Ontario Court of Appeal ruled that banning same-sex marriage was unconstitutional, he warned that, "Western civilization itself appears to hang in the balance. If it could happen in Canada, then why not here, there and everywhere?" Although Focus on the Family had affiliates in more than two dozen countries, Darrel Reid, the former president of the Canadian operation, confirms that Dobson took a special interest in this one, convinced the country was "on the leading edge of social decline."

Reid himself was not about to dispute that assesment. A former chief of staff to Preston Manning, he took over Focus on the Family Canada in 1997, vowing to transform it into more of a player on the national stage, and for the next seven years, he made good on that vow, orchestrating countless interventions at the Supreme Court to decry the use of gay-friendly textbooks in B.C. schools and protest the inclusion of sexual orientation as grounds for discrimination under the human rights act. One evangelical scholar extols his success at "Canadianizing" Focus operations in this country by declining to reprint some over-the-top tirades from Colorado headquarters, but his own rhetoric has often made unwanted headlines: Reid once told an audience that he believed it was every Christian's duty to change laws "to reflect biblical values," and declared that the Liberals' same-sex marriage bill made him "ashamed to be called a Canadian."

If he and Dobson saw that bill as merely one symptom of the country's inexorable slide toward moral breakdown, the cure he proposed was equally long-term: a think tank to provide social conservatives with the intellectual ammunition that would shift the terms of the debate. As a former academic and policy expert, Reid had a keen appreciation of the role that such idea factories could play. In Washington, a raft of conservative think tanks, from the American Enterprise Institute to the Heritage Foundation, had spent three decades crafting the ideological arguments that ultimately transformed that nation's political landscape. In 1980, the Heritage Foundation's twelve-hundred-page policy paper, "A Mandate for Leadership," became the legislative blueprint for Reagan's first term.

In Canada, few such multi-million-dollar institutions existed, and those that did generally confined their activities to shaping economic policy. For Reid, establishing a think tank devoted to family values also represented unfinished business: shortly after his appointment as Focus president, he had told *B.C. Report* that he hoped to see a day when the concerns of Dobson's organization "drive Canada's social and moral agenda." Nine years later, he realized he could never achieve that goal churning out policy studies in B.C. "Ottawa is where the laws are made," he said. "You can't be four thousand miles away. Nobody's listening to us out in Langley."

Most outsiders assumed that Focus on the Family's new Ottawa presence would be patterned after Dobson's Family Research Council in Washington, now an independent spinoff with its own six-storey building, a mailing list of five hundred thousand names and a $14 million budget. But the council has become the religious right's chief lobby on the U.S capital and after its president, Tony Perkins, raised eyebrows for alleging that the activism of the American judiciary was a greater threat to democracy than al-Qaeda terrorists, Reid preferred to cite another source of inspiration closer to home: Vancouver's Fraser Institute, which had once been dismissed as the mouthpiece for the free-market fringe. Slowly, implacably, swept along on the tides of the Reagan and Thatcher revolutions, the Fraser Institute had won coverage of its neo-conservative economic studies in the mainstream media, its name no longer qualified with labels identifying its right-wing tilt. "When they started twenty-five years ago, they were viewed with great skepticism," Quist notes. "Now they're quoted all the time."

Like McVety, Reid didn't seek to install a scholar at the new institute's helm. He wanted a political operative who knew his way around Parliament Hill, and Quist had a resume tailor-made for the job. A former municipal administrator whose wife had homeschooled their three kids, he had spent six years as an executive assistant to former Reform/Alliance MP Reed Elley—a stint which gave him an insider's understanding of what harried politicians and Hill staffers need to translate their social-conservative convictions into legislation. "I knew if we could make the research into bite-sized chunks—clearly written with five or six bullets or talking points—it would be invaluable," he says. "No twenty-page report is going to get read."

With an annual operating budget of nearly half a million dollars provided by two windfall donations—one from a foundation, the other from an anonymous Canadian philanthropist—the Institute of Marriage and Family Canada was ready to open in the fall of 2005, but the election call convinced its board to wait. "We didn't want to be seen as an offshoot of the Conservative Party," explains Quist's boss, Derek Rogusky, executive vice-president for policy. When it finally did throw open its doors less than a month after Harper's victory, twenty MPs showed up for the festivities, including two of the best-known names in the new Conservative cabinet, Jason Kenney and Stockwell Day. Excitement was high as conservative Christians contemplated being heard in Ottawa for the first time in years. "Under previous governments a lot of us were branded as bogeymen, as somehow unCanadian for our beliefs," Rogusky told a reporter. "I think that has changed with Harper becoming prime minister."

In the first issue of the glossy IMFC *Review*, the institute had the prescience—or insider knowledge—to focus on child care, the highlight of the government's first budget. While Quist hand-delivered copies to his old allies on Parliament Hill, he insisted he was not preaching only to the social-conservative choir; he also wanted to provide arguments to those MPs whose votes might be up for grabs. "It's one thing to say parents should have choice in child care," he pointed out. "It's another to say that 84 percent of parents want choice. For those who are neutral, I'm hoping it will be a tipping point."

Quist was careful to distance his think tank from Joseph Ben-Ami's Institute for Canadian Values, but they took a coordinated line of attack in the child-care debate, targeting the government's critics. While Ben-Ami slammed daycare advocates for accepting government funding, the IMFC took aim at their scholarship. Under the headline, "Don't Get Fooled By Child Care Research," the review questioned the academic independence of the leading advocates for public daycare, alleging that most of their studies "tend to be ideologically motivated and researcher bias is frequent . . . Beware."

It was an ironic critique from an institute whose own research reads less like traditional think-tank studies and more like opinion columns, long on argument and short on facts. That resemblance was no accident: one of the institute's writers was a former member of the *National Post* editorial board, and another an alumnus of the Focus on the Family Institute in Colorado Springs. In Quist's view, a measure of the institute's success was its media profile. "When we get our quote or statistics cited in the newspaper," he said, "we'll know we've started to make an impact."

By that benchmark, his organization was an immediate sensation, well on its way to emulating the Fraser Institute's feat of shaking off references to its ideological roots. When Quist was quoted, he was cited only as the head of an institute whose name was already a worthy-sounding mouthful; few reporters bothered to add that it was a subsidiary of Focus on the Family Canada and therefore part of the Colorado-based empire of James Dobson. Similarly, IMFC's research manager, Andrea Mrozek, who had worked for both the Fraser Institute and the defunct *Western Standard*, became a regular presence on the conservative commentary pages of the *National Post*, where she was almost never identified by her Focus ties. Whipping off breezy opinion pieces under titles such as "Good Riddance, National Day Care" and "The New Face of Feminism"—a tribute to Sarah Palin—Mrozek offered a contemporary spin on Focus on the Family's time-worn preoccupations without the baggage of being linked to the increasingly controversial Dr. Dobson.

After the defeat of Harper's same-sex marriage vote—and his signal that he considered the file closed—Quist announced that the institute, too, was shelving that fight. He justified that shift by citing the latest census figures, which revealed that, out of Canada's six million married couples, fewer than eight thousand or 0.1 percent turned out to be of the same sex—an "incredibly low" tally that he claimed had caught him by surprise. Instead, the IMFC was focusing its energies on promoting tax breaks for traditional marriage, an institution he declared under threat, eroded by the soaring numbers of live-in relationships. Accordingly, Mrozek and a co-author produced a report guaranteed to please economic conservatives: it claimed that marriage breakdown cost governments seven billion dollars a year in social programs for single mothers and their offspring. For an institute that had demanded the state get out of the child-care business, their paper made an unusual recommendation, calling on governments to get into the business of marriage counselling. By keeping couples together—teaching the benefits of wedded bliss in high schools and offering tax credits only to couples who had legally tied the knot—the report argued that federal and provincial authorities could save taxpayers nearly two billion dollars annually. "Families are the best social safety net we know," Mrozek declared, an assertion that came as news to many social scientists. Indeed, experts in the field questioned the study's methodology—it had only looked at government expenditures on single-parent families with no comparative data—and its simplistic approach to a complex social kaleidoscope. As Glenn Hope of the B.C. Council for Families diplomatically observed, the whole concept of modern families had become so diverse that his organization deemed it more "useful" to celebrate those differences than "try to turn back the clock."

Still, such questionable scholarship failed to dent the institute's standing. In a Parliament where 32 percent of MPs lacked university degrees, rookie Conservatives eagerly lapped up IMFC's policy papers, turning it into a well-regarded cog in the capital's proliferating theo-con machinery. Quist timed his seminars to jibe with Preston Manning's annual conservative networking conferences, which boosted their profile, but the institute's prestige soared when its architect, Darrel Reid, became a rising star in Harper's government. After a failed run as a Conservative candidate, he was hired as an adviser to embattled environment minister, Rona Ambrose, then promoted to the prime minister's own policy staff. Reid's appointment to the PMO set off a firestorm of protests in the House, where critics cited his 1997 vow to see Focus on the Family's principles drive the national agenda, but Harper shrugged off the fuss and elevated him to deputy chief of staff.

To some observers, Reid's ascension was a sign of Harper's determination to patch up frayed relations with the Christian right. In the wake of the same-sex marriage debacle, Brian Rushfeldt had warned the prime minister that, without a new issue to whip up emotions, the Canada Family Action Coalition might be unable to mobilize its dispirited troops for another election campaign, and Joseph Ben-Ami had confirmed that malaise. "I talk to people who now say, 'I've given money, given time, gone to rallies—what's the point?'" Ben-Ami confided. No sooner had conservative Christians put Harper on public notice that he could no longer count on their support than a front-page headline in the *Globe and Mail* signalled that he had been working behind the scenes to make amends.

⁂

Anyone who had tuned into Christian airwaves might have known something was up. On the radio ad, a woman's voice lays out the issue in baby-simple terms. "You pick a movie off the shelf at the video store," she says, "but after reading the description, you see that it's something you wouldn't want to lay your eyes on. As you put it back on the shelf, you're shocked to find your name printed there as one of the film's funders." The silky voice pauses to let the revelation sink in. "Sound far-fetched? Not really. Each year the Canadian government gives nearly $2 billion in tax dollars to the arts, movie and TV industry, so you're paying to produce stuff you wouldn't want to be caught dead watching."

That commercial, commissioned by the Canada Family Action Coalition, summed up everything that Charles McVety felt was wrong with the country's cultural industries. But, in September 2007, his outrage went into overdrive when he read that eighty thousand dollars of taxpayers' money had been poured into a Canadian-made movie that was the toast of the Toronto Film Festival—a low-budget feature with a title so provocative he couldn't bring himself to repeat it: *Young People Fucking.* "We expect the Canadian taxpayer to pay for something that we cannot even say the title of," he sputtered to the Senate banking committee.

Some members of Harper's caucus were equally incensed, but that indignation escaped the notice of Toronto's leading entertainment lawyers, who gathered for the regular lunch meeting of their Canadian Bar Association division a month after the film festival, expecting only a routine update from an Ottawa bureaucrat. Instead, Robert Soucy, the director of the Canadian Audio-Visual Certification Office for the

Heritage Department dropped a policy bombshell: "He said the Canadian government wants to be more selective about which cultural products it funds," recounts David Zitzerman of Goodmans LLP, one of the attendees. Films that were deemed "contrary to public policy"—which seemed to mean those featuring excessive sex or violence—would not be certified for the federal tax credits that had become the lifeblood of the country's film industry. To make that determination, a review committee from the heritage and justice departments would be set up, Soucy told the crowd, but certification would ultimately depend on the discretion of the heritage minister. "There was a stir in the room," Zitzerman recalls. "Somebody asked, 'Is this the morality police?'"

The lawyers pressed for further details, without success. Most assumed they would be invited to join the ritual consultations that had always preceded policy changes, but when no invitation materialized, Zitzerman began making inquiries of his own. To his shock, he discovered the government had done an end run around them. There would be no consultation, and it was too late to protest, he was told by a source: the legislation had already passed second reading in the House and was sitting in the Senate, waiting to be voted into law. "He said, 'David, the government has moved the agenda forward on this—it's a fait accompli,'" Zitzerman remembers. "It sounded like a cabinet-level decision."

Across the country, shocked film producers sprang into action, enlisting senatorial contacts and demanding public hearings, then leaking the news to the *Globe and Mail*. Zitzerman denounced the move as "closet censorship" and wondered aloud if such a review panel would have seen fit to certify the 2005 Oscar-winning film *Brokeback Mountain*. After all, he quipped, "They might not want to encourage gay cowboys to have sex together in Alberta."

No one doubted the measure was designed to placate Harper's disgruntled social-conservative constituency, but it was not until a day later, when a *Globe* reporter phoned Charles McVety, that those suspicions were confirmed. In the interview, McVety spoke at length about his lobbying efforts with friends in cabinet and the prime minister's office, claiming he had discussed the film initiative with justice minister Rob Nicholson and Stockwell Day. Both declared they could not recall any such talks, but, significantly, the one cabinet member McVety failed to mention chatting up was the minister actually responsible for the bill, his old pal Jim Flaherty.

As the Senate banking committee rushed to probe the measure, a parade of the film industry's star players turned its usually staid hearings into a standing-room-only sensation on Parliament Hill. Reporters who had never set foot in the upper chamber scrambled for seats to hear directors Sarah Polley and David Cronenberg warn that the provision would kill the country's film industry. Without the guarantee that a film would be certified for tax credits up front, they pointed out, no investor would risk investing in edgy Canadian productions like those that had won Cronenberg international kudos. By creating uncertainty, the bill undermined the basic economics of Canadian moviemaking, essentially sounding its death knell.

With minor bureaucratic tinkering, Harper had managed to reassure the restive Christian right that he was on the morality beat while appeasing economic conservatives who had always abhorred public funding for the arts. The only community he had offended, the country's artists and culture mavens, would probably never vote for his party anyway. He underlined his disregard by unleashing Ottawa-area MP Pierre Poilievre, an ardent social conservative, to defend the bill, sneering at the luminaries from the arts community who had captured the media spotlight. "If famous actors and actresses want to produce materials that are offensive to the majority of Canadians, they can do it on their own dime," Poilievre sniffed, "not on the backs of Canadian taxpayers."

Some pundits hailed Harper as a strategic genius for that policy sleight-of-hand, but by turning the culture wars into an attack on culture itself, he miscalculated. In the U.S., James Dobson and Pat Robertson had aimed their wrath at the National Endowment for the

Arts, but in doing so they were taking on avant-garde art galleries with nude photographs and symphony types in black tie, not Sarah Polley, the schoolgirl icon from *The Road to Avonlea*, or Paul Gross, the quintessential small-screen Mountie. In Canada, the homegrown film industry—and the arts themselves—have a national resonance, and nowhere more so than in Quebec, a reality that Harper discovered when his popularity in the province promptly took a nose-dive.

Even at the Senate banking committee, chaired by a Conservative, David Angus, Charles McVety found a chillier reception than he expected. Showing up with a poll he had commissioned, he claimed 72 percent of Canadians agreed with the government's move, and opposed public funding for offensive films. When Angus demanded to see the survey, he discovered that McVety's pollster had posed quite a different question: whether respondents favoured subsidizing pornography.

If Harper had intended to placate his theo-con supporters, the furore over the film-tax credits had the opposite effect: it put them in an unflattering public spotlight and raised questions about the extent that the prime minister was beholden to them. Evangelical scholar John Stackhouse lamented that the controversy had damaged the faith community: McVety's strident denunciations of the arts had fanned long-standing fears that conservative Christians planned to transform the country into a bastion of stern, Bible-based moralism. "Charles McVety is the nightmare that the Liberals want us to worry about," Stackhouse sighed to a *Globe and Mail* reporter.

Even within the religious right, many of McVety's former allies were furious at him: by claiming credit for the measure, they charged, he had sabotaged a bill on which a dozen social conservatives had been toiling in secret for months. "It doesn't help to go out there and say, 'Look what I did!'" steamed Joseph Ben-Ami. "This was not on people's radar, but now the opposition is growing. I can't think of a polite word to say about the fact that this might not pass the Senate because of comments from Charles McVety." Another former collaborator

confided that some members of Parliament were distancing themselves from McVety "because he's kind of become a loose cannon."

To the bill's opponents, however, it swiftly became clear that there
was more at stake than financing arrangements for feature films. When
Robert Soucy had briefed the entertainment industry's lawyers, he
mentioned that other cultural industries were also being targeted,
including recordings and books. In a country where virtually all of the
arts and some forms of the media are dependent on government funding or regulations, many in the cultural industries suddenly realized
that their work, too, was open to being declared "contrary to public
policy." The very vagueness of the phrase gave it widespread implications far beyond nixing a bout of over-enthusiastic fornication or a
surfeit of gore on the screen. A similar provision could justify denying
public money to a documentary that dared to question the government's detainee policy in Afghanistan or a book that criticized a cabinet
decision. Within the wording of the proposed film-funding guidelines
lay a template for silencing political dissent.

What some social conservatives found most unforgivable about
McVety's braggadocio was that he had exposed Harper's new modus
operandi for advancing their agenda. That approach—changing public
policy by quiet revisions to little-noticed statutes beneath the media's
radar—was exactly the sort of incrementalism that Harper had spelled
out years earlier in his 2003 Civitas speech, but it had also required
extraordinary secrecy, the collusion of federal bureaucrats and the deception of opposition MPs. The measure was confined to a thirteen-word
clause buried two-thirds of the way through a 568-page fiscal housekeep-
ing bill with a yawn-inducing title that betrayed no hint of its explosive
contents: "An Act to amend the Income Tax Act, including amendments
in relation to foreign investment entities and non-resident trusts."

The entire legislative saga was an extraordinary example of parliamentary gamesmanship and guile, and given the cast of characters
involved, it might have provided perfect material for a screenplay. The

only problem is that a version of the script has already been written and produced under the title *Amazing Grace*. The story of British MP William Wilberforce's battle to abolish the slave trade in nineteenth-century England, the 2006 film turns on a remarkably similar legislative manoeuvre. After two decades of watching his abolition bills go down to defeat, Wilberforce, a devout evangelical, was persuaded to change his tactics. At a time when Britain was at war with France, he engineered a bill that masqueraded as an act of patriotism, forbidding all British subjects, shipyards and insurers from trading with France or its allies, then he arranged for it to be put forward by another member of Parliament. The Foreign Slave Trade Act slipped through the House before the opposition twigged to its real intent: by barring British slave merchants from selling their human cargo to French plantation owners or their allies in the U.S., the law effectively outlawed two-thirds of the slave trade, striking a decisive blow at the commercial viability of slavery itself.

Among evangelicals in Ottawa, that plot line has been studied as a primer on political action. When *Amazing Grace* opened in 2007, the Evangelical Fellowship of Canada hosted a special screening for MPs, and Preston Manning turned the movie into the centrepiece of his seminars on how conservative Christians ought to wield their faith in the public square. Showing it at his lectures or simply describing the plot, Manning urges evangelical activists to study Wilberforce's strategy "backward and forward," counselling them to employ both his patience and his subterfuge.

If Harper's sly circumvention of Parliament bore an amazing resemblance to that in *Amazing Grace*—right down to undercutting the commercial viability of the Canadian film industry—it was no accident. As McVety's influence dimmed in Ottawa, Preston Manning's was on the rise.

SERPENTS AND DOVES

III

Frank Luntz paced the hotel ballroom, a study in misleading impressions. Sporting a polo shirt that had seen better days and a beard that had clearly been on the lam from the barber's shears, he prowled among the tables at Ottawa's Brookstreet Resort, microphone in hand, looking more like some stray who had wandered in off the street than the sly über-strategist of the American right who had been imported to preach spin-control tactics to a conference of star-struck Canadian Conservatives. Using his psychographic skills with focus groups and a propagandist's way with words, Luntz had made his mark teaching Republicans how to pitch neo-conservative policies in a froth of feel-good phraseology, helping them choreograph their 1994 take-over of Congress and deploy House Speaker Newt Gingrich's Contract with America. On the website of his Virginia polling firm, The Word Doctors, he takes credit for recasting the Democrats' estate tax as a "death tax" and global warming as "climate change," claiming the latter "significantly impacted the public debate."

Now, fresh from wrapping up a book on his trade secrets, *Words that Work: It's Not What You Say, It's What People Hear*, Luntz showed up in Ottawa in the spring of 2006 to help Preston Manning launch the

Manning Centre for Building Democracy, the latest addition to the capital's emerging conservative infrastructure, and, not incidentally, to dispense tips to Stephen Harper's newly installed government. After barely four months in power, Harper was already on a collision course with the Ottawa press corps, and it was no accident that Luntz's audience included the prime minister's controversial communications director, Sandra Buckler, and his health minister, Tony Clement, who took notes with the intensity of a schoolboy cramming for an exam.

Tailoring his tutorial directly to their needs, Luntz offered pointers on how to sell a free-market revolution to wary communal-minded Canadians: never use the words "free-market" or "revolution," he advised. When pitching policies such as a massive deregulation of industry or the privatization of health care, "you need a lexicon," he told the crowd. "You can change the policy—just get the language right."

For Luntz, the conference was a homecoming of sorts. A one-time Reform Party pollster, he had been in Manning's hotel suite watching the 1993 election results roll in as the ruling Progressive Conservatives were reduced to two seats and Reform emerged as the new force on Parliament's right flank. Despite all the internecine warfare and party mergers since, Luntz viewed Harper's 2006 victory as a continuation of that narrative. "I never dreamed you guys would take the government," he marvelled. "You've taken basically a socialist system and begun to turn it on its head."

Only hours earlier, Luntz had dropped by the prime minister's office for a reunion snapshot—a meeting, critics charged, that involved more than a photo opportunity. Harper had promptly borrowed a page from Luntz's media playbook, announcing that he was no longer participating in news conferences run by the parliamentary press gallery: instead, like Ronald Reagan, he would take his message directly to voters across the country, where local reporters would treat him with more reverence. Environmentalists too accused Harper of adopting Luntz's tactics on climate change, lifting them straight from a 2002 memo he wrote for congressional Republicans: in it, Luntz directed them to plant doubts about the notion of global warming. "You need to continue to make the lack of scientific certainty a primary issue in the debate," he had advised.

Luntz's tactics had earned him a reputation as the Machiavelli of message manipulation, but that image seemed at odds with the one Manning was trying to create for his centre. As *National Post* columnist Lorne Gunter had pointed out, one of the secrets of Manning's ability to rally Westerners behind Reform's untried banner was his image as a straight shooter. "With his Sunday-school-teacher appearance, his pinched, staccato speaking voice, his long, meticulously researched speeches and his genuine respect for ordinary people," Gunter wrote, "Manning didn't seem capable of guile."

But the Reform leader's vow to "do politics differently" had ended in humiliation. Within years of the 1993 breakthrough that Luntz helped plot, Manning found himself betrayed by his most trusted lieutenants, including Harper, and mercilessly lampooned by the press. His adoring wife, Sandra, persuaded him to ditch his horn-rims for corrective eye surgery and bought him voice lessons, but the makeover came too late. In 2000, he was ousted from the leadership of the 270,000-member party he had created, cast out into a political no man's land that swiftly turned into a spiritual desert. "Every Christian person of faith goes through a time when he is not conscious of God's presence," he later acknowledged, "but when I lost the leadership of the Canadian Alliance . . . that was a crisis of faith."

For Manning, who had grown up in his father's radio pulpit wearing his Baptist beliefs like a second skin, it was a devastating period. But he had not gone into politics because he felt a divine summons—"I never got a tablet of stone that dropped from heaven," he liked to joke—and his journey back to faith proved equally devoid of epiphanies. "I just chose to continue to believe in his providence and care," he told an interviewer on Vision TV. To long-time loyalists, such as

Deborah Grey, Manning was the epitome of a Christian politician, always careful to turn the other cheek, and to this day, he keeps a plaque from the gospel of Matthew on his desk: "Let he who is chief among you be the servant of all." But in his 2002 memoir, *Think Big*, he did take one shot at Harper, depicting him as neither a team player nor a team builder: "Stephen had difficulty accepting that there might be a few other people (not many perhaps, but a few) who were as smart as he was with respect to policy and strategy," Manning wrote.

The two men later reached a rapprochement, but many former Reform stalwarts were dumbfounded when Manning announced he was creating a centre to implement the sort of systematic training for political players that would ensure Harper's government was no electoral hiccup. To them, it seemed inconceivable that he would put himself at the service of a former protege once regarded as his Judas. But to Calgary political scientist Tom Flanagan, Manning's initiative was consistent with his concept of Christianity as an exercise in reconciliation, a duty to restore broken relations, no matter how onerous the personal sacrifice. In his 1995 study, *Waiting for the Wave: The Reform Party and Preston Manning*, Flanagan recounts how Manning applied that concept to his three-decade career as a management consultant: he had even drafted a paper on the crucifixion for use in corporate conflict resolution with Jesus designated as "The Mediator" and the alienated party in the dispute labelled "Mankind," under the telling subtitle: "The Theory and Application of a Model of Last Resort." "Although Manning does not say so explicitly, he invites the conclusion that, in leading the Reform Party, he is offering himself as a mediator," Flanagan writes, "perhaps even a sacrificial victim, to the entire Canadian community."

Now, as Manning returned to the political arena, carving out a role as the new godfather of Canadian conservatism, he saw himself in that sacrificial servant-leader's role, determined to reconcile warring factions—not only the squabbling social and economic conservatives in

Harper's party, but also those in the faith community who regarded politics as alien territory and viewed science and environmentalism as hostile to the Bible. Still, as he took up that task, he was no longer the earnest idealist of Reform days: he had come to regard politics as a game that could only be played with deception. When he told audiences that "politics is 90 percent communications," what he had in mind was Frank Luntz's brand of wordsmanship. Even the name of his organization is a tribute to Luntz's theories of verbal obfuscation: as he made clear in a speech introducing the Manning Centre for Building Democracy, the only kind of democracy it is dedicated to building is one where, he quipped, "peace, order and good government is delivered by conservatives."

Bringing Luntz's communications credo to Harper's uneasily united right, however, was only part of the centre's wide-ranging mandate. Another of Manning's goals was to entice more conservative Christians into the political debate and to train them on how to behave once they arrived. As he well knew, such an overture had the potential to backfire. Some evangelicals who flocked around Reform's banner had left the party with a reputation for extremism, pelting uncooperative politicians with intolerant diatribes and threatening opponents with colourful invocations of divine wrath. Harper's theo-cons offered equally ripe territory for a Luntz tutorial. "It's a sad thing on Parliament Hill," Manning conceded, "but the most vicious letters MPs get come from faith-oriented people."

⁜

When Manning announced his Calgary-based centre, funded to the tune of $10 million over ten years by an Alberta corporate angel who demanded anonymity, he spoke of emulating the campaign and political management courses offered by a handful of American universities. But in fact his model was distinctly more partisan: the Virginia-based

Leadership Institute run by veteran Republican operative Morton Blackwell, a hard-core social conservative who served as Ronald Reagan's chief liaison with the religious right. It was Blackwell who once pointed out to a co-founder of the Moral Majority that the evangelical community was "the greatest tract of virgin timber on the political landscape," and in the three decades since he established his institute in a suburb of Washington, D.C., he has trained more than seventy-six thousand Republican activists and congressmen, including George Bush's back-room Rasputin, Karl Rove, and Ralph Reed, who used Blackwell's techniques to school the foot soldiers of the Christian Coalition.

Along the way, the institute acquired seven international affiliates from Chile to Korea, and ever since some gonzo members of Bill Vander Zalm's B.C. government showed up at his seminars, Blackwell has shared his wisdom with an estimated seven hundred Canadians, including a handful of current Conservative MPs. One who remains close is Rob Anders, the controversial member for Calgary West who once denounced Nelson Mandela as "a communist and a terrorist" and sent out a mailing to constituents claiming, "It is now illegal to hold opinions that offend radical Muslim activists."

But Blackwell himself is no stranger to the Canadian political scene. In 1997, he was executive director of the Council for National Policy, an elite and ultra-secretive society of the most powerful U.S. conservatives, when it asked Harper to speak at a Montreal gathering that year. For Harper, who had just taken up his job as head of the National Citizens Coalition, the invitation marked his debut in the big leagues of the American right, and he used the opportunity to disparage Canada as "a northern European welfare state in the worst sense of the word." Blackwell still praises him as a "smart guy" who has moved this country sharply to the right, but he also credits that shift to Preston Manning, with whom he has longstanding ties. When Manning came calling for help in starting a Canadian version of the Leadership Institute, Blackwell was more than happy to oblige. As he explained in an interview, he works free of charge with any groups that, he says, "are trying to be conservative in the U.S. sense of the word."

Unlike Blackwell's model, however, Manning's self-styled "school of practical politics" is a campus without any fixed real estate. Its seminars, most patterned after those in the Leadership Institute's catalogue, are held in hotel conference rooms or college halls across the country, where Manning and a cast of experts offer weekend workshops in everything from campus activism to managing a political campaign. But the centre has also focused on training the dozens of young Conservatives who flocked to Parliament Hill after Harper's victory, signing on to do the grunt work that keeps any government ticking. In its seven-week Political Communication course, tailored for aides to cabinet ministers and MPs, two dozen hand-picked students receive weekly lectures on the nitty-gritty of interpreting polling data and selling unpopular policies—or as one syllabus called it, "the ethics of political persuasion"—from a roster of seasoned practitioners that has included Harper's former minister of human resources, Monte Solberg, and Kory Teneycke, his second director of communications. Those programs reflect Manning's determination to "professionalize" the conservative movement, creating a cadre of skilled backstage political operatives who will outlast upheavals in the Conservative Party's electoral fortunes and even his own centre's lifespan: to that end, he has begun negotiations to institutionalize his seminars under the wing of Carleton University's faculty of public administration, which could eventually reward his graduates with degrees.

For years, Manning has railed against the paradox that, in a country where nearly 70 percent of the populace professes a belief in God, faith has been banished from public debate. "There's a taboo in the House of Commons that you do not talk about your deepest spiritual convictions," he says with exasperation, "and part of the reason is that people who open themselves up just get hammered." To Manning that never seemed truer than during the 2004 and 2006 elections, when he watched pundits sneer at the evangelicals in Harper's ranks. "For all the professions of religious tolerance in this country, it's half an inch deep," he complained at the time. "There was considerable receptivity to the argument that Mr. Harper comes from the wrong part of the country and holds these religious convictions which are dangerous."

Still, no one knew better than Manning that mixing faith and politics could be rife with the potential for disaster. In *Think Big*, he cautions conservative Christians against unleashing the sort of scripture-laced screeds that prompt many MPs to recoil. "Secular politicians are afraid to open the door, even a crack, to religious discussion in the political arena," he warns, "because they fear unleashing a flood of ill-considered, ill-tempered, and contradictory statements . . . accompanied by shrill demands." Manning himself blames the loss of the same-sex marriage battle in part on the confrontational rhetoric of the Defend Marriage crowd. "Some of these faith-oriented people conduct themselves in such a way that they scare the hide off the secular," he notes in an interview. "It doesn't win friends and influence people." Determined to reconcile evangelicals to the realities of political life, he counsels a more diplomatic course—one that requires not only linguistic subterfuge but strategic wiles. It is a course that might have been dictated by Frank Luntz, but Manning prefers to cite a less contentious source of inspiration: the gospel of Matthew.

✢

In the winter of 2006, shortly after Harper's victory, more than a hundred conservative Christians gathered in Ottawa's Holiday Inn for Manning's first seminar in a series he called "Navigating the Faith/Political Interface." Writer Lloyd Mackey estimated that nearly half of the new Conservative caucus were right-wing Catholics or evangelicals, many of them freshmen who had been firmly muzzled throughout the campaign and were now anxious for a guide to the capital's alien territory. Among them was Harold Albrecht, a former Kitchener, Ontario pastor who had achieved notoriety for his letters to the editor denouncing Planned Parenthood and warning that same-sex marriage could precipitate the end of the human race. When Harper's campaign stopped by Albrecht's riding, party handlers were so nervous they hustled the candidate into an empty hotel galley to prevent him from talking to the national press corps. Not surprisingly, Albrecht was eager to accept Manning's invitation, which promised tips on "how to be faithful to democratic principles with a Christian commitment," but by the end of the weekend, an *Ottawa Citizen* reporter came up with a less earnest tag: "Mr. Manning's Charm School for Unruly Christians—or What Not to Say."

Manning's first counsel for the newly elected—especially those who'd been propelled into politics by outrage over same-sex marriage—was to curb their fervour. "The preference is to ride into Parliament with a speech that will peel the paint off the ceiling," he told them, "but you'll set your cause back fifty years." Much of his advice amounted to Luntzian spin control: ditch the God talk and avoid the temptation to play holier-than-thou. "You have to advocate righteousness," he said, "without appearing self-righteous." Then he promptly illustrated just how difficult it could be to avoid rhetorical missteps. Advising the audience to attack same-sex marriage not with quotations from the Bible but with statistics illustrating its social costs, he offered his own unscripted thoughts on the subject. "In a moment of spontaneity, Mr. Manning went off his notes," the *Ottawa Citizen* reported, "and said many people become gay after some 'horrific' experience with heterosexual relationships."

Despite that misadventure, Manning reassured evangelicals that there was no reason for them to feel like misfits in the political arena, rhyming off polls showing that more than 50 percent of Canadians shared many of their core beliefs. But those same polls revealed that a majority of Canadians are also profoundly uneasy about people of faith taking over the reins of government. "One of the greatest fears voters have of religious people," he pointed out, "is that we're going to ram religion down their throats."

That perception informed his final message—a message he would repeat countless times over the coming years. Before sending his audience out into the political fray, he drew on the passage from Matthew 10:16 in which Jesus dispatched his disciples "like sheep among wolves" to evangelize to the world. "He said, 'I'm going to give you a few guidelines first,'" Manning paraphrased. "And one of the major ones was, 'Be wise as serpents and harmless as doves.' In other words, be shrewd. Be as smart as the other guy, but be gracious. Be non-threatening."

Manning had enlisted his pal Brian Stiller to help design the seminars and to administer them he hired Wes McLeod, a former pastor and executive assistant to Reform MP Chuck Strahl. But increasingly, as he staged his faith-and-politics weekends across the country, they bore his own imprimatur. Often he twinned his cautionary serpents-and-doves parable with a staple from his repertoire as a speaker for hire: a sermon extolling the tactics of William Wilberforce, who had ended the British slave trade by circumventing his parliamentary foes with a combination of bluffing and stealth. When it came to dispensing advice for political action, Christian or otherwise, there seemed no doubt that Manning's new watchword was guile, but that raised one obvious question: to what extent were his own efforts guided by cunning and equivocation?

Despite disclaimers that he harboured no partisan goals, his workshops increasingly appeared aimed at building a religious right in Canada for the benefit of Harper's Conservatives, just as Morton Blackwell had done for Republicans in the United States. Manning bridled at such accusations, taking care to include evangelicals from other parties on his panels, and he made a point of offering seminars to Muslims, Sikhs and Jews. But those efforts merely followed the blueprint for party-building across faith lines that Harper had spelled out in his 2003 Civitas speech. Indeed, the prime minister's unwavering support for Israel's 2006 invasion of Lebanon had won him such enduring gratitude from Canadian Jews that by the time Manning threw his faith-and-politics seminar for Toronto's Jewish community a year later, Green Party candidate Rosemary Frei complained the event seemed like a "love-in" for the Conservative Party. "There's a sense that to be a good Jew, you have to be a good Conservative," she protested.

Scanning Manning's training programs, an observer would be hard-pressed not to conclude that his centre had become an annex of Harper's government. Prime ministerial staffers, either past or soon-to-be-appointed, studded every curriculum list; its campus workshops featured tutorials from Kevin Lacey, the official gatekeeper for the religious right during the government's first term, while one syllabus for the centre's political communications diploma advertised a session with Guy Giorno, the former Ontario strategist who was about to become Harper's chief of staff. That impression of a revolving door between the centre and the PMO was reinforced in the fall of 2009 when John Williams, one of Manning's senior fellows, was named the prime minister's new communications czar.

But the most powerful testimonial to the centre's partisan leanings came from its founder himself. In a column for the *Globe and Mail* a week before the October 2008 election, Manning offered a cursory review of all five party leaders, only to conclude that, in a time of unparalleled economic turbulence, "surely it must be acknowledged that Mr. Harper surpasses any other." Short of an official editorial stamp of approval, it was the most blatant endorsement to appear in the paper, and prompted a flood of objections. Allowing Manning to peg Harper as the best man to lead the country, one reader complained, was the equivalent of "Colonel Sanders recommending the best meat for dinner."

✢

When Manning unveiled his centre, he made clear that training was only one facet of its mandate. He also spelled out his intention to create a forum where the diverse strains of the conservative community could connect, patterned after another institution co-founded by Morton Blackwell: Washington's annual Conservative Political Action Conference. He had already helped foster an online version of that gathering, underwriting the creation of Stephen Taylor's website, Blogging Tories, when he launched his first Manning Networking Conference in the spring of 2008. Despite the fact that its name made no mention of conservatism, there was little doubt about its partisan tilt: one panel starred former Ontario premier Mike Harris and Canadian Medical Association president Brian Day praising privatized health care; another featured electioneering techniques from Richard Ciano, the founder of the Conservative Party's own Campaign University.

True to his personal mission of mediation, Manning ensured that every faction in the conservative movement had its requisite moment in the conference spotlight. In the exhibit hall, booths for the Fraser Institute and the Canadian Shooting Sports Association stood next to those of the leading theo-conservative groups: Joseph Ben-Ami dispensed strategy papers from his Canadian Centre for Policy Studies and Faytene Kryskow peddled her revivalist CDs across the aisle from a display manned by Dave Quist, doggedly promoting his Institute of Marriage and Family Canada. The crowd was ebullient when Harper dropped by for the opening-night reception where party faithful lined up for photos with him as if he were a visiting Hollywood celebrity. But a year later, when many of the same Conservatives gathered for the second edition of Manning's schmoozefest in the spring of 2009, the mood felt more like an insurrection in the making.

The fall election that Harper had called in the smug assumption that it would bring him a majority, had resulted in yet another minority government, and his attempt to kill opposition parties' subsidies had nearly provoked a constitutional crisis and the takeover of the government by an opposition coalition. Worse, as those political upheavals unrolled against the backdrop of an unprecedented economic tsunami, the man whom Manning had touted as the only captain fit to helm the ship of state proved to be singularly inept at grasping the full measure of the storm. Economic conservatives were furious that Harper had betrayed their shared small-government principles by embarking on a massive spending spree, and social conservatives were still fuming that, on the eve of the election, he had pulled the plug on two key morality bills designed to appease them. Even Harper's confidante Tom Flanagan reported rumblings that the prime minister's vaunted strategic sense had been overrated. "This is a dangerous development," Flanagan opined, "for if you are not to be loved, you must at least be respected."

Harper's reputation was in such a state of disrepute that some conference attendees speculated Manning was finally exacting his revenge by showcasing the talents of the prime minister's potential rival, retired defence chief Rick Hillier, as his keynote speaker. But during the packed opening reception, Harper suddenly materialized at the podium, upstaging Hillier with a lengthy riposte to his restive troops—acidly dismissing the economic libertarians who had accused him of ideological treason and attempting to placate the social conservatives he had abandoned with a tribute to the values of faith and family as key pillars of conservatism. At no other event, except a party convention, could he have reached so many of the disparate factions in his Conservative tent. By providing Harper with that opportunity, Manning cemented his own role as the movement's lofty patriarch, attempting to nudge the rambunctious members of his conservative clan toward reconciliation.

In Ottawa, in fact, Manning now wielded more influence than he had ever enjoyed as leader of the opposition. Many students who had been trained at his centre now staffed cabinet ministers' offices and two of his most devoted acolytes held top jobs in the PMO. In his monthly *Globe and Mail* column, Manning regularly rushed to the government's defence or proposed a path out of its latest predicament, constantly working to advance his thesis that, just as the Liberals had once been viewed as the natural governing party of Canada, the conservative movement he founded would assume that role in the twenty-first century.

In recognition, Harper publicly signalled their entente, showing up at a 2008 Manning tribute in Calgary to hail him as a visionary "whose legacy will define Canadian politics for decades to come." But he also offered Manning another, lower-profile reward—one that suggested he too might have heeded the parable of serpents and doves. Late on a Friday afternoon in July 2008, when most of official Ottawa was on holiday, his government quietly named Manning to the board of an obscure new science advisory body called the Council of Canadian Academies, which turned out to have a broad mandate: to make an "independent, expert assessment of the science underlying pressing issues and matters of public interest."

To the uninitiated, that act of patronage might have looked like small potatoes, but for Manning, a science buff who had reserved the Alliance portfolio on the subject for himself, it was a plum. At a time when the government faced a raft of decisions on issues such as stem-cell research, which most conservative Christians adamantly oppose, it gave him an opening to explore that daunting terrain where science and faith intersect. For Harper too, the appointment had a useful upside: in Manning, he had an unofficial ambassador to the scientific community—a constituency where one of the most pressing issues was unprecedented hostility to his government. Scarcely a week passed without headlines protesting how the PMO had silenced Environment Canada researchers or made drastic funding cuts. Even the prestigious British science journal, *Nature*, had accused it of "manifest disregard" for the field. Tensions were so high that, on the eve of the 2008 election, eighty-five of Canada's leading researchers issued an open letter calling for an end to the government's "politicization" and "mistreatment" of science.

✢

As word of Manning's appointment sped through the country's research labs so too did consternation. Optimists noted that he had cast himself as a champion of science, arguing for greater funding as well as the creation of a science czar, but others pointed out that Harper had already demonstrated his sentiments about such a move by scrapping the office of the National Science Adviser. Scrolling through Manning's writings, critics were appalled. On at least one occasion, he had argued that religion ought to play a greater role in formulating science policy. In an essay entitled, "The Genetic Revolution: Where Does Faith Fit In?"—a piece removed from his website after he was named to the council—Manning mused that "There must be a higher notion than science alone . . . that can guide scientific research and endeavour." He went on to conclude that "One of the candidates is 'faith'—religious faith—faith in the existence of God . . . and faith that there are universal and transcendent moral principles which ought to govern us in addition to the principles of physics, chemistry, and biology to which we are all subject."

In a community already irate that funding for pure research had been slashed in favour of projects with direct commercial payoffs, Manning's appointment was regarded as yet another ominous sign. "If you look back at Manning's comments about science, you see he would have been at home under the Bush administration," says James Turk, executive director of the Canadian Association of University Teachers, who had become one of the government's most outspoken critics. "It's going to have a very negative impact on the future of science in Canada."

Turk's fears seemed justified when Manning eventually proposed a solution to assuage the mood of mutual mistrust. In a *Globe and Mail* column in the spring of 2009, he suggested that the government throw a day-long conference, inviting the country's top scientists to identify ways in which their disciplines could "specifically" contribute to the nation's economic recovery. "The idea of the event would be to avoid complaints, government-bashing, excessive Obama worship and partisanship," he wrote. Six weeks later, the government followed his advice to the letter, throwing an upbeat confab in Ottawa under the banner of "Science Day in Canada," complete with a conciliatory reception where MPs could drop by to demonstrate their support. There, Manning proffered another formula for defusing tensions: a series of bureaucratic steps to ensure that decisions on science funding became more transparent. But later on the Manning Centre's website, some critics discovered his proposal had contained an additional paragraph that did not appear in the *Globe* version. It made clear that his aim was not to allay the scientific community's concerns, but to quash attacks on the government. If Harper instituted his proposed accountability measures, Manning predicted, "only a few diehard science reporters" would attend a follow-up press conference. "The story, if any," he concluded, "will be lucky to see the light of day."

✢

The attacks on Harper from the research community, however, paled in comparison to those from environmental scientists. In the same week that researchers launched their pre-election salvo over funding, the country's top climate-change experts released an open letter lambasting the government's delays and obstructionism. In a stunningly provocative move, they urged Canadians to vote "strategically" on the issue. "Global warming is a problem that must be dealt with now, before it's too late," the declaration read. "Any further delay will only increase the risks of damage and costs of action." As one signatory told reporters, whenever the government was faced with evidence underlining the urgency of reducing carbon emissions, it pursued a course of action that might have been borrowed from

Luntz's advice to congressional Republicans, adopting "the deceptive strategy of suggesting that there was scientific uncertainty when, in fact, there was none."

As it turned out, Manning had brought Luntz to Ottawa just as he was mounting a major public-relations offensive on the environment, even putting out feelers about running for premier of Alberta as a "green conservative." That prospect had failed to whip up sufficient enthusiasm, but he saw the issue as yet another opportunity for him to act as a mediator, attempting to reconcile environmentalists with the western energy and real-estate interests that had backed Reform and now funded the Manning Centre for Building Democracy. Indeed, one of his most prominent board members is Gwyn Morgan, the former president and CEO of Encana, the world's largest independent oil and gas producer, who believes the Kyoto Protocol is fatally flawed.

What made the issue all the more compelling for Manning was that some of the most vocal opponents of the environmental movement are leading voices in the Christian right. In the U.S., Oklahoma Republican James Inhofe, a biblical literalist and Christian Zionist, has led the charge in Congress, branding the theory of man-made global warming "the greatest hoax ever perpetrated on the American people" and labelling the U.S. Environmental Protection Agency "a gestapo." But the debate over climate change has also provoked a major schism in evangelical ranks. In 2007, when Richard Cizik, vice-president of governmental affairs for the National Association of Evangelicals, drafted an "Urgent Call to Action" on global warming signed by twenty-eight scientists and megapreachers, James Dobson, one of the NAE's most powerful members, demanded his resignation and castigated superstar pastor Rick Warren for signing the declaration. Scoffing at Cizik's attempts to foster a biblically inspired version of environmentalism known as Creation Care, Dobson dismissed talk of climate change as an unnecessary distraction from the truly important issues of the day—abortion and family breakdown.

Despite the increasing embrace of Creation Care, a 2009 poll showed that 40 percent of American evangelical pastors still agreed with Inhofe, refusing to blame the problem on human activity. Those attitudes pitted conservative Christians against their more environmentally engaged brethren, and nothing explained their intransigence more clearly than a scenario advanced by television journalist Bill Moyers, an ordained Baptist minister himself. In a speech to Harvard's Center for Health and the Global Environment, Moyers warned that the real reason many Christian fundamentalists showed no interest in protecting the environment was their adherence to the extremist end-times theories of John Nelson Darby. "They believe that environmental destruction is not only to be disregarded, but actually welcomed—even hastened," Moyers said, "as a sign of the coming apocalypse."

To latter-day dispensationalists, the droughts, floods and extreme weather wreaking havoc around the globe are prophetic signs foretold in the Bible that presage the battle of Armageddon and the subsequent Second Coming of Christ. Attempting to reverse them would be tantamount to defying divine providence. Besides, as Moyers noted, Darby's theory of a selective exit plan for believers eliminates any reason for personal dread. "Why care about global climate change," he explained, "when you and yours will be rescued in the Rapture?"

Among Canadian evangelicals, the Armageddon factor has played less of a role in environmental debates, but Darby's theories do motivate a handful of high-profile dispensationalists, not least among them the Reverend Charles McVety. In interviews and on his television show, McVety has repeatedly mocked the environmental movement as a secular religion that he calls "earthism." Scorning international efforts such as the 1992 Earth Summit in Rio de Janeiro, he has damned its global charter as a "pagan document" designed to spread a heretical gospel that he links to scriptural passages on the Antichrist. "The Bible talks about one-world government, and what we have developed is exactly that," McVety charges. "The false religion is the worship of Mother Earth."

But McVety is not alone in finding the inspiration for his vehement anti-environmentalism in the Bible. In the summer of 2008, Timothy Bloedow published *Environmentalism and the Death of Science: Exposing the Lie of Eco-Religion*, a 132-page attack on the "pantheistic" theory of global warming from another theological perspective. A leading Christian nationalist who runs his own website, ChristianGovernment.ca, Bloedow insists that the earth faces no environmental crisis; on the contrary, he casts its perennial resilience as part of a divine master plan of redemption. Accusing those who have raised environmental alarms of espousing an anti-Christian worldview, he argues that technological progress, private-property rights and "robust free-market competition" are all part of the "Biblical economic ethic," and, as such, are subject to the control of human beings, "the crown of God's creation."

That conviction of man's superiority, known as dominionism, has its origins in the first chapter of Genesis, where God commissions humans to exercise "dominion over the fish of the sea, over the birds of the air, and over every living thing that moves on the earth." As Bloedow and other dominionists see it, environmentalism is a direct affront to that biblically ordained mandate. "The Environmental movement treats man as a cancer, a virus, and a blight on the Earth," he writes. "Environmentalism represents the hatred of man and, by extension, of the God Whose image man bears." Bloedow's views, however disconcerting, are not easy to dismiss: his book carries a laudatory cover blurb from columnist Lorne Gunter, and he works as the chief legislative assistant to Conservative MP Maurice Vellacott, whom Harper appointed to the Commons' committee on the environment and sustainable development in his first term.

Although Preston Manning was raised a dispensationalist and his father's radio sermons regularly invoked the spectre of a coming apocalypse, he does not appear to share McVety's radical views, nor does he present himself as an unqualified dominionist like Bloedow. In fact,

Manning's philosophy on the environment, like his stand on many social-conservative issues, is difficult to pin down. Still, it comes as no surprise that his advocacy of a compromise between opposing factions is founded on a "market-based approach." He was just five years old when the first oil strike at Leduc forever changed Alberta's economy, floating his father's quarter-century reign as premier on a tide of liquid black gold. For Manning, the Athabaska tar sands also strike a sentimental chord. More than half a century ago, it was his father who, on the basis of a handshake, turned over drilling rights in that remote acreage to California oil tycoon Howard Pew, a fellow evangelical who once funded Billy Graham's crusades.

For years, Manning pondered the conflict between the energy industry's free-market rights and the passion that his children and grandchildren felt for the environment, and now he seems to embrace a brand of conservationism that climate-change experts regard as yet another excuse for putting off drastic action. A month after his appointment to the Council of Canadian Academies, he threw a conference in Calgary that shed no more light on his views. Its curious title: "Energy, Environment and Faith: Confrontation? Dialogue? Reconciliation?"

The program did not feature a single expert on global warming or spokesperson for the energy industry, nor did it include the inter-denominational eco-justice group, KAIROS, which was about to send a delegation to the tar sands to "explore the theological, social and ethical implications of fossil fuel extraction." Instead, Manning invited a theologian named Paul Williams from Vancouver's Regent College, and Markku Kostamo, the executive director of A Rocha Canada, a small Christian-based conservation organization that regards environmental decline as a reflection of man's broken relationship with God and promotes "creation care" on evangelical campuses. Indeed, the main point of the conference appeared to be the opportunity it afforded Manning himself to argue that evangelicals have a key role to play in the environmental conflict—as peacemakers. "We as Christians can bring a distinctive approach to acting as mediators," he said. "Jesus communicates constantly between God and man. As a mediator, he sacrifices his own interests to bring the parties together."

⁜

That strategy of conciliation and compromise, of carving out a middle ground between conflicting camps, is one that Manning now advocates for issues even more obdurate than global warming. In the spring of 2009, a Vancouver conservative named Terry O'Neill, co-host of Roadkill Radio, broke the news that the patriarch of the Reform Party was backing a new B.C. organization called Signal Hill, set up to take a kinder, gentler approach to the explosive debate on abortion. "Signal Hill's strategy is to put aside impassioned political and moral arguments in favour of service, education and compassion," O'Neill wrote in a boosterish op-ed for the *National Post*. He went on to recount how Manning had endorsed Signal Hill's new "third way" approach at a Vancouver fundraiser, urging the audience to employ the tactical skills exemplified in his two favourite rhetorical themes: the wily measures employed by British abolitionist William Wilberforce and the respectful cunning counselled in the New Testament parable of serpents and doves. Not that O'Neill himself needed such a nudge toward scripturally inspired doublespeak. In his piece, he neglected to mention that he was on the board of Signal Hill, or that it was simply a rebranding of a long-established anti-abortion group, the Pro Life Society of British Columbia.

He did, however, highlight a new strategy on the religious right, one which Manning was playing a key part in promoting. In the wake of O'Neill's public relations coup, the *National Post* dispatched its chief religion writer, Charles Lewis, to further chronicle the trend. Under the headline, "Born Again: Anti-Abortion Groups Try a Gentler Approach," Lewis reported that Signal Hill was not alone in adopting a less confrontational approach to reducing the ninety-six thousand abortions performed in Canada each year. As his main example, he featured Andrea Mrozek, the founder of ProWomanProLife, an Ottawa-based organization designed for female professionals who oppose abortion, but not necessarily on religious grounds. With a trendy website studded with photographs of lithe women mountain climbers and multi-tasking lawyer moms, Mrozek explained that her aim was "to change the culture" over the long term, not to demand an outright end to all abortions through some single inflammatory act of legislation. With that disclaimer, she distanced herself from the shrill absolutism of traditional anti-abortion rhetoric, which she claimed left her generation queasy. Her goal, Mrozek declared, was to "make it okay to be pro-life."

But like O'Neill, Lewis omitted one key detail from his account. He failed to point out that, while founding ProWomanProLife, Mrozek had a full-time job that gave her a high-profile stake in the anti-abortion fight: she was manager of research for the Institute of Marriage and Family, the Ottawa think tank set up by Focus on the Family Canada. Wearing that professional hat, she had authored her own op-ed piece on abortion in the *National Post* six months earlier, which left a very different impression of her views. "Deceptive language makes it too easy to ignore what Canada's abortion-on-demand status quo actually involves," Mrozek wrote. "The annihilation of some 100,000 concrete individuals every year."

Ironically, those articles heralding Manning's serpent-and-dove strategy provoked an outcry from an unlikely quarter—the pro-life movement itself. In an irate *National Post* editorial, John Hof, the president of B.C.'s Campaign Life Coalition, disputed Manning's version of Wilberforce's battle to abolish the slave trade, arguing that the driving force behind the movement was actually a lifelong abolitionist named Thomas Clarkson, who had spurred Wilberforce into action. Hof acknowledged that Wilberforce had become committed to the cause—so committed that he once chained himself to his desk in Parliament—and contrasted that unflinching grit to Manning's years in the House of Commons where, he charged, the Reform Party leader had never once raised the subject of abortion. "I watched as he avoided the issue at every single opportunity," Hof wrote. "When Preston was in Parliament and in a position of power, that was the time for him to be like William Wilberforce. Sadly, he was not."

That attack served as a reminder of the divisions within Canadian theo-conservative ranks, notably the split between incrementalists such as Manning and those end-times-obsessed believers who argue that there is not a moment to waste. The forces of Campaign Life had played a major role in unseating Manning as Reform leader, replacing him with another social conservative who strutted his beliefs without apology, Stockwell Day. Still, after his own ouster from the party, Day, too, had learned to trim the sails of his zeal. Indeed, if anyone appears to have adopted Manning's serpent-and-doves strategy, it is the determinedly low-profile cabinet minister whom many of the country's charismatic Christians still regard as "God's anointed"—an ardent Christian nationalist who has discreetly fostered almost every theo-con organization on Parliament Hill and left his fingerprints on none.

WATCHMEN
ON THE WALLS

IV

On a leafy cul-de-sac half an hour's walk from Parliament Hill, the stolid, neo-Renaissance mansion has a deceptive air. With its massive stone pillars and stately panelled salons, it looks more like the embassy of a minor foreign power than yet another redoubt of the country's brash new Christian right—an image that is not entirely undeserved. Ever since it took over a former Ottawa convent in 2005, the National House of Prayer has billed itself as a prayer mission to Parliament with a mandate that sounds both worthy and unremarkable: "to bring a positive presence by a caring church to our nation's government." Beneath that bland verbiage, however, the House of Prayer is an initiative by one of the most radical wings of the Pentecostal community, a determined company of charismatic Christians with ties to an international network of revivalists who believe Canada has a scripturally ordained role to play in the end-times. Their goal is to see the country transformed into a righteous Christian nation governed by biblical principles, one capable of fulfilling the prophetic destiny implicit in its national motto taken from Psalm 72:8: "He shall have dominion also from sea to sea, and from the River to the ends of the earth."

That mission might seem unrelated to the raucous carnival of the capital's political life, but on any given day, Rob and Fran Parker, the organization's directors, can be seen with their prayer teams huddled at the foot of the Peace Tower, where that verse is carved into the stone of the neo-Gothic window frames. On other occasions, when they aren't praying outside the Supreme Court or the Governor General's residence, they can be found inside the House of Commons visitors' gallery during Question Period, sitting upright, eyes open, sending out intercessary vibes for select policies and politicians. As Fran Parker points out, "You don't have to have your eyes closed to pray."

In another era, those efforts might have won the Parkers a reputation as religious zealots, fringe players to be given a wide berth, but in Stephen Harper's Ottawa they have been accorded a VIP welcome. Not only have they been handed the official parliamentary chapel for weekly services, but at a time of unprecedented security, they have been granted staff passes that allow them to breeze into the Commons' gallery at will or drop by MPs' offices for private prayer sessions—a level of access beyond the wildest dreams of most non-governmental organizations.

Although the Parkers insist that their mission is non-partisan, the National House of Prayer has demonstrated a marked inclination to applaud Harper and his agenda, and in return, the prime minister's office has not been reluctant to show its gratitude. During the October 2008 election campaign, the Parkers' fourteen resident interns were summoned to a private, early-morning send-off for Harper inside an Ottawa airport hangar, where each got to shake his hand in exchange for providing a backdrop of enthusiastic young faces for that night's newscasts. "The privilege of a lifetime," gushed Aleah Windsor later on the National House of Prayer blog. "All day there has been a desire on my heart to pray for him."

Three months later, when finance minister Jim Flaherty released his much-anticipated budget, the Parkers and their visiting prayer team cheered him on from reserved seats in the Commons' gallery and won invitations to the prime minister's reception. One staffer termed the opportunity "a divine assignment" in the literal sense of the word—sent from God—but the Parkers are more circumspect, at least in conversation with outsiders or the mainstream media, downplaying their ties to the government and declining to name the members of Parliament with whom they pray. "We have to be careful with the non-Christian press," Fran Parker confides to me in an interview.

One supporter who feels no need to hide his identity is Stockwell Day, with whom they joined in targeted prayer shortly after he was appointed Harper's first minister of public safety, when terrorism was an overriding concern. "We'd say, 'Let's cover our waterways, let's cover our nuclear plants,'" Rob Parker explains. "Let's pray that security would have supernatural eyes, as it were, to be able to catch any threat."

Otherwise, they remain guarded, sticking to a more personal narrative: the tale of how Rob Parker found God while toiling as a paramedic on Libya's oil rigs, then abandoned that lucrative job to study for the ministry at Irish Baptist College outside Belfast. As he prepared to graduate, the Parkers had their hearts set on a foreign mission posting, but even then they were attuned to the signs and portents that charismatic Christians regard as the bulletins of God's will. One day, reading a passage from Ezekiel 3:4—"For you are not sent to a people of unfamiliar speech and hard language"—they took it as a personal instruction. "That's when we knew we were coming back to Canada," Fran says.

After two years of ministering to a congregation in Victoria, they moved to the Community Baptist Church in Vernon, B.C. There, they were caught up in a charismatic renewal movement that took wing on a snowy January night in 1994 when a Missouri revivalist on the verge of a nervous breakdown had arrived in Toronto for a guest-preaching stint at a modest congregation in an industrial park north of the city. As Randy Clark wound up his service at Toronto Airport Vineyard Church, worshippers suddenly found themselves convulsed in spasms of uncontrollable laughter, thrashing on the floor, a few even barking like dogs. The phenomenon continued for more than two months, making headlines around the world and attracting as many as a thousand people a night, some flying in from Africa and Asia in a desperate bid to catch the miracle of holy laughter that became known as the Toronto Blessing.

To charismatic Christians like the Parkers, who rushed to Toronto to take part in the services, there was only one explanation for the mysterious syndrome: a visitation by the Holy Spirit akin to the one that had kicked off the North American Pentecostal movement at the beginning of the century, when a tiny congregation on Los Angeles's Azusa Street suddenly burst into a babble of rapturous, unintelligible tongues. In 1948, a similar manifestation known as the Latter Rain Revival broke out at Sharon Bible College in North Battleford, Saskatchewan, where thousands claimed conversion and healing before Pentecostal authorities repudiated it as the product of a false doctrine. More than two decades later, twin brothers named Ralph and Lou Sutera held prayer meetings at Ebenezer Baptist Church in Saskatoon that mushroomed to fill local arenas and spread as far away as Ottawa.

For some Pentecostals, the Toronto Blessing was not entirely unexpected. They had clung to a 1984 prophecy by a visiting South Korean pastor, David Yonggi Cho, the founder of Seoul's 800,000-member Yoido Full Gospel Church, the world's largest congregation, who had predicted a unique role for Canada in the final days of life on earth. At the time, Yonggi Cho admitted he was startled by his own prophetic decree. "I already thought that America was far greater than Canada," he confessed. "But wherever I went, the Holy Spirit spoke in my heart that God was going to raise up tremendous churches in Canada . . . and that Canada would open the way for Jesus Christ to return to this earth."

Still, most psychologists dismissed the Toronto Blessing as a case of mass hysteria, and some fellow evangelicals denounced it as "unbiblical" heresy. Even the Association of Vineyard Churches eventually expelled the airport congregation from its ranks, deeming its animal noises beyond the pale. But that rejection only served to cement the conviction of hard-core charismatics like the Parkers, who retain strong ties to the renegade church: today, Rob Parker's second-in-command at the National House of Prayer is Richard Long, whose brother Steve is senior pastor of the congregation now known as the Toronto Airport Christian Fellowship.

Those ties have linked the Parkers to a worldwide charismatic community known as the Third Wave movement, a combative brand of Christian nationalism that includes the Kenyan prophet who performed a ceremonial anointing of Sarah Palin two years before she was named the Republicans' vice-presidential candidate. While much of its growth has taken place in Africa, Asia and South America where Pentecostalism is spreading like wildfire, the Third Wave leadership is centred in the U.S., where C. Peter Wagner, a former professor of church growth, has become its chief proponent, spreading its doctrine of spiritual warfare through his Colorado-based Wagner Leadership Institute.

According to Wagner, the secular revolution of the 1960s, which put the world on the fast track to Armageddon, also ushered in an era of transformation for the Christian church, one marked by unprecedented manifestations of the Holy Spirit and the emergence of leaders with such startling supernatural powers that he deemed them worthy of the biblical titles, apostle and prophet. Claiming an apostle's title for himself, Wagner now leads what he calls the New Apostolic Reformation, urging twenty-four-hour-a-day prayer sieges waged by spiritual warriors focused intently on specific outcomes. So convinced are some Third Wave prophets of their power to change the world that they claim their prayer offensives helped provoke the collapse of the Soviet Union.

In 1999, as the new millennium loomed with predictions of Y2K mayhem, some prophets in Wagner's circle established the International House of Prayer in Kansas City, Missouri, which spawned a web of similar Pentecostal prayer houses across the continent. The movement largely escaped notice until the 2004 presidential elections, when Lou Engle, a senior pastor from Kansas City, set up the Justice House of Prayer in Washington, D.C., announcing that a prophetic vision had directed him to train his group's energies on the candidate most likely to end abortion. "We're praying for President Bush," Engle told a Christian news outlet. "God has given us dreams that he'll be a burning bush and deliver the Moses generation assaulted in the womb."

But prayer was not the only weapon that Engle and his army of young prayer warriors deployed. Inspired by another vision, they marched to the steps of the Supreme Court, standing in dramatic silence with swatches of red duct tape over their mouths inscribed with the word "life." That image, immortalized in the Oscar-nominated documentary *Jesus Camp*, made arresting news footage, and became the signature of Engle's rallies around the world, including those of TheCRY, which the Parkers helped organize on Parliament Hill.

⚜

On the National House of Prayer website, the Parkers make no mention of their ties to Lou Engle, but in 1999, the same year that the International House of Prayer was founded in Kansas City, Rob Parker set out on a spiritual pilgrimage from Calgary to Ottawa, where the idea for a Canadian version was born. At the end of a seventy-three-day prayer walk with a B.C.-based group of Pentecostal leaders called Watchmen for the Nations, Parker arrived in the capital, where he rued the fact that, in a city studded with the embassies of foreign nations, there was no embassy of prayer.

It would take another two years and the terrorist attacks of September 11, 2001, however, before he felt the need to follow up on that insight. Back in Vernon, watching the national memorial services for 9/11 victims on television, Parker was shocked when he switched from Billy Graham's stirring invocations in Washington to Ottawa's rites, where, in deference to interfaith neutrality, the service contained not a single reference to Jesus Christ. "I found out later that the name of God or Jesus was not allowed to be used," he marvels. "We were too multicultural."

Parker was not the only conservative Christian aghast at the omission. Preston Manning decried a subsequent interfaith service that added insult to injury: it went to such lengths of inclusivity that it featured representatives from the Quebec-based Raelians, a sect which believes, Manning pointed out, that humankind is "descended from aliens." While Manning used the lapse to argue for more open debate about religion in public life, Parker chose a different course. "I cried out to God that Canada has become a 'Godless nation,'" he recalls, "and asked him to intervene."

Over the next two years, the Parkers promoted the concept of a prayer embassy in Ottawa, but despite encouragement from assorted prophets, the logistics eluded them. They were ready to give up when, the morning after studying a biblical passage on the siege of Jerusalem, their eyes fell on a newspaper headline about the Liberal government's sponsorship scandal. "Paul Martin Under Siege," it proclaimed. For them, it was an unmistakable sign. "We thought, 'Yes, it's a siege of righteousness,'" Fran says. "We realized it was a wake-up call: we've got to make things right."

Not long afterward, they found an abandoned Ottawa convent once owned by Les Filles de la Sagesse that seemed made-to-order for their needs. Despite years of neglect, it boasted stained-glass windows and priceless hand-carved panelling with enough bedrooms to sleep three dozen visiting prayer warriors. Initially, the asking price was out of reach, but months later, the convent was still on the market and the price had dropped to $900,000. The Parkers were taking a second look when the real-estate agent pointed to the Chinese Embassy visible from a rear balcony. "That's China behind you," he said, a phrase that stopped them cold: those were the exact words a touring American prophet had uttered over them during an Ottawa service. Despite the fact that they had only half the required down payment, the Parkers knew their search was over.

To make up the shortfall, Dick Dewert, the head of the Miracle Channel, another key player in their charismatic network, invited them on his Alberta-based station for a fundraising telethon, which pulled in nearly $300,000 in donations. Then a Chinese Pentecostal congregation in Toronto made up the outstanding balance with a $225,000 interest-free loan. The convent's roof leaked and the rest of the once-stately building was in an advanced state of disrepair, but a handful of charismatic churches in Ottawa chipped in with funds and volunteer labour, and a Saskatchewan hotel owner shipped the Parkers forty beds. Whenever finances were stretched, they flew back to Lethbridge for another pitch on Dewert's aptly named show, *LifeLine*. "We've seen that God provides for everything we need," says Stephen Sowerby, a youth pastor whose family supplied much of the local elbow grease.

In the fall of 2005, the National House of Prayer finally opened its doors to a youth delegation from Vancouver, and other prayer teams quickly followed, including several from the Parkers' own Vernon church and one from as far away as Nunavut. At the time, other conservative Christians, such as Charles McVety, had thrown themselves into the 2006 election campaign, but the Parkers hung back, careful not to indulge in overt politicking. "We've laid low—we don't go banging on doors," Fran says. Even when Stockwell Day introduced them around Parliament Hill, they avoided public statements on hot-button issues like same-sex marriage. "No way we're going there," she insists. Still, for twenty-one days, the Parkers led a prayer fast for "the right government," and on election night they hosted a capacity crowd in their newly opened salons, where hallelujahs and tears of joy filled the second-floor prayer room as the announcement of Harper's victory flashed on the television screen. For the Parkers and their fellow

Christian nationalists, the vote was only one step toward fulfilling the vision depicted in a neo-primitive painting on their prayer-room wall. In it, the Peace Tower bends in humility before a crowd of Christians while the name of Jesus glows above in a cloudless sky—a neat précis of their mission: to see government bowing in obeisance to Christian authority and God's dominion established on Parliament Hill.

In their view, that prospect was spelled out in December 1866, when the Fathers of Confederation assembled in London, England, to hammer out the British North America Act, deadlocked over what to call their newfangled federal entity. Sir John A. Macdonald had his heart set on proclaiming it a kingdom, but the British government was leery of that presumption. The impasse persisted until Samuel Leonard Tilley, the devout, teetotalling premier of New Brunswick, showed up one morning fresh from his daily devotions to announce that his Bible had fallen open at Psalm 72:8: "He shall have dominion also from sea to sea and from the River to the ends of the earth." As his colleagues marvelled at that apparent sign of divine intervention, Macdonald agreed to designate his new nation the Dominion of Canada and, much later, a Latin snatch of the Psalm—A Mari usque ad Mare (From Sea to Sea)—was adopted for its coat of arms.

For more than a century, that anecdote remained a quirky footnote to Confederation until a California theologian named Rousas J. Rushdoony, outraged at the increasing secularization of American public life, launched a movement known as Christian Reconstructionism, which called for the restoration of biblical principles to government. While many evangelicals found Rushdoony's draconian prescriptions too hard to swallow, a smattering of his theories were blended with other theologies—some biblical literalism here, a dose of dispensationalism there—in a spiritual smorgasbord popularized by television preachers like Oral Roberts and Pat Robertson. Their on-air thunderings added a biblical gloss to the doctrine of America's Manifest Destiny, exalting the United States as the New Jerusalem, the "Shining

City on a Hill" that Ronald Reagan invoked in 1984 when he accepted the Republican Party nomination. That mix of scriptural prophecy and patriotism remained largely alien in Canada, where the populace tended to look askance at such showy displays of spirituality. But over the last three decades, as the stars of the U.S. prophetic circuit ventured north of the forty-ninth parallel, evangelicals here began to promote the notion that this country, too, had its own glorious, biblically ordained destiny.

That concept, part of a broader commitment to see Christian government established around the globe, has been fostered by a secretive group of Pentecostal leaders and broadcasters who gather periodically under the umbrella of Watchmen for the Nations, the B.C.-based organization behind Rob Parker's first cross-country prayer walk. Watchmen has played a pivotal role in establishing the National House of Prayer, but outside charismatic circles, the Parkers downplay that association, and are careful to dismiss any hints of a theocratic game plan. "It's not about getting a Christian government or a Christian nation," Fran Parker hastens to assure me. "It's about praying for our leaders to restore the nation to righteousness."

Still, one May afternoon, after giving a seminar at the National Prayer Breakfast, Parker invites me along on a dog-walking expedition to a neighbouring park, where she poses an unusual query: "Do you think nations have destinies?" she asks. As it turns out, she is ready to supply the answer before I am. "We're known as diplomatic, tolerant, laid-back, multicultural—we're different from the U.S.," she says. "God made us different for a reason." Then, letting her Wheaten Terrier loose to romp through the grass, she leans across a picnic table, her eyes ablaze with conviction. "Do I believe Canada has a destiny? Yes!"

As she explains it, this country has shattered its covenant with God by passing unbiblical legislation—abortion and same-sex marriage are just two of what she calls "sins that defile the land." Now, she and other charismatics are certain that God has put the nation on notice to correct those national transgressions. In her mind, there is not the slightest doubt that celestial warning came on May 24, 2006, when the Peace Tower clock stopped at precisely 7:28 a.m.—an hour that is the exact numerical composition of Psalm 72:8, the scriptural inspiration for the country's birth. "And what day did it stop?" Parker asks rhetorically. "Victoria Day!" In her view, only the spiritually obtuse could have missed that symbol-laden bulletin. "On the news that night, they said it might take seventy-two hours to fix," she says, pausing for effect. "Seventy-two!" she marvels. "Just so you get it!"

⁂

Understanding the Parkers' brand of Christian nationalism requires a trip back to Vancouver in the late 1960s, when Bob Birch, the founder of Watchmen for the Nations, turned his east-end church into a hub for the Jesus movement. A dour sparrow of a man, Birch was transformed into a spellbinder in the pulpit, but he refused to deliver his Sunday sermon unless he felt a direct message from God. Fasting and praying all night until he received that divine transmission, he occasionally showed up to admit that he had nothing to impart, but more often, he electrified both his congregants and the listeners of CJOR, the local radio station owned by fellow Pentecostal Jim Pattison, which carried Birch's weekly services live from Saint Margaret's Reformed Episcopal Church.

In the summer of 1969, as young people flocked to Vancouver, turning it into the hippie capital of Canada, Birch welcomed two members of a Christian counterculture movement from California who called themselves Jesus freaks. It was not the most natural of spiritual alliances. Already in his fifties, Birch had no sympathy for the sexual revolution, denouncing it as "a problem of Satanic proportion," but with one ear cocked to the celestial messaging system, he had bunk beds built in his church basement for the influx of homeless youth besieging the city. As word spread of the charismatic preacher who spoke in tongues and welcomed flower children on a quest for their own form of ecstatic abandon, Saint Margaret's Sunday services became a standing-room-only attraction. Crowds lined up for hours vying for a seat in Birch's pews, the overflow sprawled on the adjoining grass, listening through open windows to a preacher they dubbed simply Pastor Bob. Inside, barefoot rock 'n' rollers coming down off bad trips found themselves next to bankers in pinstripes, the whole congregation often babbling unintelligibly or jumping about in such exuberant worship that one *Vancouver Sun* reporter described the resulting cacophony as "like the entire Peruvian Army singing backwards—overwhelming, almost frightening."

As Birch won international acclaim as a revivalist, he was not reluctant to put his celebrity to political use. When his friend and fellow evangelist Bernice Gerard became a Vancouver alderwoman, he joined her crusade against nude sunbathing at the city's Wreck Beach, and tried to block a concert by the Rolling Stones. Years later, when he was in his eighties, he launched a campaign to stop Vancouver from hosting the 1990 edition of the international Gay Games. After organizing a group of pastors to blanket B.C.'s lower mainland with protest flyers, Birch greeted the news of an earthquake in the gay mecca of San Francisco as a sign that more drastic measures were required to avert a similar act of divine retribution against Vancouver. In November 1989, he took out full-page ads in the city's newspapers that proclaimed "time is running out" above a nearly empty hourglass. Invoking the spectre of Armageddon, the text warned that the games would "bring God's judgment upon all in this city" and demanded they be banned "in the name and authority of Jesus Christ."

Even some of Birch's pastoral colleagues took their distance from that wrathful proclamation and Protestant leaders across the country rebuked him for hate-mongering, but a year later, he remained unrepentant. Instead, he founded a new group based on a passage from Isaiah 62:6:

"I have set watchmen upon thy walls, O Jerusalem, which shall never hold their peace day nor night." In the cauldron of anger and intolerance that Birch had helped ferment, Watchmen for the Nations was born.

At first, the group held monthly spiritual warfare events, drawing as many as two thousand charismatics to each, but from the outset, it was no ordinary organization. In keeping with Birch's insistence on prophetic omens, he decided that the only route to salvation lay in assembling Pentecostal leaders for what he called Gatherings of the Nations—invitation-only weekends unfettered by goals or agendas, where they would wait for the will of the Lord to reveal itself. At the first gathering in the B.C. ski resort of Whistler, the group waited for more than a day until it finally discerned a clear command: Canada must atone for its transgressions against its First Nations.

That 1995 decree reflected the influence of Peter Wagner's New Apostolic Reformation movement, which argues that nations not only have divinely ordained destinies, but those destinies can be marred by collective sins such as racism and bigotry. Only by engaging in what Wagner terms "identificational repentance"—mass appeals for forgiveness by today's citizenry—can such national scars be healed and the population released from Satan's grasp. The repentance ceremonies to Canada's aboriginals at the Whistler gathering prompted a rash of Pentecostal missions to native communities, above all in the Arctic, regarded as the scriptural "ends of the earth" referenced in Psalm 72:8. Since then, charismatic congregations have sprouted across the North with a focus on ecstatic worship and miraculous healing, thanks in part to the evangelizing influence of two Inuit preachers from Iqaluit who now serve on the Watchmen council. Those ceremonies of national repentance may have also influenced some Pentecostals in Harper's caucus who are regulars at Watchmen gatherings, helping build support for the government's formal apology to the First Nations for abuse at residential schools among a constituency that once had little sympathy for native issues.

In 1998, when Birch was in his nineties, he passed his mantle on to David Mohsen Demian, an Egyptian surgeon whom he had anointed his spiritual son. Under Demian, the Watchmen for the Nations gatherings took a new turn that was both more political and low-key. With Quebec separatism still threatening to rend the national fabric, he stressed the need for reconciliation between French and English, launching a cross-country performance called La Danse, which acted out a mock courtship and wedding between the two founding nations, complete with an exchange of vows presided over by televangelist David Mainse, one of Watchmen's most high-profile members. Later, Demian would credit those symbolic matrimonial ceremonies with helping to vanquish the separatist threat—an assertion that might astonish political scientists unfamiliar with the claims of the Third Wave prayer movement.

For years, Demian had fasted and prayed for a prophetic insight into what God required of Canada to fulfil its end-times destiny, and finally, on a flight from Vancouver to Ottawa, he received his response. The word "Israel" surged into his consciousness, he reports, and he concluded that the chief obstacle blocking the country from its scripturally ordained path was the stain of anti-Semitism. Demian traced that blot on Canadian history to a fateful 1939 decision by Frederick Charles Blair, the top immigration official in the government of William Lyon Mackenzie King, who turned away a German merchant ship named the *St. Louis* with nearly a thousand Jewish refugees on board. Having already been refused landing privileges in Cuba and the U.S., the ship's final hope was Halifax, a hope Blair swiftly dashed by invoking a regulatory requirement that effectively barred its human cargo from disembarking. In doing so, he perpetuated the government's de facto policy on wartime Jewish immigration, as chronicled in Irving Abella's history, *None Is Too Many*, and the *St. Louis* limped back to Europe where hundreds of its passengers perished or were killed in Nazi concentration camps. "For the destiny of this nation, for the full purpose of God to be realized, and for a solid unity between the French and English," Demian wrote, "a national repentance towards Israel has to take place."

As a Coptic Christian from Egypt, he felt a doubly pressing need to make amends. Tracking down the two dozen remaining survivors of the *St. Louis*, Watchmen for the Nations held a moving dinner of repentance for them in Ottawa, where Frederick Blair's grandson, who is now an Ontario pastor, offered an official apology for his ancestor's brutal rebuff. But for Demian that November 2000 ceremony was only the first step in a much larger reconciliation process. The following year he led more than five hundred conservative Christians on a visit to Israel, where, at the Holocaust memorial, Yad Vashem, he begged the country's chief rabbi for forgiveness on behalf of the Canadian people.

In the years since, Watchmen for the Nations has become one of this country's leading Christian Zionist organizations Demian has twice hosted visits by the Knesset Christian Allies Caucus, a group of Israeli parliamentarians whose mandate is to foster ties with their counterparts in governments around the world, and he has vigorously applauded Harper's pro-Israel policy in the Middle East. Nor has that show of support gone unrewarded: in the summer of 2009, Jason Kenney named Demian to a newly created advisory committee tasked with erecting a monument that commemorates the *St. Louis* tragedy and celebrates Ottawa's refurbished ties to Jerusalem.

Despite that success, Demian's remarks at a gala honouring the Knesset delegation that spring sounded an oddly ominous note. Before an Ottawa audience that included the Israeli ambassador and officials from Canada's leading Jewish organizations, he warned that "Time is of the essence. I feel that very soon there will be a rising up against the Jewish people." If his message stood in stark contrast to the prevailing mood of international boosterism, it also offered a telling glimpse into the dispensationalist mindset that has driven his reconciliation efforts with Israel.

For years, Demian's speeches and newsletters have left no doubt that he believes the final days are at hand. But in the fall of 2008, as the global economic crisis felled corporate giants, he sent out an alert to Watchmen faithful warning of further havoc to come. "There will be a great acceleration in the shakings that are coming as He makes clear His end-time purposes for the nations," Demian wrote. For him, the implications of the crisis were obvious: it was time for God-fearing believers to seize the reins of power. "As things on this earth become more confused and more chaotic, God intends the Church to carry His governmental authority," he counselled, "and to become His mouthpiece in the earth in a way we have never seen before."

Six months later, another of Demian's bulletins sounded an even more certain note of finality under the title, "It's Sooner Than You Think." As he explained, "God spoke to me that we had entered into a season of acceleration. This is also the season when we are going to begin to see the kingdom of God being established on earth as it is in heaven."

Reading those missives, it seems clear that Demian sees reconciliation with the Jewish people as an essential precondition for Canada to fulfil its own prophetic fate. When he pleaded for an official apology to the *St. Louis* survivors, he admitted his belief that "It will bring Canada into its end-time purpose." Indeed, the Watchmen's website spells out its mission in unvarnished terms: "We believe God means Canada to play a role in preparing the end-time bride of Christ," it declares, "and that this preparation will be catalytic to a global revival that will precede Christ's return."

Just what form that end-times preparation will take is unclear, but Demian offered a hint in an e-mail alert he dispatched to Watchmen members only hours after the 9/11 attacks. "We have moved more firmly into God's accelerated timetable for the last days," he wrote. "It is in this time that Canada must rise up. Our flag represents our spiritual destiny; the leaf is for the healing of the nations." As American planes were diverted to Canadian airports and Newfoundlanders opened their homes to stranded international passengers, Demian saw the country already beginning to fulfil its prophetic role. "We are to be a refuge for the nations," he declared. "Let us cry out to the Lord to release Canada fully to her destiny to bring healing and wholeness to the nations of the world."

A week later, with the memory of the imploding World Trade Center still etched in their minds, Rob and Fran Parker were among more than a hundred charismatic leaders from across the country who gathered for an emotional Watchmen conference at a Bible college outside Kelowna, B.C. Pondering the apocalyptic portents, the group agreed to establish a National House of Prayer in Ottawa and took a startling oath: "to lay down their lives and ministries for one another to see God's kingdom advanced in Canada."

At the time, Stockwell Day, one of Watchmen's most prominent members, was under attack as leader of the Canadian Alliance, and there, on the shores of Lake Okanagan, the group made a point of performing a ceremonial anointing, encircling him for a laying-on-of-hands and praying for "God's purposes over his life." A year later, when Day was defeated by Harper, becoming the Alliance foreign affairs critic, he was considered so close to Watchmen for the Nations that Lloyd Mackey detailed its apparent impact on his portfolio for *B.C. Christian News*. Only months after Demian had called for closer relations with Taiwan, Mackey reported, Day rounded up a delegation of like-minded MPs for a trip to Taiwan's national prayer breakfast—a provocative gesture at a time when the Liberal government of the day was striving to forge relations with the rival regime in Beijing.

But the Watchmen's ceremonial anointing is not the only blessing that Day has enjoyed from those in the ranks of the New Apostolic Reformation movement. According to a Colorado prophet named Cindy Jacobs, the founder of Generals of Intercession, which claims to concentrate on "world influencers," she delivered Day a confidential prophecy when he turned up at one of her conferences in Red Deer in 2005. Although neither Jacobs nor Day has elaborated on that impartation, there appears to be a firm belief among the radical charismatics tied to Watchmen for the Nations that Stockwell Day's finest political days are yet to come.

⊹

Ever since the National House of Prayer set up shop under the spiritual wing of Watchmen for the Nations five years ago, it has emerged as a hub of evangelical activity in the capital, hosting hundreds of prayer teams and offering a haven to conservative Christian MPs who find themselves sidelined from Ottawa's cocktail circuit. On the House blog, one staff member even suggested its prayer warfare had influenced the 2008 election. "There have been more members of Parliament who would consider themselves as 'Christian' elected into office than there have ever been in the history of our government!" exulted Terry Long. "That is what I call substantial fruit from a praying nation."

Leading their prayer delegations to MPs' offices, Rob and Fran Parker have helped to destigmatize the notion of charismatic Christians in the corridors of power and have made the rhetoric of Christian nationalism increasingly routine. In the process, they have shifted the debate on the role of faith in the country's political life. Under the guise of hosting a parliamentary prayer mission, they are engaged in a massive demystification effort designed to lure wary evangelicals into activism or even to run for office themselves. Nor are their three-month youth internships some hapless afterthought. Just as the Parkers were preparing to open the doors of the National House of Prayer, David Demian announced a new prophetic revelation: the key to securing Canada's end-times role lay in the hands of a younger generation. "Gen X will reverse the curse in Canada," he decreed.

Months later, the Parkers found themselves organizing a daylong youth rally on the lawns of the Parliament Buildings, which marked the Ottawa debut of Faytene Kryskow, a Gen-Xer whom Demian had designated to lead that spiritual charge. At the time, Kryskow had not yet moved to the capital, but she arrived with credentials that were anything but humdrum. Landing in Ottawa, she introduced herself to Lloyd Mackey as an "extreme prophet," and, as she makes clear in her autobiography, she had received her political marching orders not from David Demian, but directly from God.

ROCKING THE VOTE

V

As the lights go down in Hamilton's Copps Coliseum, the chant goes up. "Je-sus! Je-sus!" It starts slow and insistent, punctuated by rhythmic clapping, then builds to a mighty, foot-stomping roar. In an arena that has hosted the driving decibels of Metallica and The Tragically Hip, that refrain normally cues an encore, but the thousands of teens jamming these stands for a Christian youthfest called "Acquire the Fire" have a different kind of return appearance in mind. All day, in passionate exhortations from youth pastors and the compelling lyrics of Christian rock, they've been warned that the Second Coming of Jesus Christ is at hand.

To underline the point, a two-part drama unfolds onstage, its plot set in a high-school hallway on the last day of life on earth. By the time the play's denouement arrives, its celestial courtroom scene hardly comes as a surprise. The voice of God rumbles over the coliseum, an unseen baritone delivering his final judgment on each of the six student characters, enumerating every lapse in soul-saving or faith. Even the hero, a likeable youth leader with the archetypal moniker Adam, is indicted for dispensing his good deeds fuelled by ego, not a selfless heart. Chastened, Adam whirls to confront the audience. "How would you live your life differently?" he demands. "Because time is ticking away. Make no mistake: his kingdom is coming."

A hush falls over the arena as Ron Luce, the boyish evangelist behind the two-day extravaganza, bounds onstage wearing a black leather jacket and aviator sunglasses to lead a mass prayer of repentance that segues into a rousing call to Christian arms. "Now listen, we've got to march out of here as a victorious army, ready to shine God's light in this world," he shouts as the stage erupts in a blaze of pyrotechnics that brings the crowd to its feet, clapping and jumping, hands raised to the heavens in a frenzy of praise.

That high-voltage mix of Christian bands and artfully orchestrated emotion has turned Luce's Texas ministry, Teen Mania, into a multi-million-dollar operation hailed for its success in selling Jesus to the bubblegum set. For nearly a decade, he has filled stadiums across the continent with more than twelve million teens for "Acquire the Fire" and its newer, more militant sister show, "BattleCry," baptizing thousands of sobbing adolescents a night at his revival-style altar calls. But Luce's message is not simply an old-time summons to good works and sexual purity. In the combative vocabulary of a military mission, he challenges his young audiences to rise up in revolt against the demonic designs of Hollywood, MTV and the shopping mall. "We're here to stage a reverse rebellion," he proclaims.

One year, Luce implored his audiences to toss out their worldly temptations, collecting mammoth garbage cans full of condoms, cigarette packs and punk rock CDs. The next, his volunteers carted a giant cowhide onto the stage and seared it with a red-hot branding iron—a graphic scene-setter for his tirade against the TV programmers and corporate advertising wizards who target the $150-billion youth market. "They think of you as cattle," Luce declared. "They don't care that if you buy the clothes on their show, you might get date-raped. They don't care that if you listen to their show, you are more likely to have sex and get STDs."

In the iconoclastic age of *Adbusters* magazine, those rants strike a receptive chord, albeit one laced with irony: at least two of Teen Mania's top executives are former marketing experts from Procter & Gamble. But Luce's impassioned sermons aren't meant as tutorials in consumer literacy; they are a calculated attack on secularism. Urging teenagers to turn their backs on the touchstones of popular culture, he calls them to a cosseted, Christ-centric lifestyle circumscribed by family and church—no sex, drugs or secular rock 'n' roll. Not that shopping of all kinds is verboten. Booths litter the coliseum corridors peddling an array of Teen Mania wares, from Luce's pocket-sized books to T-shirts that read "Branded by God."

At a time when video games grow ever more gory and online predators lure young girls to seedy motel rooms with the bait of modelling contracts, it's not difficult to understand Luce's drawing power. What parents wouldn't leap at the chance to drag their sullen offspring to a concert where the emcee denounces the perils of "point-and-click porn," then prays for anyone who has "dissed" Mom or Dad? But surveying Copps Coliseum, the only Canadian stop on the annual twenty-five city tour of "Acquire the Fire," it seems that on this particular night, Luce is preaching to the converted. Most of these teens have been bussed here from small towns across Ontario by their church groups or sit under the watchful eyes of parental chaperones. Some clutch well-thumbed Bibles or sport oversized crosses beneath their blonde cornrows and backward baseball caps, but no Goth makeup or multiple piercings mar the panorama of earnest wholesomeness, nor does the pungent haze of any controlled substance waft toward the arena's rafters. The biggest breach of the peace in this crowd seems to be a rainbow spill of Smarties abandoned on a washroom floor.

Not that anyone would know it from the alarmist statistics flashing across the coliseum's three giant video screens. "This is a generation in crisis," the pulsing graphics announce. "One out of twelve attempt suicide each year. Forty percent have experimented with self-injury (are cutters). One in ten high-school females report being raped at some point in their life." In an era when an undetected case of adolescent alienation can explode into a bloody rampage such as that at Montreal's Dawson College, those numbers tap into every parent's worst nightmare. Other statistics are aimed expressly at conservative Christians. "This is a generation without morality," a bulletin warns from the video screens. "Seventy-five percent believe the Bible says God helps those who help themselves. Fifty-three percent believe Jesus committed sin." Those findings are meant to back up Luce's most contentious claim—that only 4 percent of today's Bible-believing youth will remain true to their faith into adulthood. Scholars have dismissed it as blatant fearmongering, and Christian Smith, an expert on teen spirituality at Notre Dame University, debunks the figure in a 2007 essay entitled "Evangelicals Behaving Badly with Statistics." But Luce continues to repeat it as a wake-up call to churches, admonishing them to beef up their youth groups and to shell out for advance blocks of tickets to Teen Mania events.

Fanning fears has become Luce's leitmotif—the secret behind his transformation from itinerant youth preacher to CEO of a teen empire whose influence reaches far beyond his stadium blockbusters, which are broadcast around the globe on GOD TV. A frequent guest on Pat Robertson's 700 *Club* and James Dobson's radio show, Luce was appointed to the White House Advisory Commission on Drug-Free Communities by George W. Bush in 2002. While other youth ministries are struggling to stay current—Campus Crusade for Christ jettisoned any outdated reference to "crusades" from its recent rebranding as c4c—no other evangelical leader has proven as adept as Luce at mobilizing the Facebook generation.

But what worries many of his critics is just where that mobilization may lead. At rallies, he rails against the "namby-pamby, kum-bayah, thumb-sucking babies that call themselves Christians," urging a "wartime mentality" and an "attacking church." With his paramilitary metaphors and take-no-prisoners message, some fear that he is whip-ping up his young Christian soldiers with an angry, us-against-them worldview—one in which there is no shortage of enemies and the Christ-like virtue of tolerance has become a dirty word.

Luce has nursed that sense of resentment since he himself was a teen. Raised by a single mother so out of control that he claims to have turned her in to the police, he ran away at fifteen to stay with his estranged father, who promptly used him as a pipeline to a steady supply of marijuana. Rebelling against that exasperating permissive-ness, Luce had a personal encounter with Jesus which he signalled by donning a gigantic metal cross in such an obvious show of defiance that his stepmother locked him out of the house. It was only after he was taken under the wing of his pastor that he turned the pain and fury of that personal narrative into his life's work. In 1986, armed with his guitar and a master's degree in psychology from Oral Roberts University, Luce set out across the U.S. with his bride, Katie, to call other lost kids to Jesus, running his fledgling teen ministry from his Chevy Citation.

At first, his audiences barely filled church basements, but that changed when he introduced the strobe lights and electronic bass that had become de rigueur at rock concerts, and rechristened his show "Acquire the Fire." As word of its appeal spread through Pentecostal circles, Anthony Does, a youth pastor at Toronto's Evangel Temple, organized a bus trip for his adolescent flock to catch a performance in an auditorium outside Detroit. Among his charges was a thirteen-year-old named Kemtal Glasgow, the son of a Toronto postal worker, who was blown away by Luce's hip revival with its emotional altar calls. "I'll never forget that weekend as long as I live," Glasgow recalls. "It was very simple: Ron played the guitar and Katie sang back-up, but the message was presented in such an innovative, cutting-edge way that it seemed specially designed for me as a kid. This wasn't church as usual."

So impressed was Anthony Does with the show's effect on his youth group that he imported "Acquire the Fire" to Evangel Temple's thousand-seat auditorium in north Toronto, where he found himself with an overflow crowd. In the following years, it outgrew each new location he booked, but what gave Teen Mania its liftoff was not rave reviews alone. On a sunny April morning in 1999, two disgruntled students in black trench coats pulled up to Columbine High School in Littleton, Colorado, unleashing their revenge fantasies in a fusillade that left a dozen students and one teacher dead before they turned their guns on themselves. Three days later, more than seventy-three thousand teens from across the continent found themselves hustled to Michigan's Pontiac Silverdome, near Detroit, for an "Acquire the Fire" weekend that set all-time attendance records. The panic on parents' faces was unmistakable: Luce's rants against video games and Hollywood hits like *Natural Born Killers* had just been trumped by brute reality.

Within two years, the show's Canadian crowds were big enough for Copps Coliseum and Does had set up Teen Mania Canada, now run by Glasgow, his former protege, out of Luce's East Texas headquarters. There, Glasgow doubles as marketing director for the ministry's Global Expeditions, sending three thousand high-school students—nearly two hundred of them Canadians—on foreign mission trips each year. For those less inclined toward altruism, Luce runs Extreme Camps where pastimes include a paintball course riddled with bunkers and trenches that would be the envy of the U.S. Army. But Teen Mania's most elite training ground is its Honor Academy where, for an eight-thousand-dollar fee and a pledge not to date for the entire year, Luce puts eight hundred young believers through a gauntlet of physical and spiritual challenges aimed at steeling them for their appointed task: infiltrating what he and other Christian nationalists call "the high places"—jobs in the godless bastions of government, the media and the entertainment industry. The centrepiece of that year is a three-day boot camp where a mock general in combat gear drives the class through punishing obstacle courses and an arduous forced march dragging mammoth wooden crosses, night and day. Some never make it through that opportunity "to crucify your flesh," as one graduate terms it, but others, like Glasgow, have turned the ordeal into a springboard to full-time jobs in the Christian right.

Critics have accused Luce of using the symbols and techniques of authoritarian movements to rally his youthful zealots, but stories abound of young people transformed by Teen Mania's overseas trips. And who can fault a spiritual impresario for offering churchgoing teens a sense of belonging and a stronger backbone for their beliefs? "Ninety-eight percent of the people in the world are followers of culture, only 2 percent are shapers," Luce says, prowling the stage. "Shouldn't we be that 2 percent? Why should it be the secular people who shape our world?"

Tapping into the wellsprings of adolescent idealism, he exhorts his young listeners to become dreamers, not zombies glued to computer games or celebrity gossip sheets. Settled in my seat for the finale of "Acquire the Fire," I'm about to be engulfed by an attack of the warm fuzzies when Luce's sermon takes a discomfiting turn. "You've got people who not only don't believe the Bible, they're so fervently against it, they want to shape everything," he declares. "When HIV started, they got together and made a plan: let's make people love us even if we have to lie."

It takes a few seconds to register: Luce is invoking the spectre of a vast gay and lesbian conspiracy. "They want to get into education," he continues. "In almost every sitcom, there's a homosexual who's nice and funny. And these guys with this agenda—we'll call it the homosexual agenda—they come up with songs that are fun." On cue, the band breaks into the bouncy strains of "YMCA," but before the crowd can join its infectious chorus, Luce shuts it down. "If we don't dream, somebody else will dream for us," he whispers ominously. "We'll be sucked into somebody else's dream. It's time for the men and women of God to rise up and shape our culture."

Although his call to arms is subtle—he never once mentions same-sex marriage—it is a summons to stamp out the increasing acceptance of homosexuality in both the media and politics. As the crowd rises in a fervent ovation, it becomes clear why Teen Mania is seen as such a threat by liberals and secularists. With his talk of dreams, Luce taps into the inchoate longings of every teenager in his audience and ties them to an agenda that is less about self-realization than the conservative Christian vision of a biblically based nation, free from gay role models and gay rights.

Luce has also been accused of another, more overtly political goal: recruiting new foot soldiers for the Republican Party. Although many in his audience are not old enough to vote, they have frequently been enlisted for door-to-door canvassing, staffing party phone banks and leading noisy cheering sections at campaign rallies. During the 2008 presidential election, Luce played a key role in attracting fifty thousand young people to TheCall, a massive rally on the Washington Mall, organized by revivalist Lou Engle. The event was ostensibly aimed at praying for an end to abortion, but it appeared more concerned with countering Barack Obama's hold on the youth vote. Later, on the eve of the election, Luce and Engle packed three hundred thousand of their young shock troops into San Diego's Qualcomm Stadium for a one-night simulcast, beating the drums for ballot amendments to ban gay marriage in Arizona, California and Florida—all of which passed.

While Luce has confined his campaign efforts to the United States, he is expanding his $1.4-million Canadian operation and has surprising ties to this country's political scene. In 2001, when he first booked "Acquire the Fire" into Copps Coliseum, one of his guest speakers was Stockwell Day. At the time, Day was fighting for his job as Canadian Alliance chief, beset by a caucus mutiny and calls for his resignation, but clad in a black leather jacket for Luce's show, he won the sort of ovation usually reserved for a rock star. Urging the crowd to shun drugs and "get real with God," he might have been any other politician grabbing a chance to boost his image in the generational spotlight, but unbenownst to the audience, he and Luce were old friends. For nearly a year, Day had served on the board of Teen Mania Canada.

Six months later, in the summer of 2002, when Anthony Does helped organize a Christian youth revival on Parliament Hill, Luce flew up for a star turn onstage. Drawing a crowd of five thousand, the first edition of TheCRY demonstrated that evangelical young people in Canada could be mobilized with the same mix of moral exhortations and Christian rock that Luce had pioneered in the U.S. But despite its success, the high-voltage prayer rally wasn't held again for four years. Then in 2006, after Stephen Harper's victory, another youth group backed by Day hatched plans for a new version, which they called TheCRY2(Him).

By that time, Day ranked as the most committed evangelical in Harper's cabinet, with ties to many of the Christian-right groups that had helped bring the Conservatives to power, but he had learned to keep those ties below the media radar. Quietly and far from the cameras, he has served as a backstage mentor to the star of TheCRY's 2006 edition, Faytene Kryskow, who could not be accused of harbouring a modest sense of her mission. In one of the biographical sketches she hands out, Kryskow informs readers that she "has been described by many as a modern-day Joan of Arc."

⚓

Her voice, edgy and urgent, bursts over the sound system even before she hits the spotlight. "Omigosh, we're at Missionfest!" she enthuses as she races onto the Toronto Congress Centre stage, a determined cheerleader decked out in a strawberry-coloured shirt and chandelier earrings. In one hand, Kryskow brandishes a Bible, in the other a portable microphone, but the prop she wields to most effect is her trademark waist-length hair, which has just undergone a dramatic transformation. Weeks earlier, she had ordered her hairdresser to turn the wild, blonde-streaked curls featured in a dizzying number of photos on her website into a more demure auburn mane. Now she plays with it constantly, as if she has not quite settled on the gee-whiz persona she has adopted for the evening—one that is light years from the brisk, no-nonsense organizer I had encountered at a conservative networking conference only days earlier.

"I'm a Jesus freak," Kryskow burbles to the Missionfest crowd. "I'm a worshipper to the core." As the conference's chief youth speaker, she is a bundle of upbeat intensity, pitching her target demographic with the vocabulary of a hyperventilating teen. Being at Missionfest is "awesome," she enthuses, God's sacrifice of his only son to redeem human sin is "cool" and, taking up her Bible, she reads a passage from the book of Jeremiah that she says "really rocked me." Her speech is peppered with tales of divine revelations that God has "downloaded," but preaching in the verbiage of the iPod set is only part of Kryskow's appeal. With a mastery of spin that she picked up in her college communications studies, she is working to turn the goody-two-shoes stereotype of young Christians on its head. Borrowing the military terminology of Teen Mania, she bills her cross-country rallies as "Sieges" and her Bible-believing followers as "hard-cores" and "dread champions of the Lord."

Four years after setting up shop in Ottawa, Kryskow has emerged as one of the country's evangelical stars. She is the director not only of 4MYCanada, her four-thousand-member youth lobby, but also the chief organizer for TheCRY and the Canadian branch of a U.S. anti-abortion group called Bound4life. When she is not whipping her followers into a burst of activism—tapping into an e-mail network she estimates at thirty thousand—she is flying across the country on her own crammed preaching schedule. Still, her chief role is leading teams of young evangelicals on blitzes of Parliament Hill, where she has snagged meetings with more than three hundred Members of Parliament and senators to argue that the voice of the country's socially conservative youth has been ignored. "The perception of young people was that we were all just off the rails, morally," she says. "We are here to say that this is not true."

With her striking looks and tactical smarts, Kryskow has cut a swath through the capital, and two years ago the faith-based Bridgeway Foundation named her one of the country's top thirty-five Christian leaders under thirty-five. Calling her young evangelical troops to political action, her website spells out the instructions for engagement, chapter and verse: how to choose a candidate and enlist in a campaign; how to bombard MPs with letters and e-mails, either supporting or decrying specific legislation; and how to land an internship or full-time job in the government. On 4MYCanada.ca, ablaze with hyper-patriotic graphics and red maple leaves, she leaves no room for misguided civic passion or error: she lists "bills we are watching," and lays out the desired response step by step, even providing printable postcards and petition forms. "This is our Canada and we are taking responsibility for her," she tells one gathering of MPs. "We are committed to working in any and every way that we can to support you as you bring forth legislation on issues that we are excited about."

At a time when pollsters regularly report the disengagement of eighteen to thirty-four-year-olds from the electoral process, her lobby has become the toast of Stephen Harper's caucus, which hardly seems a surprise. In her 2009 book, *Marked: A Generation of Dread Champions Rising to Shift Nations*, Kryskow claims to be non-partisan, but she can't hide her elation at Harper's ascension to power, hailing him as "the first practicing Christian prime minister"—a designation that might come as news to Paul Martin, who attended mass at least once a week. Harper's victory brought in "the most socially conservative government that we have had in decades," she notes, rejoicing that more than 40 percent of MPs are professed born-again believers. "For a nation that has been defiled to the core by an anti-God agenda for decades," she declares, "this is a miracle."

When Harper winds up his speeches with "God bless Canada," she calls it "one of the most awesome blasts of fresh air my generation has ever experienced." Betraying no impatience with the prime minister's incrementalism or failure to deliver on policy promises, Kryskow praises his tenure as "one of the most incredible national reformation periods our nation has seen in recent history." So enthusiastically has 4MYCanada applauded Conservative policies, in fact, that an observer could be forgiven for confusing it with a junior cheering section of Harper's theo-con constituency. As the Conservative Party remains deadlocked over whether to create its own youth wing, Kryskow even attended the party's 2008 policy convention in Winnipeg, reporting back to her troops, "We are teary eyed with gratitude . . . Pretty much EVERY resolution that we asked you to pray for today passed."

Winding up her spiel at Missionfest, she summons the crowd to political activism with an unusual pitch. "Imagine an army of young people five million strong," she says. "Imagine their passion to arise as a youth force that effectively decided who would get elected to political office—a force so powerful that it literally began to change their nation." Her audience is warming to her message when it takes a bizarre turn. "This actually happened," Kryskow says. "They called themselves the Hitler Youth and they changed the face of their nation and the world." As her listeners sit in stunned silence, she delivers her closing call to arms: "If they could mobilize their cause to become that mighty with the power of evil backing them," she tells the crowd, "how much more could we accomplish with the power of God backing us up?"

⁜

Kryskow's political role is all the more remarkable in a former street-corner evangelist who had never voted before she set out for the capital five years ago, arriving with such a dearth of knowledge that she "didn't even know we had senators," as she told an Edmonton radio host. "This was like a crash course in national stuff."

Just who chose her for the mission and how she was groomed are facts that Kryskow prefers not to discuss, but snippets of her life story slip out in what she calls her "preaches" and in the three books she has written. One detail that she seldom mentions to her audiences is that celebrity runs in the family: her father Dave spent six years playing left wing for a half-dozen National Hockey League teams, including the Chicago Black Hawks and the Washington Capitals. In 1979, he retired to Lesser Slave Lake, northwest of Edmonton, where Faytene grew up, the second of his three daughters, a self-proclaimed wild child. "From fourteen to twenty, I was a textbook hellraiser," she says. She was also a textbook study in eating disorders, a decade-long struggle with binging and purging that connects her to many of her young conscripts. "On the outside, I looked like I had everything together, but on the inside, I had this emptiness," she says. "I'd throw up just because I thought I'd be more perfect."

Raised a Ukrainian Catholic, she lost her bearings in the New Age nirvana of Vancouver's Simon Fraser University, where she found "people were preaching Buddha and Islam—all these ideologies were being tossed around." In her second year, she holed up in her dormitory and defied God to appear: "I remember sitting on my bed saying, 'God, if you're real, I believe you have the power to speak to me in a way that I'll know it's really you.'" The response was unmistakable—a "supernatural encounter" she calls it—but she had no desire to become one of those cheery born-agains who got on her nerves: "the glow-worm people," she dubs them, always bursting with an annoying sense of bliss. "I wanted to wipe the smile off their face."

Kryskow brought her angst to Lisa Dewar, who ran a campus ministry called Ambassadors for Jesus, and Dewar swiftly saw through the facade of an A student who had won a spot on the college karate team. "To the naked eye, you'd never know she was struggling with anorexia,"

153

Dewar recalls. "She seemed like a very in-control girl, but she was definitely going down a road of personal destruction."

Kryskow was on the cusp of committing her life to Christ when she came down with a case of cold feet. "I got scared. I thought, 'Oh, no, there are all these things I can't do—I can't go party anymore,'" she recounts. "For a lot of people, Christianity is a list of Dos and Don'ts." The don'ts eventually cost her the affections of her long-time boyfriend, who was less than thrilled about her new incarnation as a passionate moralist. "I ended up breaking up with this guy I once thought I might marry," she says wistfully. "I can remember looking up and saying, 'Jesus, I'm yours,' and suddenly all the anger and fear just poured out of me."

Joining the Dewars' Pentecostal congregation prompted another estrangement. Kryskow's parents were aghast to discover she had embraced an ecstatic form of worship, punctuated by shout-outs and speaking in tongues. "They thought I'd joined a cult," she says. Equally shocking to them was the fact that she turned her back on a promising business career. She had worked her way through school with the Southwestern Company, a Tennessee-based direct-sales outfit that relies entirely on summer students, many of them evangelicals, to peddle its publications door-to-door through a system best described as Bootstrap Capitalism 101. Obliged to buy their inventory up front, its recruits must pay their own way to a week-long sales school in Nashville, then fund the trip to their assigned territories, rustle up their own lodgings and calculate the gross sales and price points that will permit them to rack up a profit by summer's end. A third of the students quit within weeks, defeated by the solitude and slammed doors, but those who survived include Kenneth Starr, the special prosecutor best known as Bill Clinton's nemesis. Kryskow thrived in that sink-or-swim environment, becoming a top performer who netted seventy thousand dollars in one summer alone. "I was as psycho then for money as I am now about Jesus," she says. The staff job that waited after graduation would have meant even bigger paydays, but she realized she could no longer obsess over a balance sheet. "At twenty-two, I was on track for making six figures," she tells her Missionfest audience, "when the Lord hijacked my heart."

Ironically, it is that path not taken—the secular path of dogged salesmanship and entrepreneurial spunk—that best prepared her for her current task: organizing a cross-country youth lobby to peddle the cause of traditional Christian values to wary MPs and cabinet ministers. Not that Kryskow could have imagined such a vocation at the time. Although she felt a calling to ministry, it was one she didn't dare voice: she had never studied theology and, as a Catholic, had only a nodding acquaintance with the Scriptures. Sensing her ambition, Lisa Dewar steered her to Pacific Life Bible College in nearby Surrey, a school she chose expressly for a young woman who was convinced that misogyny lurked at the heart of Christianity. "I thought the Bible had been written by men to control women," Kryskow admits. "That's what I'd been told at university and it seemed to make sense."

In 1997, shortly before Kryskow arrived, Pacific Life had become the official college for the Foursquare Gospel Church of Canada, the California-based branch of Pentecostalism founded by one of the continent's most famous female evangelists, a Canadian farm girl named Aimee Semple McPherson. As Dewar anticipated, Kryskow was fascinated by tales of the 1920s revivalist known simply as "Sister" whose birthday and rural roots she shared. Born on a dairy farm in southwestern Ontario and widowed at nineteen, McPherson had set off across the continent with two toddlers and her mother to become a self-styled "soul-winner for Jesus." On the eve of the Roaring Twenties, in a culture awash in flappers and bootleg gin, she preached a no-nonsense mix of temperance and "old-time religion" that never failed to attract crowds or headlines. A genius at snagging publicity, she criss-crossed the U.S. in a seven-seat Oldsmobile that she dubbed her "Gospel Car," its doors stencilled with apocalyptic alerts: "Prepare to Meet Your God" and "Where Will You Spend Eternity?"

Tales of McPherson's miraculous cures kept her tent revivals packed until she finally settled in Los Angeles, where she built her own Angelus Temple, a domed, white wedding cake of a church that seated more than five thousand. Only a stone's throw from Hollywood, her services blossomed into theatrical pageants, in which she occasionally appeared as a milkmaid, and once wheeled a motorcycle onstage, dressed as a traffic cop. Attracting standing-room-only crowds and stars like Charlie Chaplin, she founded her own radio station to become the first female evangelist on the airwaves. Then, as the twin threats of Nazism and Communism loomed in the 1930s, McPherson threw her energies into patriotic productions, urging a return to America's Christian roots. Her stage sets blossomed with forests of U.S. flags, and her billboards, streaked with fighter planes, hyped war-bond sales. Taking to the road with a touring production called "America, Awake!" she introduced a strain of Christian nationalism into public discourse that made the star-spangled spectacles of today's U.S. religious right look like models of restraint.

For Kryskow, McPherson was a powerful role model who had mixed politics and Pentecostal revivalism to become one of the world's most influential megapreachers, founding a denomination that has grown to fifty thousand churches in more than a hundred countries. Certainly, she was on Kryskow's mind in the fall of 2005 during a prophetic conference in Stratford, Ontario, only miles from McPherson's birthplace. Urging her audience to get involved in the next federal election, Kryskow grew increasingly emotional as she summoned her listeners to become "nation-shakers," to join riding associations and get out the vote. "Somebody's got to pick up that mantle of Aimee Semple McPherson," she cried. But by then, it was already clear: that somebody would be Kryskow herself.

⁜

Her route from Pacific Life Bible College to Parliament Hill was hardly direct, and McPherson was not her only feminist inspiration. Dropping out of the college in her third year, Kryskow leaped at a job coordinating food deliveries from churches to Vancouver's housebound poor, but found herself frustrated, tethered to a desk. She longed to be a real missionary, out in the field. With Liberia in the grips of a savage civil war and heart-wrenching footage of its starving orphans dominating the news, she volunteered to go there under the wing of Hope for the Nations, a B.C.-based charity run by a Kelowna pastor named Ralph Bromley.

By then, Kryskow had hooked up with a network of radical Pentecostals that included Bromley and his wife, Donna, as well as their fellow pastors, Stacey and Wes Campbell, the founders of Kelowna's New Life Vineyard Church, a congregation tied to the Toronto Vineyard fellowship of holy laughter fame. Within that close-knit charismatic world, Stacey Campbell was already a budding luminary with an arresting prophetic style. In the midst of a service, the fresh-faced mother of five would suddenly metamorphose into a blur of swirling blonde hair, her head whipping from side to side as if in neurological overdrive, pronouncements pouring forth in breathy, yet lucid paragraphs. When Kryskow set off for Africa, she was still a neophyte in those circles, but she had received her instructions in a prophetic vision of her own. "All I saw was the faces of African children," she says. "I knew that God had called me to be the hands and feet of Jesus."

She spent seven months in Liberia, finding lodging with Catholic nuns at a leprosy centre in the town of Ganta, where fourteen-year-olds toted AK-47s and a nest of tiny, tree-dwelling poisonous snakes called green mambas lurked in the branches outside her back door. On her website, Kryskow claims she organized "miracle crusades where she saw multitudes saved and healed," but in the Salvation Army's *Journal of Aggressive Christianity*, she comes across as an enterprising pragmatist, who found medical care for a band of malnourished children and rescued a fifteen-year-old from prostitution by setting her up in business as an egg seller. Returning to Vancouver, she recorded a CD called *King of Justice: Songs of a Missionary*, and was already organizing her next trip, this time to Russia, when, driving back from a conference in Alberta, she had another vision, the image of a massive red maple leaf suspended over the Rockies. Once again, she heard the voice of God: "He was saying, 'Who's going to rise up for Canada?'" she recalls. "'Who's going to fight?' He was looking for a generation who would be a voice in this land."

Kryskow would not discover what form her celestial assignment would take for another four years, but she scrapped her travel plans and threw herself back into evangelizing with another controversial local prophet: Patricia King, a flamboyant bleached blonde with a punk haircut and no patience for those spouting "Christianese." Based in Mission, B.C., Pat Cocking, as King was then known, made no attempt to hide her own heretical past practicing witchcraft—whipping up health cures and love potions, even casting spells to banish the lumps from gravy. "And you know what?" she wrote later in an essay for a Christian news service. "It all worked." It was while dabbling in astrology—another New Age pastime deemed by most evangelicals as the devil's handiwork—that King found Christ, or at least his horoscope. "I was drawn toward this wonderful Man who had such an unusual chart," she wrote, but admitted to another epiphany that also contributed to her conversion. "I had a moment of spiritual enlightenment concerning the person of Jesus," she confessed, "while I was totally stoned on marijuana."

Not surprisingly, some in the West coast evangelical community considered King an outlandish figure, an image she played up by christening her ministry Extreme Prophetic. But Kryskow had been an acolyte since her days at Simon Fraser, often making the hour's drive to Mission to take King's courses with titles like "Glory School" and "Prophetic Boot Camp." After her return from Liberia, she joined King's staff as an itinerant evangelist, taking her ministry to the hookers and homeless addicts haunting the sidewalks of Vancouver's infamous Downtown Eastside. Kryskow had begun leading church groups there while she was still in university, staging impromptu guitar concerts and handing out food and warm clothes, and insists she was never afraid. "I always had a sense of divine protection," she says.

Under King's influence, however, her evangelizing trips to the concrete jungle around Hastings and Main took a novel turn. Where once she had arrived with sandwiches and sweaters, she now set up her grandmother's folding card table and chairs on the sidewalk with a sandwich board offering "Free Prayers" and "Spiritual Readings." Occasionally, King or Stacey Campbell accompanied her, always careful to point out that this was no psychic fair, but the lineups for their prophetic readings stretched around the block well past midnight, and won them coveted media coverage. "People are just so starved for words of affirmation," Kryskow told *B.C. Christian News.* "People who would never sit down in a church to pray will sit down on the street."

When King won her own TV show on the Miracle Channel, Kryskow became a regular guest, introduced as a "budding prophetess," but she was not King's only protege. The Extreme Prophetess had also played spiritual godmother to a young Abbotsford revivalist named Todd Bentley, a burly former jailbird with face piercings and tattoos from ankles to neck. Founding his own Fresh Fire Ministries, Bentley became celebrated for sporting a biker's black leathers and regaling audiences with tales of divine lightning bolts and his encounters with an angel named Emma. His career was undimmed by a 2001 exposé in Alberta's *Report* magazine, which revealed a past considerably more checkered than he had confessed: at fifteen he had been convicted of molesting a minor.

Still, by the spring of 2008, Bentley was the hottest name on the global revival circuit. His services in Lakeland, Florida, were attracting eight thousand worshippers a day and carried live on GOD TV in more than a hundred countries, where they became known as the "Lakeland Outpouring." The ill and the desperate flew in from around the world for his rumoured miracles of healing and claims of resurrecting the dead. His crowds continued to grow even after YouTube footage showed him taking a run at a colon-cancer patient, planting a black boot in his stomach with cries of "Bam!" and "Ka-boom!"

In *Charisma*, the chief magazine of the Pentecostal movement, Bentley was hailed as a prophet whose revival might well eclipse the Toronto Blessing and herald the global outbreak of signs and wonders expected before the end times. For some Canadian charismatics, his cures were sure signs of the coming Apocalypse—a confirmation that the country would play a healing role in the final days. Kryskow made a video recounting how, years earlier, Bentley had cured her of an apparently hopeless medical condition, autoimmune hepatitis, by revealing that a coven of witches had laid a hex on her. "He began to reject specific voodoo curses that had been set over my life," she recalls. "The Lord showed me it was the devil's plan to suck my vision out."

She remained so convinced of her friend's powers that, in August 2008, after bannering Bentley's revival on 4MYCanada's website, she flew to Lakeland for "some refreshing," joining Patricia King and Stacey Campbell at an "apostolic commissioning ceremony" organized by apostle-in-chief Peter Wagner. Intended to counter reports by Fox News and ABC's *Nightline* that called Bentley's cures into question, the televised ceremony was a theatrical tour de force: Bentley collapsed onto the stage, felled by the Holy Spirit, grinning and twitching as the assembled prophets anointed him with oil. Stacey Campbell uttered a prophetic benediction over him in a blizzard of flying hair, and Wagner decreed, "Your power will increase, your authority will increase." But their prophetic sonar turned out to be less than reliable. Within weeks, Bentley admitted to an affair with a staffer that broke up his marriage and shut down his tent.

To some critics in the charismatic community, the Lakeland revival was already a spiritual travesty—"a circus of whacked-out manifestations," as one defector put it—and the public anointing ceremony, led by the same cast of characters behind the disputed Toronto Blessing, the final straw. Certainly, the Bentley debacle was not the first brush with controversy for Patricia King and the Campbells. In 2003, a group of American charismatics had denounced King's Glory School teachings as New Age heresy, and she was obliged to submit to what she termed an "intensive theological audit," posting testimonials on her behalf from family and friends: "Patricia is the most faithful person I know," Kryskow's submission read. "I am continually amazed by her Christ-like character."

The same summer, Stacey and Wes Campbell received unwelcome news of another kind: the Federal Bureau of Investigation had raided the headquarters of a California pastor named Gregory Setser who was eventually convicted of fraud in a $160 million Ponzi scheme that targeted evangelicals on both sides of the border. In Canada, the scheme operated out of the Campbells' Kelowna church, defrauding nearly seventy investors, but it would not hit the Canadian media until three years later, when the B.C. Securities Commission found several New Life pastors guilty of misconduct for selling securities without a licence. Among them were Wes Campbell and Ralph Bromley, the president of Hope for the Nations, who had sent Kryskow to Liberia. The pair was barred from serving as directors or officers of a public company in the province—Bromley for five years, Campbell for two—and the Campbells were later ousted from the church they had founded. Undaunted, they started two new ministries before resurfacing on the staff of another congregation, Kelowna Christian Center, which has featured local MP Stockwell Day at its fundraisers.

Both Patricia King and Stacey Campbell, whom Kryskow calls her "spiritual mothers," have headlined her conferences and prayer rallies, and appear to be part of the secret "leadership" to which she defers. That may be one reason she has been reluctant to admit the mainstream media to many of her prayer weekends and guards the contents of her preaching with care. When I asked to attend one Siege, she explained that the presence of a journalist would inhibit her attendees, interfering with their unbridled worship experience, but there seemed to be more to her objections. Later, when she noticed that I had purchased CDs of one such event from 4MYCanada's booth at a conference, she snatched them from my hands. "I don't want you to have those," she said, returning my twenty dollar bill to me.

⊹

In Kryskow's charismatic circles, prophetic pronouncements are regarded with the same reverence that the Vatican reserves for papal edicts. When David Demian declared at a Watchmen for the Nations gathering that Canada's end-times destiny would be realized by Generation X, she knew she had received a divine commission. But, unlike papal edicts, Demian's decree carried a cryptic corollary: "This next generation must learn to walk backward before they run forward," he declared, leaving the assembled Watchmen mystified. For Kryskow, the riddle was soon solved. During a Watchmen gathering in Montreal, she had a vision of a broom sweeping away debris to expose forgotten ruins, and she took it as a more tangible job description: to write a book unearthing the country's Christian origins.

That project coincided with a push by the continent's leading dominionists to recast the historical record in a Christian light, demonstrating that their call for biblically inspired government is actually a return to the way things once were before decades of secular spin. In the U.S., the campaign was led by the late Florida televangelist D. James Kennedy, who promoted books on the faith of the founding fathers, and convened an annual conference, Reclaiming America for Christ. Here, Kryskow set out to pen a Christianized version of the Canadian narrative, fully cognizant of the wry observation that appears in one of her books: "History will be kind to us," Winston Churchill quipped, "for we intend to write it."

Still, it was a daunting undertaking for a communications major with no scholarly background or inclinations, who nearly failed a course in archival research. Her solution was to borrow from a glossy tome entitled *Canada: Portraits of Faith*, which features fifty-two eminent Christians from Jean de Brébeuf, the martyred Jesuit, to Ernest Manning. Kryskow lifted chunks from three dozen of its thumbnail profiles, often word for word, acknowledging the debt in her footnotes, then tacked on a sampling of hymns and religious headlines from the time of Confederation, and called the rejigged package *Stand on Guard: A Prophetic Call and Research on the Righteous Foundations of Canada*.

What made the book all the more unusual was her own text: a florid account of her prophetic visions, including one that arrived after a Watchmen for the Nations gathering in Quebec City, when she threw herself down on the Plains of Abraham and felt "the flag running (almost literally) through my blood. I felt tied to this nation at a depth that was so intense it was overwhelming."

Although Kryskow refers to the book as a bestseller whose marketing agent was the Holy Spirit, its publication was underwritten by a one-thousand-dollar donation from a Seattle congregation. She herself served as its chief distributor, mailing a copy to every senator and MP, as well as key government offices, which allowed her to claim that *Stand on Guard* is in the Library of Parliament and on Stephen Harper's bookshelf. As she headed to Ottawa with her first youth delegation in the summer of 2005, the book became her calling card.

If its title was not enough to stir patriotic sentiments, a cover blurb from Stockwell Day was guaranteed to catch the eye of most readers on Parliament Hill. In the telling lexicon of dominionism, he applauded Kryskow for demonstrating that the country's major institutions "are resting on pillars of principle built by Canadians who were unassuming and unswerving in living out their faith in the public square."

That tribute was not the only support Day contributed to her mission; he was, it turns out, its chief instigator. During the final late-night debate on the same-sex marriage bill in June 2005, he was dismayed to see the Commons visitors' gallery packed with young gay and lesbian activists; not a single member of an evangelical youth group had showed up to provide a counterweight. Afterwards, as he and his wife, Valorie, picked their way through the jubilant crowd on the Centre Block steps, they were struck by how politically astute their young opponents appeared. As Day later told a Watchmen for the Nations assembly, it was time for the Christian right to respond with its own plugged-in youth contingent dedicated to the defence of traditional values.

A month later, Kryskow and a band of friends set out across the country on an eight-city tour they called "Siege: Storm the Hill." Financed by Patricia King's Extreme Prophetic ministry and Watchmen for the Nations, they unveiled their crusade on the steps of the B.C. legislature. Although they attracted only small crowds—most recruited from local churches and pro-life groups—Kryskow's spiel was so novel that they garnered media coverage at every stop, including a story in the *National Post*. "Politicians believe the aggressive liberal voice represents the next generation," she told reporters. "I'm here to say it doesn't." In each city, she warned young Christian conservatives that the time for manners and meekness had passed: "Speak up and be unashamed of your traditional values," she urged.

Working their way eastward, the group stopped in the Okanagan Valley, where Day and his wife welcomed them into their home, sharing prayers and a testimonial for Kryskow's promotional video before shepherding them to a prime networking opportunity: the annual garden party that ailing Conservative MP Darrel Stinson hosted for constituents and former Reform Party cronies in his adjacent riding. There, with television cameras rolling, Day introduced Kryskow like a proud parent, leaving her to plug her fledgling crusade to an audience that included veteran Alberta MP Myron Thompson, a former high-school principal, who choked up during her presentation and declared he had spent thirty years praying for just such a youth brigade.

Two months later, when Kryskow returned to Parliament Hill with her first Josiah Team of Christian youth, Thompson made sure their visit did not go unnoticed. Inviting them to the Commons' gallery before Question Period, he flouted parliamentary protocol to introduce them from the House floor, their presence recorded in Hansard as he led a standing ovation of fellow Conservatives. Kryskow cites the incident as an example of the "ridiculous favour" bestowed on her group, which landed private meetings with thirty members of Parliament. Still, she was careful not to claim credit for that coup. "It's not a glory issue," she said later. "It's a strategy issue. God showed us the strategic way to do it."

God, it appears, was not the only strategist on the case. She hired a Vancouver public-relations company, and her political overtures betray the hand of an insider with a seasoned knowledge of Parliament Hill. Each member of her cross-country delegation asked for a meeting with his or her member of Parliament—a request no politician was likely to refuse—then showed up with the rest of the Josiah Team to deliver a wildly flattering message: instead of the usual litany of constituent complaints or demands, they expressed gratitude for the sacrifices exacted by a life of public service. As New Brunswick Conservative Mike Allen later admitted, "I had to do a total mental reboot when they opened the meeting by saying they appreciated me."

In those encounters, Kryskow's team prayed with each MP, and young women occasionally professed taking vows of sexual purity or recounted their regretted abortions. For some conservative Christian politicians, such intimate exchanges opened unexpected veins of emotion. One of Kryskow's twenty-year-old interns was amazed when a veteran politician "just started to weep with us." But Kryskow also spoke in the unsentimental language of the ballot box. Her cohort of eighteen-to-thirty-five-year-olds might have a woefully low turnout rate at the polls, she conceded, but she and her Josiah Teams were committed to changing that. "We are the untapped vote," she said. "When you are

facing pressure and need the courage to stand, remember our faces."
Lest they forget, she ended every meeting with a parting gift. One
memento was an elegant, postcard-sized prayer in a silver frame: "May
you have the courage to do good government," it read, "even when it
is unpopular or contrary to your partisan lines."

In the course of that lobbying, Kryskow's group has benefited from
support unavailable to most non-governmental organizations. Like her
allies at the National House of Prayer, she enjoys Commons' passes
and the use of prestigious salons on Parliament Hill for her receptions,
where Day and a handful of conservative Christian MPs have been
regular guests. When she led her second Josiah Team to the Hill in the
spring of 2006, they were welcomed by the Conservatives' first caucus
chair, Rahim Jaffer, on the floor of the House, and invited to try out
the MPs' leather seats, even before Harper had convened his first session of Parliament. Later, the government accorded Kryskow and three
of her interns another rare privilege: reserved spots in the Senate gallery to watch the 2007 Throne Speech and an invitation to the prime
minister's reception afterward.

That honour provoked an ecstatic e-mail report to 4MYCanada's
membership, which no PMO press release could have matched.
Describing the occasion as "a mix between a family reunion and a
Stanley Cup playoff," Kryskow heaped praise on the government's
agenda, before rhapsodizing over the speech's closing nod to divine
providence. "Amazing, phenomenal, awesome!!!" she declared.
"Divine Providence!! Come on!! This is an open invitation for God to
invade our Parliamentarians hearts and minds on these issues! . . . If
you could see us right now you would know we are JUMPING like
freaks! I just want to say WE ARE SO IMPRESSED WITH OUR
PRIME MINISTER!"

Her cheerleading soon took a more tangible form. Kryskow testified
before the Justice Committee in favour of the government's bill to raise
the age of consent—a key show of support for a measure that some

other youth groups warned would criminalize teenage sex—and backed another controversial measure targeting minors: adult sentences for young offenders with long rap sheets, which was later overturned by the Supreme Court.

Meanwhile, Kryskow has spent much of her time recruiting new activists to 4MYCanada's rolls, staging regional editions of her Sieges at locations chosen to underline the country's Christian roots. "Reverse the Curse!" she proclaimed, parroting David Demian in her promotional video for a 2007 prayer weekend in Saint John, New Brunswick. There, she later claimed, her group tapped into the spirit of the province's former premier, Samuel Leonard Tilley, whose daily Bible study had inspired the nation's designation as a dominion. Months earlier, convening a conference in Ottawa starring Patricia King, Kryskow rented Dominion Chalmers United Church, trumpeting it as the site where the nation's first prime minister, Sir John A. Macdonald, "got saved." (In fact, the church was not built until after his death, and despite the assertion of one Ph.D. thesis, most historians dispute any suggestion that the notorious tippler ever had a born-again experience.)

For Kryskow, those historical allusions are meant to show that a nation's fate can be changed by spiritual warriors wielding the weapon of strategic prayer. In her third book, *Marked*, she claims that intercessions by a Vancouver group directly provoked the downfall of former New Democratic MP Svend Robinson, once the country's leading gay-rights activist. She also makes an extraordinary case for the flipside of that thesis, blaming legislative missteps for precipitous plunges of the Canadian dollar. The Supreme Court's 1988 decision to overturn the country's abortion law, she asserts, sent the stock market into a freefall. "It seemed to me like a spiritual law kicked in," she writes, "and the heavens of blessing were shut over our nation because of our massive bloodguilt." In October 2008, she saw the same principle at work when abortion pioneer Henry Morgentaler was awarded the Order of Canada, an honour her group vehemently contested with a petition and a protest outside Rideau Hall. "On that very day, the Canadian dollar plummeted to an eighty-four cent low," Kryskow asserts. "Coincidence? Maybe, but again I doubt it."

That unique view of economic history can be traced back to her stint helping to found the Vancouver House of Prayer, where she led teams on "spiritual mapping" expeditions across the city, charting locations they believed were subject to demonic possession, then conducting a Pentecostal form of exorcism. Now she sees her Ottawa advocacy work in the same light, banishing the legislative "strongholds of Satan" that she believes are keeping the country from its biblically ordained fate. In one prophetic vision, she received "clear and intense" instructions to establish a group of young believers devoted to praying away the sin of abortion in fifteen-minute shifts around the clock, seven days a week. She promptly launched Bound4life, the Canadian branch of a U.S. anti-abortion group founded by Lou Engle.

At her prayer and fasting weekends, Kryskow's rhetoric and themes are a direct echo of Engle's tearful, keening performances, and he has appeared at a handful of her rallies, both in person and via video greetings. With Stacey Campbell, who serves on one of his boards, Engle has clearly fostered Kryskow's work in Ottawa. In a glowing foreword to *Marked*, he calls her "like a daughter to me" and compares her to the Old Testament heroine, Esther, for having "risked everything to step onto the stage of Canadian history . . . Amazingly, the scepter of favor has been stretched out to her and the benevolent Kingdom of Heaven is transforming the halls of justice," he writes approvingly. "Laws and ideologies are changing."

⁎

In the summer of 2007, the CBC announced a Great Canadian Wish List to drum up interest among the Facebook set: young Canadians were

invited to log onto the social networking site and vote on their generation's leading wish for the country's 140th birthday. To the shock of its
organizers, the contest was commandeered by Christian youth groups
such as 4MYCanada, who pulled off an online putsch. On Canada Day,
the CBC hastily announced that the leading wish, which had chalked up
9,500 votes, was to abolish abortion. While the results were largely
ignored—they countered every recent poll on the subject—they demonstrated the leverage that young, tech-savvy faith groups can wield.

It is a lesson that informs much of Kryskow's political organizing,
and never more so than when she threw her support behind a private-
member's bill called The Unborn Victims of Crime Act. On Parliament
Hill, where private members' bills are regarded as niceties, routinely
ignored by MPs and the press, the measure was dismissed as a lost
cause—yet another pro-life initiative by Ken Epp, an evangelical backbencher from Edmonton who had already announced his retirement.
But Kryskow and her allies at the National House of Prayer had helped
Epp conceptualize the proposed legislation—modelled on the Unborn
Victims of Violence Act that George Bush signed into law in 2004—
which made a criminal assault against a pregnant woman also a separate
crime against her fetus, and they set out to turn it into a cause célèbre.

On 4MYCanada's website, Kryskow launched a slick, multi-faceted
campaign. It featured a petition designed to demonstrate the extent of
Epp's support and downloadable postcards showing romantically lit
pregnant bellies, with detailed instructions on how to inundate MPs
with weekly mailings. Heightening the suspense, she announced that
one of her divine visitations had ordered a three-day fast to ensure the
bill's passage. Then, posting a video of the House debate, she advised
her members to borrow its arguments in another, eleventh-hour barrage of letters to lawmakers. Her instructions, urgent and precise,
showed an informed knowledge of the political mindset: one tip warned
followers against form letters "because MPs tell us they are less effective than personal ones you write."

Late on the night of March 5, 2008, as a blizzard crippled the capital, closing roads and turning sidewalks into obstacle courses, Kryskow and a team from 4MYCanada stood in the Commons visitors' gallery to watch a vote that most in the parliamentary press gallery had dismissed. For pro-choice activists, the reference to the "unborn" in the bill's title had already set off alarms: recognizing the rights of a fetus, they warned, could open the door to a Supreme Court challenge and the prospect of new abortion legislation. "It's very sneaky," Joyce Arthur, head of the Abortion Rights Coalition of Canada worried. But only an hour before the vote, a backroom Liberal operative had informed me that the bill did not stand a chance, and the party leader, Stéphane Dion, had already left the House.

To the shock of pro-choice critics, Epp's bill sailed through second reading by a fourteen-vote margin. While Dion was among the missing, the government benches were packed, led by Harper himself. As he stood to register his assent, Kryskow and her young crew unleashed a round of cheers from the visitors' gallery. They had braved the storm to show social conservatives, and particularly Stockwell Day, that times had changed since the 2005 same-sex marriage debate: not only had they shown up, but they had helped orchestrate a victory in which the government itself was clearly complicit. "Way to go!" Kryskow crowed to her online followers later that night. "You guys are amazing and this little act of advocacy is rippling through Parliament Hill."

In *Marked*, Kryskow also suggests that the hand of God played a role in the results. At a parliamentary reception after the vote, a key cabinet member puckishly asked her what she thought of the blizzard that had been raging outside all night. "His grin and the twinkle in his eyes told me he was getting at something," she writes. "I then realized that there were several MPs who had not made it to the House of Commons that night for the vote because of the harsh winter storm . . . God wins!"

In the end, the shock waves generated by the vote mobilized the pro-choice movement, and some of its leading voices accused Harper of using the ploy of a private-member's bill to test the waters on anti-abortion legislation. While Epp denied that he had any intention of reopening the explosive abortion debate—pointing out that he had specifically included an exemption for the procedure—Kryskow conveyed the opposite impression when she spoke to the crowd at Missionfest, hailing the measure as "the first winnable pro-life bill that this nation has seen in two decades."

Although she and other groups kept up their pressure, Harper's fear of reopening the Pandora's box of abortion prevailed: on the eve of his surprise 2008 election call, he quashed the measure—an exercise in overkill for a bill that would have died anyway with the end of the parliamentary session. For Kryskow and her supporters, that about-face was a blow, but while some of the country's pro-life groups denounced the Conservatives for their treachery and vowed to boycott the polls, she held her fire. Writing on the subject in *Marked*, she suggested that Harper had been punished for his betrayal by a force far more potent than the miffed conservative Christian electorate. His popularity, like the global economy, promptly went into a tailspin, she noted, forcing him to settle for yet another minority government. Once more, "God's law" had worked in mysterious ways, she said, suggesting that Harper would be well advised to take the hint.

With that, Kryskow also signalled that the abortion fight was far from over. Indeed, she appears to have been chosen as the new face of the pro-life movement by a group of social conservatives affiliated with the National House of Prayer, and her role championing Epp's bill was part of a larger plan. "We knew if the same old cast of characters walked onto the Hill saying the same old things, we'd never get anywhere," one confided. "We needed a new face to get their attention."

⁜

At a glittering post-election reception in the panelled splendour of a parliamentary ballroom, Kryskow was in high spirits as she thanked the seventy members of Parliament who had turned up as 4MYCanada's guests. "Plainly put, we think you are awesome!" she enthused, while noting that she and her group had helped elect many of the social conservatives in the room. That candid admission was in stark contrast to the 2006 election, when her electioneering was confined to making coded statements on the Miracle Channel and supplying directions to a list of approved theo-con candidates on an affiliated website. Back then, 4MYCanada had an application pending before Revenue Canada for accreditation as a religious charity, which precluded direct partisan activity, but the agency eventually turned Kryskow down. She tried to put a happy face on the verdict, which made it impossible for her to offer tax breaks to donors. "We had a choice to make!" she announced on her website. "We decided the future of Canada was more important than an ability to give charitable receipts."

In fact, the choice was not hers to make, but the rejection did have an upside. It put her group's finances beyond the scrutiny of prying media eyes—she insists that her organization is entirely financed by individual donors—leaving 4MYCanada freer than most conservative Christian organizations to agitate for legislation and work on election campaigns. During the fall 2008 contest, Kryskow published a list of candidates that 4MYCanada "wholeheartedly" endorsed: of the 111 names she recommended, ten were members of the Liberal Party, none were New Democrats, and neither Michael Ignatieff nor Jack Layton made the cut. Since then, she has become even more engaged in the political process. Amid the constant threats of another election call in the spring and summer of 2009, she held campaign training seminars, each with an impressive roster of instructors, including Joseph Ben-Ami, Tristan Emmanuel (who had just run Randy Hillier's campaign for the leadership of Ontario's Progressive Conservative

Party), and Winnipeg MP Rod Bruinooge, the energetic new chair of the parliamentary pro-life caucus.

One byproduct of 4MYCanada's lack of charitable tax status is that other faith-based think tanks and advocacy groups have quietly come to regard it as a collective political arm, steering supporters to its online campaigns, and helping to turn Kryskow into the telegenic face of the country's emerging Christian right. Making herself available to the media to comment on one social conservative bill, she admitted she was doing so at the urging of her friends from the National House of Prayer. "I can say things they can't," she conceded.

In the process, Kryskow's influence has grown, bolstered by a group of heavyweights in the charismatic community, who include both prophets and politicians. Stockwell Day, who had originally played a backstage role at her events, has increasingly moved to centre stage; he was billed as the keynote speaker at her Toronto Siege in December 2009 until a mission to China obliged him to cancel and send video greetings. Stepping in to replace him, televangelist David Mainse, who once convened his own crowds on Parliament Hill, called Kryskow his spiritual heir. "The mantle I used to carry she's picked up," Mainse says.

It is a mantle that Kryskow seems happy to assume. In her speeches and a CD on the subject, she compares herself to Joan of Arc, the sixteen year-old French farm girl who, driven by the divine commands in her head, rode to the rescue of France's reluctant boy king. Like her heroine, Kryskow regards her mission in Ottawa as infinitely broader than serving a political party or legislative agenda and clearly at the service of a higher power. In *Marked*, she describes being "planted smack in the centre of my nation's affairs—prophesying to leaders and influencing policy," for the express purpose of turning Canada into God's dominion. Laying out that theocratic agenda, she offers a dissertation on dominionism: Jesus came to earth not simply to save souls, she insists, but to save entire countries, and she calls on her young faithful to form an "army of God," as the prophet Joel once did in the

Old Testament, battling to "disciple" the nation, indeed to see it "completely submitted to Christ." Government is not the only target, she points out; there are other "gateways of influence" that must also be taken over by her latter-day version of Joel's army: the arts, media, science, education, medicine and the law. Whatever field her followers choose to tackle, Kryskow offers an unusual note of encouragement: "You are going to kick major devil butt!"

IN THE BEGINNING

VI

In the beginning, there were words—a shouting match that exploded onto the pages of the *Globe and Mail*. Two officials from the Canadian Association of University Teachers (CAUT) had asked for a meeting with Gary Goodyear, the secretary of state for science and technology, to plead for a boost in basic research funding that would keep the country's top scientists from fleeing to the United States. For months, consternation in the scientific community had been mounting after the Conservatives had frozen spending for the leading academic granting agencies and warned of another $150 million in cuts to come. Already, researchers were being lured away to American universities and key projects on cancer and climate change were at risk. But when David Robinson, CAUT's Ottawa lobbyist, informed Goodyear that the association had received unprecedented protests from its sixty-five thousand members on the subject, the minister went ballistic.

So heated did the discussion become that Goodyear finally picked up his papers and stormed out of the ministerial conference room warning that CAUT had burned its bridges with the government. "We've been lobbying politicians for a decade and we've been very critical of some governments, but it was always civil, always proper," says executive director James Turk. "Now there's a real pit bull attitude."

As word of the confrontation sped through the academic grapevine, so too did speculation about what had prompted Goodyear's outburst. For many, it reflected a broader pattern of hostility not only toward pure scientific research, unrelated to commercial spinoffs, but toward the entire field of science itself. At a time when Barack Obama had just named a Nobel Prize–winning physicist as his secretary of energy, many in academic circles winced when Harper handed the science portfolio to an obscure Conservative backbencher who had dropped out of university to become a chiropractor in Cambridge, Ontario. With budgets and scientific independence increasingly under attack, one question kept recurring: was that antipathy provoked by the fact that Goodyear, a devout Baptist, embraced a personal belief in creationism? Had Harper exacted revenge on his academic and environmental critics by appointing a minister who regarded evolution as a theory concocted by scheming secular humanists in academia to undercut the very foundations of Christian doctrine?

It was a question that any self-respecting journalist had every right to pose, but the *Globe*'s veteran science reporter, Anne McIlroy, was more diplomatic. In an interview with Goodyear, she asked if he believed in evolution. Once again, he blew a fuse. "I'm not going to answer that question," he bridled. "I am a Christian, and I don't think anybody asking a question about my religion is appropriate."

In fact, McIlroy had done no such thing, but by dragging religion into his answer, Goodyear turned a potentially routine profile into a front-page sensation. "Science minister won't confirm belief in evolution," announced the *Globe*'s headline. For James Turk, the minister's prickly riposte confirmed his members' worst fears. "It is inconceivable," he told McIlroy, "that a government would have a minister of science who rejects the basis of scientific discovery and traditions."

Goodyear went on television to protest that, of course, he "believed in" evolution, and then proceeded to undercut that assertion with a rambling explanation that included an observation on how footwear had evolved from sneakers to high heels. As his statement sent another round of shock waves through the country's research labs, Elizabeth Elle, a biology professor at Simon Fraser University, pointed out that he had demonstrated "a fundamental misunderstanding of how evolution by natural selection works."

The incident riveted the scientific community, even making the pages of the American journal *Discover*, but it also served as a cautionary reminder that a debate, which most in the media and urban mainstream regard as settled, can still send tempers off the charts in a substantial slice of the population. As a subsequent Canwest News Service poll showed, nearly one-third of Canadians believe that humans were created by a "spiritual force"—up from 22 percent two years earlier—while 41 percent accept the premise that we have evolved "from a lower species such as apes."

Those numbers can't compete with the public embrace of creationism in the United States, where it remains such a cultural litmus test that candidates in the 2008 presidential primaries were grilled on the subject and three of the leading contenders for the next Republican nomination, including former Alaska governor Sarah Palin, have advocated teaching it in public schools. In Canada, the debate is more muted, in part because no politician has dared utter a word on the topic since Stockwell Day's sentiments about Adam and Eve cavorting with dinosaurs turned him into a national laughingstock, effectively torpedoing his leadership of the Canadian Alliance. But eight years later, the reaction to Goodyear's outburst showed a marked shift in the public mood. This time, a handful of conservative columnists launched withering attacks not on the politician but the reporter, accusing McIlroy of gotcha journalism and anti-Christian bias. One source even leaked a comment to the *Globe* that Harper's caucus believed the media would "do anything to make people of faith look dumb." With the Conservatives beholden to their theo-con constituency, Harper stuck by his minister, squiring Goodyear to a round of funding announcements, even if most of them were for infrastructure projects, not research. It didn't hurt that Goodyear's friend and former campaign manager, philanthropist Reg Petersen, was an influential figure in Conservative evangelical circles, or that Petersen had just survived a minor scandal of his own. Months earlier, he had negotiated a settlement with Elections Canada for allegedly violating campaign laws on political contributions to Goodyear's campaign.

Still, the most resounding show of solidarity came from Conservative MP James Lunney, another evangelical chiropractor, who appeared on the floor of the House to defend his colleague against the "arrogance and intolerance" of media and scientific elites. In the course of his speech, Lunney made clear that Gary Goodyear and Stockwell Day were not the only figures in Harper's caucus with reservations about the fundamental principle of modern biology. "Any scientist who declares that the theory of evolution is a fact has already abandoned the foundations of science," Lunney claimed. "Given the modern evidence unavailable to Darwin . . . I am prepared to believe that Darwin would be willing to re-examine his assumptions." To many, that assertion was even more alarming than Goodyear's. In a year when scholarly institutions around the globe were celebrating the bicentennial of Darwin's birth and the 150th anniversary of his contentious theory, the forces of creationism appeared to be alive and well in Canada, even playing a role in the policy calculations of Harper's government.

Nowhere are those forces more unapologetic than in the rolling Alberta ranchland south of Red Deer. Here, in this stronghold of Conservative support, which some locals still call "Stockwell Day country," an oil worker named Harry Nibourg opened the country's first creationism museum in the hamlet of Big Valley, population 351.

❖

"So, what bias are you coming from?" Harry Nibourg demands over the long-distance line. "Everybody has a bias. If they say they don't, they're a liar." Fresh from a six-day shift in a remote natural-gas field in northern Alberta, Nibourg is on the phone dispensing directions to his Big Valley Creation Science Museum, 150 kilometres northeast of Calgary, where journalists are welcome, albeit warily. I sidestep his question, but on the way, I stop at Drumheller, home to the Royal Tyrrell Museum of Paleontology, where scientists find themselves on the front lines of an ongoing conflict over the origins of the universe.

As I approach the town, the serene prairie vista gives way to the stark, surreal moonscape of Alberta's badlands: dome-topped mountains of striated sandstone heave up from treeless coulees through which the highway winds in steep hairpin turns. Here, on a chilly August day in 1884, a young geologist named Joseph Burr Tyrrell who'd been hired by the government to scout for coal stumbled on another sort of bonanza: a gigantic prehistoric skull. That discovery, sent to a renowned fossil finder in Philadelphia, turned out to be the mandibles of a creature dubbed the *Albertosaurus sarcophagus*—a smaller cousin of the fierce, flesh-eating *Tyrannosaurus rex*—the first of the extinct theropods to be unearthed in what is now hailed as the world's largest dinosaur graveyard.

It wasn't until nearly a century later that townsfolk grasped the potential riches Tyrrell had unearthed. Until then, Drumheller thrived as the hub of Alberta's coal country, shipping millions of tons of the black ore across the continent from more than 130 local mines. In 1984, a year after the last of those mines was shuttered, the Royal Tyrrell Museum threw open its doors to unveil the massive reassembled skeletons that paleontologists had been quietly chipping out of the same sedimentary rock and shale. In one nearby bonebed, they found the remains of twenty-two Albertosauri dating to the Late Cretaceous period more than seventy million years ago. Now nearly 400,000 tourists a year descend on the museum's sleek, modernistic galleries where towering models of those mammoth beasts romp through simulated rainforests, their imagined roars reverberating through the mossy gloom.

The former coal town has not been reluctant to cash in on its rebranding as the Dinosaur Capital of the World. On almost every street corner, a lumpen pink or purple dinosaur statue prances in toothy welcome, all of them dwarfed by the monstrous eighty-two-foot concrete *T. rex* rearing up outside the tourist bureau, where intrepid visitors can climb the hundred steps through its innards to a viewing platform perched between its jaws.

But even in the larky heart of dinosaurland, not everyone is enthusiastic about the Royal Tyrrell's chronicle of life on a four-billion-year-old earth. Nowhere in the museum's version of events—from the emergence of single-cell organisms 600 million years ago to the advent of the first dinosaurs more than 500 million years later—is there any mention of a species known as *Homo sapiens*, let alone a legendary duo named Adam and Eve. According to the prevailing paleontological wisdom, humans did not appear until long after some unexplained extraterrestrial calamity, possibly a crashing meteorite, had rendered dinosaurs extinct, leaving them buried under the glacial rubble of the ice age.

That timeline, which directly contradicts the Genesis account of the Garden of Eden, is heresy to young-earth creationists, who insist that the earth is a mere stripling created by God barely six thousand years ago and thus fully capable of hosting both *T. rex* and Adam and Eve in the same time frame. Pilgrimaging regularly to the museum, they tuck creationist tracts under its benches in the hope that they'll be found by touring schoolchildren. But not all of Drumheller's Bible-believing visitors come from out of town. A sizable portion of the local citizenry is made up of conservative Christians who regard the museum's account of history as secular propaganda, and help stage the town's other main tourist attraction, the annual Canadian Badlands Passion Play. For six days every summer, a volunteer cast of two hundred, many from a local Christian arts college, depict the life, death and resurrection of Jesus Christ in a setting billed as a dead ringer for ancient Israel: a natural amphitheatre hollowed out from the rock along South Dinosaur Trail. What the Alberta tourist brochures fail to mention is that the Dinosaur Capital of the World turns out to be ground zero in the Canadian debate over creationism—an ideological standoff captured in a documentary called *The Cross and Bones*.

Among those leading the charge on behalf of the cross is the Reverend Blaine McDonald, a former general manager of the the passion play who doubles as a town councillor and associate pastor at Elim Pentecostal Tabernacle. Not only has McDonald hosted seminars featuring some of the biggest names on the creationist lecture circuit, he has waged a war of words with David Eberth, senior research scientist at the Royal Tyrrell, on the letters page of the *Drumheller Mail*. "It's a weird, bizarre kind of mix in the Valley," McDonald concedes. "But the debate isn't really addressed in any kind of a serious way here, which I think is absurd."

For Eberth and his colleagues in the scientific community, the creationist campaign of McDonald and other biblical literalists is exasperating—a slap to decades of accepted scientific theory and exacting scholarly research. "These people are scary," he says in an interview. "Their numbers aren't great but they have a very loud voice and that voice is getting attention."

He was shocked by a 2007 Angus Reid poll, which showed that although a majority of Canadians believe in evolution, an almost equal number are convinced, like Stockwell Day, that humans and dinosaurs once coexisted—a paleontological impossibility. "We don't have any rocks that contain the fossil remains of ancient humans," says a frustrated Eberth. "We tell the story based on the evidence that we have."

Equally irksome are the constant challenges from McDonald and other creationists to a public debate—an opportunity that Eberth and most paleontologists have steadfastly declined. "It would be like debating whether the world was flat," he shrugs. "The scientific approach is truly based on the notion that there are natural explanations for natural phenomena which we see evidence for. A creationist point of view adheres to the doctrine of supernatural phenomena, and there's no way to test or prove supernatural events."

Still, for many conservative Christians, the Royal Tyrrell's science calls into question the very cornerstone of their faith: a belief in the inerrancy of the Bible as God's divinely dictated word. British religious scholar Karen Armstrong explains it as a theological domino theory: if the book of Genesis is merely a charming fiction, then why should anyone accept the truth of the rest of the narrative that lies at the heart of Christianity—the crucifixion and miraculous resurrection of a carpenter named Jesus of Nazareth whose death is believed to have redeemed human sin? What's at stake in the creationist debate is not just the factual authenticity of the six-day Genesis story, but the authority of the Bible itself.

Ironically, as Armstrong points out in *The Bible: A Biography*, the insistence that every word of the Good Book represents divinely inspired truth is a relatively new wrinkle on the theological scene. It wasn't until the late nineteenth century that a group of conservative American Protestants—already appalled by the twin assaults of Charles Darwin and Karl Marx upon their faith—were spurred into action by allegations from a German literary movement that Moses had not authored the first five books of the Old Testament, and King David had not composed the Psalms. Hammering out the core principles of Christianity at a series of conferences that included an annual gathering in the Ontario resort town of Niagara-on-the-Lake, they explained those precepts—including the inerrancy of the Bible—in a twelve-volume series that was published between 1910 and 1915 as *The Fundamentals: A Testimony to the Truth*.

A decade later, those self-styled fundamentalists found their insistence on biblical literalism put to the test. In 1925, the newly formed American Civil Liberties Union hired attorney Clarence Darrow to defend a schoolteacher named John Scopes against charges of teaching the banned subject of evolution in the rural backwater of Dayton, Tennessee. In response, the World Christian Fundamentalist Society commissioned William Jennings Bryan, a three-time presidential candidate and creationist crusader, to champion biblical authority in an epic courtroom clash that Hollywood later immortalized in the movie *Inherit the Wind*. Although Bryan and the fundamentalist camp won the legal case, they lost in the court of public opinion as big-city reporters like H. L. Mencken descended on Dayton, mercilessly lampooning creationists as Bible-thumping throwbacks and "rustic baboons."

In the wake of that mockery, fundamentalists beat a hasty retreat from public life. Nursing their decades-long resentment of both intellectualism and the media, they threw themselves into building Christian schools. For them, creationism would become a defining issue—one that drove their sense of persecution and mistrust of the political process. So raw did the memory of the Scopes "monkey trial" remain that nearly a century later, when a Kentucky-based ministry named Answers in Genesis opened a $27 million creationist museum on the outskirts of Cincinnati, Ohio, in May 2007, its founder Ken Ham cast it as an instrument to avenge the humiliations inflicted in that long-ago Tennessee courtroom. "It was the first time the Bible was ridiculed by the media in America," Ham told his opening day audience. "We are going to undo all of that here at the Creation Museum. We are going to . . . show that belief in every word of the Bible can be defended by modern science."

Only days after Ham unveiled his 65,000-square-foot showplace designed by a former special-effects wizard from Universal Studios, Harry Nibourg opened his one-room creation-science museum in Big Valley, Alberta, earning a front-page spread in the *Globe and Mail*. The contrast was stark, but the timing was not coincidental. Like most Canadian creationists, Nibourg and his collaborators have ties to Ham and the fractious network of biblical literalists in the U.S., and the museum's website minces no words about its mission: "to refute the lie of evolution."

‒

Driving north from Drumheller on Highway 56, I almost overshoot the turnoff to Big Valley, a former railroad whistlestop where the largest roadside sign heralds its identity as home to the Canadian Railway Hall of Fame. As I pass the red Alberta Wheat Pool elevator and the 1912 train depot, it becomes clear that the town has seen better days. Once, its eight-bay roundhouse serviced dozens of locomotives a week and Big Valley boasted a population of more than a thousand, with three hardware stores in one block and even a brothel of some renown. But disgruntled wives burned down the cathouse, and, after the railway closed the roundhouse, the town fell on desperate times. One summer, residents watched as more than twenty houses were hoisted onto flatbeds and trucked off to Drumheller.

Today, the railroad is once again Big Valley's lifeline. bringing thirty thousand tourists a year aboard Alberta's last steam train for an old-time roast beef dinner at Outriders Family Restaurant and a stroll down the Jimmy Jock Boardwalk to sample the enormous glazed cinnamon buns at Hulley's Hideaway, where Vivian Hulley dubs herself as "the lady with the best buns in Alberta." Despite such novel civic offerings, the Big Valley Beautification and Cultural Affairs Committee spent years trying to drum up other attractions to lure more traffic to town. What nobody bargained for was a museum that would drag residents into a raging theological debate. "There's 50 percent that love us and 40 percent that hate us," Harry Nibourg says, "and 10 percent that want to burn the place down."

Nibourg himself is an unlikely idealogue, a rangy bachelor in his mid-forties who describes himself as "politically incorrect, redneck and proud of it." The fifth in a Dutch family of eight kids, he grew up in a succession of neighbouring towns, helping out on his father's dairy farms until he lit out for the bigger paycheques of Alberta's oil rigs. He never got past high school and paints himself as a reformed party animal once devoted to building hot rods, drinking beer and chasing girls. But one night in 1994, manning the control room at Canadian Crude Separators on the outskirts of town, he borrowed a Walkman from a co-worker and found himself listening to a tape about the final days before the Battle of Armageddon.

His colleague turned out to have a whole library of such doomsday fare, most of it churned out by Peter and Paul Lalonde, two brothers based in Niagara Falls, Ontario, who produced some of the *Left Behind* movies based on the apocalyptic bestsellers by Jerry Jenkins and Tim LaHaye. The more Nibourg listened, the more he became hooked, and there, on the night shift monitoring an oil company's thermal oxidizer, he says he "found the Lord." Never one for half measures, Nibourg decided to mark his conversion with a baptism by total immersion in the Red Deer River, undeterred by the fact that it was November and the shallows had already frozen over. As dozens of townsfolk gathered to watch, a pastor in hip waders lowered him backwards into the frigid waters, only interrupting the service briefly when, Nibourg recalls, "a big chunk of ice came floating by."

Already intrigued by end-times prophecies, Nibourg turned his attention to another subject equally rife with conspiracy theories: the origins of the universe. On one of his pal's tapes, he encountered a controversial American creationist named Carl Baugh who claimed to have found fossilized human footprints together with dinosaur tracks in the Paluxy riverbed outside Glen Rose, Texas, a landscape not unlike Alberta's badlands. Other creationists accused Baugh of doctoring both his fossil finds and his academic credentials, but he dismissed his critics as part of a global scientific plot to suppress any evidence that threatened the theory of evolution—a notion that fired up Nibourg's sense of outrage. He was wondering how to help set the record straight when he heard about a three-day seminar organized by a Red Deer pastor named Vance Nelson, the founder of Creation Truth Ministries.

Wandering into the workshop late, Nibourg found Nelson reeling off geological data with the relentless intensity of a semi-automatic. The son of a Manitoba bear-hunting guide, Nelson had grown up with no interest in religion, even if he did acknowledge mysterious forces prowling the vast beyond: a teenaged *Star Trek* fanatic, he could rhyme off the most arcane plot twists to befall Captain Kirk and his starship crew. "I believed in UFOS, I believed in aliens from outer space," he says. "I just didn't believe in God."

Nelson was on track to study electrical engineering when he was born again. Within a year, he had enrolled at North American Bible College outside Edmonton, now known as Taylor College, where he met his wife, Korelei. There, he stumbled on DVDs by Ken Ham, which argued the case for young-earth creationism, claiming that geologists' radio-metric system for dating the earth was severely flawed. In Ham's view, the fact that dinosaur bones are perfectly preserved in ancient rock was not proof of a multi-billion-year-old earth, where sedimentary deposits are stacked on top of each other like chronological pancakes. Instead, it was a clear demonstration that the gigantic beasts were piDinioned in place by a sudden cataclysmic torrent—a global flood from which only Noah and his hand-picked zoo escaped on their homemade ark. No matter that neither geologists nor anthropologists have found evidence of any such worldwide catastrophe. To young-earth creationists, Noah's flood—or the Noahic Deluge, as they prefer to term it—is the key to wiping out the presumptions of paleontology.

For Nelson, the implications were clear: if the earth is only six to ten thousand years old, an epoch in which the first human traces were found, then dinosaurs could indeed have roamed the Garden of Eden and science was no longer at odds with the six-day Genesis story. He was perplexed when his professors failed to share his enthusiasm for taking that defence of creationism into the pulpit. "It was too controversial," he now concedes. "Most of them didn't want to know."

After two frustrating years as an apprentice minister in Calgary, Nelson enrolled at Clearwater Christian College, a bastion of biblical literalism founded on fifty beachfront acres outside Tampa, Florida, to combat the flaccid morals and feel-good ecumenicalism that were infecting other Christian campuses in the 1960s. A glance at its current science curriculum reveals courses unlikely to be found on any other university syllabus: one, Vampire Bats and Wisdom Teeth, details "some of the bizarre imperfections in nature brought about by sin"; another, Desert, Anyone? casts global warming as a portent of the approaching end-times ("Deserts are growing as the grip of sin tightens on the earth," the course description reads. "The earth is slowly dying and becoming unfit for life, and Christ must purge all sin from His creation to make all things new [Rev. 21:1]").

But for Nelson, Clearwater's main draw was the head of its science department, Gary E. Parker, one of the best-known scholars in the creationist movement. Once an atheist and evolutionist with a doctorate of education in biology, Parker had authored five college textbooks before he and his wife joined a faculty Bible-study group and committed their lives to Christ. In a pamphlet on sale at the Big Valley museum, Parker recounts his intellectual odyssey, including the moment when he realized he had once regarded Darwin's theories as his true religion—"a faith commitment and a complete world-and-life view that organized everything else for me . . . God was unnecessary."

At Clearwater, Nelson became one of Parker's most avid proteges, winning introductions to many of the other big names in the small world of scientific creationism. After graduation, he set up his own creationist ministry in Red Deer, carving out a niche speaking to church and homeschooling groups from an alliterative lecture repertoire that included "Biology and the Bible" and "Geology and Genesis." In the summer, he and his wife ran creationist Bible camps, using the props of paleontology—fossils and petrified dinosaur eggs—to explain how the world was created by a crackerjack designer named God in six twenty-four-hour days. Setting aside a tenth of their income over several years, they acquired more than $100,000 worth of museum-quality fossils and a five-foot mahogany model of Noah's Ark, which they loaded onto a one-ton diesel truck to create a mobile creationism museum. At one of their first stops, Red Deer's Bethany Baptist Church, Nelson met Harry Nibourg and the Big Valley Creation Science Museum was born.

For Nibourg, Nelson's kid-friendly displays were the ticket to realizing his own fantasy of a permanent argument for creationism. By the end of the seminar, they were huddled in the church basement, hammering out the details. While Nelson had the scientific expertise, Nibourg volunteered an equally essential ingredient: his fat paycheques as an energy-services worker to finance the $300,000 scheme. Ruling out a site in Calgary, Edmonton or Red Deer as prohibitively expensive, Nibourg snapped up a lot across from the Big Valley train station for a mere $2,000 just months before Alberta's building boom sent prices soaring. In his spare time, he erected the museum's frame, but kept his plans under wraps. "I said, 'If the Lord wants it to happen, it'll happen,'" he says.

After he and Nelson toured a handful of the two dozen creationist museums scattered across the United States, even stopping by Carl Baugh's Texas headquarters, they organized an expedition to the world's largest gem and fossil show in Tucson, Arizona, where thirty-five hundred dealers offer their wares in a madcap bazaar that takes over the city for a week. The Big Valley contingent converged on a motel that had been converted into Fossil Central. "It was like kids in a candy store," Nibourg recalls. "The maids were amazed what we were dragging back to the room." Stumbling on the deserted studio of a sculptor who had crafted the mammoth life-sized casts for "Dinosaur

Adventures" at the West Edmonton Mall, they scored five gigantic dinosaur heads—a deal Nibourg credits to divine intervention. "It was like the Lord was keeping people away," he says. "We came back a few hours later and the prices had gone through the roof."

They hired Ian Juby, a creationism consultant from Chalk River, Ontario, to map out the museum's displays, and a board member donated an exhibit that now occupies a place of honour near the front counter: a genealogical scroll that traces Henry VIII's family tree back to Adam and Eve. The scarlet paint was barely dry on the museum's walls when Nibourg got word of Ken Ham's gala launch outside Cincinnati and rushed to inaugurate his own vinyl-sided version on Big Valley's main street. More than five hundred people flocked to the official opening, where the pastor who'd baptized Nibourg in the ice-slicked Red Deer River delivered the benediction and an accordionist from the local Cowboy Church house band pumped out gospel favourites. The whole town joined in the hoopla, including Big Valley's mayor, a teacher who had made no secret of the fact that he was a staunch evolutionist. "Lots to learn!" he wrote cryptically in the guest book.

By summer's end, more than eight thousand visitors had trooped through the museum, some from as far away as Korea and New Zealand, and Nibourg was swamped with booking requests from private Christian academies. But the one group that had never darkened the museum's door were the students from Big Valley's only public school. "There's still a stigma attached," he says. "The teachers don't want their students comin' in here, askin' the questions because then they'd have to deal with it."

⚜

At 9:55 a.m. on a chilly Friday in November 2007, a yellow school bus pulls up outside the Big Valley Creation Science Museum. On board are sixteen sleepy-eyed teenagers under the wing of Pastor Mike Maahs and his wife Gail, who have driven from Birch Hills, Saskatchewan, a rocky nine-hour bus trip away. As the teens straggle into the museum, gleefully catching sight of Nibourg's mounted dinosaur heads, one confides his surprise. "I was expecting it to be bigger," admits Halsten Rust, a precocious thirteen-year-old, who still treasures the memory of a trip to the Royal Tyrrell Museum when he was four.

Pastor Mike, as he calls himself, soon takes over from Nibourg, quickly proving that he's no amateur at playing tour guide. He points to a geological sample meant to bolster the thesis that the earth is not billions of years old. "It gives a different explanation, a biblical explanation, than the one you get in school," he alerts the group. Unlike most of Big Valley's student visitors, his charges are products of the public education system who had to beg the day off for this excursion as part of their confirmation classes for the Church of the Lutheran Brethren. Leading the way to a display called Icons of Evolution, which disputes the conclusions that paleontologists have drawn from famous fossil finds, Maahs fires off another shot at the provincial science curriculum. "These are the pictures in all your textbooks," he says. "And they will be labelled differently in your textbooks than how it actually happened."

Creationism, it turns out, is Pastor Mike's shtick. A former broadcaster on a country music station in Fargo, North Dakota, he noticed an announcement that Ken Ham was coming to town with a seminar called "Back to Genesis" and after signing up for it, he began teaching creationist courses in his spare time. A decade later, when he felt a call to the ministry, he qualified as an official speaker for Answers in Genesis, and was one of six hundred special guests invited to the launch of Ham's Creation Museum. Now, newly posted to his first parish in Saskatchewan, Maahs is revelling in this chance to put his expertise to use. "My motivation is to help others see the Word is true," he says.

He is also intent on arming his adolescent flock with arguments to counter their teachers. Standing in front of a wall studded with authentic fossils, he throws out a well-practiced question: "So what happens when a fish dies?" Lolling on the carpet, the students exchange blank looks. "It floats to the top!" he says. "It decomposes. It rots and it stinks and other fish eat the bones. There's nothing left to form a fossil." Heads nod in vigorous agreement. "Yet we have these perfect fossils of fish, so what happened?" he asks.

Suddenly, Halsten's face lights up. "The flood!" he shouts.

"That's right," Pastor Mike beams. "A lot of water, a lot of mud, real fast. That fish is completely sealed and entombed in there. Scientists know the only way for that to happen is what I just explained, but they don't want to accept a worldwide flood story."

For nearly an hour, the teens ponder the exhibits as Maahs occasionally chimes in. Contemplating a mechanized model of a DNA double-helix strand, he notes that each contains an intricate computer-like code. "To have a code, you have to have a person who writes that code and a way to decode it," he points out. "How can you have a code and a decoder just by chance?" He pauses for a moment to underscore the visit's theme. "It's so amazing that God has created all this together," he exults. "Isn't that a great God?"

As the students pack up, Nibourg hands out dinosaur snacks and the class poses for a photograph amid the cement Albertosaurus tracks studding the front lawn. In the museum guest book, Gail Maahs signs for the group. "Thank you!" she writes. "Keep spreading the truth." Then it's time to get back on the bus for their next stop: the Royal Tyrrell Museum. Maahs insists he isn't worried the class will be swayed by the high-tech dazzle of the province's multi-million-dollar showcase of paleontology. He has equipped himself with a guide to the museum written by Margaret Helder, an Edmonton grandmother with a Ph.D. in biology who heads the Creation Science Association of Alberta. "When we go to the other museum, remember how all this fits in," he counsels, "and remember what great lengths they've gone to in order to explain the evolution theory."

In fact, despite its halls of prehistoric bones and slick interactive displays, the Royal Tyrrell can't deliver the one commodity that Nibourg's postage-stamp gallery serves up: absolute certainty. A stroll past its Albertosaurus skeletons and awe-inspiring *T. rex* ends with only a wan conjecture about what provoked their sudden demise. "Dinosaur extinction remains one of the great mysteries of paleontology," acknowledges one exhibit.

As the Tyrrell's David Eberth admits, when scientists lack empirical evidence, they are loathe to proffer conclusions, and that fastidiousness has left them hobbled against creationists who have built entire careers tallying evolution's theoretical gaps. Watching their foes pounce upon every unexplained phenomenon, Eberth and his colleagues fear creationism is gaining ground in Canada as the number of evangelical Christians climbs and right-wing radio hosts turn it into a sacred cause. Almost every province now claims its own creationism association, and Creation Ministries International—which split from Ken Ham's Answers in Genesis in a bitter legal and doctrinal battle—has set up shop in Kitchener, Ontario, next door to Gary Goodyear's riding. Its speakers, led by a Romanian geologist named Emil Silvestru, tour churches and Christian schools from coast to coast.

That rash of creationist activity has passed largely unnoticed in the mainstream media, but emotions on the subject run deep. When the Royal Ontario Museum mounted its Darwin exhibit in 2008, not a single corporate sponsor could be found to underwrite it. At the eleventh hour, the Humanist Association of Canada, the *United Church Observer*, and an upscale Toronto private school stepped in—the only organizations willing to risk a consumer backlash from the country's Christian right.

For conservative Christians like Harry Nibourg, an attack on the factual accuracy of Genesis calls into question biblical quotations on issues such as homosexuality that have provided the rationale for the culture wars. To them, undermining the Garden of Eden story leads inevitably to unleashing the libertine flood tides of Sodom and Gomorrah. No one stresses that connection more firmly than Ken Ham, who routinely warns that "compromise on Genesis has opened a dangerous door"—one that has led to nothing less than a breakdown of society. At his museum, one exhibit, called Culture in Crisis, illustrates the results of scorning the scriptures: a sinister city alley is plastered with news reports of terrorism attacks and shooting rampages, while videos show teenagers glued to laptop pornography and contemplating abortions. Given those perceived stakes, it seems no wonder that the front lines of the culture wars are now the continent's classrooms, where creationists are striding back into the spotlight, flexing their ideological muscles and waging an aggressive new campaign to see their subject taught under a new label: intelligent design.

⚜

In 2004, when Bible-believing Christians took over a rural school board in Dover, Pennsylvania, few North Americans had heard of intelligent design, a newly devised theory which argues that the staggering complexity of the universe can only be explained by an unseen designer, although not necessarily a designer named God. By attempting to force its science staff to teach the concept, the Dover board landed in a court case that was declared a rerun of the Scopes trial, complete with lawyers from the American Civil Liberties Union and its own national media circus. By then, creationism had been cast out of American classrooms in a series of federal-court rulings that found it violated the constitutional amendment ensuring the separation of church and state. The Dover case presented a new challenge to that legal status quo.

The school board's lawyers argued that intelligent design was a revolutionary way of looking at science that had nothing to do with the six-day Genesis story or religion of any sort. In fact, its leading academic proponents—most on the payroll of a Seattle think tank called the Discovery Institute—scoffed at Ken Ham and the young-earth creationist crowd. They had no problem agreeing with mainstream geologists that the earth was, indeed, billions of years old; what they objected to was teaching evolution as scientific orthodoxy. Darwin's theory of natural selection, they insisted, was incapable of explaining the intricate patterns of design present in even the most primitive cells. That argument was spelled out in a biology textbook that the Dover School Board had attempted to impose upon its science teachers, *Of Pandas and People*, published in 1989, which makes no mention of God or the Bible but does underline the presence of an unseen genius as a cosmic architect.

After six weeks of expert testimony, a federal-court judge ruled that intelligent design was a "mere re-labeling of creationism," and, as such, had no place in Pennsylvania's public schools. A key piece of evidence was a discovery about *Of Pandas and People* that might have come straight from the television whodunit *CSI:* an early version of the manuscript revealed that every mention of intelligent design had, in fact, replaced the original term, "creationism," which was covered by typographic correction fluid.

For most Canadians, the Dover case seemed a foreign phenomenon, yet another example of the litigious extremism of the American religious right that could never happen here. But Brian Alters, a McGill professor of education who served as an expert witness against the Dover school board, warns against that smug assumption. As director of the university's Evolution Education Research Centre, Alters has spent nearly a decade amassing evidence to prove that the push to teach creationism is underway in Canada, but in a country that has no constitutional separation between government and religion, he worries opponents lack any legal means to block its incursion. Every victory against pressures from the creationist lobby in the United States has come when parents took school boards to court for violating that amendment to the American Constitution.

In one of Alters's surveys, more than one-third of B.C. science teach-ers reported pressure from parents to offer some version of creation-ism; so determined were most to avoid a dust-up that they admitted turning a blind eye to the curriculum's mandate to teach only evolution. Instead, they either treated both worldviews as equal or skirted the thorny subject of life's origins altogether. In the most highly publicized example, the province's Ministry of Education was stunned to discover that the Abbotsford school board had quietly adopted a policy allowing teachers to discuss "scientific creationism" as a concession to evangeli-cal parents. When that breach of provincial policy came to light, the board members, most of whom were evangelical Christians them-selves, protested that it had not displaced evolution on the curriculum, and that teachers could only wade into creationist waters if students broached the topic first—which they invariably did. But what most shocked investigators was that the unauthorized practice had been going on for twelve years without a word leaking out. Even after a set-tlement with provincial officials, the board did not capitulate swiftly or with any signs of remorse: chairman John Sutherland, who was then a business professor at Trinity Western University, accused the minister of being "more interested in indoctrination than education."

As it turns out, B.C. schools have not been alone in giving Darwin short shrift. In Ontario, the neo-conservative government of Mike Harris unveiled a new high-school curriculum in 1999 that relegated evolution to the equivalent of a scientific afterthought. According to its guidelines, only those students enrolled in an elective Grade 12 biology course were to be exposed to a theory that scientists regard as founda-tional; the rest would graduate with what one irate professor termed "a gaping hole" in their basic knowledge. "Ontario education is missing a link," hooted the *Sudbury Star*. "Evolution nearly extinct in class-room," headlined the *Ottawa Citizen*, adding that the "new science curriculum tries to avoid controversy." But unlike the nineteen American states that had dropped evolution from their curricula,

Ontario authorities faced no controversy whatsoever. "When something happens in the U.S., people tsk, tsk and say it couldn't happen to us," notes Jason Wiles, a former member of Alters's McGill team. "But in a way, it's worse here. They're not even teaching evolution in most provinces and there's definitely less resistance to teaching creationism in Canada than there would be in the U.S."

In Quebec, where the government has ordered some private evangelical schools to teach evolution, the forces of creationism have found support from an unlikely quarter. Parents in a remote Inuit community on Ungava Bay complained that their children arrived home from school claiming their ancestors were apes. When the local principal reprimanded his new science teacher for teaching evolution to an increasingly evangelical population, the minister of education himself stepped in to order the provincial science curriculum restored, an intervention that won no applause from at least one aboriginal mother in the town of Salluit. "The minister may have come from apes," Molly Tayara told the *Montreal Gazette*, "but we're Inuit and we've always been human."

So concerned are some scholars about the steady erosion of scientific literacy in schools that, in November 2007, they launched a journal aimed at helping teachers grapple with the thorny subject. The quarterly *Evolution: Education and Outreach*, is edited by Niles Eldridge, chief paleontologist at the American Museum of Natural History, and its editorial board includes four Canadian academics, among them Brian Alters and Dan Brooks, a veteran zoology professor at the University of Toronto. "Academics have been way too passive in the face of the culture wars," Brooks says. "The thinking was: 'This is so patently stupid, how can anybody buy into it?' But it's time for us to start fighting back."

At the journal's launch, its publisher, Germany's giant Springer Press, made no attempt to conceal the fact that it was designed to play catch-up with the relentless efforts of the Christian right, but the company was not only concerned about the growing backlash against science in the United States. It had discovered that creationism was making a comeback on its own doorstep: a year earlier, Poland's deputy minister of education, a leading member of the government's Catholic coalition partner, had publicly denounced evolution as a lie.

For some Canadian educators, the journal came not a moment too soon. In Abbotsford, education officials discovered that teachers had been covertly discussing creationism using classroom guides supplied by California's Institute for Creation Research, which promotes what it terms "creation science." The concept was designed to circumvent the American constitutional ban on religion in public schools, but the institute's roots undercut the claim that its version of creationism was scientific, not spiritual: it was founded as part of San Diego's Christian Heritage College by a former hydraulic engineer named Henry Morris and Reverend Timothy LaHaye, the ubiquitous Baptist pastor behind both the Moral Majority and the bestselling *Left Behind* novels. For nearly two decades, the institute's approach gained traction in American education, even inspiring a Louisiana bill that guaranteed instruction in creation science wherever evolution was taught. Then, in a landmark 1987 ruling, the U.S. Supreme Court overturned the Louisiana law and, with it, the institute's prospects. Declaring there was nothing scientific about creation science, the court effectively banned it from the nation's public schools.

Within three years of that legal setback, a new strategy for teaching creationism was taking shape in Seattle, where two former players from the Reagan administration had launched a conservative think tank in Seattle named the Discovery Institute. Recruiting academics with mainstream credentials, they spun off a subsidiary, the Center for Science and Culture, devoted solely to promoting "intelligent design," a theory popularized by a former Berkeley law professor, Phillip Johnson, in his 1991 book, *Darwin On Trial*. According to a leaked fundraising memo that Johnson drafted, the only way to sell intelligent design was to downplay its proponents' religious views. "Get the Bible and the book of Genesis out of the debate," he advised.

Instead, Johnson argued, intelligent design should be presented as an ecumenical force, one that could unite secular scientists and believers of all sorts in a theoretical "big tent," a phrase he borrowed directly from Reagan's revamp of the Republican Party. Not that Johnson's own sentiments were secular. A convert to Roman Catholicism, he has admitted that, "I start with John 1:1: 'In the beginning was the word.' In the beginning was intelligence, purpose, and wisdom. The Bible had that right."

One of the leading figures bankrolling the Discovery Institute is Howard Ahmanson Jr., the reclusive heir to a California fortune, who is best known for funding Christian nationalist causes. By 2005, with Johnson's strategy and Ahmanson's millions, intelligent design was winning a tentative toehold in some American academic circles, at least until the Dover school-board verdict exposed it as creationism in disguise. With that federal-court decision, the scientific establishment broke out the champagne, predicting the concept was on its way out. In fact, exactly the opposite proved to be true. Basking in unprecedented publicity, the Discovery Institute turned the defeat into a fundraising opportunity, hatching a sophisticated new public relations strategy.

Rather than lobbying states to teach intelligent design, it pushed for them to "teach the controversy," a phrase which became the institute's mantra. In the absence of any real controversy, Discovery officials created one with the help of an influential new cast of characters, including right-wing pundit Ann Coulter. In her 2007 bestseller, *Godless: The Church of Liberalism*, Coulter acknowledges the "generous tutoring" of three of the institute's senior fellows and devotes an uncharacteristically turgid four chapters to attacking evolution as "bogus science," dubbing its proponents "Darwiniacs" enrolled in their own private cult.

But Coulter has not been the Discovery Institute's only media cheerleader. Another key figure promoting its work is Toronto writer Denyse O'Leary, a birdlike wordsmith known for her omnipresent hats and prolific output, who has become one of the leading bloggers on what she likes to call "the ID [intelligent design] controversy." Although virtually unknown in this country's mainstream media and literary circles, within the cozy continental cosmos of intelligent design, O'Leary is a minor luminary—a feat that is all the more remarkable considering that she has no formal scientific background. A single mother who turned an honours English degree into a freelance writing and editing career, she has focused her efforts on the faith-based press. When her editor at *Christian Week* asked her to undertake a monthly column tackling the scientific issues such as cloning that were challenging Christian doctrine and beliefs, O'Leary leaped at the opportunity. Those essays were later collected in a 2001 book, *Faith@Science: Why Science Needs Faith in the Twenty-First Century.*

During her research, O'Leary happened on the furor over intelligent design, and in 2004 she turned out a primer on the subject published by Augsburg Fortress Press, an arm of the Evangelical Lutheran Church in America, called *By Design or By Chance?* In it, she positions herself as simply an inquiring journalist with no personal stake in the outcome of the debate. "I'm not in any sense a creationist, but I'm very doubtful of Darwin's theory," she tells me. "There's good reason there's an intelligent design controversy: the most popular theory about the origins of life is not performing well."

I would read the same claim—astounding to scientists—repeated almost word for word by an official at the Discovery Institute. Although O'Leary insists that she was halfway through her research before she first heard of "Disco," as she breezily refers to it, her book features glowing cover blurbs from institute fellows as well as from Phillip Johnson, the father of the intelligent-design movement, who hails her for "a magnificent introduction" to "the greatest intellectual controversy of our time." Having spoken at Discovery seminars and been hooked into its strategic conference calls, O'Leary admits that she has an unusually close relationship with the institutional fountainhead of intelligent design. "I am, if you like, an embedded journalist," she says.

Her insider's status was solidified in 2005 after she broke a news story on her Post-Darwinist blog that won the institute headlines around the world. Tipped off by a "Disco guy," she reported that Washington's august Smithsonian Institution, an internationally recognized bastion of evolution, had inadvertently agreed to host the screening of a Discovery Institute documentary called *Privileged Planet: The Search for Purpose in the Universe*. When the *New York Times* picked up her scoop, Smithsonian officials were left red-faced. In the end, they allowed the screening to proceed but withdrew the museum's sponsorship and returned a sixteen-thousand-dollar rental fee that had appeared on its books as a donation from the Discovery Institute. The brouhaha established O'Leary's reputation and confirmed her appetite for controversy. "It made me hated in many places," she says with pride. Still, she underlines the fact that she has never been on the institute's payroll. "I write about the Discovery Institute so I'd never accept money from them," she says. "It might cramp my judgment."

The same consideration did not prevent her from becoming a paid correspondent for the Access Research Network, a non-profit organization based in Colorado Springs that supplies homeschooling guides on intelligent design, most of them written by Discovery Institute scholars. Nor has it kept her from the employ of the Foundation for Thought and Ethics, an obscure Texas outfit known chiefly for publishing *Of Pandas and People*, the textbook that sparked the Dover school-board trial. In 2006, when the foundation set out to produce a sequel, *Design of Life*, by the Discovery Institute's William Dembski, it recruited O'Leary as an editorial consultant and later hired her to take over Dembski's promotional blog.

With Dembski's website in her stable, O'Leary has become one of the most influential voices on intelligent design in the blogosphere, a key gatekeeper of news and opinion on the subject, tirelessly championing her Discovery Institute pals and taking the mickey out of their critics with a crafty mix of Irish wit and scathing asides. From the midtown Toronto apartment she shares with her mother, she launches withering broadsides at enemies like McGill's Brian Alters and hails breakthroughs such as Louisiana Governor Bobby Jindal's signature on a 2008 bill allowing his state's educators to teach intelligent design ("Right on, Bobby!").

Like her friends at the Discovery Institute, O'Leary claims she has no personal investment in pegging the ultimate intelligent designer as the God of the Old and New Testaments; her only interest is establishing the existence of design itself. But that disclaimer seems to belie her personal and professional odyssey. Once a devout Anglican, she left the denomination during its debate over same-sex marriage, converting to Roman Catholicism and joining one of Toronto's most conservative parishes, which celebrates the age-old Latin mass reinstated by Pope Benedict XVI. Although she refers to her conversion in a recent book, O'Leary omits another biographical detail. For more than a decade, she was on the front lines of the anti-abortion movement, running a Protestant pro-life weekly and editing at least two pro-life anthologies.

Faith also appears to be a motivating factor for the academics she chooses to promote on her Post-Darwinist blog. One of her most frequently quoted experts is Kirk Durston, a doctoral candidate in biophysics at the University of Guelph, who has trumpeted the merits of intelligent design in seminars on more than thirty Canadian campuses as head of the New Scholars Society. What O'Leary fails to mention is that the New Scholars Society is a ministry of the U.S.-based evangelical powerhouse, Campus Crusade for Christ.

O'Leary's blog has endowed her with sufficient stature to teach a night-school course on intelligent design at St. Michael's College, part of the University of Toronto, and to air her opinions on other pet peeves in the culture wars. Quoting her attacks on human rights commissions as "the nanny monster," and "the human face of fascism," one Christian news service identified her not as a science writer or even a blogger, but as a "Christian leader." O'Leary is not unaware that the Internet has expanded her reach as well as that of her sometime foes, those young-earth creationists whose voices had long been marginalized. "The Internet and the blogosphere are having a tremendous impact on shaping many issues," she says, "including the ID controversy."

In the summer of 2008, O'Leary brought that online impact to bear on the most ambitious public-relations effort yet to promote intelligent design: a controversial Canadian-backed documentary called *Expelled: No Intelligence Allowed*, which alleges a conspiracy in American universities to suppress the theory and damage the careers of its proponents. On her blog, she hyped protests from irate scientists who helped the film rake in $7 million in the first month. "The Darwin trolls are rude and noisy," she wrote, "but they do fill the theatres." Just in case the film's Canadian launch failed to generate an equivalent outcry, O'Leary posted the times and dates for every advance press screening on her blog, along with a helpful hint: "Picketers please note, there is a wide sidewalk, and plenty of coffee shops nearby."

⁜

O'Leary was not alone in turning *Expelled* into a cause célèbre. In his monthly *Evangelical Christian* magazine, Charles McVety—fresh from attacking the Canadian film industry on Parliament Hill—hailed it as "the best movie I have ever seen." That plug was enclosed in an email he sent to every member of Parliament, inviting them to an exclusive screening at Ottawa's Chateau Laurier Hotel, followed by a gala reception featuring executive producer Walt Ruloff, the B.C. software mogul who poured more than $3.5 million into making the film. To promote it, Ruloff hired Motive Entertainment, the marketing firm that had turned Mel Gibson's crucifixion epic, *The Passion of the Christ*, into a multi-million-dollar blockbuster. Following the same grassroots model aimed at cultivating an evangelical audience, Motive arranged advance

screenings of *Expelled* for churches and Christian schools, offering a
$10,000 charitable donation for the largest group ticket sales. If that
campaign did not come cheap, it was well within Ruloff's means: a
one-time high-tech wunderkind, he had sold his logistics software
company to Microsoft for US$160 million.

From his estate on an island near Vancouver, Ruloff was researching
an investment in biotechnology when he claims that scientists began
confiding their doubts about Darwinism. "There's a real sense of not
being able to speak up against this machine that is big science," he
told *Education Week*. But his self-portrait of a maverick venture capitalist
who stumbles on an intellectual conspiracy is, like *Expelled*'s own plotline, only part of the story. According to a fellow producer, the idea for
the movie hit Ruloff in an airport while reading about the Discovery
Institute's public relations strategy to rally support for intelligent design
by stressing the notion that academic freedom was under threat. By
the time Ruloff's plane landed, he had sketched out the script for a
documentary patterned after the box-office hits of Michael Moore.

For the role of intrepid narrator, the pesky Moore clone who con-
fronts establishment leaders in their corporate lairs, Ruloff conscripted
Ben Stein, the bespectacled polymath best known as the irksome
teacher in the 1986 teen flick, *Ferris Bueller's Day Off*. A trained attorney,
game-show host and former business columnist for the *New York Times*,
Stein was also a speech writer for Richard Nixon, giving him the ideological stature to tackle the strongholds of evolutionary science, including the Smithsonian, which he makes a show of trying to storm in the
film. But Ruloff had another reason for casting Stein as the documentary's front man and star. He had met his co-producers, Logan Craft
and John Sullivan, while auditing a course at Vancouver's Regent
College, an evangelical postgraduate school where both were studying
for a master's degree in theology, and was worried that *Expelled* might
be slammed as a screed from the Christian right. As a secular Jew,
Stein inoculated them against that charge.

Not only did Stein supply the star power, but, as one of *Expelled*'s screenwriters, he is credited with giving the film a didactic drift that has enraged critics. Although the narrative claims that a half-dozen American scientists lost their jobs or were denied tenure for touting intelligent design, Stein never probes those allegations. (In fact, one research associate who claims he was fired from the Smithsonian was on a contract that had expired; another, who recounts being blacklisted, went on to teach at two other colleges). Instead, Stein spends much of his screen time blaming Charles Darwin for the atrocities of the Holocaust, underlining that assertion with a visit to a Nazi death camp.

Even show-business dailies like the *Hollywood Reporter* decried the link as "offensive," while the *New York Times*, Stein's erstwhile employer, lambasted the film as "a conspiracy-theory rant masquerading as investigative inquiry" and "one of the sleaziest documentaries to arrive in a very long time." Canadian critics were no kinder. Under the damning headline, "No intelligence, and no laughs, either," the *Globe and Mail*'s Liam Lacey refrained from awarding the movie a single star. Opening with grainy newsreel footage of the Berlin Wall, every allegation of academic persecution seems to end with a cutaway shot of Soviet leader Nikita Khrushchev banging his shoe on a United Nations desk or the Gestapo herding Jews onto trains. As the *National Post*'s Chris Knight wryly observed, "Apparently, Darwinists can be both Communists and Fascists at the same time."

For most first-time film producers, those reviews might have been devastating, but for Ruloff, they were neither unexpected nor bad news. From the beginning, *Expelled* was intended to fan the intelligent-design controversy; as he argued in interviews, "In its very nature, the backlash proves the central premise to our film."

Part of the backlash came from zoologist Richard Dawkins and a trio of other scientists who protested that they had been tricked into appearing in a benign-sounding documentary called *Crossroads: The Intersection of Science and Religion*—a deception that Dawkins reported in an extensive Internet posting entitled "Lying for Jesus?" But Ruloff shrugged off the accusations. "They're trying to come up with a way to discredit us," he told the *Los Angeles Times*. "The best they can come up with is that we changed the title? Gosh, let's get real and talk about the issues."

In fact, *Expelled* gives the issues themselves exceedingly short shrift. Veering off on assorted tangents, the film fails to interview a single scientist who believes in both God and evolutionary theory, of which there are many. Instead, it focuses on a handful of curious testimonials that underscore one conclusion: evolution leads to an outright rejection of religion. That thesis seems to have motivated the screenings Ruloff held for lawmakers in Florida and Missouri, two states where bills to teach intelligent design have surfaced on the legislative agenda. But if his aim is to win the theory a niche in North American classrooms, his bid to reach Canadian MPs struck many in Ottawa as passing strange. Education, after all, is a provincial issue and in his invitations to the film, Charles McVety made no mention of a threat to academic freedom in this country.

But McVety's missive is an indicator of why the battle for creationism and its updated twin, intelligent design, is unlikely to disappear anytime soon. In lengthy paragraphs of overwrought prose, he rails against Darwin for spawning the social applications of his theory, including the practice of eugenics, which flourished in the early twentieth century, long after Darwin himself was laid to rest in Westminster Abbey. As it turns out, some of the most vocal proponents of eugenics were the continent's early feminists, including Alberta's Emily Murphy, one of the Famous Five who won Canadian women legal status as "persons" in 1929, and thereby the right to vote. In *Expelled*, it seems no accident when Stein points out that Margaret Sanger, an American champion of eugenics, was also the founder of Planned Parenthood, now the largest provider of surgical abortions in the United States. For conservative Christians, evolution has become the equivalent of the serpent's apple in Eden, a symbolic catch-all for what they see as the evils of the secular world.

Similarly, it is not without significance that McVety's invitation to *Expelled* was issued through the parliamentary office of Conservative MP Maurice Vellacott, whose legislative assistant, Timothy Bloedow— like McVety—has attacked the environmental movement. To Bloedow and McVety, who are Christian nationalists from different theological streams, environmentalism is an assault on the biblical verities in the book of Genesis. Indeed, just as the campaign to teach creationism has been aimed at re-establishing biblical authority, the drive to discredit evolution has always targeted a much broader ideology: the concept of secular humanism, which many evangelicals blame for unleashing a flood tide of biblically proscribed practices and attitudes on society.

For them, the first step in remaking Canada as a Christian nation is to rein in the forces of secularism and science, and they show no sign of scaling back their efforts to do just that. From Big Valley to the big screen, they are becoming more sophisticated in tailoring their message—perhaps newly emboldened by the knowledge that they now have allies on Parliament Hill.

RAISING THE JOSHUA
GENERATION

.

VII

In the Grade 12 social-studies class at Riverside Secondary School in Port Coquitlam, twenty-five teenagers turn their attention from text messaging to the well-tailored retiree who is their guest speaker of the week. Immaculate in grey flannels and a buttoned-down shirt, he is far from an imposing figure, easily dwarfed by the tallest girls in the class, but as these students well know, this is no ordinary visitor dropping in on Social Justice 12, the controversial new course designed to combat discrimination in British Columbia schools. Murray Corren is its inspiration and driving force—one half of the gay couple behind the most provocative revamping of the provincial curriculum since the government first dared to inform students about the verboten subject of sex.

In online Christian chat rooms and the right-wing blogosphere, he and his spouse, Peter Corren, have been called every epithet imaginable since they launched a 1999 human rights complaint against B.C.'s Ministry of Education for "systemic gender discrimination." Seven years later, just as the case was finally scheduled to be heard, the government settled, seizing on the Correns' proposal for an elective course to combat not only homophobia but bigotry of every kind, including biases against the disabled, the homeless and the poor. To thousands of evangelical and Catholic parents, those topics were mere window dressing to mask the true aims of the course: foisting what some like to call a "homosexualist agenda" on impressionable teens.

For two years, they attempted to block both the course and another product of the settlement that caused even greater consternation: a curriculum guide to teaching diversity in select subjects from kindergarten to high school on which the Correns were given an unprecedented advisory role. One evangelical group, the Canadian Alliance for Social Justice and Family Values Association (CASJAFVA), collected seventeen thousand signatures on a petition condemning the agreement and staged a noisy demonstration outside the provincial legislature, while Vancouver's former Roman Catholic archbishop, Raymond Roussin, warned parents that the proposed guide would infect the classroom with "morally objectionable material." After the debut of Social Justice 12 in the fall of 2008, its foes stepped up their efforts. A half-dozen organizations, including REAL Women of B.C., formed a coalition called Take Back Our Schools, which blasted the Corren agreement as a blatant attack on parents' rights.

In Abbotsford, the epicentre of the province's Bible belt, the same school board that had once covertly okayed the teaching of creation science refused to offer the course for a year—its reluctance bolstered by a group called Parents for Democracy in Education, which sounded the equivalent of an Amber Alert. "Government Dictatorship?" its online advertisements screamed. "Are you alarmed about the revised school curriculum? Is it challenging parental rights, cultural values and religious freedom?" The group's website featured a plug from the former Social Credit premier, Bill Vander Zalm, who donated half the profits from his most recent book to the cause and denounced "the growing trend of student indoctrination."

While the outcry over the Corren agreement has become one of the most polarizing skirmishes in the Canadian culture wars, it is only the latest standoff in a half-century struggle to determine which values are taught in the public-school system and who has the final say over what a child learns: parents or the government. Ever since any mention of creationism was banned from biology lessons in the name of science and prayers were pulled out of schools in the name of interfaith harmony, many conservative Christians have come to view state-run education systems with mistrust and outright hostility. As they see it, liberals and secular humanists have conspired with the courts to wipe out all symbols of Christianity from the classroom and impose an alien agenda on their offspring.

In Quebec, where the government has orchestrated a decade-long secularization of education, some Catholics and evangelicals have launched lawsuits against the Ministry of Education over a new ecumenical course called Ethics and Religious Culture that has been declared mandatory. Designed to boost cross-cultural understanding in a province where that commodity sometimes appeared to be in short supply, the course has provoked outrage for giving the same weight to Hinduism, Judaism, Islam, aboriginal spirituality and even Wicca as it does to Christianity. Last year, a Quebec judge dismissed a case filed by two Drummondville families who had charged the ministry with violating their constitutional rights by refusing requests to exempt their children from the course, but, with other cases pending, this is unlikely to be the last word from the courts.

Meanwhile, the Alberta government found itself under fire for introducing a contentious measure that guarantees parents the very right their Quebec counterparts were refused: the opportunity to yank their children out of any classes dealing explicitly with religion or sexual orientation. Despite objections from the provincial teachers' federation and a warning from the Canadian Civil Liberties Association that the bill would help "promote a regime of religious intolerance," it survived five stormy weeks of debate in the legislature to become law in the spring of 2009, prompting former Conservative senator

Ron Ghitter to observe that "we're kind of stepping back into the Middle Ages."

Alberta's move was clearly a pre-emptive strike designed to prevent the Corren precedent from spilling across the border, a fear that conservative Christians have fanned in every province. Still, not all the objections to B.C.'s Social Justice 12 have come from the family-values camp. While the minister of education was hailing it as a global milestone in teaching diversity, some of the loudest objections emerged from the very communities who make up the province's diverse demographic patchwork: Hindu, Sikh and Chinese Canadians who have demonstrated that, on issues like same-sex marriage, they can be as socially conservative as the Christian right.

That realization was not lost on Stephen Harper when he drafted his theo-conservative strategy, nor was it any accident that Harper kicked off his 2008 election campaign clad in a blue sweater, indulging in a round of baby-kissing in the B.C. riding of a three-time candidate named Alice Wong. Now the Conservative member of Parliament for Richmond, Wong had been an enthusiastic speaker and fundraiser for CASJAFVA, the right-wing advocacy group whose mostly Chinese membership had organized the largest protest against the Corren agreement.

But the furor over Social Justice 12 was also fostered by cross-border ministries like Focus on the Family Canada, headquartered on the outskirts of Langley, east of Vancouver. Fresh from his radio campaign against same-sex marriage in this country, its founder, James Dobson, warned the millions of subscribers to his monthly newsletter of yet another threat: a cabal of gay activists had drafted a sinister plot against the continent's schools. In elaborate detail, he spelled out their "audacious attempt to reshape the beliefs of an entire generation, beginning with the youngest and most vulnerable." Summoning his followers to block any attempts to portray homosexuality as an acceptable lifestyle, Dobson pulled out all the rhetorical stops. "Not since Adolf Hitler prepared a generation of German and Austrian youth for war," he fumed, "has so grand a strategy been attempted."

Standing before the Social Justice 12 class, Murray Corren looks incapable of provoking such inflammatory prose, but as a veteran of nearly every gay-rights fight in the province, he is clearly the incarnation of James Dobson's worst nightmare—a symbol of everything the religious right deems wrong with public education.

⁙

Murray Corren might have rhymed off statistics to the class: 82 percent of gay students report being bullied and 48 percent confess to contemplating suicide. He could have recounted the tragedies of two American adolescents who'd actually been driven to kill themselves, one found hanged by an electrical cord in his closet after being taunted as a "fag" by classmates. Instead, Corren relates a condensed version of his own biography, growing up as Murray Warren in a bleak Newfoundland mining town where he was mocked at school as a "sissy" and occasionally limped home with a bloody nose. It is a calculated strategy, he admits, to stress the personal, not the political. "All the research shows that if you actually know somebody who is gay," he says, "it's much harder to discriminate."

Coming of age in the 1950s, Corren was haunted by a book he'd found at the local public library, *Abnormal Sexuality*, which, he says, detailed "this sickness, this mental illness I had." Even when he escaped to Memorial University in St. John's, then to Montreal, where he taught for two years, he lived in terror of revealing his sexuality. That changed when he went to England to complete his M.A. thesis. Helping out at one of London's private gay clubs, he caught sight of a dashing Englishman with piercing blue eyes named Peter Cook, the beginning of a forty-year relationship that lasted until Cook's death in December 2009. Five years earlier, when they became one of Canada's first same-sex couples to marry—their garden ceremony featured in the National Film Board documentary *Why Thee Wed*—they signalled their status by legally amalgamating their surnames, Cook and Warren, to Corren, a moniker that has become a household word in religious right circles.

Still, they had been together for nearly two decades, running florist businesses in England and South Africa, before it occurred to them to enlist in the movement for gay rights. Moving to Vancouver on the eve of the 1990 Gay Games, they found a city where homosexuals were celebrating a newfound sense of freedom, but at the Coquitlam elementary school where Corren had landed a teaching job, he kept his live-in relationship under wraps. Then, on a trip to San Francisco, watching its notoriously flamboyant Gay Pride parade, he was stunned to see a contingent of gay and lesbian teachers marching under a banner proclaiming their sexual identity. So moved was he by their openness that he jumped out of the crowd to join them, only to have his euphoria shattered by a stinging rebuke from the crowd. "Where were you when I needed you?" a young spectator yelled at the teachers' contingent. The incident left Corren shaken. "I realized it was a question I had to answer," he tells the class. "Where was I for the students I taught who were wrestling with their sexuality?"

Helping to found a support group called the Gay and Lesbian Educators of B.C. (GALE BC), Corren became its public face and a lightning rod for social-conservative fury. When he asked his school board to investigate the plight of gay pupils, he received his first death threats. Months later, at a tumultuous meeting of the B.C. Teachers' Federation, his resolution calling for an official policy to end homophobia passed by a landslide, but that victory opened the way to a more determined backlash—one that would galvanize conservative Christians across the country.

In the wake of the federation vote, the school board in Surrey brought in a resolution pointedly banning any resource material recommended by educators who were members of GALE. The move hardly came as a surprise—among the most outspoken Surrey trustees was Heather Stilwell, a former leader of the Christian Heritage Party—but GALE set out to test the board's stand. Weeks later, an openly gay kindergarten teacher named James Chamberlain asked for permission to use three supplementary storybooks depicting same-sex families: *Asha's Mums*, *Belinda's Bouquet* and *One Dad, Two Dads, Brown Dads, Blue Dads*. As Corren rhymes off the titles, the Riverside students nod in recognition—for most, the books had been standard primary-school fare—but the Surrey trustees vetoed all three. Testifying at a crammed board meeting on Chamberlain's behalf, Corren showed up sporting a T-shirt that announced "Bigots Ban Books," only to find himself caught up in a near-riot. As a reporter hustled him to safety in a waiting car, parents in hot pursuit, one bruiser branded him a pervert and pedophile.

The episode steeled his resolve. He and his partner hired the human-rights lawyer Joe Arvay, who had defended Vancouver's lesbian bookstore Little Sisters, to mount Chamberlain's constitutional challenge against the Surrey board. Although the Correns were only tangentially involved, they guaranteed Arvay's legal fees, which would eventually exceed $1 million as the case made its way through two appeals to the nation's highest court. Five years later, the Supreme Court ruled that the Surrey board had defied the nature and intent of the B.C. Schools Act by banning the three storybooks. Writing for the majority, Chief Justice Beverley McLachlin refused to acknowledge the supremacy of parents' rights. "Parental views, however important, cannot override the imperative placed upon the British Columbia public schools to mirror the diversity of the community, and teach tolerance and understanding of difference," she declared.

For many conservative Christians, the decision still stands as a watershed, a legal Waterloo that galvanized them into the sort of grassroots activism that Ralph Reed pioneered in the U.S., taking over local school boards and town councils in the first step toward building a nationwide resistance movement. A social-conservative coalition called

the Surrey Electoral Team emerged to control the board and city government for nearly a decade, and one of its leading members, the
former school-board chair, Mary Polak, would go on to become a cabinet minister in Gordon Campbell's provincial government.

But the biggest evangelical star to emerge from the Surrey book battle
was Kari Simpson, a U.S.-born mother of four who had set up an advocacy group called the Citizens Research Institute. Despite living in
Langley, Simpson threw herself into the Surrey fight, launching a recall
movement aimed at B.C.'s minister of education and publishing a
controversial "Declaration of Family Rights," which forbade teachers
from exposing designated Christian students to any discussions that
suggested a homosexual lifestyle was even remotely normal. At rallies
across the province, she attracted overflow crowds and her tirades grew
so inflammatory that a former ally, Vancouver talk-show host Rafe
Mair—no mealy-mouth himself—compared her anti-gay rhetoric to
that of Nazis and Southern segregationists. In return, Simpson slapped
him with a defamation suit, resulting in a decade-long legal saga that
appeared to end in June 2008 when the Supreme Court ruled that
Mair's remarks, however insulting, were within his right to fair comment. In newsrooms across the country, the decision was celebrated as
a breakthrough in the defence of free speech, but Simpson had no
intention of leaving the courts with the last word. After failing in an
attempt to reopen the case, she filed a human rights complaint that
could hardly fail to make headlines. She accused the B.C. Human
Rights Tribunal, the very body that would decide her case, of seven years
of systemic discrimination against Christians—an echo of the Correns'
original complaint against the Ministry of Education.

Now the co-host of the syndicated right-wing webcast, Roadkill Radio,
with conservative writer Terry O'Neill, Simpson has been championed
by California's Chalcedon Foundation, the chief redoubt of Christian
reconstructionism founded by Rousas J. Rushdoony. Long before
Rushdoony penned his signature treatise on that theological school, he

unleashed a scathing denunciation of U.S. public schools as hotbeds of secular humanist indoctrination in a study entitled *The Messianic Character of American Education*. His sentiments were taken up by a generation of evangelical leaders, including Jerry Falwell and James Dobson, who helped turn Christian schooling into one of the chief crusades of the religious right. In a speech to fellow fundamentalists, Falwell once rhapsodized about "a time when, as in the early days of our country, we won't have public schools. The churches will have taken them over again and Christians will be running them."

So explosive was the mood in B.C. after the Corren agreement that Derek Rogusky, the vice-president of Focus on the Family Canada, predicted it would provoke an exodus of evangelicals from the province's public schools. But when the Ministry of Education tallied enrollment, no such mass defection had materialized. Instead, statistics revealed what some provincial educators regard as a more unsettling trend: a steady 2 percent annual increase in the number of B.C. students attending private schools, most of them faith-based, over the past two decades. Despite the ministry's determination to ensure diversity in the classroom—or maybe because of it—nearly 11 percent of the province's school-age population now attends private Christian, Jewish, Sikh or Muslim academies, more than twice the ratio in any other province.

Clearly, one reason for that relentless growth is that B.C., along with Alberta, pays up to 50 percent of the fee for students registered in accredited private schools. But that subsidy also prompted many Christian school boards to fear that the province could pressure them to comply with the Corren agreement. Although the ministry issued a vaguely worded letter assuring them that they had nothing to fear, the controversy revealed an important distinction: not all Christian schools are cut from the same reactionary cloth. In Surrey, Dennis deGroot, the principal of Fraser Valley Christian High School, shocked some colleagues by offering Social Justice 12 to his students. As he pointed out, the course fits perfectly with the school's mission to produce evangelical graduates inspired to tackle the problems of poverty, inequity and racism—a mission that includes an annual senior-class trip to an impoverished African village. "If we are not teaching about justice," deGroot wrote in *B.C. Christian News*, "then who will?"

⁜

What does a Bible-based education look like? In Betty-Anne Rozema's Grade 3 class at Knox Christian School in Bowmanville, Ontario, twenty pint-sized tykes sit cross-legged on a carpet beneath a handmade mobile of rocket ships, their tinfoil fuselages sprouting sequined fins and orange tissue-paper flames. Clapping to command attention, Rozema holds up an oversized picture book featuring a gigantic burst of light. "Many astronomers believe the universe was born from one big explosion called the big bang," she says. "It all began with tiny, tiny particles—that is, matter."

One six-year-old is quick to catch her drift. "It's not true!" he squeals. "Well, this is what scientists believe," she says patiently. "What do you believe?" The answer comes back twentyfold, loud and clear: "God made it!"

Rozema doesn't pause to debate the issue, moving on swiftly to describe the solar system and the fragile protection afforded by the earth's atmosphere. "I'm very glad God put us on this planet just the right distance from the sun," she says. "What people have to do is be very careful we look after this atmosphere or we won't have air to breathe." Between that pitch for environmentalism and the school's allegiance to the inerrancy of the Bible, Rozema walks a careful line, well aware that some parents embrace the literal six-day creation story while others prefer a Christian version of the big bang in which God choreographed the cosmic fireworks. "I don't tell them which to think— I leave that up to the parents," she says. "Either way, it makes God sovereign. He initiated it: order came from chaos. God knows what he's doing." In later grades, these students will hear about evolution or stumble on television shows about the origins of the universe that make no mention of a deity, but that is not a message Rozema conveys to her class. "I would never promote a theory where God is absent— where it's a fearful thing," she says. "I believe children want to have parameters that can be trusted. If what they're hearing at home and here is consistent, their worldview becomes more solid."

That deference to both parental and biblical authority is one reason why 134 families pay up to $12,500 a year to send their children to Knox Christian School, one of an estimated 1,500 private evangelical schools across the country. In Ontario, as in other provinces, the precise number defies easy calculation since many Christian schools refuse to register with the assortment of fractious organizations that lobby on their behalf. "There are some schools that don't want to be recorded," says Adrian Guldemond, executive director of the Ontario Alliance of Christian Schools, who claims 80 members in his association but estimates that as many as 650 such institutions actually exist in the province. "They're what we call invisible schools—usually in homes or church basements," he explains. "They have a view of the government as being anti-Christian and uncooperative, and they like to stay below the radar."

The number of Canadian evangelical schools is but a fraction of those in the United States, a disparity that can be traced back to the origins of public education in each country. In the U.S., it was championed by Horace Mann, the first secretary of Massachusetts's board of education, who banished God from the classroom. In Canada, Egerton Ryerson, a former evangelist who was the superintendent of schools for Canada West (now Ontario), drafted the education model later followed by most provinces. Working in the 1840s, both shared a conviction that education must be free and accessible to all—a vehicle to instill common values in volatile immigrant populations from vastly different backgrounds and often hostile faiths. But the two disagreed on the means to accomplish that task. In a country founded by pilgrims fleeing religious persecution, Mann decreed that education must be secular, reflecting the Founding Fathers' insistence on a constitutional separation of church and state, while Ryerson argued only that it must be non-sectarian—free from control by any single denomination. An evangelical convert who had been booted out of the family home by his Anglican father, Ryerson knew all too well the price of denominational passions, but as a former preacher on the Methodist revival circuit he was not about to toss God out of the schoolhouse entirely.

Later, Ryerson agreed to the existence of a separate Roman Catholic school system in Ontario as long as Quebec guaranteed the education of its Protestant minority—a stipulation that sealed the terms of Confederation. But his chief battle for control of education was not with Catholics but with Anglicans, who demanded a special role as the province's established church. Thus, the public system Ryerson designed was aimed at surmounting Protestant power struggles with an ecumenical appeal based "upon the broad basis of our common Christianity." His education bills stipulated that teachers must be persons "of Christian sentiment," and that each day must begin and end with prayers and Bible study, including specific instruction in the Ten Commandments.

It wasn't until nearly a century later, in the secularized wake of the Second World War, that debate over the role of God in the classroom erupted again in the Canadian public square. Some non-Christians protested that Ryerson's requirements for religious instruction amounted to indoctrination, while their Christian counterparts saw the mushrooming postwar demands to strip all symbols of faith from schools as the imposition of a dangerous new theology: secular humanism. At a time when the writings of Sigmund Freud and Dr. Spock were trumping traditional theories of child rearing, many parents regarded such calls for permissiveness as the final insult. Few were more offended than the immigrants who had flooded into the country from Holland after World War II, certain that a more robust response from Christians might have halted Hitler's takeover of their homeland. Forgoing public funding in exchange for the right to shape their children's worldview, they set up private religious schools such as Knox, where the motto unapologetically promises a "Christ-centred education."

Founded in 1957 by Dutch farmers determined to ensure that their offspring were raised in the strict Calvinism of the Christian Reformed Church, the school no longer limits admission to members of that denomination, but its application form contains six biblical statements with which at least one parent must agree, including the opening verse of Genesis: "In the beginning, God created the heavens and the earth." As its principal, George Petrusma, puts it, "We want to be on the same page."

In surveys, most parents say they chose Knox because its teaching reinforces what their children hear at home and at church. But an increasing number of social conservatives, including many immigrants, are also seeking out Christian schools as a refuge from the alien, anything-goes culture they perceive in the public system, where classes are often twice the size and drug dealers can infiltrate even the most remote rural playgrounds. Winston Quintal's parents, newly arrived from India, pulled him out of a nearby public school, worried about the rumoured presence of drugs and the preoccupation their son had with wearing the right brand names. "My parents are very attentive about my social life," Quintal says during a seventh-grade break at Knox. "Here, the principal knows every single student and the teachers are much more strict. I had to get used to it. In my old school, all that mattered was if you were cool."

While Quintal's parents might once have had to trade academic excellence for that tighter rein, Christian schools like Knox no longer qualify as scholastic backwaters. In the basic skills test it administers every two years, students consistently score a grade ahead of their actual status, and on provincial tests, secondary students from the Ontario Alliance of Christian Schools ranked in the eighty-first percentile on all subjects while those in the public system averaged only a median passing grade. "The reality of a private school is that it's a consumer-driven model," Petrusma says. "If we weren't doing the job, our desks would be empty."

At Knox, every day begins with a prayer and half an hour of devotions, and the curriculum is set out in thick white plastic binders from the Ontario Association of Christian Schools, designed to meet provincial academic requirements while linking each segment to a verse from the Bible. Broaching the subject of aboriginal history, the guide includes a cautionary note: "Not only we, but also God, is offended by stereotyping." As Grade 8 teacher Stephen Janssen admits, "We march to a different drummer here."

The son of a Christian school principal, Janssen concedes that his approach to some subjects is unlikely to resemble that of his public-school colleagues. "The Christian conception of history is definitely linear," he points out. "God guides history and there is a culminating moment: Christ's return." A query scrawled at the top of his blackboard provides a reminder of that point: "When Christ returns," it asks, "what will things look like?"

For students who go on to high school at Knox's sister institution down the road, then graduate to a Christian university or Bible college, it is possible to spend an entire academic lifetime, as Janssen has, inside the cocoon of faith-based institutions. Still, he insists the school is "not about setting up walls and saying, 'We're a fortress of Christian faith.'" He invites students to contemplate what he calls "the messiness of the world," from Afghanistan and the Middle East to the consumer messages that bombard them through the mass media. "By the time a student leaves, we want to make sure that they are equipped to make wise and discerning choices," he says, "that are in agreement with what they believe."

But occasionally, the school's theological principles are also apparent in its omissions. In social studies, there is no mention of newfangled family permutations such as same-sex parents, and although some students are the products of single mothers or divorced parents, their situation is considered such an anomaly that they are offered a special counselling program during lunch hour. "The definition of family here is one mom, one dad and children," Petrusma says. Those who show up with bare midriffs or revealing attire can expect a friendly chat with teachers who keep a watchful eye on pubescent hormones, and sex education at Knox is confined to extolling abstinence—no lessons on how to fit a condom over a banana are dispensed on these premises. In health class, sexuality is hailed as a gift from God reserved for men and women who are married, and the curriculum guide leaves no room for mixed messages. "Write on the board," it instructs teachers, "that No Sex + Married Sex = Safe Sex."

While few would dispute a private school's right to present its own theological perspective, another question burst into the headlines in the summer of 2007: should provincial taxpayers in Ontario, like those in B.C. and Alberta, subsidize such faith-based lessons?

⊹

That question was a political hot potato—one that had been dodged by Ontario politicians for more than two decades, ever since former premier William Davis extended the same public funding to Catholic high schools that their elementary counterparts had won at Confederation. Davis had deflected the howls of protest from other faiths by commissioning a study from his former education minister, Bernard Shapiro, who concluded that the government was on questionable moral ground, but Shapiro's plan for redress sat ignored. Nearly a decade later, a Toronto mother who sent her kids to a private Hebrew day school launched a lawsuit charging that, without the same public funding accorded Catholics, her family was the victim of religious discrimination. The Canadian Jewish Congress backed her Charter challenge and the Ontario Alliance of Christian Schools convinced an evangelical couple to join the case, which eventually landed on the docket of the Supreme Court. Although they lost, the ruling offered an unwelcome nudge to the political establishment: while the province was only obliged by the terms of the Confederation deal to fund Catholic schools, the justices conceded that the constitution did not prevent it from underwriting the education of other religious minorities.

Still, no politician dared touch the question until Conservative premier Mike Harris, intent on wooing the suburban evangelical vote, promised tax credits for private schools. But his proposal never made it into law and the issue appeared to drop off the political map. Then, in June 2007, Conservative leader John Tory left many in his party dumbfounded when he unveiled an election promise to fund the fifty-three thousand students in the province's religious schools at an estimated cost of $4 billion—a bombshell that unleashed such passions it swamped the provincial election and effectively torpedoed Tory's political career.

The surprise was that Tory didn't see the uproar coming. He had, after all, been an aide to Davis in 1984 when the subject of Catholic school funding had first set off a political firestorm. Although his move was meant to restore fairness, to some it looked like crass political opportunism, an attempt to curry favour with those conservative Christians in the suburbs outside Toronto who had just helped bring Stephen Harper to power. Ironically, Tory's proposal had the opposite effect. One of the groups most infuriated by his platform was the Ontario Alliance for Christian Schools, which had warned him against any such move. "We were officially on record as saying to Mr. Tory, 'Don't do it,'" confirms Adrian Guldemond. "We've gone through this before so we've got a fairly good bead on what Ontario voters think."

True to Guldemond's predictions, the greatest opposition came not from secular proponents of a single public-education system who wanted an end to all religious-school funding, but from those harbouring ethnic fears. "We had people canvassing across the province and we heard it at the door," Guldemond says. "People said, 'We're not going to fund these Christian schools because it will only allow Muslim schools. They turned it into a racial issue.'"

Tory was trounced at the ballot box, having managed to alienate virtually every side in the debate. In the midst of the furor, he had set off further alarms by admitting that, to qualify for public funding, faith-based schools would have to conform to provincial curriculum requirements. As Tristan Emmanuel, a veteran of the Defend Marriage campaign, pointed out, he doled out twelve thousand dollars a year to send his three children to a Christian school precisely because no provincial bureaucrat could stride in and impose a Corren-style course promoting gay tolerance. "We say, 'Hey, wait a minute, the reason we left the public system was the curriculum,'" Emmanuel bristled at the time. "I don't need the money if it means ceding control over that ground."

Guldemond shrugs off those objections. "They used to say that in B.C. before they got funding," he notes. "Now you never hear a word about it." But the demand for public subsidies of religious schools is unlikely to disappear, above all in the wake of the 2008 economic collapse that left many evangelical families reeling. In the U.S., Christian Schools International reports a 10 percent drop in continental enrollment, and in pockets of Ontario such as Bowmanville, where many residents' fortunes are tied to the auto industry, the fallout has been devastating. More than a dozen families have been forced to withdraw their children from Knox, including the great-granddaughter of one of its founders.

But Dave Koetje, the president of Christian Schools International, sees another threat to evangelical education, one barely noticed outside religious circles: the mushrooming homeschooling movement. Not only can transplanting the classroom to the kitchen table turn out to be more cost effective, it has become increasingly trendy. "The homeschooling movement is the fastest growing educational movement in the country," Koetje says. "Five years ago, there were a lot of stigmas attached, but now it's sort of bandwagonish. It's gotten lots of great press and lots of colleges are ignoring traditional high school transcripts." In Koetje's view, homeschooling is not just a threat to Christian schools. "It's a threat to the entire school program," he says.

⁜

Diane Geerlinks hardly looks like a menace to the country's educational foundations. A blonde extrovert in a lace-trimmed T-shirt, she might be any garrulous evangelical from a small town north of Toronto who married young and found herself the mother of five. Having acquired a diploma in early childhood education, she was running a daycare centre out of her Georgetown home when she realized she and her husband were faced with a bizarre choice: she could take in more toddlers so they could afford to send her firstborn to a Christian school or she could focus her skills on her own offspring. "That got me hooked," she says. "I thought, 'Why am I looking after other people's kids so I can pay someone to look after mine?'"

Now Geerlinks has become a regular on the homeschooling circuit—a wise-cracking ambassador for a booming subculture that many regard as eccentric, if not downright anti-social. Kicking off the annual conference of the Ontario Christian Home Educators' Connection (OCHEC) in Hamilton's convention centre, she regales a ballroom full of anxious parents—some homeschoolers, some merely exploring the option—with tales from her own domestic classroom. "As you begin home education, I'd like to say, 'There's not one right way,'" she declares. "God has a plan for you. It's a designer education."

Some parents may want the reassuring trappings of a traditional school, she points out, complete with textbooks and curriculum guides like the hundreds on sale in the crammed exhibit hall downstairs. Others may trade in book learning for what pedagogical rebels call "unschooling"—field trips and hands-on experiences directed by a child's interests. "There are people who have never used a textbook until Grade 8," she notes. Geerlinks herself settled on a blend of the two styles known as "unit learning," but makes no attempt to glamorize her own hit-and-miss course as she grappled with tantrums, claims of terminal boredom and agonizing moments of self-doubt. "There will be times when your children will say, 'I wish I were in school,'" she admits, "and in your head you're thinking, 'You know, I wish you were too.'"

She panicked when one daughter demanded more sophisticated science lessons. "I thought, 'I don't even like science. How am I going to teach it?'" but she insists that God showed her the way. "He taught me how to teach her, and you know what? The next thing I knew we were dissecting a cow's heart at the kitchen table." When both her sons balked at reading, she despaired: "I thought, 'I can't do this. I've failed. I've ruined their lives.'" Then out of the blue, one picked up a book and has been devouring a volume a week ever since. The other now retreats to reading whenever he's stumped by math. "I had to remind myself that this is not about finishing a math page or whatever lesson we're working on," she says. "It's about instilling Godly character and teaching them to lead Christian lives."

That opportunity to mould a formative mind far from peer pressure and the siren song of pop culture is swelling the continent's home-schooling ranks. In the United States, more than two million children are being home educated, dwarfing the number in this country, but even here the movement has been growing at a rate that is difficult for authorities to ignore. In 1979, an estimated two thousand children were being taught by their parents; today, the Home School Legal Defence Association of Canada puts that tally at sixty to eighty thousand. While Ontario claims the largest number of homeschoolers, the movement's chief momentum is in the West, where B.C. foots the bill for home-computer costs and Alberta picks up 16 percent of the tab for those who comply with the provincial curriculum and submit to periodic tests. As home educators like to point out, the Internet has put even the most isolated students only a keystroke away from a vast electronic library and distance-learning tutorials.

To outsiders, homeschooling numbers might seem negligible, but the movement's collective clout is no longer dismissed—at least not since the last U.S. presidential primaries. As the results from the Republican caucuses in Iowa rolled in late one January night in 2008, pundits were astonished to discover that the key factor responsible for transforming an obscure, guitar-playing former Arkansas governor named Mike Huckabee into the upset winner was his grassroots network of fellow evangelicals in the homeschooling movement.

While once most homeschoolers were left-wing hippies who'd dropped out of the straitlaced consumer culture of the 1960s, today more than three-quarters are conservative Christians recoiling from the moral free-for-all they blame on those long-ago summers of love. According to a 2003 survey, more than 85 percent of Canadian families who opted to homeschool their children did so in order to teach them a particular set of religious and moral beliefs. In the foyer outside the OCHEC convention, Amy and Ryan Bromilow aren't reluctant to own up to that motivation. They've just driven in to Hamilton from Wyoming, a hamlet outside Sarnia, Ontario, where Amy is teaching their three kids just down the road from where she was once homeschooled herself. "We want to keep our children pure the way my parents wanted to keep us pure," she says, "and to teach them Christian values."

With her flowery skirt and fortress mentality, Bromilow might seem to fit the prevailing stereotype of the homeschooler, but that profile is changing as swiftly as the country's demographics. At the OCHEC conference, a handful of women sporting Islamic headscarves push strollers through the crowd—one reminder that Muslims now make up one of the fastest-growing segments of the movement—and homeschooling is no longer a strictly rural phenomenon. One former bookstore manager with a gold earring glinting beneath his shaved pate could pass for any urban hipster in the downtown Hamilton neighbourhood where he and his wife have chosen to teach their two daughters.

Even some of the leading players in Stephen Harper's Ottawa have jumped on the homeschooling bandwagon. Two Conservative MPs, Ontario's Jeff Watson and Ed Komarnicki, a former president of the Saskatchewan Home Based Educators, have homeschooled their children, and one of Harper's closest friends and advisers, former Conservative Party strategist Ken Boessenkool—a lobbyist whose clients have included TASER International—has opted to oversee his kids' education at home in Calgary.

Still, the biggest revolution is not in the size or the makeup of the movement but its public image—a shift summed up in the title of a 2007 Fraser Institute study, "Homeschooling: From the Extreme to the Mainstream." In 1985, only 16 percent of Canadian families approved of homeschooling, but by 2001, the number had ballooned to 41 percent. Some experts tie that jump to mounting disaffection with a one-size-fits-all education system, but another reason for the surge is the stratospheric test scores that homeschooled students have racked up. Research shows that children taught at home regularly outperform students from both public and private schools. One 2003 study found that homeschooled students averaged 80 percent in reading, 76 percent in language skills and 79 percent in math on the standard Canadian Achievement Test while their public-school peers averaged only passing grades.

Homeschoolers have consistently captured top prizes and publicity in continental spelling bees, but nothing has destigmatized the movement more than the fact that almost every Canadian university now accepts students who have been educated by their parents, as do the top addresses in the American Ivy League. Still, no matter how astonishing their academic achievements, homeschoolers face the assumption that they're social misfits—shy, reclusive and inept at interacting with their peers after a life sequestered around the family hearth. In fact, one Canadian study reported the contrary: most homeschoolers were involved in at least eight outside activities a week, from church groups and field trips to sports teams. In Hamilton, which boasts a home-schoolers' choir and a handful of learning cooperatives where families get together to stage plays and go on bird-banding expeditions, one mother, Beatrice Ekoko, launched *Radio Free School,* a half-hour weekly newsmagazine on McMaster University's FM station, which her three daughters help produce, occasionally conducting interviews with their favourite authors. Even without that smorgasbord of activities, Paul Faris, executive director of Canada's Home School Legal Defence Association, argues that students who are educated by their parents may actually be better socialized than their public-school counterparts. "They don't look at people and think, 'If you're not in my class we have noth-ing in common,'" he says.

Not that Faris is unbiased. The oldest of seven growing up on a goat farm in southwestern Ontario, he was homeschooled himself, and insists he never felt deprived. He played on local hockey teams, went to high-school dances and won a scholarship to the University of Western Ontario, where he graduated from law school. Now married to another homeschooled graduate, he is the new spokesman for the movement in Canada, a fervent advocate for the cause who defends families in court against overzealous social workers and lobbies for greater parental rights on Parliament Hill. As he points out, every legal clampdown on homeschoolers is provoked by the same question: "Whose child is it anyway? Is it your child or the government's?"

Intense and goateed, Faris is careful to tailor his message to his audi-ence, as required. On the phone with me, he is cautious and low-key, downplaying his organization's Christian underpinnings and American ties. But addressing an insider crowd at the OCHEC convention, he metamorphoses into an aggressive cheerleader for a movement that some critics see as one of the most radical wings of the religious right. Listening to him, it becomes clear that he is not simply championing some homespun, do-it-yourself educational alternative—a retreat from the rowdiness of the secular mainstream. For Faris and his American allies, homeschooling is a political act with a profoundly subversive goal: to groom a new generation of fiercely motivated evangelical leaders capable of taking their place in society's power centres and creating a form of Bible-based government.

With their ability to think outside the box and their enforced history as self-starters, homeschoolers are perfectly positioned to become "spiritual change agents who are advancing the Kingdom of God," Faris tells the OCHEC crowd. "Homeschooling I believe is the most important movement in Canada right now," he says, "because we're out to change our culture."

✢

How do you change a culture? In the homeschooling movement, the answer comes without hesitation: one child at a time. Not that most attendees at the OCHEC conference need persuading on that score. For those who do, Faris brandishes figures from The Barna Group, the U.S. religious right's favourite pollster, whichs warn that, by the end of a public-school education, 70 percent of evangelical children will have lost their core beliefs. "You're putting your five-year-old in something that's designed to destroy his faith for six or seven hours a day," Faris says. "You think you'll counter that with what you teach him at home for an hour a night?"

If Faris's rhetoric sounds alarmist, it turns out to be only a pale Canadian imitation of that proffered by his mentors at the Home School Legal Defense Association in the U.S. "Satan has a good thing going in the public school system," writes HSLDA's senior counsel,

Christopher Klicka, in his primer, *Homeschooling: the Right Choice*. One of two Americans on Faris's Canadian board, Klicka blames that demonic romp on the courts which, in the name of neutrality, have "censored God and His principles" right out of the classroom. "The future of liberty in our country and the very survival of the family may depend on our commitment to homeschooling," Klicka writes.

The same argument has galvanized the modern homeschooling movement since the early 1960s when Calvinist theologian Rousas J. Rushdoony first promoted home education as the cornerstone for reconstructing a Christian nation. Among those who latched onto Rushdoony's theories was Tim LaHaye, the San Diego pastor who was one of the key organizers of the Moral Majority. In 1980, in the midst of the Cold War, LaHaye took Rushdoony's attack on secular education a step further in *Battle for the Mind*, warning that liberals and humanists were waging a propaganda campaign in schools that was paving the way for a Soviet takeover.

Unlike LaHaye's later *Left Behind* thrillers, the book failed to make a dent on bestseller lists, but it did win one convert: a brash, born-again law student named Michael Farris—no relation to Paul Faris—who had turned the Washington state chapter of the Moral Majority into its largest branch. So impressed was Farris with *Battle for the Mind* that he became the author's protege. He landed a job as national director of Concerned Women for America, the anti-feminist lobby set up by LaHaye's wife, Beverly, and moved to the outskirts of Washington, D.C., where he and his wife, Vickie, began homeschooling their ten kids. But what began as a private experiment soon turned into a full-time crusade. In 1983, Farris founded the Home School Legal Defense Association and soon earned a reputation as a media-savvy evangelist for the cause, grabbing headlines for branding the American education system "a multi-billion-dollar inculcation machine." Taking on laws that made homeschooling illegal in forty-five states, often by requiring parents to hold a teacher's certification, he turned HSLDA into one of the most effective Christian lobbies, championed by the likes of Joseph Farah, founder of the ultra-right-wing news website WorldNetDaily, who sees homeschooling as the equivalent of a Christian survivalist movement—a choice that "denies the government school monopoly what it craves most: the minds and souls of your children."

In 1993, Farris scored a major breakthrough when the Michigan Supreme Court ruled that a lack of state teaching certificates did not prevent a dairy farmer and his wife from exercising their constitutional rights to homeschool their ten kids. That decision prompted a rash of other legislatures to rewrite their statutes easing the legal pressures on homeschoolers, but critics have accused Farris of constantly fanning their fears with his relentless code-orange rhetoric. Still, those scare tactics have kept HSLDA's coffers and membership rolls filled: from an initial two hundred families, it has grown to more than eighty-two thousand and expanded to Brazil, Germany, Japan and Taiwan. In 1994, Dallas R. Miller, an Alberta lawyer and homeschooling father of five, opened a Canadian branch in Red Deer, complete with HSLDA's U.S. logo, mission statement and two of Farris' top lieutenants on its board.

A year later, Miller played a key role in a Canadian case that sent shivers through homeschoolers across the continent. In Newfoundland, a Seventh Day Adventist couple was charged with truancy for refusing to enroll their children in public schools, despite the fact that they had asked two different school boards to okay a curriculum drafted by their church. When they still refused to comply, social workers descended on their home, seizing their three kids, including a five-year-old not yet legally required to be in class, and placing them in foster care for ten traumatizing months. A judge finally overturned the order, but Miller later cited it as an example of bureaucracy gone wild, the sort of consequences that could arise from the United Nations Declaration of the Rights of the Child, which the homeschooling movement opposed as a direct threat to parents' rights.

In Virginia, Michael Farris decided to use his homeschooling celebrity as a springboard to politics, running for the lieutenant governor's job. But in a 1993 race that commanded national attention, his rivals had no trouble painting him as an extremist, a pal of Jerry Falwell's who had once tried to ban *The Wizard of Oz* from schools. His political career was over before it began, but he was determined to ensure that a new generation of young evangelicals would not meet the same fate.

In September 2000, in a former cornfield outside Purcellville, Virginia, Farris threw open the doors to a cluster of red brick, neofederalist buildings that he christened Patrick Henry College, an elite training ground for the cream of the Christian homeschooling crop. Financed in part by the profits from Tim LaHaye's *Left Behind* bestsellers, the college has been dubbed "Harvard for homeschoolers," but its goal was not merely to create a fundamentalist version of the Ivy League. Farris set out to produce a new breed of crack spiritual warriors who could take over key seats of influence in government, law, business and even Hollywood. As he saw it, his own generation had played the role of Moses, bringing Bible believers to the brink of political power. Now, it was time for a new generation—what he calls "the Joshua generation"—to lead the way into the promised land, establishing a true Christian nation in Rushdoony's theocratic mold. As Farris likes to tell every class, "You are the tip of the spear."

It was a remarkably ambitious mission for a fledgling institution whose code of conduct might have been lifted straight from some backcountry Bible school: its "Statement of Biblical Worldview," which every student must sign, includes a ban on all handholding except when a couple is walking. Equally old-fashioned, its curriculum stresses a grounding in the classics, even Greek and Latin, and divinity-school-style courses in Christian apologetics. But a decade after its opening, Patrick Henry boasts a waiting list. Skeptics rolled their eyes when Farris told the *New York Times* that some parents expected him to churn out a new crop of Christian Supreme Court justices, but four years later, they were stunned into respectful silence when Patrick Henry's debaters beat the Oxford University team in an international moot-court competition staged in England under British law—a triumph they repeated the following year.

Still, Farris's overriding goal is to groom Christian foot soldiers who will, as he euphemistically puts it, "take back the land." Students collect academic credits for working on election campaigns—almost all of them toiling for Republicans—and courses include hands-on instruction on how to run a politician's office and interpret polling results. But it is the college's mandatory three-month internships in government that have turned its rolls into a farm team for Washington's right-wing power structure. In 2004, that program came to light when one sharp-eyed media scribe noticed that, of one hundred interns in George Bush's White House, seven were from tiny Patrick Henry, an institution so obscure that few liberals were even aware of its existence. One of those students worked as an aide to Bush's shadowy strategist, Karl Rove.

Known for their unwavering patriotism and Puritan work ethic, Patrick Henry grads have also been sought out by the military and the CIA, and dozens now work as full-time congressional aides or analysts within the bureaucracy which makes up Washington's powerful permanent village. When talking to the mainstream media, Farris downplays the implications of seeding politics and the public service with his young Christian guerillas. "The goal is not a political coup or the establishment of a new Israel," he wrote in *The Joshua Generation*. "It is about raising men and women of faith who, because they love God, refuse to sit silently by while their nation hates what He loves and loves what He hates."

For most Canadians, Patrick Henry College sounds like a pipe dream—yet another product of the superior numbers and zeal of the American religious right that could never happen here. What few seem to realize is that such an institution already exists in this country, one that shares many of the same aims and access to power, and is already making its mark on Parliament Hill.

⁜

Driving north from Langley, British Columbia, past ragged woodlots and weathered horse barns, it's not difficult to miss the turnoff to Trinity Western University. No triumphal gates mark the entrance to the country's leading evangelical institution of higher learning tucked away in this rural pocket of the Fraser Valley. Vancouver is half an hour's drive to the west and Ottawa seems light years away, but it was here in the rolling fields of the former Seal Pak Dairy Farm that the elders of the Evangelical Free Church planted their vision of a Christian institution of higher education unlike the countless Bible colleges dotting the country: a private liberal-arts college with a distinguished reputation and an undisguised political aim—to "develop godly Christian leaders."

It was a grandiose goal for a school whose beginnings were humble in the extreme. Making its debut in 1962 as Trinity Junior College, its first seventeen students took lectures in the old farmhouse and played sports in the refurbished barn. The only new structure on the grounds was a gull-winged chapel that doubled as a dormitory and library when not in use for the mandatory daily prayer service. Now, nearly fifty years later, on a manicured campus strewn with bustling low-rises—each bearing some wealthy benefactor's name—the chapel sits condemned, fenced off like some mid-century-modern relic of the school's long struggle for respectability. That struggle entailed decades of government lobbying and a lawsuit before the Supreme Court, but today most of Trinity Western's four thousand students sail between classes blissfully unaware of the controversy that dogged its ascension to a unique niche in the country's academic pantheon.

Most are drawn by its cozy communal atmosphere and a top spot in the *Globe and Mail*'s annual ranking of small universities where it has scored an A+ for quality of education and faculty interaction—with no class larger than twenty students—but a D for its proximity to the nearest pubs. For many evangelical parents, that lack of temptation is precisely the reason they dispatch their offspring to a school that, like Patrick Henry College, requires every enrollee to sign a thirteen-page Responsibilities of Membership agreement that bans smoking, drinking, swearing, drugs and dabbling in the occult, while noting that the university "does not condone dancing at clubs where alcohol is liberally consumed." Abortion is included in the list of forbidden activities, as are all coed living arrangements, even off-campus, and the separate dorms reserved for men and women have regulated hours for commingling. "Sexual intimacy is to be practiced only within the context of marriage between a husband and a wife," the agreement states.

It was precisely those stipulations that kept Trinity Western University classified as a two-year junior college for more than a decade, and in the 1970s, with B.C.'s New Democratic government adamantly opposed to recognizing any private religious institutions, that status seemed unlikely to change. The school's only hope lay in a private member's bill sponsored by a Social Credit MLA, which had been put off until the last day of the spring legislative session in 1979. Then, with twenty minutes left on the clock, the premier, Dave Barrett, suddenly stood up and walked out. It turned out that Barrett, who'd been educated by Jesuits, had agreed to support the measure but felt philosophically compelled to sit out the vote. As cries of "hypocrite" and "mugwump" flew across the chamber, the bill squeaked through in what Bob Burkinshaw, Trinity's dean of social sciences, hails as "one of the most significant religious events in a century." Most of the country's major universities had been founded as religious institutions, Burkinshaw points out, but all have since been secularized. "It was the first time in a century there was a new university in Canada that was confessional," he says. "Basically, it broke the state monopoly on higher education."

Still, it would be another five years before the powerful Association of Universities and Colleges of Canada would confer its official imprimatur on Trinity Western. The sticking point was a doctrinal statement, which even members of the science faculty must sign, acknowledging the biblical account of creation. A committee of university presidents swooped in to grill Jack Van Dyke, the chemistry professor who then headed Trinity Western's science department, on whether the college taught evolution. "My answer was yes," Van Dyke says, "but you need to understand that we teach evolution within a context and that context is creation. Anybody who says there is no evolution is not opening their eyes—you just have to look at the mutation of viruses—but what we at Trinity try to avoid is 'evolutionism,' which is a religion."

That response might have sent shock waves through most mainstream science faculties, as would the university's later "Statement on Creation," which includes a nod to intelligent design, but after a year of heated debate, the association finally recognized Trinity Western's degrees for international accreditation. "They were satisfied that we weren't hiding theories from our students," Van Dyke says. Still, even today, in an interview with me in the university cafeteria, he admits to a foundational belief that "God created mankind" and vents his pique at newspaper headlines that refer to apes as the ancestors of humans. So what would he say to those evolutionary biologists who insist that God had no part in the origins of the universe? "Well, I feel sorry for those people!" Van Dyke exclaims, slapping the table. "They've missed the richness of life."

Buoyed by its newfound status, Trinity Western launched a decade of feverish expansion, adding an interdenominational seminary, nursing school and faculty of education, but once again, its Christian precepts threw up a stumbling block. For years, its education students had to spend their final year at Simon Fraser University in order to win certification from the British Columbia College of Teachers (BCCT), but, in 1995, a BCCT committee finally signalled that Trinity Western had met the necessary conditions to grant its own teaching degrees. Then, at the eleventh hour, one official noticed the definition of marriage in the "Responsibilities of Membership" agreement. While it didn't declare homosexuality a sin, its assertion that marriage was reserved for a man and a woman left little doubt about its implication. At a time when the Correns had just overturned the Surrey school board's ban on same-sex storybooks, the university suddenly found its application rejected on the grounds that the teachers it trained might spread a disapproval of homosexuality in the province's public schools.

As the veto unleashed protests from conservative Christians across the country, Trinity Western filed a lawsuit alleging religious discrimination, which eventually landed in the Supreme Court. Half a dozen evangelical organizations filed supporting briefs, including the Christian Legal Fellowship, represented by Dallas Miller of the Home School Legal Defence Association. But for Trinity Western, the case also provoked institutional soul-searching. Some uncompromising evangelical allies urged the university to use it as a direct constitutional challenge to the concept of gay rights, and an Alberta group offered to foot the legal bill. Despite the temptation, Trinity Western's legal team declined to turn its quest for academic standing into yet another vitriolic clash in the culture wars. "We decided we weren't going to go on the attack," Burkinshaw says. Besides, the university didn't need the proffered funds. "We had more donors for that case," he says with a chuckle, "than for any other campaign."

On May 17, 2001, the Supreme Court ruled that the B.C. College of Teachers had failed to prove that Trinity Western students exhibited anti-homosexual bias. Merely holding a belief, it said, did not necessarily translate into discriminatory acts. In Langley, there was jubilation. Now students no longer had to contemplate concealing their faith like some humiliating skeleton in the closet that might block them from their chosen careers, but the ruling also had implications far beyond the campus. In Calgary, constitutional lawyer Gerry Chipeur, who had intervened in the case on behalf of the Seventh Day Adventist Church, called it "the most important freedom-of-religion decision that the Supreme Court has ever made." Had the B.C. College of Teachers succeeded, he argued, it could have squelched the professional aspirations of evangelicals in every field across the country. "They would basically have kept all Christians out of public service," Chipeur says now. "Not just teachers, but doctors, nurses and lawyers—even judges."

The ruling came at a convenient time. Months earlier, Trinity Western had embarked on a mission not unlike that of Patrick Henry College: to put more evangelicals on the fast track to jobs in the civil service and the country's political power structure.

⁜

On a flight from Ottawa to Vancouver, a Trinity Western official got a confidential tip from his seatmate: an historic mansion in Ottawa was going on the market for a song. For Don Page, the dean of graduate studies at the university, the news was the answer to a decade-old prayer. A former Ottawa mandarin, Page had been lured to Trinity Western to groom a new generation of Christians for the federal public service—a determination fuelled, in part, by his own disenchantment. As a senior policy adviser in the External Affairs Department, stickhandling international crises, he had been appalled when some of the country's most promising young diplomats were caught smuggling contraband and accepting bribes. "These were not stupid people," he recalls, "but they didn't see anything wrong with what they were doing. In fact, they'd rationalize it: 'You aren't paying us enough so we have to make money on the side.'"

To Page, who had started a Bible study group at External Affairs and inspired prayer cells in thirty other departments under the Public Service Christian Fellowship, there was only one solution: to enlist more people of faith in the government. "I realized we had to find a better class of public servant," he says, "and Trinity Western was the only university that was committed to doing something about it."

But for more than a decade after his arrival, as he lectured on servant leadership in every faculty and laid the groundwork for a master's
degree in the subject, Page had watched the essential ingredient of his
scheme—a hands-on internship program in Ottawa—bog down in a
bizarre tangle of interprovincial red tape. He was ready to shelve his
dream when he got the news that the Metcalfe Street mansion built by
J. R. Booth, the lumber baron who had supplied the timber for the
original Parliament Buildings, had been put up for sale by the dwin-
dling membership of the elite Laurentian Club. Not only was it an ideal
location for Trinity Western's interns, it was an architectural gem—a
certified national historical site which would give the obscure western
university a prestigious satellite campus in the capital.

In March 2001, Trinity Western took possession of its new Laurentian
Leadership Centre for less than $2 million, only to discover that there
was a reason for the bargain basement price: the mansion was a tony
ruin. The roof was a sieve and the rest of the structure had to be gutted,
every inch of plumbing and wiring replaced. The hand-carved wood
panelling stank from a fish left mouldering in the commercial kitchen,
and a decontamination unit had to excavate the backyard where a
buried oil tank had leaked its toxic contents. But for Page, the million-
dollar renovation became a labour of love. In the summer of 2002, he
and his wife camped out in Ottawa with an interior decorator to put
the finishing touches on the restoration, polishing the mansion's eight
marble fireplaces and its antique sterling silver sconces, even hand-
washing all two hundred crystal pendants in the giant chandelier that
Booth had given his daughter as a wedding present. "There were a lot
of things I was involved in that weren't academic," he admits with a
sheepish grin.

Still, it wasn't those palatial digs alone that turned the Laurentian
Leadership Centre into an unprecedented evangelical training ground.
Contacting MPs and former colleagues across the capital's bureaucracy,
Page rustled up three-month unpaid internships that have become the

envy of other student programs in the capital. Under the contracts he drafted, every intern receives a semester's worth of real work writing speeches or policy papers with no fear of being used as a glorified secretary.

In September 2002, the centre's first class of twenty-three students fanned out to assignments in almost every government department and key capital power centres like the *Ottawa Citizen* and the Royal Canadian Mounted Police. Nearly a dozen found themselves on the staff of MPs, including Stephen Harper and Stockwell Day, and two of their most eager bosses were Chuck Strahl and Diane Ablonczy, both of whom are Trinity Western alumni. So intent was Page that his charges make a good impression, he gave them tutorials on etiquette and office dress codes. Not that he was worried they would show up for work nursing hangovers: for once, Trinity Western's moral code was a plus. "They recognized they were going to get a student with strong moral values," he says. "That's what every MP wanted to know: can I trust this student with documents?"

To run the centre, Page enlisted Paul Wilson, who had arrived in Ottawa in 1994 to work as director of research for Preston Manning's Reform Party, and stayed on to perform the same duties for Stockwell Day. Later, Wilson would serve as senior policy adviser for one of the most hard-line evangelicals in Harper's new government, former justice minister Vic Toews. But before he left the Laurentian Leadership Centre for that post, he helped organize Manning's first Ottawa conference on faith and politics, coaching the newly elected crop of evangelicals in Harper's caucus on how to navigate the pitfalls facing Christians in public life. At the time, Wilson was furious at press reports that compared the Laurentian Leadership Centre to Patrick Henry College. "This is not a political training program," he told the *Ottawa Citizen*. "It's about understanding citizenship and faith." Not everyone at the paper appears to have accepted that disclaimer. "Onward Christian soldiers," read the headline, hinting that, like

Michael Farris, Wilson was bent on grooming Canada's own Joshua generation for government. "Evangelicals are mobilizing in Ottawa to put their stamp on public policy and opinion."

✢

At 8:20 on a Wednesday morning in October 2007, students litter the magnificent, main-floor salons of the Laurentian Leadership Centre, some sprawled on damask sofas under priceless antique tapestries, others straggling out of the eat-in kitchen, a dazzling mix of marble and stainless steel that could pass for an upscale Italian café. But as the clock strikes the half hour, they scramble up the panelled staircase to an ornate conference room for that day's class on politics and government. Janet Epp Buckingham, who has replaced Paul Wilson as the centre's executive director, opens with a reading from the book of Joshua, whose hero led the Israelites across the Jordan River to conquer Jericho. "We have an example of some pretty serious leadership here," Buckingham observes. "Joshua is the guy who gets things done. He got a very clear message from God and the Bible says people followed Joshua without hesitation."

As she points out, the same could not be said about the two prime ministers whom her students are profiling that day. Matt Pasiuk, a business major from Abbotsford who has spent his entire academic life in Christian schools, is upbeat about his subject, Brian Mulroney, praising him for the Free Trade Agreement with the U.S. while slamming his imposition of the "horrendous" Goods and Services Tax. But Pasiuk seems hazy on the failed Meech Lake Accord—"It's a bit over my head," he says—and he makes no mention of the corruption charges then hanging over Mulroney, a lapse that Buckingham chooses to leave unexplored.

Reporting on Kim Campbell's ill-fated four months in power, Irene Cadrin, a political-science student from northern Alberta, appears to view the country's only female prime minister with undisguised scorn. "She's very popular among the feminist movement in Canada," Cadrin says in a tone that makes clear this is not a desirable distinction. "She's their poster girl." Cadrin barely mentions Campbell's tenure as justice minister, but notes that when she was in the B.C. legislature, she fought restrictions on abortion and has the most "complicated" marital situation of any prime minister. "She was married once, she was married twice, then she didn't bother to get married again," Cadrin says, making no attempt to mask her disapproval.

Only weeks earlier, the *National Post* had run a flattering, full-page profile of the Laurentian Leadership Centre, celebrating it as a new haven for the "sharpest edge of intellectual evangelical Christianity," but on the day I visit there is little evidence of that acuity. If this is history filtered through a biblical worldview, it is a version that seems hopelessly skewed by conservative bias and a marked disregard for the facts. When students refer to the *Toronto Star* as "the Red Star" and deride Canada as a "welfare state," I feel as if I've stumbled into the ornate clubhouse of some fresh-faced relics from the Reagan era.

That impression only deepens after a mid-morning break when Buckingham steers the discussion to the Charter of Rights, her own legal specialty. As the former chief counsel of the Evangelical Fellowship, she had been one of the leading advocates for the Christian right and, during the incendiary same-sex marriage debate, she won a reputation as a reasonable and nuanced voice. Today, however, Buckingham makes little attempt to temper the arguments of her students who, almost without exception, slam the Charter as "bad" or "frightening" and a threat to evangelical Christians. Decrying the fact that the courts "have gone too far on social issues," she notes that religion in Canada has been "privatized," as she puts it, which turns out to mean that it has been banished from the public sphere.

Sitting in on the discussion, it seems no wonder that critics see the centre as an elite finishing school for Harper's Conservatives. Every class has been invited to a photo session with the prime minister, and his office has hosted at least one intern each semester. Despite the centre's repeated insistence that it is non-partisan, a seven-year review of its internships shows that, of the fifty-one MPs who employed students, forty-two were Conservatives—most of them evangelicals. It's a critique for which the students themselves are well prepared. "Sometimes I can see people trying to paint us as a Conservative breeding ground," Matt Pasiuk volunteers, unasked, after class. "But there's a lot of different views here. In the halls or at dinner time, there are some pretty interesting arguments about things like abortion and same-sex marriage."

Pasiuk's internship with his Conservative MP, Ed Fast, whose daughter was a friend back in Abbotsford, convinced him he would never want a career in politics, but for others, the experience has opened coveted doors. Matthew Laine had never set foot in Ottawa before he arrived at the centre, but, interning with the Green Party, he discovered an organization in chaos where he could carve out his own niche. After two weeks helping out in a cliff-hanger of a provincial campaign, he felt "totally empowered. I was calling these bureaucrats all over Ontario on behalf of candidates to get them registered," he says. "It was pretty cool." Laine snagged a seat on the party's youth council, and months after graduating from Trininty Western, he landed the Greens' nomination in the B.C. riding of Delta-Richmond East, where he racked up 8 percent of the 2008 vote. A year later, he ran in the provincial election, and he argues that a Green Party candidacy is consistent with his faith. "If you want to be a Christian, you need to be a good steward of the planet," he says. Still he admits his wariness of hyper-righteous rhetoric. "I say, prove to me you're a Christian," Laine says. "It can't be just a now-and-then thing. That's why the pro-life movement bugs me. It's okay to be pro-life, but I say, 'Be pro all life—be pro the homeless guy, not just pro-fetus.'"

With those views, Laine admits he was the ideological odd man out at the centre—"pretty much the token liberal," he says. Many alumni have gone on to work for Conservative MPs or cabinet members, and Jared Kuehl, a graduate of the Laurentian Leadership Centre's first class, went straight from university to a job in the issues management branch of Harper's office. Another graduate, Mark Penninga, has taken another sort of political path. After an internship with Conservative MP Maurice Vellacott, Penninga landed a job as a spokesman for Focus on the Family Canada before founding his own Christian nationalist lobby, the Association for Reformed Political Action (ARPA), backed by the country's Reformed churches. Announcing its arrival on the political scene, he threw a Parliament Hill seminar for MPs co-hosted by Vellacott and the Liberals' leading evangelical, John McKay, which featured a lecture from a respected Christian Reformed theologian entitled "God and Government: A Biblical Perspective on the Role of the State." While the seminar was an exercise in gentility, ARPA's website is less so. "Canada is perishing—both physically and spiritually—because we have turned our back on God," it declares. One of the main objects of its wrath is the Corren agreement, which Penninga paints as a threat to religious freedom. "In the name of tolerance," he argues, "tolerance is being thrown out the window."

Was this then what Don Page envisaged for the country's Joshua generation? Page answers by recounting a moment when, watching the proceedings of a parliamentary committee on television, he noticed three familiar figures in the front row. All were Laurentian Leadership Centre graduates, researching departmental policy papers or speeches for MPs. "Where else do we see another university having such a positive influence?" he beams. "I'm hearing that our students are the people MPs want to hire in their offices."

At least thirty of the centre's young Christian soldiers have won jobs in Ottawa's permanent policy-making apparatus and every semester produces new recruits. That is no mean accomplishment at a time when the federal civil service is facing an imminent labour crisis, aging faster than the general population, with one-third of its members due for retirement within the next decade. Nor is it a development that Stephen Harper would frown upon. Before he was prime minister, Harper railed against the liberalism of the civil service, and Trinity Western is not alone in attempting to help him reverse that tilt. More than a dozen well-regarded Christian colleges and universities now exist in this country, and the Conservatives are quietly fostering their growth. When economic stimulus funds were being doled out, Harper funneled more than $26 million their way, including $2.6 million to Trinity Western—a windfall that was announced by Conservative MP Mark Warawa, a TWU alumnus himself.

What effect those graduates will have on Canadian politics remains to be seen, but as Page recalled from his experience with the Public Service Christian Fellowship, it doesn't take huge numbers to get things done on Parliament Hill. He once managed to solve an overseas crisis with phone calls to senior bureaucrats he knew from departmental prayer cells, and he credits the backstage intercessions of a handful of evangelical mandarins with convincing cabinet ministers to take a stand on tobacco advertising. "In today's society, there are important issues and Christians have a role to play," he says. "I think our students are already influencing the thinking of government."

THE ELECTRONIC PULPIT

VIII

He lopes to the stage in front of the Parliament Buildings, a ruddy, square-jawed giant whose face is as familiar to conservative Christians as the family-room TV set and iconic enough to make heads turn. Even in his seventies, David Mainse still radiates the unmistakable wattage of Canada's only real televangelical superstar. Scores of other preachers have used television as an electronic pulpit, but Mainse was one of the first to grasp its power in bringing the intimacy of the faith experience to the country's most remote living rooms. In 1962, he and his wife Norma-Jean forked over fifty-five dollars to a small-town Ontario TV station for their first live broadcast, a late-night slot after the eleven o'clock news. Fifteen years later, they converted that on-air audition into a full-time television ministry with *100 Huntley Street*, the daily talk show that turned Mainse into the patriarch of Canadian religious broadcasting and spawned his multi-million-dollar Crossroads Christian Communications empire. Today, *100 Huntley Street* ranks as one of the longest-running shows on this country's airwaves, outlasted only by *Hockey Night in Canada* and Canadian Football League telecasts, with more than two million Canadian viewers and almost as many in the U.S., where Mainse was once hailed as a possible successor to televangelist Jim Bakker. So secure did he deem his legacy that, in 2003, he handed the show and much of the Crossroads domain over to his sons Ron and Reynold, retiring to assume a self-styled role as the country's "spiritual statesman."

Now, as Faytene Kryskow hands him the microphone at the 2008 edition of TheCRY, her daylong fast and prayer rally on Parliament Hill, she hails him as one of her "spiritual fathers," and Mainse seems only too happy to play the part. "You know, a friend of mine, a union leader, says the world belongs to those who show up at the meetings," he tells the crowd of young conservative Christians. "It's time the people of God showed up to the meetings, whether it's a school board or a riding association." With a federal election less than two months away, Mainse's call to political activism could not have been more timely, and as a violin wails over the loudspeakers, he instructs his listeners to gaze up at the second-storey windows of Stephen Harper's office, focusing their prayer vibes on the need for anti-abortion legislation. "God, we pray for our prime minister to have great courage to protect the little ones in the womb," he cries out, breaking into the tears that have become his onscreen signature. "Please convict those who oppose it of sin and unrighteousness," he sobs. "Help them to know they've got to live with their consciences."

For Mainse, Kryskow's Ottawa rally is a trip down memory lane. Three decades earlier, he had assembled five thousand Christian faithful on these grounds for a live telecast of *100 Huntley Street* that included politicians from every party and Prime Minister Pierre Trudeau. It was only one stop on a televised twenty-five-city tour that he christened a "Salute to Canada," but it was not an entirely original initiative: a year earlier, America's most prominent televangelists had summoned 250,000 evangelicals to the U.S. capital for a "Washington for Jesus" rally that put the religious right on the map. Cynics dismissed Mainse's copycat exercise in Christian patriotism as a public-relations ploy designed to boost his bid for the country's first satellite network licence, then pending before the CRTC, but his "Salute to Canada" had the opposite effect. At a time when the U.S. religious right was regarded with fear and loathing in this country, Mainse's network application was rejected by the CRTC, which would refuse to issue a licence to any English-language faith group, either on radio or television, for more than a decade.

That ban on religious broadcasting may be the single most important reason why Canadian evangelicals have lagged behind their American brethren in both numbers and political clout—a restriction that has put the CRTC at the top of the Christian right's hit list and prompted the Evangelical Fellowship of Canada to demand changes in the country's telecommunications policy. As scholars have amply documented, the on-air cheerleading of televangelists like Jerry Falwell and Pat Robertson played a pivotal role in making the religious right the dominant voice of the new conservative movement that was unleashed by the Reagan revolution in the 1980s. In his 1978 book, *The Emerging Order*, economist Jeremy Rifkin noted that, with their unparalleled access to mass telecommunications, American evangelicals possessed "a base of potential power that dwarfs every other competing interest in society today." Driven by their need to solicit on-air donations, they created massive data banks that provided the contact lists essential to political organizing, but as Rifkin pointed out, those burgeoning Christian broadcasting empires were not interested only in swelling Republican ranks. Their aim was far more ambitious: "to build a total Christian community."

Five years after the publication of Rifkin's book, Gary North, a Texas economist and Christian Reconstructionist, drafted the guidelines for doing just that. In *The Tactics of Christian Resistance*, he laid out a six-point action plan on how to remake America into a nation governed by biblical principles. One of the key levers of power he stressed—along with education and political mobilization—was the creation of independent Christian satellite and cable networks.

In Canada, where the CRTC's regulatory restrictions barred any such development, not all evangelicals were as patient as Mainse, who circumvented the commission's veto of his satellite scheme by quietly cobbling together his corporate communications conglomerate, one syndication deal at a time. But if he had no appetite for confronting the government's enforced secularization of the airwaves, a band of renegade Pentecostals in Alberta did not have the same reservations, tackling the CRTC's ban on religious broadcasting with a bravado that some commentators found distinctly un-Canadian.

⁜

It is, to say the least, an unlikely site for a broadcasting rebellion: an angular mass of red brick under a blue metal roof plunked down in a remote pasture on the outskirts of Lethbridge. But it was here, on Alberta's Highway 3, just across from Marshall Auto Wreckers' yard, that a clandestine transmitter hidden inside a closet in a half-finished church put Canada's first Christian television station on the airwaves. That unlicensed 1986 broadcast was the brainchild of George Hill, the senior pastor of Victory Christian Fellowship, who gambled that Ottawa wouldn't risk incurring Western wrath by clamping down on a breakaway prairie congregation just trying to spread the gospel's Good News.

For Hill and his wife, Hazel, the founders of the Victory Church movement, it was only one of countless rolls of the dice in an improbable evangelizing career built largely on faith and chutzpah. He was a gregarious British-born electrician and she was a drop-dead gorgeous brunette from Australia who had decided to work her way around the world as a hairdresser. When they met in a northern Ontario mining town, they were instantly smitten by the kind of chemistry that tends to produce spontaneous combustions, but eighteen months and one daughter later, their fights had become so volatile that they agreed the only solution was to split up.

He took to the road again and she moved west to Vancouver, leaving no forwarding address. There, a friend invited her to Saint Margaret's

Reformed Episcopal Church, where Pastor Bob Birch, who would go on to found Watchmen for the Nations, had become a magnet for the 1970s Jesus freaks. At one of Birch's standing-room-only services, Hazel pledged her life to Christ. "My search for real love was over," she would write in her memoirs, although she hadn't entirely given up on the temporal variety. A month later, she had just sent up a prayer for a man in her life when the telephone rang. It was George Hill, who had decided to search for her in the Vancouver phone book. "I had prayed for a man," she said later, "but I never thought I'd get the old one back."

Starting over, the Hills moved to Lethbridge, where he landed an electrical contracting job and she found work in a beauty salon. When he, too, was saved, they began a weekly Bible study group that soon outgrew their rural ranch house, and on Mother's Day 1979, they held their first service for two dozen friends and neighbours in a nearby hall. Over the next three years, the Hills spent their nights taking correspondence courses for their ministry credentials as word spread about their lively brand of charismatic worship and miracle cures. When their first mass baptism, held in a friend's backyard swimming pool, made the front page of the *Lethbridge Herald*, their congregation swiftly outgrew the space they had rented in a high-school gymnasium, then three ballrooms at the Sandman Inn and the local labour hall. They bought an abandoned downtown church only to find themselves fielding complaints about the noise levels of their freewheeling services and the unholy shouts that split the air whenever they were engaged in banishing demons. Finally, a member of the congregation tipped them off about a forty-three-acre lot for sale east of town and they grabbed it, drafting plans for a $3-million complex that would include a school, day-care centre and television studio. Now, three decades later, that redbrick complex is the cornerstone of Victory Churches International, a Calgary-based movement with 1,700 churches in dozens of countries, including Kenya and Thailand, that also spawned Brian Rushfeldt's family-values lobby, the Canada Family Action Coalition.

But for George Hill, church-planting was only part of a grander plan to carry out Christ's Great Commission to reach every unsaved soul by every available means. As he saw it, one of those means was the God-given gift of telecommunications technology that his idol Pat Robertson had already employed to considerable effect in Virginia, turning a der-elict UHF channel into the Christian Broadcasting Network (CBN), the fifth largest cable network in the U.S. Setting out to emulate Robertson's feat in Canada, Hill was furious to discover that, for more than fifty years, the CRTC and its predecessors had blocked all applications from single-faith groups for religious media licences. He had no intention of complying with a policy that he saw as evidence of the government's anti-Christian bias.

When a new parishioner told him that an enterprising type back home in Grande Prairie, Alberta, had set up a giant satellite dish to suck in contraband signals from California's Trinity Broadcasting Network (TBN), Hill saw his opening. His flock didn't blanch at the prospect of turning their church into a pirate broadcaster and devoting the take from one Sunday's collection plate to the project, they raised a whopping twenty thousand dollars, more than enough to cover equip-ment costs. Once the electronic infrastructure was in place, the chief expense was a twenty-dollar-a-month hydro bill—no pesky Canadian content required—since TBN's founders, bejewelled televangelists Jan and Paul Crouch, were happy to supply their signal free to fellow Pentecostals who might respond to their on-air appeals for "love gifts" during the network's frequent Praise-a-Thons.

In the midst of a February blizzard, Hill's associate pastor Dick Dewert—or De Weert as he was still known in those days—offered a prayer of dedication, then flicked the switch on the ten-watt transmit-ter in Victory's half-finished sanctuary, sending out TBN's pirated signal from a thirty-metre antenna outside the back door. The recep-tion was as snowy as the weather, but suddenly the citizenry of Lethbridge could tune in to the high-glitz gospel broadcast from TBN's rococo Orange County studios twenty-four hours a day, from the teary hallelujahs of Jimmy Swaggart to the eyelash-batting chatter of that still-blissful duo, Jim and Tammy Faye Bakker. Having access to that brand of Christian fare was essential, Dewert argued, if Canada was to "experience a significant spiritual breakthrough."

When the CRTC got wind of Victory's retransmissions, it issued a cease-and-desist order that Hill and Dewert ignored. Their gamble paid off: the commission didn't want to be seen prosecuting a breakaway prairie church, and lacked any real powers of enforcement. But three years later, when the Hills raised another pirate antenna on the roof of a new Victory church in Medicine Hat, the signal accidentally bled into a hockey game on the local cable channel, interrupting a tense face-off between Calgary and Edmonton with shouts of "Praise the Lord!" The objections echoed all the way to CRTC headquarters outside Ottawa, and the Hills received another cease-and-desist order, this one hand-delivered by two sombre federal bureaucrats. Tearing open the envelope, Hill scanned the threat of exorbitant fines and possible jail time. "I said, 'Go ahead,'" he recalls taunting them. "It would be the best advertisement I have ever had!'"

By 1992, when half a dozen other stations were brazenly beaming TBN rebroadcasts across the prairies, CRTC chairman Keith Spicer realized that the commission's inaction had become a national joke. Increasingly, the media cast the outlaw Christian broadcasters as electronic Davids battling a stern regulatory Goliath. When a federal official insisted that "even God has to apply to the CRTC," the pirates invoked a higher authority—the Charter of Rights—and muttered about taking their fight to the Supreme Court. It was no idle threat. George Hill had enlisted the support of Pat Robertson, who devoted a CBN special to the plight of Canada's persecuted Christian broadcasters and dispatched high-priced help: Jay Sekulow, the formidable constitutional attorney who headed Robertson's answer to the American Civil Liberties Union: the American Center for Law and Justice. In Ottawa, Sekulow recruited four lawyers to set up the Canadian equivalent of his legal defence group and began building a court challenge against the CRTC for violating Christians' constitutional rights.

In October 1991, when Spicer summoned the unlicenced operators to an Edmonton hearing, Dick Dewert greeted the prospect of a showdown with relish. "I take no pleasure in breaking the law," he told the *Lethbridge Herald*, warning that he intended to prove the CRTC had been "blatantly discriminating" against Christians' freedom of expression. Spicer had assured his fellow commissioners that they had nothing to worry about beyond a few unflattering headlines, but to his astonishment, more than a thousand irate evangelicals showed up with their children in tow, waving placards that read, "Say No to CRTC dictatorship" and "CRTC biased and intolerant toward religion." Inside, the tribunal erupted into a revival-style protest, complete with hymns, shouted snatches of Scripture and an atmosphere so raucous that the commission had to call in security. "It was lively to say the least," recalls Nick Ketchum, the CRTC's former director of television policy. "It brought to the commission's attention that there was a big constituency out there that was frankly pissed off—and not likely to disappear anytime soon."

Shaken, the CRTC panel retreated to Ottawa for closed-door consultations. Ten days later, a letter from Spicer to a Lethbridge MP was leaked to the *Ottawa Citizen*: "The commission," Spicer wrote, "is now considering a re-examination of its policy regarding religious broadcasting."

⁜

At CRTC headquarters, the mere mention of Jimmy Swaggart and his preacherly ilk made Keith Spicer's blood boil. "I couldn't stand that stuff and neither could any of my colleagues," he admits now in a phone interview. "We saw all that as shoddy, manipulative and dishonest broadcasting. We had stories of these guys calling up people on the day they got their pension cheques. They were quite obviously preying on weak, vulnerable people."

Still, it wasn't the commission's personal tastes that had kept Christians from owning a slice of the Canadian broadcasting pie. It was a volatile history dating back to the 1920s, when a dozen denominations set up their own wireless ministries, often denouncing rivals in terms so vitriolic they made today's shock jocks sound like choirboys. So inflammatory was some of their on-air slagging that, in 1928, William Lyon Mackenzie King's cabinet revoked the licence of the International Bible Students Association, the precursor to today's Jehovah's Witnesses, for attacking the government and the Roman Catholic Church as satanic institutions. Nor did it help that Father Charles Coughlin, the Hamilton-born priest known as the pioneer of hate radio, unleashed his pre-war rants against Jews from a thirty-station network headquartered just across the border in Michigan. When Ottawa finally codified its control over the country's airwaves in the original Broadcasting Act, the spectre of that intolerance haunted Canadian regulators. No matter how powerful "Bible Bill" Aberhart and Ernest Manning became on their paid-time Sunday broadcasts, no single-faith group, Christian or otherwise, would be granted the right to own an English-language radio or television station for nearly half a century. At the CRTC, what the commissioners liked to call "balance" became the prevailing regulatory obsession.

Even when the commission partially relented in 1987, a year after Victory's pirate broadcasts began, the exception it made was for Vision TV, a multi-faith channel expressly designed to meet that requirement. In its mandate, Vision expressly guaranteed that every claim to the ultimate spiritual truth would be granted equal air time. But to conservative Christians, offering every religion an equal voice was tantamount to saying they all guranteed an equal road to salvation— outright blasphemy and a rejection of Christ's insistence in John 14:6: "I am the way, the truth, and the life: no man cometh unto the Father, but by me."

In 1992, with a round of CRTC hearings on religious broadcasting looming in Ottawa, Dewert and a handful of his counterparts created the National Christian Broadcasting Association to confront the government with a united voice. As chairman, they chose Willard Thiessen, a grandfatherly Winnipeg televangelist who had launched his syndicated talk show, *It's a New Day*, sixteen years earlier. But the undisputed star of their inaugural press conference was David Mainse, who lost no time conveying his thoughts about the commission's preoccupation with ecumenical programming. "Each channel or radio signal does not have to have the balance," he thundered. "We're talking about an exclusive Bible-believing channel here."

Before the hearings opened, the CRTC was inundated with a record 2,600 written submissions and 56 petitions from witnesses who asked to appear, including a request from James Dobson's U.S. radio ministry, Focus on the Family, which had more than a passing interest in opening up the Canadian airwaves. But compared to the circus that had unfolded in Edmonton, the Ottawa hearings were a model of decorum. Now that Dewert and his fellow evangelicals had snagged Spicer's attention, they were on their best behaviour, with nary a Christian protestor in sight.

They were also quick to distance themselves from their American televangelical cousins, who had become not only an embarrassment, but a threat to their regulatory hopes. For the second time in five years, Jimmy Swaggart had been caught with a prostitute, while baby-faced Jim Bakker had been defrocked for cavorting with his receptionist and packed off to prison on twenty-four counts of financial fraud. Those sordid shenanigans were a public-relations disaster for Canada's television preachers, and some, like Mainse, who had been a frequent guest host on Bakker's show, were already paying the price. In 1987, the year the first scandals broke, donations to *100 Huntley Street* plummeted by 40 percent and he was forced to bow out of a planned partnership with Vision TV.

But the most serious threat to a new religious channel came from David Nostbakken, the moving force behind Vision TV, which was still struggling to make ends meet. Despite its lofty interfaith mandate, a quarter of its revenues came from selling air time to U.S. television ministries, and, Nostbakken warned, competition from a new religious channel could deal Vision a death blow. In the end, it was not the bromides from broadcasters or men of God that carried the day. The witness who had the greatest impact on the hearings was a high-school student named Dayna Dixon, the seventeen-year-old daughter of an Ottawa Pentecostal minister, who testified that all she and her siblings wanted when they came home from class was some light-hearted family sitcom or Christian rock, not the bed-hopping sirens of television soap operas or the bleak refrains of Kurt Cobain and gangsta rap. If teens were struggling to resist sexual pressure, she said, the current radio and TV fare made them feel like aliens from another galaxy.

Dixon turned out to have been recruited for her role by her father's friend, Bob Du Broy, who went on to co-found CHRI, Ottawa's Christian hit radio station. But at the CRTC, Nick Ketchum still pegs her testimony as the moment when "Keith had, if you'll forgive the expression, his conversion experience." Spicer himself admits that he was "totally moved" by what she said. "I guess I'm a sentimental fool," he shrugs, "but I thought of my own daughter and I said, 'Let's look at this. Let's listen to these people who are saying there's nothing acceptable for our kids on radio or television.'"

At the commission, Spicer's capitulation caused consternation. His deputy and at least three other commissioners—including Bev Oda, a former TV Ontario (TVO) executive who would become a member of Stephen Harper's cabinet—were dead set against opening the airwaves to televangelists. After months of debate, Spicer finally cast the deciding ballot that broke their deadlock. Announcing the commission's first religious broadcasting policy, he was uncharacteristically defensive, depicting it as a "Canadian-style compromise" and underlining its demands for strict fundraising rules and the inclusion of other faith views. Horrified by the ethnic massacres then bloodying Bosnia, six of Spicer's fellow commissioners issued a dissenting opinion, warning that such licences could "promote social, cultural and racial intolerance which is often rooted in religious intolerance."

Across the country, however, Christian communities cheered the CRTC's about-face. David Mainse and Willard Thiessen rushed in applications for the country's first single-faith television licence, but once again the commission caught the broadcasting community by surprise. Instead of choosing either one of those veterans—both of whom boasted ample financing and a two-decade track record of producing their own shows—the CRTC awarded the first over-the-air religious TV rights to Victory Christian Fellowship, the ringleader of the country's pirate broadcasters. At the Victory complex outside Lethbridge, Dick Dewert and his staff were watching the O.J. Simpson trial on the office television set when the CRTC's call came in—the first of countless developments that earned the Miracle Channel its name.

To some critics, the commission's decision was nothing short of perverse. After months of heaping scorn on the excesses of American televangelists, Spicer and company had licenced the one group guaranteed to adopt their high-pressure fundraising strategies. The Miracle Channel's business plan allowed for no commercial advertising, and as a registered religious charity, its only revenues came from donations and the sale of air time to other ministries, most of them U.S. televangelists trolling for donors themselves. So strapped for cash was the organization that Dewert had to buy four hours on a Lethbridge cable channel for a telethon just to meet its start-up budget. Despite those hurdles, in the midst of a blizzard in January 1996, a studio aide held up a hand-lettered cardboard sign reading CJIL—the call letters for Christ Jesus Is Lord—and Lethbridge's channel 17 burst onto the air with a Sunday-night service from Victory Christian Fellowship.

Later, on the Miracle Channel's flagship talk show, *LifeLine*, Dick and Joan Dewert regaled viewers with a litany of the miracles that proved their venture had divine sanction: just when they feared they could never afford to put the channel on the air, a stranger had walked into their offices with a $50,000 cheque. Then when the deal for their new studios was about to fall through, a Regina businessman called out of the blue, offering to wire them $250,000. But one particular miracle reported over Christian wire services was not the sort that Dewert liked to recall: during a 1999 telethon, he claimed God had suddenly planted a gold tooth in his mouth. When his dentist surfaced to dispute the claims, pointing out that he had installed the gold filling ten years earlier, Dewert recanted, calling it "an honest mistake." He explained that he'd been carried away by reports of gold dust and jewels inexplicably materializing among a group of American Pentecostals—a rationale that was as implausible as it was telling: increasingly, Dewert's infatuation with the Christian broadcasting scene in the U.S. put him at loggerheads with the CRTC.

In 2002, when his licence first came up for renewal, the commission was so furious with the Miracle Channel's failure to meet basic balance and Canadian-content requirements that it put the station on a two-and-a-half year probation and, in a blistering reprimand, threatened to pull the plug entirely. "The future of CJIL weighs in the balance," its decision read, warning that the channel's licence could be revoked or its signal confined to the rural regions of southern Alberta "indefinitely." But by the time the probationary period was up, the commissioners seemed mollified and renewed the Miracle Channel's licence for a full seven-year term.

No sooner had officials at the channel breathed a sigh of relief than they faced a new threat: a series of complaints unlike any the CRTC had dealt with before. Each was meticulously documented, accusing Dewert and his on-air fundraisers of eliciting donations by promising viewers answers to their prayers about life-threatening illnesses or financial ruin if only they coughed up a contribution. All of the complaints came from the same address: a post-office box in Humboldt, Saskatchewan, where Keith Spicer's worst fears about religious broadcasting were being realized.

⸎

Tim Thibault can still recall the day when the Miracle Channel finally flashed onto his television screen. A self-taught technology whiz, he had moved to Humboldt in the winter of 1998, recruited by the town's only hospital to upgrade its computers in case the apocalyptic predictions of the Y2K scare came true. By the time his contract was up, the new millennium had dawned without incident, and he and his wife Marina decided to stay in the prosperous farming town east of Saskatoon. When the Miracle Channel won a berth on their satellite service, they were convinced the decision was preordained. "This was the first Christian—Godly—channel we could get," he says. "It fit with our belief system."

Thibault set up a new company to create a centralized database for Saskatchewan's health care system, but two years later, provincial officials nixed the scheme. By then, his savings were running out, but he cashed in his RRSPs to start another high-tech venture called PTL Systems, whose initials—in a sly nod to Jim Bakker's Praise the Lord club—stood for Thibault's co-founders, Pedro, Tim and the Lord. To Thibault, it seemed only natural to name God as a business partner. Raised a Roman Catholic, he'd once traded in religion for rock 'n' roll, touring the West with his own band in a booze and drug-fuelled haze until a friend had dragged him to a Regina Pentecostal church. "For the first time in my life, people were genuinely concerned with who I was," he recalls. "I fell hook, line and sinker and promised a hundred-and-eighty-degree turn-around." Becoming a lay pastor, he had intended to start a Humboldt branch of the church, but instead, he and his wife became avid members of the Miracle Channel's electronic congregation, watching up to eight hours a day. "We were Miracle Channel junkies," he admits. "It was like a daily heroin fix."

They came to regard Dick and Joan Dewert as family, but the Dewerts were by no means the only draw. Tuning in to the Miracle Channel meant hooking up with the top names in American televangelism, including Kenneth Copeland, Creflo Dollar and Benny Hinn, all of whom, like the Dewerts, preached the prosperity gospel. That theological movement, sometimes known as the "Word of Faith" or the "name-it-and-claim-it" school, was founded by a folksy Oklahoma pastor named Kenneth Hagin based on his particular reading of Galatians 6:7: "For whatsoever a man soweth, that shall he also reap." In dozens of books, with titles like *How to Write Your Own Ticket with God* and *You Can Have What You Say!*, Hagin insisted that God wanted his followers to be blessed with material wealth—all they had to do was cultivate positive thoughts and contribute generously to the collection plate. Mainstream theologians have dismissed the concept as the product of a bizarre, even heretical, misreading of the Scriptures, but their objections have failed to tarnish its allure. The followers of the prosperity gospel that Hagin begat became the fastest-growing segment of evangelical Christianity and his message the dominant theme of the electronic church.

Some scholars blame its growth on a 1960 decision by the Federal Communications Commission, which allowed U.S. broadcasters to charge religious groups for air time. As a result, most American mainline denominations decided to bow out of television, preferring to put their money into bricks and mortar, but those Pentecostals who saw themselves as the heirs of the old-time tent revivalists had no hesitation about turning to the new electronic big top or shilling for donations to fund their on-air evangelizing. When Pat Robertson announced that he needed ten dollars from seven hundred viewers or else his fledgling station would go off the air, his *700 Club* was born. Some televangelists like Robertson and Paul Crouch became so wealthy they bought or built networks of their own, and to viewers, their lavish lifestyles bore witness to the apparent payoffs of the prosperity gospel. In Lethbridge, George and Hazel Hill became apostles of Hagin, but they were not the only Canadians who bought into the early Word of Faith boom. By 1979, the year the Hills founded their first Victory church in Lethbridge, Canadians were already sending $15 million a year to televangelists, more than half of it to those south of the border.

While most mainline Protestants recoil at the first hint of a financial pitch from a silver-tongued man of the cloth, the Thibaults felt no such reservations. "We were already on the same theological track," Tim explains. They knew the scriptural code of the prosperity gospel—"sow a seed for your need"—and they embraced it with fervour, pledging automatic deductions of thirty dollars a month from their bank account as Miracle Channel "partners." During the channel's periodic Partner Weeks, they called in extra donations to the station's glass-walled phone banks, where a team of volunteers prayed over huge bowls of pink telethon chits in what the Dewerts called their "war room." Thibault was elated when Joan Dewert read out the prayer request that accompanied one of his pledges. "Tim from Humboldt, Saskatchewan, is calling," she announced. "He says, 'Pray for my company; it's struggling.'" Clutching the prayer chit, she closed her eyes as if receiving a telephathic communication. "Tim," she said, "your company is no longer struggling."

In fact, PTL Systems was in desperate straits. Thibault was nearly fifty thousand dollars in debt, maxed out on his credit cards and hounded by the bank, but like some compulsive poker addict, he was afraid not to gamble on one more donation: after all, if he wasn't prospering, maybe it was because he hadn't given enough. "We no longer had any money for ourselves and our kids were going hungry," he says, "but we were so sold on this that we actually had other family members contributing on our behalf." Nor was the Miracle Channel the only beneficiary of the Thibaults' generosity. They sent cheques to Kenneth Copeland and Benny Hinn, and when Missouri spitfire Joyce Meyer came to Saskatoon, they drove into town to hear her—an outing that cost more than one hundred dollars. Thibault detested Meyer's wise-cracking homilies, but he didn't dare risk God's wrath by snubbing her offering call. "When that collection plate comes around," he explains, "you want to be part of it." Now he sees a divine purpose in those years of misguided magnanimity. "God was causing us to fall into a deeper and deeper rut," he explains, "until we woke up and realized we'd been duped."

It was then that Thibault began phoning the Miracle Channel, demanding theological justification for its claims. Soon, the station's operators started refusing his calls. He picketed an appearance by Dewert at Regina's Apostolic Church and organized Under the Son Ministries for other disillusioned donors who began meeting in his home. "It was almost like Alcoholics Anonymous," he says. "There was a lot of de-programming that had to go on."

Using his high-tech talents, Thibault mounted a website called the Miracle Channel Review, prompting letters from CJIL's lawyer that threatened to sue him for copyright infringement and demanded he take the site down. Instead, he posted video clips showing the Dewerts and their telethon guests drumming up donations with questionable come-ons. In November 2004, Thibault filed a formal complaint with the CRTC, attaching footage of guest host Bill Prankard, an avuncular Ottawa evangelist who ran a bikers' ministry and sat on the Miracle Channel's board. "There is somebody right now watching and God is speaking to them about RRSPS," Prankard declared in one prophetic fundraising pitch. "They've got RRSPS and they've got a sizable amount and it's a security thing. Well, it's not a security thing. Your security is in God. And God's speaking to you to cash those in. I dare you to do it."

Another video clip showed Fred Bennett, a Tennessee preacher who headed the Miracle Channel's U.S. operations, urging a businessman facing bankruptcy to donate the last dollars left in his chequing account.

"You're about to lose it all anyway," Bennett counselled, "so you need to sow it into the miracle of the Miracle Channel, and your whole business is going to turn around."

It took the CRTC more than a year to rule on Thibault's complaints. Part of the delay came from the difficulty of weighing pitches couched in the biblical metaphors of the prosperity gospel that couldn't be measured in the same way as Canadian-content hours. But in 2005, the commission ruled that the Miracle Channel had contravened its fundraising guidelines for religious broadcasters, even daring to suggest "divine consequences" if viewers failed to send in a donation. It also ordered the Miracle Channel to come up with its own internal ethics code, an exercise that took nearly a year. By the time the code was okayed in February 2007, Dewert was facing another regulatory showdown. After repeatedly being refused a spot on Alberta's leading cable system, he had applied for religious broadcasting licences in Calgary and Edmonton, but on the morning of the hearing, he woke up to a front-page story in the *Globe and Mail* that recapped the Miracle Channel's questionable fundraising practices. When the CRTC awarded both Alberta licences to David Mainse's Crossroads Communications, one of Dewert's top aides hinted that the *Globe* story must have been planted by the competition; in fact, the piece had been inspired by Dewert's nemesis, Tim Thibault, who had finally been forced to close down his business. In the process, Thibault became a one-man Christian broadcasting watchdog, painstakingly recording every misstep of the country's electronic preachers, although his sights were mainly set on the Miracle Channel. "From conversations with Mr. Thibault," one bureaucrat confided, "I can only conclude that he won't rest until the channel is off the air."

Three months later, that prospect seemed like a distinct possibility. Without warning, Dewert summoned his staff to the station's in-house church and announced he was stepping down after what he termed "a moral failure." Like so many of his American televangelist heroes, he had fallen prey to the temptations of the flesh, confessing to an "adulterous affair" with a married woman who turned out to be a senior employee, but unlike U.S. sex scandals, this one never made national headlines. George Hill flew in from his California retirement, and overnight, all traces of the Dewerts were expunged from the Miracle Channel's walls and website, *LifeLine* yanked off the air. The station's traffic manager declared that Dewert was "on another career path," his whereabouts unknown, but as almost everyone in Lethbridge knew, he was still in town, selling shares in an Alberta real-estate investment firm run by Roy Beyer, another former Victory Fellowship pastor, who had co-founded the Canada Family Action Coalition.

To Tim Thibault, it seemed no surprise that Dewert was being bailed out by his politically connected colleague, who had served as operations director for Stockwell Day and the Defend Marriage campaign. A year earlier, Thibault had asked Revenue Canada to investigate the Miracle Channel's charitable tax status, helpfully providing footage that showed Dewert weighing in with some strong opinions during the 2006 federal election campaign. In one segment from a New Year's Eve special that aired only three weeks before the vote, he decried same-sex marriage legislation as "the greatest betrayal of the Canadian public in the history of the nation" and urged viewers to check out a pro-marriage website for a list of acceptable candidates. While he never came right out and plugged the Conservative Party, it was clear that Dewert was not endorsing the Liberal status quo. "We need to see our nation change," he exhorted viewers. "The goal here is to get a pro-marriage, pro-family Parliament, right?" After Stephen Harper's victory, he implied on another show that his station had played a role. "It's interesting to me that, politically, there has been a change in our nation everywhere the Miracle Channel is," he declared.

But if Dewert had a political agenda, it was not the same one that Thibault or the tax department's auditors had in mind. They were on the hunt for partisan endorsements, not for the pronouncements of the Miracle Channel's guest prophets, urging viewers to transform Canada into a Christian nation with a prophetic role to play in the coming Apocalypse.

⸕

In the soaring steel and glass atrium of the Crossroads Broadcasting Centre outside Burlington, Ontario, the walls depict a simulated Victorian streetscape—the ancient brick of a dry-goods shop here, the pillars of a mock concert hall there—the whole airy space converted into the idealized stage set of an old-time town square. That nostalgic foyer seems an ironic counterpoint to the high-tech studio complex hidden behind its painted façade, a $20-million-telecommunications showplace that David Mainse opened in 1992, with a personal appearance by his pal Pat Robertson, whose *700 Club* had been Mainse's model for *100 Huntley Street*.

At the time, Crossroads seemed golden, already a syndication success story with an overseas mission division and a broadcasting college where foreign students could prepare for careers at the Christian radio and television stations springing up across the developing world. Among Canadian Christian broadcasters, Mainse seemed the only figure capable of turning a television licence into the sort of bully pulpit that Robertson and Jerry Falwell had created in the U.S., and he had not been reluctant to demonstrate that inclination. When critics accused him of aping Falwell with his "Salute to Canada," he was quick to deny the charge. "We're not a Moral Majority type of movement that lobbies politicians on issues," he hastened to reassure Ottawa's wary elite. "What we want to do is . . . lobby God through prayer rather than politics." But his disclaimer seemed less convincing a year later when he led his crew to the U.S. capital for a week-long series entitled "The Maple Leaf Salutes the Stars and Stripes," where he snagged a personal welcome from Ronald Reagan. If that weren't enough to discomfit some in high places, Crossroads erected its own pavilion at Vancouver's 1986 Expo, as if it were a nation unto itself, complete with its own anthem for world peace. Then, with a pivotal referendum on sovereignty looming in Quebec, Mainse launched a hundred-city tour to stump for federal unity, a subject he termed a "burning passion."

Despite such forays into national affairs—or perhaps because of them—Mainse had watched the country's first single-faith TV licence go to the Miracle Channel, a renegade rebroadcaster in an Alberta backwater that couldn't hold a candle to Crossroads' slick, seasoned operations. The snub left him steaming, but some colleagues argued that he ought to regard it as a reverse compliment: clearly, the CRTC had decided to test the risky waters of religious broadcasting far from the country's largest media market, in a place where Mainse's mix of righteous patriotism and charismatic passion couldn't pose a political threat.

He continued to build Crossroads' audience, but it wasn't until 1998 that he finally won the CRTC's okay for a twenty-four-hour television licence. Then, barely five years later, fans were stunned when Mainse suddenly walked away from that windfall. In the summer of 2003, he announced that he was trading in the 100 *Huntley Street* spotlight to hit the road on a personal crusade against same-sex marriage, which he damned as "the most destructive move that any society could make." Christening himself Crossroads' "minister of evangelism and social action," as one press release put it—he denounced the Liberals' prospective legislation from pulpits coast to coast. When the measure finally passed, he was so infuriated he mounted a last-ditch letter-writing campaign to the Queen, begging her to order the Governor General not to grant the bill royal assent. "Our beloved Queen Elizabeth II," he wrote. "Millions have nowhere else to turn but you. Should you act in this, millions of us would surely become more fervent supporters of the monarchy than ever." Not surprisingly perhaps, Buckingham Palace declined to provoke a constitutional crisis in return for a few more far-flung royalists, but even after same-sex matrimony became law, Mainse refused to give up the fight.

Within months, he abandoned his lifelong facade of non-partisanship—in fact, he'd once served as a Liberal scrutineer—announcing that he had joined the Conservative Party. In Crossroads' Burlington riding, he threw his weight behind one of the Conservatives' most controversial candidates, David Sweet, an evangelical who had just stepped down as president of Promise Keepers Canada, and when Stephen Harper showed up at a nearby campaign stop, Mainse hand-delivered a letter that, he suggested, might contain helpful hints for a Conservative agenda.

After Harper's promised free vote on whether to reopen the marriage debate went down to defeat, Mainse refused to throw in the towel. On Crossroads' website, he listed the stand taken by every member of Parliament and urged viewers to keep up the pressure. "Drop them a note or pop in for a visit," he counselled. "Bring along some baked goods or a small token of blessing." But after handing over the muffins, his fans were instructed to mince no words, informing those politicians who had failed to support the traditional definition of marriage to expect consequences at the ballot box. Turning up as a guest on *100 Huntley Street*, Mainse was no longer the laid-back diplomat of the airwaves. He proudly recounted the uproar he'd once provoked at Nova Scotia's Dalhousie University, where he denounced "the homosexual agenda" and accused professors of "brainwashing those students in the destruction of traditional values." Cued by his son Ron, the *Huntley Street* heir, he launched into an exhortation that might have been mistaken for a campaign speech. "We need to get involved, we need to join political parties and reopen the question," he thundered. "Shame on you if you don't get out there . . . if you don't work for it."

To some, Mainse's militancy was wildly out of character for an evangelical TV star who—thanks to the CRTC's demands for balance and interfaith programming—had cultivated the image of an amiable, ecumenical paterfamilias. But while eschewing the sort of partisan tirades that have turned the U.S. religious right into a wing of the Republican Party, he had, in fact, spent most of his career promoting another political agenda that had largely escaped mainstream notice: the flag-waving brand of Christian nationalism that he first brought to Parliament Hill.

Indeed, while the CRTC was zealously restricting religious broadcasting in order to prevent a partisan like Falwell or Robertson from commandeering Canadian airwaves, it inadvertently issued most of its single-faith radio and television licences to charismatic Christians who share an equally unsettling political goal: a determination to return the country to what they claim are its Christian roots—the first step toward ultimately refashioning it as a theocracy. From Crossroads and the Miracle Channel to the thirty Christian radio stations that have sprung up in the wake of the CRTC's revamped religious broadcasting policy, most are controlled by a radical wing of Pentecostalism determined to see biblical precepts guide every level of government and conservative Christians installed in the key seats of power.

Three of the country's leading evangelical broadcasters, Dick Dewert, David Mainse and Willard Thiessen, have all played key roles in Watchmen for the Nations, the chief Christian nationalist organization, promoting its vision on their airwaves, and at a 1999 Watchmen conference in Winnipeg, the trio pledged to throw their telecommunications might behind the movement's agenda. Before a national assembly of national Pentecostal leaders, they trooped onstage with their wives to sign what they called a "Covenant of Christian Broadcasters," acknowledging Jesus Christ as "the Supreme Ruler of the airwaves," and vowing to use their media outlets "for the sake of Canada and her destiny."

Just as in the U.S., where Christian nationalists like Pat Robertson have been instrumental in turning their rhetoric of religious patriotism into routine discourse, so, too, the stars of Christian broadcasting in this country have propagated the notion of Canada's prophetic destiny as spelled out in Psalm 72:8: "He shall have dominion also from sea to sea, and from the River to the ends of the earth." On the Miracle Channel, that verse inspired the title of evangelist Bill Prankard's daily talk show *From the River*, as well as his mission ministering to the Inuit populations of Nunavik and Labrador who, he likes to remind viewers, inhabit the proverbial "ends of the earth."

During Mainse's 1981 "Salute to Canada," his cameras panned lovingly over that Psalm on the Peace Tower, and he liked to remind viewers that Billy Graham had once proclaimed Canada a potential "spiritual superpower." Patriotism, Mainse conceded, doesn't tug Canadian heartstrings the way it does those in the U.S.: this country is too multicultural and fractious, constantly under the threat that one of its founding nations will secede. "In fact, it suddenly struck me," he wrote in his 1981 book *God Keep Our Land*, "the only uniting force available in Canada was Jesus Christ."

But it was during Dick Dewert's heyday on the Miracle Channel that the lexicon of Christian nationalism became daily fare on Canadian airwaves. As he frequently pointed out, "Canada is the only nation to have its borders described in the Bible." Unveiling the channel's new Lethbridge studios in 2002, Dewert convened the first of what he called his Dominion Conferences, designed to promote the country's prophetic end-times role, where his keynote speaker was the most prominent Christian nationalist in Ottawa, Stockwell Day.

To outsiders, even to many evangelicals, the idea of remaking Canada as a Christian nation might seem derivative, a concept borrowed from TV preachers like Pat Robertson and Jerry Falwell who blamed the 9/11 attacks on God's wrath at America for legalizing homosexuality and abortion. But to Miracle Channel and Crossroads' viewers, it has become a familiar, even humdrum theme, demystified by frequent references on their talk shows. Both regularly feature the key figures in the New Apostolic Reformation movement, from Faytene Kryskow and her pals Rob and Fran Parker at the National House of Prayer—whose down payment was raised on a Miracle Channel appeal—to an international cast of prophetic stars such as Cindy Jacobs, who have dispensed a steady stream of predictions touting Canada's unique preordained role in the final days.

Shortly before Stephen Harper's 2006 election, a Tennessee pastor named James Goll appeared on Dewert's *LifeLine* to offer a prophecy about this country's immediate political prospects. The new Canadian government would have a three-year window of opportunity to reverse certain "decrees" that were threatening the nation's destiny, Goll declared. To Miracle Channel regulars, there was no mystery about what legislation he had in mind: American religious right leaders had repeatedly denounced Canada's legalization of same-sex marriage as a dangerous precedent. "Canada is like a lead domino at this time among the nations," Goll intoned in an apparent prophetic trance, then, sounding more like a state department strategist than a cleric in the grip of the Holy Spirit, he urged Canadians to overturn their offending laws. "For the U.S.'s sake, seize your moment," Goll beseeched his Miracle Channel audience. "For family values' sake! For the Kingdom's sake!"

Before the cameras, Dewert and Mainse cast themselves as spiritual warriors, using the airwaves to do battle with the forces of the Antichrist—a position that came in handy when their broadcasting ministries came under siege from the temptations of more mundane powers. In the summer of 2008 when Dewert re-emerged from his enforced exile from the Miracle Channel for a confessional interview about his transgressions, he blamed his adultery on "demonic factors" that were intent on subverting his mission to see Canada fulfil its scriptural destiny. "Joan and I were at the foreground leading the prophetic voice of the nation," he declared, "and we were targets."

A year later, Mainse took a similar line of attack when his sons Ron and Reynold were named as alleged "finders" in a $14 million cross-border Ponzi scheme by the U.S. Securities and Exchange Commission. As both were abruptly relieved of their on-air duties despite their insistence that no ministry funds were involved, Mainse returned to host a telethon dedicated to making up Crossroads' $500,000 shortfall in donations, telling viewers that "There's a Wicked One out there that is trying to destroy the ministry."

For Mainse, the scandal was a devastating blow. Only months earlier, he had shared an award with Billy Graham from the Canadian Council of Christian Charities for a lifetime of ministerial integrity. But he seemed to prefer pinning the humiliating debacle on the work of the devil than on the seductions of the Word of Faith movement, which had convinced his sons that there was nothing untoward about an investment scheme that promised returns of up to 20 percent on their money and prompted them to talk an estimated sixty friends and family members into forking over their savings. So prevalent were such scams among believers besotted by the prosperity gospel that in 2003 the B.C. Securities Commission hired an evangelical pastor and a Catholic priest to counsel faith communities about the pitfalls of get-rich-quick investing schemes, dubbing the pair "God's fraud squad."

Indeed, the prosperity credo was considered such an essential element of Christian broadcasting that in late 2009 when the Miracle Channel was on the brink of financial ruin in the wake of the Dewerts' departure, its board's solution was to hire a new CEO: Manitoba pastor Leon Fontaine, an entrepreneurial whirlwind who has turned Winnipeg's Springs Church into a ten thousand-member megacongregation by preaching the message that God wants nothing more than to reward his faithful with an "abundant" life.

That conviction, like the belief that the devil is warring for the nation's soul, rests on a nostalgia for a simpler time—one when moral choices were stark and easily defined, with a law forbidding abortion and homosexuality considered an abomination punishable under the Criminal Code. It was a time that Christian nationalists paint as halcyon when their Bible-believing predecessors were in charge of the government and most national institutions. No matter that their mythological

Eden actually saw Irish Catholic immigrants beaten bloody by Ontario's Protestant Orange mobs, or that demagogues like Father Charles Coughlin used the airwaves to denounce Jews as "Christ-killers." The Christian nationalists who now control most of the country's faith-based broadcasting outlets are convinced of the need to recreate that imagined past—a past that is as idealized, and false, as the painted facades in the Crossroads atrium.

⁜

On a warm fall day in 2007, that neo-Victorian setting served as the unlikely backdrop for the annual conference of Equipping Christians for the Public Square. Originally founded to combat the growing power of gay rights, the ECP Centre, as it is now known, is the creation of Tristan Emmanuel, a brash former rock singer who won his ministry credentials from an ultra-conservative South Carolina seminary and emerged as one of the chief spokesmen in the Defend Marriage campaign. In the wake of that legislative defeat, Emmanuel castigated fellow Bible believers for espousing what he called "the politics of reaction," letting secular humanists and the mainstream media set the agenda while conservative Christians lagged behind in the battle for hearts and minds. "This is a culture war," he tells the crowd gathered in the Crossroads atrium. "If we don't have our own infrastructure and institutions, nobody is ever going to take us seriously."

Emmanuel had convinced a handful of conservative Christian high rollers to back an Internet webcast and news site unfettered by the secular filter of the country's traditional media outlets. To some, it might seem paradoxical that he was unveiling his new media strategy in the heart of an old-media empire, but the setting was no accident. Ever since Emmanuel first stepped into the political spotlight, David Mainse had quietly served as one of his backroom angels, giving him free office space in Crossroads' headquarters and a more priceless resource: his personal mailing lists with more than twenty thousand names. Eventually, Emmanuel's outspokenness prompted him to find other accommodations, but even afterwards, he enjoyed regular guest spots on Crossroads' programs and used its atrium for his annual fundraisers.

Now he was trying to persuade his membership, many of them Calvinists of the Christian Reformed persuasion, to help underwrite his online news service, No Apologies, whose motto betrayed his appetite for controversy: "Punching a Hole in Political Correctness." A one-time acolyte of the late evangelist Ken Campbell, the provocative founder of Renaissance Canada whom he'd met on an anti-abortion picket line, Emmanuel had long argued that Canadians were too timorous, a trait he could hardly be accused of harbouring. He had publicly applauded Billy Graham's son, Franklin, for describing Islam as "a very evil and wicked religion," and denounced gays and lesbians as "sexual deviants" whom he would never allow to teach his children. "I've had Christians write me, saying, 'You don't sound like a Christian,'" Emmanuel admits. "People in this country are very nervous about my edgy approach to cultural engagement, but I'm calculating this is one style that's lacking in Canada, and I'm happy to fill the bill."

In a column for No Apologies, Emmanuel berated his countrymen for an excess of tolerance and declared that Canada needed its own Rush Limbaugh. In the meantime, the keynote speaker at this ECP fundraiser was Rush Limbaugh's former ghost writer, Joseph Farah, the founder of WorldNetDaily, an extreme right-wing Web service that Emmanuel acknowledges as the model for No Apologies. Although virtually ignored by the established press, WorldNetDaily has become a platform for some of the most incendiary voices in U.S. conservatism, including Limbaugh, Ann Coulter and its own staff writer Jerome Corsi, author of *The Obama Nation*, the pre-election bestseller that helped to perpetuate the myth that Barack Obama was a clandestine Muslim on a nefarious anti-American jihad.

Founded in the wilds of Oregon at the end of the Clinton administration as Etruth.com, WorldNetDaily is now headquartered in Washington and claims eight million readers a month. Although Farah shrinks from labels, in this crowd of fellow believers he feels free to describe it as America's only major Christian media outlet, and is not averse to suggesting that it is an instrument of the divine. "We have been severely tested over the years," he says, relating its roller-coaster financial history. "There were many times God reminded me just whose project this was." He insists that his editorial mission is to reflect a "biblical worldview," but a look at what he has published over the past three years reveals a consistent diet of right-wing sensationalism with a pro-life and pro-Republican tilt, stories lauding creationism and homeschooling interspersed with relentless attacks on global warming as a sly "power grab" by an "international tyranny."

For the benefit of his Canadian listeners, Farah argues that it is time for conservative Christians to wrest the means of mass communication away from the tyranny of left-wing secularists—an assertion that ignores the soaring ratings of right-wing soapboxes like Fox News. But, as he points out, founding an alternative newspaper or television network today would cost millions, while the cost of starting a website is a pittance. "Don't just complain about the state of the media," he upbraids the crowd. "Fix it."

Chronicling the growth of the American right, Farah highlights a turning point in 1987, when Ronald Reagan scrapped the Fairness Doctrine, which required U.S. broadcasters to ensure balance on the airwaves. Overnight, anyone with a microphone could let his or her opinions rip without fear of licencing repercussions. Less than a year later, Farah notes, Rush Limbaugh emerged as a nationally syndicated phenomenon, heralding a new era that swept in on a tide of vitriol and intolerance. With the stroke of a pen, Reagan had unleashed radio's shock jocks who have been dubbed the single most effective recruiting tool for the American right.

In the U.S., Christian broadcasters like James Dobson are now fighting congressional attempts to restore the Fairness Doctrine, which they fear could limit their on-air opinions, but in Canada, where the CRTC's obsession with balance has served the same purpose, pressure is building to move in the opposite direction. The Evangelical Fellowship, among other organizations, is demanding an end to the commission's restrictions on faith-based broadcasting, charging that they constitute a form of religious discrimination.

Ironically, that request to deregulate Christian broadcasting may prove irrelevant. As Joseph Farah and Tristan Emmanuel point out, the Internet has already replaced television and radio as the Christian communications medium of choice. Today, no self-respecting megachurch lacks its own website, and many evangelical congregations are passing up expansion plans in favour of live-streaming video of their services to the not-so-faithful at home. An estimated 65 percent of North Americans use the Internet for religious and spiritual information, and even Pope Benedict XVI, who boasts his own Facebook page, has ordered his preists to embrace the wonders of online technology. In the fall of 2009, 1,800 American conservatives attended the "Values Voters Summit" in Washington, while live webcasts of the event drew an online audience of 175,000. For Christian nationalists like Faytene Kryskow, the online reach of GOD TV has proved a particular boon, zapping webcasts of TheCRY to thousands sitting at their home computers, who otherwise couldn't afford the time or expense of going to a rally on Parliament Hill.

As Emmanuel stressed at his conference, the chief virtue of the Internet is that, unlike the airwaves, it remains largely unregulated, beyond the scrutiny of the CRTC or any bureaucratic equivalent. No one appreciates that free-for-all more than Timothy Bloedow, the parliamentary aide who took over both the ECP Centre and the No Apologies news service in 2008, when complications in Tristan Emmanuel's personal life forced him to step aside. As one of the country's leading Christian nationalists, Bloedow runs his own website, Christiangovernment.ca, where he promotes "the urgent need for a Christian theocracy" and hammers away at secular bureaucracies like human rights tribunals as "commie commissions."

Reading Bloedow's online diatribes, it would be easy to dismiss him as a solitary extremist, but the chief backers of the ECP Centre and No Apologies include a Hamilton steel tycoon named Al Schutten and Rob Wildeboer, chairman of Martinrea International, the country's second-largest auto-parts manufacturer, an enthusiastic supporter of Stephen Harper who won an appointment to the government's new Science, Technology and Innovation Council. Neither financier has shown any interest in taming the rhetorical excesses of Bloedow or his like-minded brethren in the blogosphere. On the contrary, Schutten and Wildeboer applauded the ECP's chief focus: funding the legal defence of those conservative Christians accused of discrimination for expressing their sentiments on homosexuality. Indeed, as Christian nationalists such as Emmanuel and Bloedow vent their views in the unregulated ether of the Internet, their chief worry is a complaint filed against them with one of the country's assorted human rights commissions, which have become the religious right's new bêtes noirs—the latest gatekeepers of balance and secular humanism forcing Bible believers to measure their words.

JUDGMENT DAY

IX

A t the annual Civitas conference, elation was mingled with a
sense of disbelief. Barely three months after Stephen Harper's
2006 election, the secretive conservative fraternity that had spent
most of the previous decade fulminating against the outrages of
Liberal governments suddenly found one of their own in power. Still,
the victory had come at a price. In a party where freedom was the
mantra, whether extolling free markets or the freedom to tote unregistered guns, there had been one casualty on the way to the ballot
box: freedom of speech within the Conservative caucus. MPs had not
merely been gagged; under Harper's centralized communications
command, even the most gregarious theo-conservatives had been
transformed into proverbial church mice, bolting in terror at the sight
of a media microphone.

Given that vaunted party discipline, it was all the more astonishing
when, between Civitas's off-the-record sessions, veteran Saskatchewan
MP Maurice Vellacott sought out a CBC reporter to accuse Chief Justice
Beverley McLachlin of claiming "God-like powers." This was not simply
his opinion, Vellacott insisted. Citing a speech McLachlin had made to
a New Zealand conference, he charged her with comparing the process

of applying unwritten constitutional principles to acquiring prophetic gifts. "Suddenly there's some mystical kind of power that comes over them," he railed, "by which everything that they've ever decreed is not to be questioned."

As McLachlin hastened to point out, she had said no such thing, but in the ensuing uproar—as Vellacott apologized and the government declared that the opinions he expressed were strictly his own—some in the Canadian legal community wondered whether his outburst was as much of a blooper as it seemed. His rhetoric might have been overheated and his reading of McLachlin's speech skewed, but his sentiments mirrored what Harper and others in his circle had been saying for years. Intentionally or not, Vellacott had put the federal bench on notice that, under the new government, it would not be business as usual.

Not that the judiciary had been under any illusions. Harper's views were no secret: three years earlier, after an Ontario court ruled in favour of same-sex unions, he accused the Liberals of stacking the bench with left-wing ideologues likely to take progressive stands on hot-button social issues that the government was afraid to touch. "They didn't want to come to Parliament, they didn't want to go to the Canadian people and be honest that this is what they wanted," he charged. "They had the courts do it for them."

Those views had been formed, in part, back at the University of Calgary by two of Harper's colleagues in the political-science clique known as the Calgary School: Ted Morton and Rainer Knopff had built their careers as constitutional experts attacking the Supreme Court and the 1982 Charter of Rights and Freedoms. In the course of interpreting the Charter, they charged, Beverley McLachlin and her fellow justices wielded more influence over public policy than any duly elected government. "The Supreme Court is no longer a court, but an overtly political censor," they wrote in their 2001 study, *The Charter Revolution and the Court Party*, calling the court "an oracle ready to second-guess disputable political judgments whenever it sees the need."

Still, some Ottawa observers contended that Harper's attempt to rein in the courts was driven by more than ideology. As head of the National Citizens Coalition, he had launched a 2001 lawsuit to overturn the restrictions on election spending by third-party groups such as the NCC, steering the case through two appeals to the Supreme Court. Three years later, the high court had ruled against him in a decision immortalized as *Harper v. Canada.*

Harper had never been the type to forget slights and it came as no surprise when, soon after taking office, he shook up the Supreme Court appointments process. His first nominee, Justice Marshall Rothstein, had been shortlisted by the previous Liberal government, but Harper agreed to appoint him if he submitted to questions from an all-party Commons committee under the heat of television lights. Critics protested the move as an attempt to Americanize the judiciary, invoking the media circus of U.S. Supreme Court nomination hearings, but the prime minister refused to budge. For many, his subtext seemed clear: a good grilling by MPs might remind Rothstein and his colleagues just whose job it was to stake out new legislative frontiers.

Harper's intransigence was ironic considering that Rothstein could hardly be considered a hostile candidate. Vic Toews, the newly appointed justice minister, had been one of his students at the University of Manitoba law school and, as an appeals court judge, Rothstein's rulings were regarded as restrained. Still, Harper insisted that a parliamentary vetting was the first step toward a "more open and accountable approach" to judicial nominations. Although Rothstein later admitted that cribbing for the event had been excruciating, the three-hour televised hearing turned out to be anti-climactic, an exercise in mutual politesse. But, by then, the Canadian legal community had gotten the message: under Harper, the judiciary itself would be on trial.

That strategy was guaranteed to please virtually every faction in his conservative coalition, but none more so than theo-cons such as

Maurice Vellacott, who had accused the Supreme Court, of assuming the role of a secular priesthood, one whose decrees superceded not only the legislative powers of Parliament, but the supremacy of God's law. Every policy that was anathema to the Christian right, from striking down the country's abortion law to sanctioning same-sex marriage, had originated in the courts. In the United States, evangelicals had come to regard the legal system as such an instrument of Christian persecution, bent on removing all vestiges of belief from public life, that one 2005 conference was called "Confronting the Judicial War on Faith."

For Vellacott, a former pastor in the Evangelical Free Church who had earned his doctorate at a Christian university in Chicago, that perception was bolstered by his legislative assistant, Timothy Bloedow, one of the leading Christian nationalists on Parliament Hill. As an acolyte of Rousas J. Rushdoony, the godfather of Christian Reconstructionism, Bloedow sees the Supreme Court as one of the chief obstacles to Reconstructionism's overriding goal: establishing a theocracy that will govern according to biblical law. In *State vs. Church*, his book-length argument for the "re-Christianisation" of Canada, Bloedow denounces the current "judge-ocracy" and calls for dismantling most federal institutions, including the courts. According to his ideal of a Christian nation, the central government would only direct foreign relations and national defence; almost all other powers would be handed over to sovereign local communities, where justice would be meted out through the sort of tribal councils that held sway back in the days of ancient Israel.

Bloedow paints that form of biblical justice as benign and practical— a cozy, communal alternative to the lofty pomp and bureaucracy of the current system—but declines to offer concrete details. Rushdoony, however, displayed no such reluctance. In *The Institutes of Biblical Law*, his three-volume treatise published in 1973, the Calvinist patriarch examines what Bloedow terms "Old Testament case law," and concludes that, for crimes such as sodomy, adultery and blasphemy, or even consulting a fortune teller, the sentence prescribed in the book of Leviticus should apply: death by stoning.

Such draconian measures might seem like the stuff of an ominous science-fiction plot, but they are not as implausible as they might appear. Bloedow admits that he has attended conferences where Christian Reconstructionists have hammered out the conditions under which such punishments would be phased in to a society, and one African country already offers a glimpse into that thinking. In Uganda, where many members of the government are evangelical Christians, homosexuality has been a crime punishable by life imprisonment for two decades, but a 2009 private-member's bill proposed even more stringent measures: in cases classed as "aggravated homosexuality"— gay sex with anyone disabled, under eighteen or infected with HIV/AIDS—it mandated the death penalty.

Rushdoony's scrupulous adherence to Old Testament codes is one reason that his doctrines have fallen out of fashion with most contemporary fundamentalists—but today a wider circle of Christian nationalists have adapted and popularized many of his themes. Instead of dismantling federal institutions, they urge Bible believers to take dominion over every aspect of government, including the chief objects of Rushdoony's wrath: education and the courts. To that end, both Jerry Falwell and Pat Robertson have created law schools at their universities to produce a new generation of Christian lawyers as well versed in constitutional precedent as they are in the Scriptures. Robertson, one of the leading U.S. Dominionists, has also launched a campaign in Washington for what he calls the "de-liberalization" of the courts. That term was one Harper himself might well have borrowed as he set out to do the same in Ottawa.

⸎

In February 2007, on the twenty-fifth anniversary of the Canadian Charter of Rights and Freedoms, Harper rose in the House of Commons to declare that he intended to select judges who respected his legislative agenda. What shocked most onlookers was not the statement itself, but its brazenness. That confirmation of his government's intention "to imprint its views on the judiciary," a *Globe and Mail* editorial marvelled, was unprecedented in the Charter's quarter-century history, but no one doubted his resolve. By then, his first justice minister, Vic Toews, was so busy orchestrating what the *Globe* decried as "an overt ideological makeover" of the courts that he had been upbraided by the Canadian Bar Association.

A Mennonite who had served as Manitoba's attorney general, Toews spent years as the Conservatives' justice critic railing against "these radical liberal judges who have their own social agenda," and once delivered a speech entitled "Abuse of the Charter by the Supreme Court." As the party's point man during the same-sex marriage debate, he was such an impassioned moralizer on U.S. Christian radio shows that critics labelled him the "minister of family values." It was a sobriquet that would later come back to haunt Toews: in the summer of 2008, a story in the *Winnipeg Free Press* revealed that he was engaged in a "messy" divorce from his wife of thirty-two years after fathering a child with a younger woman.

Still, for a politician who had regularly castigated the Liberals for stacking the courts with partisan faithful, Toews wasted no time in following suit. At first, his appointments were greeted with a resigned shrug. A five-year study of Liberal judicial appointments between 2000 and 2005 had revealed that 60 percent had party ties, leaving the opposition on shaky ground to berate the Conservatives for larding the bench with its own failed candidates and former party pooh-bahs. But when Toews tampered with the makeup of the judicial advisory committees that vet nominees for the 1,100 federal court posts, the legal community howled in protest. He had not bothered to consult either the Canadian Bar Association or Parliament when he added a new delegate from the law-enforcement community to the panels, weighting them in the government's favour. Even Chief Justice Beverley McLachlin issued a rare objection, warning that the shift put the independence of the judiciary at risk.

Many of Toews's new appointees to those panels were long-time Conservative loyalists who made no attempt to hide their party ties, including a Nova Scotia firefighter who had twice run as a Tory candidate, three former aides to Mulroney cabinet ministers and Harper's best friend, John Weissenberger, a Calgary geologist who was obliged to step down from the Alberta committee when he accepted another patronage job as a ministerial aide. But during an interview one panelist admitted that he had been specifically instructed to redress the liberal leanings of the courts. "Look, my job is to get Conservative judges," he told me, asking for anonymity. "There's nothing wrong with that. We'll get back to where the courts rule in a very limited area and the legislature will be left to make the laws."

Now, three years later, Toews's revamped screening committees appear well on the way to fulfilling that mandate. According to some assessments, approximately half of the two hundred new superior court judges appointed by Harper have Conservative connections or have made donations to the party's coffers. If their views on interpreting the law are correspondingly conservative, Harper may be in the process of changing the tenor of the courts, pushing the judicial consensus to the right for the first time in nearly half a century.

But as legal scholars point out, a Conservative Party membership does not necessarily dictate a conservative judicial temperament; in the best-known example, Roy McMurtry, the former chief justice of Ontario, whose court opened the way to same-sex marriage, was appointed by Brian Mulroney. What worries critics of Harper's judicial strategy far more than partisanship is his appointment of committed social conservatives who have acted for the religious right on some of the most contentious moral issues before the courts. In December 2006, Toews named Dallas K. Miller, the founder of the Home School Legal Defence Association, to Alberta's Court of Queen's Bench. As a lawyer in private practice, Miller had acted for conservative Christians in so many culture-war cases that REAL Women of Canada accorded him its National Defender of the Family Award. Another controversial appointment went to Nova Scotia lawyer Lawrence O'Neill who, as a former Tory MP, introduced a bill that would have required a fetus to be represented by legal counsel before an abortion. But it was when Toews named a dapper Toronto barrister named David Moseley Brown to the Ontario Superior Court of Justice that the first alarm bells went off in the country's gay-rights community.

Although listed as an expert in energy law at the prestigious Bay Street firm of Stikeman Elliott, Brown became better known as an advocate for Christian conservatives in most of the key court challenges pitting religious convictions against the Charter of Rights. He had acted for almost every theo-con organization in the country, from the Evangelical Fellowship and the Catholic Civil Rights League to Focus on the Family Canada, sometimes separately but often as part of a faith coalition. In 2004, he had argued for REAL Women of Canada in an anti-spanking case before the Supreme Court, and for its president, Gwen Landolt, Brown had an added distinction: he was one of the first male members of a major blue-chip firm willing to intervene on behalf of anti-abortion protestors. At EGALE Canada, the country's equal-marriage lobby, his name elicited strong emotions of a different sort. As Gilles Marchildon, its former executive director, told the *Globe and Mail*, Brown seemed to have been involved in "representing opponents of equality in virtually every big lesbian-gay-bisexual-trans case" to go before the judiciary.

A devout Catholic, Brown has described himself publicly as a Christian lawyer, and, at a 2006 conference shortly before his appointment to the bench, he reminded law students motivated by similar beliefs that, "As a Christian lawyer, you are called to practice your trade and conduct your life in accordance with your faith." Legal principles were important, he told them, but a barrister's dignity springs from "membership in the community founded and sustained by God . . . not in some free-standing notion of freedom or autonomy." Earlier, during a debate on same-sex matrimony, he made clear that he objected to the proposed legislation, warning that "Within a few generations, marriage will have no practical meaning and society will be the worse for that."

Still, it was one thing for a lawyer to bring his faith into the courtroom, quite another for a judge to do the same. As critics pointed out, Brown's appointment raised questions about his impartiality should he be assigned a case involving gay rights or pro-choice issues. "I think people should be aware of the views he has," said Carolyn Egan of the Abortion Rights Coalition of Canada, "and how they could potentially impact on future decisions."

But that task was one largely left up to the press. Ironically, while Harper had pressed for hearings to grill Supreme Court nominees, there were no such hearings to explore the views of his hundreds of other appointees to lower levels of the bench. For those probing Brown's judicial philosophy, the chief clues came from an organization he had often represented in court, the Christian Legal Fellowship, whose founding principle is a rebuttal to every damning lawyer joke. "The vocation of law is a calling from God," it declares, and barristers themselves are "instruments through which the Holy Spirit of God works."

⁂

In the ballroom of Toronto's Delta Airport West Hotel, the annual meeting of the Christian Legal Fellowship would never be confused with some high-glitz convention of the Canadian Bar Association. As silence falls over the crowd, more than a hundred lawyers stand shoulder to shoulder in prayer, some with heads bowed, others with their palms raised heavenward. For the country's leading faith-based legal group, those devotions are essential agenda items at a conference where each day begins with a pre-breakfast session of "corporate prayer and praise," and every seminar, no matter how disputatious, ends with a blessing. Quite apart from that public show of piety, it seems difficult to imagine the denizens of Bay Street's Gucci Gulch signing up for seminars with titles like "Influencing Your Canada for Christ" and "Human Rights: What Are They and Does God Want Us to Defend Them?"

Founded thirty years ago and inspired by the Christian Legal Society in the U.S., the fellowship was set up by a half-dozen law school graduates, all of them evangelicals, led by John McKay, now a Toronto Liberal MP, and Paul Mack, his former partner. "As Christians, you're inundated continuously with perspectives that aren't necessarily your own," McKay says, "so part of it was self-help."

Today, the fellowship's five hundred members meet in local chapters once a month, each endorsing a Statement of Faith that declares the Old and New Testaments the "supreme and final authority" in their personal and professional lives. But mindful of the group's origins, Calvin Beresh, a graduate of Oral Roberts University who now practices in Niagara Falls, heads a special division aimed at inspiring more young Christians to enrol in law schools—and once there, to join the Christian Legal Fellowship's rolls—offering scholarships and a mentoring program with some of the organization's biggest legal names. Already, one of his former students has won a job on the legal staff of the Evangelical Fellowship, but Beresh's ultimate dream is to establish the country's first Christian law school, patterned after Pat Robertson's at Regent University in Virginia, whose graduates held top posts in the White House of George W. Bush "We're not looking just for the gifted students," Beresh says. "We're looking for the ones who'll stand up and witness for Christ."

For two decades, the fellowship kept a determinedly low profile, but, in 1996, it suddenly ventured into the values wars. That change in course was prompted, in part, by a controversial Alberta case that turned a shy chemistry instructor named Delwin Vriend into a reluctant hero of the gay-rights movement. Seven years earlier, Vriend had been fired by The King's University College in Edmonton, a private school run by the Christian Reformed Church, after admitting that he was gay. Complaining to Alberta's Human Rights Commission, Vriend found his petition dismissed on the grounds that the provincial human rights code made no mention of discrimination based on sexual orientation. When he appealed the ruling in a regular Alberta court, a judge upheld his argument, and more importantly, ordered the province to change the wording of its legislation.

Instead, Alberta's then premier, Ralph Klein, fought back. For Klein and social conservatives across the country, Vriend's case became a symbol of the sort of "judicial activism" that some had been denouncing for years: the judge was not merely bringing a liberal interpretation to legislation, they charged; she was attempting to rewrite existing laws. But to Vriend's backers in the gay-rights community, "judicial activism" was a canard: every decision requires some interpretation, they argued; cries of "activism" only surfaced when social conservatives disagreed with the verdict.

Klein's forces cheered when the Alberta Court of Appeal overturned the Vriend ruling, but that victory proved short-lived. Vriend promptly appealed to the Supreme Court and it was then that the Christian Legal Fellowship decided to flex its members' collective legal muscle by intervening in support of the province. The move was part of a new strategy borrowed from the U.S. religious right, where groups of like-minded evangelical organizations filed a flurry of complementary briefs in a tactic known as "judicial lobbying," intended to persuade the court that their position had widespread support. So numerous did interveners become that one Canadian Supreme Court justice complained they had turned the courts into "an ancient jousting contest, with each side gathering up as many spear bearers as they can." Although the Christian Legal Fellowship's factum was one of four in the Vreind case—another came from Focus on the Family Canada—it failed to sway the outcome. On April 2, 1998, the Supreme Court issued a landmark ruling in favour of Vriend, ordering Alberta to bring its human rights code into line with the equality guarantee that is implicit in the Charter of Rights—a decision that remains controversial to this day.

The ruling rested on the argument that, although sexual orientation had not been spelled out as grounds for discrimination in the Canada Human Rights Act, it was implied, and thus could be "read in" to provincial codes. Critics, such as Harper's pal Ted Morton, denounced the decision as a "partisan judicial power grab" that robbed the provinces of their rights—proof that the court was in "the political vanguard of the social left." Although Klein threatened to use the "notwithstanding" clause in an attempt to override the ruling, he never followed through on that vow. Instead he demonstrated his own brand of defiance: for the next nine years of his premiership, Klein refused to make the court-ordered adjustment to Alberta's laws.

It was not until the spring of 2009 that his successor, Ed Stelmach, finally complied, but so charged did that concession remain that he did so as part of an even more controversial horse-trade with the party's conservative Christian base. In the same bill that inserted the contentious clause into the provincial human rights code, Stelmach also enshrined parental rights, allowing Albertans to pull their children out of classes dealing with "religion, sexuality or sexual orientation," and thus sparking another controversy.

In the decade since the Vriend decision, the Christian Legal Fellowship has emerged as a major player on the constitutional scene. It has intervened against a bid by three Toronto sex workers to challenge the legality of prostitution laws and argued on behalf of pro-life militants in the "bubble zone" case, a ten-year legal saga that began when two Operation Rescue veterans were convicted of violating the security perimeter outside a Vancouver abortion clinic in a manner that could hardly have escaped notice: they were toting a nine-foot wooden cross inscribed with the words "You shall not murder." The fellowship's activism has coincided with its increasingly close ties to Focus on the Family Canada. Not only did Cindy Silver, a former in-house counsel for Focus, serve as the fellowship's executive director, but over a five-year period, the group received nearly forty thousand dollars in tax-free grants for litigation training seminars from the Canadian affiliate of James Dobson's ministry.

Unbenownst to most Canadians, however, Dobson's influence on this country's legal battles has not been restricted to financial support. At a 1994 convention of American religious broadcasters, he and a handful of other evangelical heavyweights—including Florida televangelist D. James Kennedy and Bill Bright of Campus Crusade for Christ—announced a new initiative intended to remedy a source of increasing frustration: despite having taken over both houses of Congress, the Christian right was still losing most of its battles in U.S. courts. In the last sixteen years, their Alliance Defense Fund (ADF) has grown from a one-man Arizona office with a borrowed photocopier to a litigation giant with thirty-nine staff attorneys who have chalked up more than thirty victories before the Supreme Court.

Most of ADF's cases are aimed at challenging the U.S. constitutional separation between church and state. Often representing Christian clubs and churches that have been barred from holding their meetings in publicly funded premises or students punished for singing hymns in school, it also played a leading role in the most sensational, and sensationalized, euthanasia case to date, underwriting the two-year battle by a Catholic family to keep a Florida hospital from removing the feeding tube of their brain-damaged daughter, Terri Schiavo. "We try not to file frivolous cases," says ADF's chief counsel, Benjamin Bull. "We're interested in creating precedents, not press releases."

For nearly a decade, the Alliance Defense Fund paid scant attention to the legal skirmishes beyond America's borders, but, in November 2003, that oversight ended with a shock. The Supreme Judicial Court of Massachusetts handed down a ruling in *Goodridge v. Department of Public Health* that paved the way for the legalization of same-sex marriage for the first time in any state. Writing the landmark decision, Massachusetts's chief justice cast about for a precedent on the subject and found one fresh off the presses from Ontario's Court of Appeal. At ADF's Arizona headquarters, that move served as a wake-up call. Suddenly, the chief legal arm of the American religious right turned its gaze north of the forty-ninth parallel. "Our courts are increasingly citing foreign precedents," Bull says. "The legal decisions made in Canada and Europe have an incredible influence on us, and if we just worry about what happens in the U.S., we'll be the losers."

❖

Tall and crisply handsome, betraying his upbringing as an army colonel's son, Benjamin Bull has flown to Toronto to spur the foot soldiers of the Christian Legal Fellowship on to greater militancy. "Christians aren't as organized here," he confides to me between conference sessions. "At least, I know Christian lawyers aren't." A former federal prosecutor who specialized in pornography cases, he has spent most of his career strategizing for evangelical interest groups, including the American Family Association, which specializes in mustering mass boycotts of corporations that support gay-pride events. So well-versed is he in the fundamentalist worldview that, in his speech to the fellowship, he addresses one theological question even before it can be posed: why should believers bother to take their battles to the courts when Armageddon seems so close at hand? "Some will point out that the Bible says persecution just increases in the end times so why should we try to stop it?" Bull concedes. "But the Bible also tells us that if greater persecution comes . . . we must never stand idly by."

As a prelude to his pep talk, he shows a ten-minute promotional video that leaves no doubt as to why the Alliance Defense Fund is not standing idly by when it comes to Canadian courts. Called "Protecting American Sovereignty," it features U.S. Supreme Court Justice Antonin Scalia and Reagan's former attorney general, Edwin Meese, denouncing the perils of foreign legal precedents, and brandishing Ontario's same-sex marriage ruling as exhibit A. The video is so alarmist that, as the lights come up, Bull feels moved to apologize. "It works one way in front of donors," he says sheepishly, "another way here." So well has it worked with donors, in fact, that ADF can now afford to plunge into court actions around the world. In 2004, Bull quarterbacked an international protest against the conviction of an obscure Swedish pastor named Ake Green, who had delivered a sermon declaring homosexuality "a deep cancerous tumour" on society. Fearing the case could be used as a precedent against American clergy venting similar views, he helped propel appeals all the way to Sweden's highest court, where Green was acquitted, in part thanks to a flurry of sympathetic amicus curiae briefs that Bull had orchestrated from global allies, including the Christian Legal Fellowship. "When the judgment came out, it quoted your amicus brief," Bull reminds his audience. "The whole purpose of that case was local, but it was the international briefs that turned it around."

That flattery is a prelude to his pitch for ADF's National Litigation Academy, which offers intensive, four-day training sessions for Christian lawyers on how to mount constitutional challenges, offered in Phoenix free of charge. In return, each graduate pledges to donate 450 hours of his or her time over three years on cases of ADF's choosing. More than a thousand attorneys around the world have taken advantage of that quid pro quo, two dozen of them in Canada, including the fellowship's director Ruth Ross.

In selecting its battles, one of ADF's main preoccupations has been defending the right of pastors to air their political views—an issue in which James Dobson has a personal stake. Four years ago, when accounts of his pivotal role in Bush's election hit the media, his Colorado ministry suddenly found itself under investigation by the Internal Revenue Service, faced with the threat of seeing its charitable tax status revoked. After a gruelling year-long audit, Focus on the Family was cleared, but its patriarch was not in the mood to forgive and forget. During the 2008 presidential elections, ADF challenged the authority of the Internal Revenue Service, enlisting three dozen pastors in twenty states to openly endorse candidates on what it called Pulpit Freedom Sunday, daring federal authorities to swoop in and swamp the court system. "It is the job of the church and pastor to decide whether they should talk about political issues from the pulpit," a spokesmen declared. "It is not appropriate for the government to draw that line."

A similar rationale lay behind ADF's decision to take on its first Canadian case: defending an Alberta youth pastor named Stephen Boissoin, who had been hauled before the province's human rights commission in 2002 for a letter he wrote to the *Red Deer Advocate* denouncing "the homosexual machine." Initially dismissed, the complaint was reinstated three years later and the Alliance Defense Fund got wind of it on a Christian radio show, where Boissoin announced that he intended to represent himself. Tracking him down in Calgary, Bull's staff informed him that he would do no such thing. "He said, 'We can't take the chance you might lose,'" Boissoin recalls, "because what's going on in Canada will affect us in the U.S."

To mount that defence, Bull called in an IOU from an ADF litigation academy graduate, whose reputation as one of Canada's top constitutional experts was only rivalled by his political connections. Gerald Chipeur had acted as legal counsel to the Reform Party and the Canadian Alliance before signing on with Stephen Harper's Conservatives, and, as he liked to joke, he was one of the few survivors of that internecine warfare who knew where the bodies were buried. "But it's not the time to talk about that," he says with a cautionary glance as I settle into his office for an interview. "There aren't enough people dead yet."

⁜

From his twenty-third floor suite in one of Calgary's Husky towers, Gerry Chipeur can see the distant snow-slicked foothills of the Rockies, but his office decor bears witness to an even more extensive reach. On one wall, a framed photo shows him with Republican presidential candidate John McCain, for whom he threw a thousand-dollar-a-head fundraiser, raking in nearly fifty thousand dollars from American expatriates working in Alberta's oil patch. On another wall, a snapshot of Stephen and Laureen Harper is inscribed with "thanks for being on the winning team"—a reference not only to Chipeur's professional services for the Conservative Party, but his pre-emptive strike on the prime minister's behalf. Only days before the 2006 election, he had contacted Paul Weyrich, the late chair of Washington's Free Congress Foundation, asking him to warn fellow American conservatives against interviews with Canadian reporters on the lookout for dirt about Harper's U.S. ties.

Chipeur's loyalties, however, are nothing if not complex. The largest expanse of his wall space is reserved for a portrait of Harper's former rival, Stockwell Day, who had hired him years earlier for a damaging defamation suit filed during his days as Alberta treasurer. Nearly a decade later, Day had barely been installed as Harper's first minister of public safety, when he named Chipeur his department's lobbyist in Washington. That perk was not Chipeur's only reward. In 2007, during the Conservatives' controversial revamp of its screening panels for federal judges, Chipeur won a slot on the judicial advisory committee for Alberta, an unpaid appointment that he regards as a sacred calling. "There's absolutely nothing wrong with a Conservative government appointing Conservative judges," he says with undisguised passion. "We need to get some good judges in, and we need Christian law schools."

The implications of his thoughts on the subject are best revealed in a column that Paul Weyrich wrote shortly after the pair had a post-election chat in 2006. At the time, American conservatives were disheartened that Harper had won only a minority government, but after talking to Chipeur, Weyrich reported, he realized that all was not lost: the new prime minister still possessed extraordinary powers to appoint judges at every level of the courts. "If Harper were to alter the composition of the courts," Weyrich pointed out, "the anti-abortion issue could again be contemplated."

While Chipeur's political ties have brought him coveted corporate contracts, they have also helped subsidize the less profitable side of his practice, defending religious rights, an interest that inspired his legal career. As a Seventh-day Adventist, he grew up in an evangelical denomination whose members routinely face dismissal for refusing to work on their Saturday Sabbath. "I'd always had a selfish interest in that aspect of the law," he admits.

Graduating from the University of Alberta law school in 1984, two years after Trudeau introduced the Charter of Rights, Chipeur was called to the bar just as that new addendum to the constitution was turning Canada into a more litigious and, some say, Americanized society—one where individual and minority rights would come to rival those of the community at large. After writing his M.A. thesis on religious liberty, he joined an Edmonton law practice that was already testing those new legal waters. In one of his first cases, he acted for his Seventh-day Adventist Church, intervening on the side of Big M Drug Mart, a Calgary pharmacy chain convicted of violating the Lord's Day Act. When the Supreme Court overthrew that verdict—and the decades-old ban on Sunday shopping—their argument turned out to have played a defining role: since the ban offered no protection for the Adventists' own sabbath, the justices ruled it discriminatory and therefore unconstitutional.

Now, more than two decades after that decision, Chipeur is a partner in the Calgary offices of Miller Thomson, where his client list reads like a who's who of the Christian right: he submitted a brief to the Supreme Court opposing same-sex marriage on behalf of Senator Anne Cools, and when Calgary's outspoken Catholic bishop Fred Henry found himself under investigation by Revenue Canada, it was Chipeur who rallied to his defence. He had already carved out a reputation in constitutional law when Dallas Miller, the first Canadian to sign up for ADF's litigation academy, invited him to Phoenix for one of its conferences. The trip turned into a networking bonanza: through ADF, he dined with James Dobson in his Colorado boardroom, and hobnobbed with Antonin Scalia, a personal hero who is one of the most conservative voices on the U.S. Supreme Court. Despite that rapport, Chipeur failed to rouse any ADF interest in his Canadian caseload—a source of frustration. "They didn't think there was a role for them north of the border," he says. "Then suddenly, after a decade of them largely ignoring Canada, they called me out of the blue."

That request to take on Boissoin's case brought Chipeur a chance to make constitutional history, but it also raised an awkward reality: a legal battle that could determine the parameters of free speech in this country was being financed and overseen by a consortium of ministries in the U.S. religious right, including Focus on the Family.

⁜

Stephen Boissoin is running late when I arrive at the Black Knight Inn on the outskirts of Red Deer. Waiting for him, I try to picture the youth pastor at the heart of the debate over Canada's human rights commissions, a man being championed by almost every leader in the country's Christian right. I've barely had time to conjure up an image of some slight, earnest martyr—kind-eyed and priestly, perhaps sporting a clerical collar—when I find myself shaking hands with a black-clad former bodybuilder, his shaved head highlighting his ear piercings, his cheek scarred from stab wounds incurred during his career as a gang enforcer. Even the "pastor" honorific that Chipeur and other supporters stress in their pitches for his defence fund turns out to be defunct. Two years earlier, Boissoin surrendered his ordination papers with the Evangelical Christian Church, he says, after doctrinal differences over when the Battle of Armageddon was expected to occur.

On the Saturday we meet, he has just quit his job as the service manager at a Red Deer car dealership, hoping to make a killing in Alberta real estate. Four hours later, it becomes clear why Chipeur has not scheduled more interviews with his star client: like many characters at the heart of landmark legal challenges, Boissoin is a problematic poster boy for the cause of free speech. Not that he is a man of few words. For two hours, I hang, riveted, on his tale of how an angry young boy from Oshawa, Ontario, ended up as an angry young man in Calgary's gang wars, running with Asian drug dealers and Jamaican posse types, then settling scores for them with his .44 magnum Desert Eagle—the kind of handgun, he likes to point out, that Clint Eastwood used as Dirty Harry. His anecdotes pour out in vivid and often gory detail: the time he was escorted behind a derelict hotel and shot in the kneecap as a suspected stool pigeon; the ambush outside a nightclub, where, thanks to a semi-automatic stashed under the passenger seat, he was able "to blast up these guys' cars." When police raided his apartment, they found an arsenal that included two AK-47s and a sawed-off shotgun. "I got involved with some pretty hard-core stuff," he concedes, "but I did it for two reasons—the money and the ego."

Thrown into solitary confinement in the Calgary Remand Centre and swaddled in restraints for letting his temper blow one time too often, Boissoin found himself weeping inconsolably when he overheard an inmate reading the Bible in an adjacent cell. It was there that he began his halting journey to salvation and eventual ordination, earning his ministerial degree by correspondence from an

Indiana institute. In Red Deer, where he married, he opened a drop-in centre for troubled teens, who flocked to hear his tales of gangs and guns. "Everybody loved my story," he says. "I was the big, buffed, ex-bad boy."

In June 2002, Boissoin was surfing online, researching grants for his youth centre, when he discovered that the Alberta Human Rights Commission was funding an Alberta chapter of PFLAG—Parents, Families and Friends of Lesbians and Gays—to promote tolerance for homosexuality in the province's schools. Weeks earlier, a Red Deer high school had celebrated Gay Day, and for Boissoin, the PFLAG grant was the last straw. He fired off his sentiments to the letters page of the *Red Deer Advocate*, alleging it was the work of a nefarious plot: "From kindergarten on, our children, your grandchildren are being strategically targeted, psychologically abused and brainwashed by homosexual and pro-homosexual educators," he warned. "Come on, people, wake up!... Where homosexuality flourishes, all manner of wickedness abounds." He raged on for four more paragraphs, ending with a dramatic call to arms: "My banner has now been raised and war has been declared," he wrote. "Will your child be the next victim that tests homosexuality positive?"

The letter prompted blistering responses, both pro and con, then two weeks later, the *Red Deer Advocate* reported that a gay teenager had been attacked by a trio of toughs, who shattered his cheekbone, taunting, "You're a faggot, right?" With that news, Darren Lund, then a Red Deer high-school teacher who had pioneered an award-winning tolerance program, filed a human rights complaint against Boissoin, alleging his tirade had provoked the assault. By the time the Alberta commission finally agreed to hear the case three years later, Boissoin's youth centre had closed, and he had moved to Calgary, where his cause was championed by a former member of the provincial legislature named Craig Chandler, founder of the Concerned Christian Coalition, who had his own knack for making headlines.

Dubbed by one local columnist as "a roaming rottweiler in the far-right kennels of Alberta politics," Chandler was already infamous in some Conservative circles for lambasting Peter MacKay's support of gay rights and warning that Belinda Stronach was leading a takeover of the Conservative Party by the "militant homosexual movement." He would become an increasingly problematic ally—so problematic that he was later barred from running for the provincial Conservatives—but he put Boissoin's case on the map.

For a fundraising dinner he threw in Calgary, Chandler lined up an appearance by Tristan Emmanuel, the founder of Equipping Christians for the Public Square, who had just authored a provocative, self-published volume called *Christophobia*, arguing that a tiny homosexual elite was foisting anti-biblical legislation on the country because of a "blind revulsion to Christ." No slouch at grabbing media attention, Emmanuel found himself upstaged when a band of masked protestors in camouflage fatigues stormed the hotel ballroom, chanting, "Right wing bigots go away, Gay Militia here to stay." Thanks to their raid, Boissoin's plight hit wire services across the continent, and was later featured in a thirteen-part American television series entitled *Speechless: Silencing the Christians.*

The ruckus helped nail the support of Emmanuel's backers at the ECP Centre, a half-dozen evangelical entrepreneurs, led by auto-parts magnate Rob Wildeboer, who would eventually raise an estimated twenty-five thousand dollars for Boissoin's defence. Most had been propelled into political action when an Ontario human rights tribunal fined a Toronto printer five thousand dollars for declining to fill an order for a lesbian group—an incursion into business they regarded as outrageous. "This is a private enterprise being told what to print," Wildeboer says, still horrified. "That just wasn't right."

Under Emmanuel and his successor, Tim Bloedow, the ECP Centre has become one of the most strident voices calling for the demise of human rights commissions, casting them as instruments of Christian persecution. "Other than an outright ban on Christianity," Bloedow writes, "there isn't much more these thugs can do to marginalize Christians."

On his websites, Bloedow brands them "kangaroo courts" and "commie commissions," lambasting them as "the primary tool by which leftists seek to crush dissent in this country." But, as a Christian Reconstructionist, his objections run much deeper: to him, the very notion of legally protected individual rights is an unthinkable heresy, a repudiation of God's sovereign law. In his book, *No Sacred Ground: 'Human Rights' Thought Police Clamping Down on Christians*, Bloedow chronicles the case of Christian Horizons, an evangelical charity for the developmentally disabled, which fired an employee who owned up to a live-in lesbian relationship that breached the code of conduct she had been required to sign. For Bloedow, the most disturbing aspect of the case was not the Ontario Human Rights Commission's finding of discrimination; it was the order that the charity scrap its morality pledge. Predicting that the decision could prompt an exodus of faith-based charities from the social-service field, he painted an even more sinister scenario: without a pledge that screened out non-believers, he warned, sexual predators would soon be prowling Christian Horizons' hallways, taking advantage of the weak. "Any rise in the number of cases of abuse," he wrote, "should be placed squarely at the feet of the OHRC."

If that sabre-rattling verged on the hysterical, it was symptomatic of the emotions that have come to characterize the increasingly volatile human rights debate. When Janet Epp Buckingham, the former legal director of the Evangelical Fellowship, cautioned fellow conservative Christians against rushing to dismantle the commissions—pointing out that they had often protected people of faith—she found herself pilloried by two former allies, Gwen Landolt and Denyse O'Leary, who blasted the tribunals as "the human face of fascism."

Just when the vitriol appeared to have peaked, a new player appeared on the scene to ratchet it up another notch: in January 2008,

Ezra Levant, the former publisher of the *Western Standard* magazine, showed up before Alberta's Human Rights Commission to explain why he had chosen to reprint a dozen Danish cartoons depicting the Prophet Mohammed in a less than reverential light. For Levant, who had carved out a reputation as a provocateur in both politics and the press, the hearing provided an opportune stage. Bringing along his pregnant wife to film the encounter, he posted it on YouTube, garnering four hundred thousand hits, the launching pad for his one-man scorched-earth campaign against what he termed the "rogue courts" masquerading as human rights commissions.

By then, an Alberta human rights commissioner had found Stephen Boissoin guilty of promoting "rampant" hatred and "fearmongering," ordering him to pay his complainant five thousand dollars and to proffer an apology. But what sent conservative Christian tempers off the charts was the tribunal's demand that he never again repeat his sentiments about homosexuality—a condition that he promptly rejected. Later, Chipeur reported a rash of phone calls from panicked clergy preparing to water down their sermons. "Pastors have been coming to me saying, 'I'm afraid,'" he told an ECP conference. "They're saying they're going to change the policies of their church or school to be totally whitebread."

Rushing to Boissoin's defence, Levant denounced his sentence as "Stalinist" and a dangerous precedent. Suddenly, after years of having only a passle of fellow evangelicals in his corner, Boissoin had the benefit of Levant's relentless noise machine. What few knew was that the pair were no strangers. Long before his colourful forays into politics and journalism, Levant had been a junior lawyer in Gerry Chipeur's firm, where Boissoin was one of his clients.

⊹

No one would deny that Ezra Levant has a way with words. As Stockwell Day's short-lived spokesman in the Canadian Alliance Party, he coined the term "Stockaholic" for loyalists such as himself, although others have described him in less flattering terms. In his memoir, *Think Big*, Preston Manning offers a harsh assessment of Levant's stint as the Reform Party's Question Period coordinator, charging that "Ezra got us into trouble on several occasions because of difficulties in discerning, in the heat of battle, that line between 'the truth, the spin, and the lie.'" Even Mark Steyn, the *Maclean's* columnist whose own human-rights case Levant championed, acknowledged in the foreword he wrote to Levant's book, *Shakedown*, that "Ezra is an unlikely hero . . . a blow-hard, a loudmouth, a self-promoter, a 'controversy entrepreneur,' etc. I speak as one myself."

Denouncing the federal human rights commission as a "$25 million boondoggle" and its head Jennifer Lynch as "chief commissar"—"an angry bigot . . . temperamentally unsuitable for any public office"—Levant has been careful to foster his reputation as a rhetorical flame-thrower. But no matter how inflammatory his verbiage, his two-year war against the country's assorted human rights tribunals succeeded in a strategy that he called "de-normalization"—changing the popular perception of them, and raising widespread questions about their ethics and raison d'être.

In his blog and his book, Levant hammered repeatedly at their flaws, including their failure to follow normal court procedure or rules of evidence, and their members' frequent lack of legal training. Created a generation ago, the commissions were originally intended as a quick and low-cost means of redress for minorities who found themselves victims of discrimination, barred from renting an apartment or applying for a job, but they have become a sounding board for a broad array of complaints, Levant charged, transformed into a "costly grievance industry."

Instead of offering a speedy resolution, some commissions now take more than a year to deal with a file, he argues, and while any citizen can lodge a complaint, leaving the commission's investigators to shoulder the cost of proving its worth, those who find themselves on the receiving end of the charge are forced to pony up their own legal fees to defend themselves. As Chipeur points out, without the Alliance Defense Fund's largesse, Boissoin could never have afforded his services: "One argument is that this is a strategy that some leaders of secular humanism have said, 'Let's use these human rights commissions because they're free; we'll exhaust the other side into submission, and then they'll retreat.'" And just who does Chipeur see spearheading such a plot? "There are those within the homosexual community," he says, "who are trying to use human rights laws to limit the freedom of Christians."

That conspiracy theory might be more convincing if it weren't for the fact that one of Boisson's most vocal allies was the gay-rights lobby, EGALE. While deploring Boissoin's sentiments about homosexuals, EGALE officials testified on his behalf, arguing that even the most offensive opinions have the right to be heard. "We want Pastor Boissoin's assertions aired, debated and subjected to public scrutiny," said a spokesperson. "Sunshine is the best disinfectant."

Indeed, one of the most edifying by-products of the human rights debate is the mind-boggling bedfellows it has convened. Conservative Christians accustomed to regarding the Canadian Civil Liberties Association as the enemy—the chief agent for secularism in public life—suddenly found it, too, backing Boissoin's right to offend. Alan Borovoy, the association's founder and long-time legal counsel, who had been one of the moving forces behind establishing the country's first human rights tribunal, agreed with Levant that the commissions were being used for purposes that were never intended and for which they were singularly ill-equipped, above all to arbitrate allegations of hate speech. "It's one thing to invoke the law against discriminatory deeds," he wrote in the *Calgary Herald*. "It's another thing entirely to employ it against discriminatory words." If that trend toward judging hate speech cases continued without modifying the provisions of the Human Rights Act, Borovoy predicted, the result would be a "legal quagmire."

For some, that legal quagmire already appeared to have arrived. With the allegations that Levant and Mark Steyn had fanned hateful feelings against the Muslims who lodged complaints against them, most of the country's mainstream media organizations scrambled aboard what had been a largely Christian bandwagon: the push to scrap a specific clause of the Canadian Human Rights Act known as Section 13 (1), which bars any acts that could incite hatred or contempt. At the 2008 Conservative policy convention, party delegates voted to kill it by a huge margin, and a year later, the House of Commons justice committee held hearings into that possibility. Even a Canadian human rights commissioner declared the clause unconstitutional in a ruling that Steyn pronounced "the beginning of the end" for the problematic provision. In December 2009, an Alberta appeals-court judge offered an unexpected endorsement of that trend, overturning the 2008 ruling by the provincial human rights tribunal against Boissoin: while his letter to the *Red Deer Advocate* was "jarring, offensive, bewildering, puerile, nonsensical and insulting," Justice Earl Wilson wrote, it did not qualify as hate speech.

By then, Levant and Steyn too had been exonerated, but they were no longer content merely with quashing Section 13 (1) of the Human Rights Act; Levant wanted the whole human rights apparatus, both federal and provincial, dismantled and consigned to oblivion. "The answer is not to tinker with these bureaucracies or try to reform them," he wrote, "but to gut them, uproot them and abolish them." That left him at odds with many of his old allies, including his mentor Gerry Chipeur and the leaders of the Canadian Jewish Congress, who argued that, with eight thousand new anti-Semitic websites on the Internet, the need for the commissions was greater than ever.

It also left Stephen Harper with a strategic dilemma. While he had once campaigned on amending the provisions of the Human Rights Act—a move sure to please many of his evangelical supporters—he now risked alienating much of the Jewish vote and those ethnic minorities he had so assiduously courted as part of his theo-con outreach. The battle over regulating human rights turned out to be one between conflicting sets of rights—the right to free speech versus the right not to suffer a sense of offence.

Only one thing seemed certain: the issue was unlikely to disappear. On the contrary, it dominated the 2009 Conservative leadership race in Ontario, thanks to many of the same evangelicals who had rallied to Boissoin's cause. In fact, the figure chiefly responsible for pushing it to the forefront of the Ontario Tory contest was the man behind the dark-horse candidacy of MPP Randy Hillier: his campaign manager, Tristan Emmanuel. Later in the race, the issue was taken up by the winner, the Conservatives' new leader, Tim Hudak.

But as *Toronto Star* columnist Haroon Siddiqui pointed out, the debate over human rights commissions also had a dark side. "The subtext here is Muslims," he argued. "For years, human rights agencies across Canada have been adjudicating complaints against anti-Semites, homophobes, etc. But when some Muslims cited *Maclean's* magazine for Islamophobic content, a storm broke out."

⁜

Siddiqui's observation reminded me of two conferences that I attended while researching this book. One in the fall of 2008 was sponsored by Tristan Emmanuel's ECP Centre, "Islam: The Threat at the Door." In a promotional e-mail, Emmanuel's website sounded the requisite alarms: "The one threat that is greater to Western Civilization than Secular Humanism," it thundered, "is the tyranny of Islamic Fundamentalism." Accordingly, the conference featured a mysterious former Islamic jurist from an unnamed North African country who had converted to Christianity after reading the Bible, which made him the subject of an Islamic fatwa. Under the cover of a protective identity, Sam Solomon, as he called himself, spent his time touring the West with Ravi Zacharias International Ministries, warning against the perils posed by his former faith.

Despite the mystery about his origins, Solomon turned out to be a regular on the evangelical conference circuit—such a regular, in fact, that it turned out I had seen him months earlier as the keynote speaker at the closing banquet of the Christian Legal Fellowship's annual conference, where he delivered a show-stopping performance. There, wiry and immaculate in a tuxedo, a microphone pinned to his lapel, Solomon roamed the ballroom floor, his timing worthy of a Vegas pitchman and his script packed with vivid and chilling details. His speech was punctuated by abrupt geysers of Arabic quotations from the Koran, barked out in the tones of a vengeful imam, then, just as suddenly, his voice dropped to a theatrical whisper as he recounted the heinous plot by fanatical Muslims to take over Canada. "Islam is not a religion in the Western sense of the word," he declaimed. "It's a socio-political, socio-economic, socio-educational judicial and militaristic system, often garbed in religious terminology. There is not one word in the Koran about peace. The Koran is full of hate, violence, rape and the spoils of war."

At times, his speech smacked of an anti-immigration tirade as he brandished the spectre of a day when Canada would boast a non-white majority. That impression was reinforced when he pinpointed the government's defining misstep: the moment it adopted multiculturalism as an official policy. Other countries, including Britain, had done the same, Solomon declared: "Now the whole of the Western world is sinking under the weight of Islam." For more than an hour, he spelled out the growing influence of Muslims in Europe: unsanctioned shariah courts were springing up across Britain, and French imams had agreed to end ghetto riots in exchange for the right to run their own Islamic schools. Holland, he claimed, was "overrun" by Turkish and Moroccan Muslims, concluding, "The multicultural experiment has failed."

What most shook his audience of Christian lawyers, however, were his tales of an economic jihad being waged around the globe, complete with shariah-compliant banks in Britain and the launch of an Islamic index on the New York stock exchange. A listener might have been forgiven for concluding that a devastating financial coup d'état was on the horizon, but it turned out that at least one of Solomon's shibboleths was three decades old.

Still, reminding his listeners how Ontario had come within a whisker of introducing a shariah law, Solomon did his best to whip the hall into a panic. Someone at the conference had taken him for a drive around Toronto, he said, which left him in shock: on every street, he'd seen Muslim women wearing the hijab. "Mosques are everywhere, Islamic schools are everywhere," he sputtered. "My word, I thought I was back in Saudi Arabia."

As if that were not angst-inducing enough, he warned of a possible terrorist attack, naming Montreal as the probable target. At the back of the crowd, I sat speechless, fighting off a pervasive sense of dread, but not for the reasons he might have hoped. Solomon's performance was a tour de force of fearmongering unlike any other I had ever witnessed, including a week I once spent in rural Louisiana watching white supremacist David Duke play the race card during his campaign for governor. But in this crowd, I was clearly alone in failing to be swept up by Solomon's rhetorical spell. En masse, the ballroom of Christian lawyers rose at his bidding, pledging to take a stand against the sinister prospects he invoked. As a worship band broke into a soft-rock anthem of praise, the fellowship's executive director Ruth Ross, clad in a cocktail suit with a collar of pearls, summoned her members to pray over the kneeling Solomon, joining with him in a solemn covenant to fight off the looming Islamic hordes. "I believe in the truth we've heard tonight," she proclaimed. "We've covenanted with Sam and one another. Lord, we join hands as we prepare to go forth and do battle across this land."

Outside in the hallway, I ordered a CD of Solomon's presentation, but months later, it still had not arrived. Later, Ross informed me that she had cancelled that particular recording and torn up the cheques.

The sound quality of Solomon's speech was not satisfactory, she said, and besides, she and her board had realized that such inflammatory material might provoke "some issues of liability" for the Christian Legal Fellowship—perhaps even a human rights complaint. It was one thing for the fellowship to defend Christians against persecution by secular humanists, it seemed; quite another for them to be accused of spreading hate by another faith.

THE ARMAGEDDON FACTOR

X

On the car radio, the weather report sounded an aptly apocalyptic note. Environment Canada had just issued a severe thunderstorm warning for Toronto, and already the sky north of the city had turned an ominous charcoal. Even the most cynical Hollywood screenwriter could not have dreamed up a more fitting backdrop as a ribbon of cars turned into the parking lot at Canada Christian College in search of a more precise forecast on just when to expect the outbreak of Armageddon. Yellow police tape blocked the driveway and plainclothes officers were jumpy, eyeing the crowd for threats to two of the visitors inside, Israeli ambassador Alan Baker and Major General Aharon Zeevi Farkash, then chief of Israel's military intelligence, although neither was the night's main draw. That distinction was reserved for Reverend John Hagee, the Texas televangelist who packs eighteen thousand born-again Christians into his Cornerstone Church in San Antonio every Sunday, and whose fiery televised sermons reach an estimated ninety-three million homes around the globe.

Seated onstage in the Elmer S. McVety Centre, Hagee hardly looked capable of exuding such star power. A squat fire plug in a brown shirt, brown suit and beige striped tie, he stared out from behind owlish wire rims, no hint of a smile creasing his jowls, but the moment he took command of the microphone he had the audience in thrall. "As we sit here in safety and security, a nuclear time bomb is ticking in the Middle East," he intoned, his drawl gathering decibels as he rhymed off the litany of threats against Israel from Iranian President Mahmoud Ahmadinejad, who had vowed to see the nation wiped off the map. "In the twenty-first century, the president of Iran is the new Hitler of the Middle East," Hagee thundered. "I believe Israel is in the greatest hour of danger it has known since statehood."

In his 2006 book, *Jerusalem Countdown*—on sale in the college lobby for fourteen dollars—he had already spelled out the exigencies of that scenario: a military strike against Iran's nuclear bunkers like the one Israel had launched against Iraq's nuclear reactor years earlier. Lest anyone question the tactical necessity of such a move, Hagee provided supporting arguments from top Israeli intelligence sources and the prophet Ezekiel. "We are facing a countdown in the Middle East," he wrote with urgent certainty. "It is a countdown that will usher in the end of this world."

No matter how alarming that prospect, Hagee counselled readers that they had nothing to fear. This was, after all, part of God's plan as foretold by the Old Testament prophets and the gospel of Matthew, which lists wars, famines and earthquakes as "birth pains" before the return of Jesus to the world. "We are racing toward the end of the age," Hagee exulted. "Messiah is coming much sooner than you think."

No one in a crowd that included senior Israeli officials and Frank Dimant, the executive director of B'nai Brith Canada, seemed fazed by Hagee's invocation of global annihilation to pave the way for the Second Coming of Christ. His tirade against Iran was merely the latest update of the dispensationalist credo that lies at the heart of the Christian Zionist movement, the volatile blend of biblical prophecy and realpolitik that has become an indispensable adjunct to Israeli foreign policy.

Not only have Christian Zionists ensured support for Israel's annual multi-billion-dollar grant from the U.S. Congress, they have also been a godsend to the nation's economy. Ever since the second intifada broke out in the fall of 2000, devastating the Israeli tourist industry, the majority of the country's visitors have been evangelicals, steadfastly signing up for Uzi-escorted tours of the Holy Land and marching through the tense streets of Jerusalem, flags waving, in a defiant show of solidarity during the festival of Sukkot. Benjamin Netanyahu, the Likud leader who is now prime minister, has hailed Christian Zionists as "the best friends Israel has in the world"—a sentiment he voiced at a Jerusalem rally where Hagee presented Israeli charities with a six-million-dollar cheque.

As criticism of Israel's military and settlement policies has mounted, that friendship has become even more vital in the battle for global public opinion. In February 2006, with the possibility of an Israeli air strike against Iran escalating, Hagee summoned fellow televangelists to San Antonio to lay the foundations for a new grassroots lobby called Christians United for Israel (CUFI). Months later, as Israeli jets pounded Iranian-backed Hezbollah forces in southern Lebanon in what analysts saw as a dry run for an attack on Tehran, Hagee called more than three thousand of his CUFI conscripts from every state to Washington, D.C., for a day of targeted lobbying, instructing them to seek support from their congressmen for Israel's bombing campaign. At a glittering banquet, he warned the crowd that any calls for a ceasefire ignored "God's foreign policy statement" for the Jewish people. "Leave Israel alone," he told U.S. lawmakers. "Let them do the job."

It was the same pitch Hagee made to the evangelicals assembled at Canada Christian College by his Toronto lieutenant, Charles McVety. "I challenge you to be bold, be fearless," he exhorted the audience. "Christians, stand up and speak up for Israel." Not that Hagee felt that Stephen Harper needed any corrective arm-twisting. Within weeks of taking office in 2006, Harper had greeted Hamas's victory in the

Palestinian territories by becoming the first world leader to cut off its funding, beating even George Bush to that sanction. "God has promised to bless the man, the church, the nation that blesses the Jewish people," Hagee purred from the podium. "I am so delighted that Canada's prime minister immediately denounced Hamas terrorism when he became the leader of this great nation."

Since then, Harper has backed Israel with such fervour that veteran scholars and diplomats rank it as the most dramatic shift in the history of postwar Canadian foreign policy. During Israel's 2006 invasion of Lebanon—a bombing campaign that won international condemnation for killing dozens of civilians and a Canadian peacekeeper in a clearly marked United Nations post—Harper declared the action a "measured response" to Hezbollah's rocket attacks. Two years later, when Israel launched a three-week military campaign against Hamas militants in the blockaded Gaza Strip—killing more than a thousand Palestinians and wounding five thousand—he left the rhetoric to others, but Canada was the only nation among forty-seven on the United Nations Human Rights Council to vote against a motion that condemned the offensive and called for an investigation into possible war crimes. Nor did Ottawa show any enthusiasm for a subsequent fact-finding report by Justice Richard Goldstone, the former chief prosecutor for war crimes tribunals in Rwanda and Yugoslavia, which condemned Hamas's rocket attacks on Israel but found the Israeli response "deliberately disproportionate . . . designed to punish, humiliate and terrorize a civilian population." As Ezra Levant wrote in the *Toronto Star*, "No world leader has been as clear as Harper has been in his support for Israel's right to defend itself."

Although the prime minister has reiterated Canada's commitment to a two-state solution, that stand merely echoes Bush's Roadmap to Peace, a plan roundly condemned by all sides. Instead, on an issue where every public utterance carries seismic ramifications, Harper has shown little inclination for staking out a middle ground, openly ignoring the counsel of his Foreign Affairs Department and the political fallout on his relations with this country's mushrooming Muslim population. No sooner had he marked Israel's sixtieth anniversary with a pledge of Canada's "unshakable" support than his government lived up to that vow, showily banning Britain's grandstanding MP George Galloway, a Hamas booster, in a move that appeared more successful as a gesture of solidarity than as a gag on the publicity-loving Scot.

So unflinching has Harper's backing of Israel been that some critics have questioned his motivation. Is it merely another by-product of the big-tent strategy he spelled out in his 2003 Civitas speech—an electoral ploy designed to lure the Jewish vote away from the Liberals? Or is it an illustration of the influence that Christian Zionists like Hagee and McVety have come to exert over Canada's foreign policy? If so, it leads to another question that might well give voters pause: to what extent is this country's role in the Middle East being influenced by the dubious theology of a renegade nineteenth-century Anglican priest obsessed with the idea that the end of the world is at hand?

⁂

Even in his own day, the father of dispensationalism was a controversial figure. Intense, ascetic, with a notorious scorn for the status quo, John Nelson Darby quit his parish in the Irish county of Wicklow rather than obey an edict from the king on how the church must conduct of its affairs. While meeting regularly with a band of equally zealous believers who became known as the Plymouth Brethren, Darby suffered a debilitating fall from his horse and, in the course of his convalescence, had an epiphany that would provoke a theological schism in evangelical ranks. Suddenly, he saw the vast sweep of the biblical narrative in a new schematic light. According to his revised reading, all of scriptural history, past and future, had been divided into seven epochs or dispensations: the first was man's idyll in the Garden of Eden and the last would be Christ's thousand-year reign of peace on earth. With the crucifixion, Darby warned, the world had entered into the sixth dispensation, one he called the Age of the Church, which would end with the Battle of Armageddon against the forces of the Antichrist.

If that theory was not entirely original, Darby added a pivotal twist. Based on a single verse in Paul's letter to the Thessalonians, which describes how the godly would "rise in the clouds to meet the Lord in the air," he postulated that true Christian believers would be summoned to heaven in a secret Rapture before the fateful battle, thus sparing them the horrendous tribulations that would mark the final days.

On seven mission trips to North America between 1862 and 1877, which included stops in Toronto, Montreal and Ottawa, Darby preached his spellbinding thesis, but it was in the United States, still reeling from the devastation of the Civil War, that he found his most receptive audiences. There, evangelical crowds were captivated by a theology that fit the recent national bloodbath into a grand celestial design while promising the faithful their own preordained exit plan. Darby's ideas were taken up by some of the leading turn-of-the-century revivalists and became a staple at a handful of Bible colleges from Toronto to Los Angeles, notably Chicago's Moody Bible Institute. Later, one of his most effective publicists proved to be Cyrus Scofield, a former U.S. attorney and convicted forger who, after a jailhouse conversion, produced a version of the Scriptures annotated according to Darby's dispensationalist timeline. Published in 1909 by Oxford University Press, the *Scofield Reference Bible* brought new respectability to Darby's theory; by the end of the Great Depression, it had sold nearly two million copies and become the first end-times bestseller.

As dispensationalism swept the Midwest, an Alberta teacher named William Aberhart was sufficiently entranced by Darby's apocalyptic scenario that, in 1927, he founded a school devoted in part to the subject: the Calgary Prophetic Bible Institute. Among those who signed up for the first class was Ernest Manning, a Saskatchewan farm boy who was so moved by "Bible Bill's" radio sermons that he stayed on after graduation to run the institute for more than a decade, while Aberhart pursued his twin careers as premier of Alberta and host of *Canada's National Back to the Bible Hour*. After Aberhart's 1943 death, Manning took over both the premier's office and his radio pulpit and if his preaching lacked the fire-and-brimstone of his mentor's, it was driven by the same dispensationalist fervour. In his sermons, Manning routinely parsed the Old Testament prophets for clues to the identity of the book of Daniel's wicked "king of the north," and, like others in the 1950s, he saw Satan's stand-in as the Soviet Union. As he once explained to the *Edmonton Free Press*, the Soviets posed more than a military and ideological threat; Christian leaders could not negotiate in good faith with such godless atheists.

For the first half of the twentieth century, most evangelicals dismissed dispensationalists as marginal showboaters peddling cataclysmic scenarios to fill their revival tents, but in the wake of the Second World War, their credibility and numbers received a sudden boost. According to Scofield, the Second Coming could not occur until the Jewish people had returned to their biblical homeland, and in 1948, with the creation of the state of Israel—seen as the "budding of the fig tree" in the gospels of Matthew and Mark—that prophecy appeared to have been fulfilled. For Manning and his fellow dispensationalists, the countdown to the final days had begun. As the monthly magazine of the Moody Bible Institute put it, "God's clock has struck."

Dispensationalists were already poring over the Bible as a prophetic puzzle, searching for other eschatological clues, when Israel's 1967 capture of the West Bank and Gaza ramped up their sense of urgency. The victory put all of Jerusalem under Israeli control, paving the way for the restoration of the second temple—the prelude to the Battle of Armageddon, which, some dispensationalists decreed, would unfold on the plain of Har Megiddo northwest of the city. When Hal Lindsey's 1970 bestseller, *The Late Great Planet Earth*, turned Darby's theory into a pop-culture sensation, launching an entire apocalypse industry, the Israeli government was forced to confront the implications of a dooms-day theology in which its real estate played a pivotal role.

Shortly after the 1967 war, Israel's Ministry of Religious Affairs sent a young scholar named Yona Malachy to the Bible College of Los Angeles, a bastion of dispensationalism now known as Biola University, to bone up on Darby's theories. His study, *American Fundamentalism and Israel: The Relation of Fundamental Churches to Zionism and the State of Israel*, was published in 1977, the year that Israeli Prime Minister Menachem Begin came to power. Only months earlier, America's first born-again president, Jimmy Carter, had declared that Palestinians had a right to their own homeland—a prospect that was anathema to Begin and his right-wing Likud allies. They had no intention of ceding the land captured in the Six Day War, territories which Begin scrupulously referred to by their biblical names, Judea and Samaria.

Using Malachy's study as a guide, Begin set out to cultivate a grass-roots religious and political force among Carter's fellow evangelicals that would oppose calls for a Palestinian state and, in the process, lay the foundations for a lasting pro-Israel bloc within the American politi-cal system. One of the first signs of that strategy surfaced within months. On the eve of a Untied Nations peace conference, Jerusalem's Institute of Holy Land Studies took out full-page advertisements in U.S. newspapers that declared: "The time has come for evangelical Christians to affirm their belief in Biblical prophecy and Israel's divine right to land."

Shrewdly, Begin focused his courtship on America's leading televan-gelists, and not merely because of their electronic reach. From Oral Roberts to Pat Robertson, most were Pentecostals who preached a pop version of dispensationalism. Within a year of his election, Begin hosted sixty of them on an all-expense-paid tour of the Holy Land, complete with briefings from top political and military officials who stressed the security considerations that prevented Israel from handing back its conquered territories. But he lavished special attention on Jerry Falwell, who had just been drafted by backroom Republicans to lead the evangelical juggernaut that would help oust Carter from power. Not only was the Moral Majority committed to preserving family values and America's military might, but one of its four founding principles was a pledge to defend Israel. As international headlines hailed Carter's Camp David Accords for forging a breakthrough in the Middle East, winning Begin and Egyptian President Anwar Sadat a joint Nobel Peace Prize, Falwell made no attempt to hide his reservations: "You and I know that there's not going to be any real peace in the Middle East," he declared, "until the Lord Jesus sits down upon the throne of David in Jerusalem." A year later, Falwell was back in Israel as Begin's guest, trekking with reporters to a disputed West Bank settlement where he linked America's survival to its treatment of the Jewish state. "I believe if we fail to protect Israel," he intoned to the assembled TV cameras, "we will cease to be important to God."

In 1981, when Israel bombed Iraq's Osirak reactor, Begin called Falwell even before he alerted the Reagan administration, but the Moral Majority leader was not alone in mustering a public show of support. John Hagee, another of the evangelical pastors whom Begin had hosted three years earlier, organized a solidarity rally in San Antonio, the first of what would become his signature Nights to Honour Israel. As Hagee likes to tell his audiences, he went to Israel as a tourist "and came back a Zionist."

Under Reagan, dispensationalism flourished within the U.S. government, largely escaping the media's scrutiny. To the horror of his diplomats, the president hired Hal Lindsey, a former tugboat captain-turned-end-times maven, as a Middle East consultant. At the height of his Cold War brinkmanship with the Kremlin, Reagan's rhetoric often echoed the apocalyptic thunderings of the television preachers who had helped bring him to power. Certainly, it was no accident that he first branded the Soviet Union an "evil empire" at a conference of the National Association of Evangelicals. For years, former administration officials have dismissed reports that Reagan, like his mother, had a personal belief in dispensationalism, but when his diaries were published in 2007, it became clear that the final days were frequently on his mind. Informed of Israel's strike on the Osirak reactor, the man in control of the U.S. nuclear arsenal noted in his journal, "I swear, I believe Armageddon is near."

Analysts have repeatedly blamed the alliance that Begin forged with U.S. evangelicals as one of the greatest obstacles to peace in the Middle East. In January 1998, when the Clinton administration chided Benjamin Netanyahu for his failure to hand over West Bank land in keeping with the Oslo accords, Falwell organized a hero's welcome for Netanyahu in Washington, where Hagee led the crowd chanting, "Not one inch." So vehement has Christian Zionist opposition been to any territorial concessions that Pat Robertson attributed former prime minister Ariel Sharon's incapacitating stroke to divine punishment for bulldozing four Jewish settlements in the West Bank.

In the wake of the terrorist attacks of September 11, 2001, Paul Boyer, a University of Wisconsin historian, estimated that more than 40 percent of Americans subscribed to a popular version of end-times theology, viewing the nightly news through that "filter of prophetic belief." But by then, the Soviet Union had been supplanted by a new candidate for the Antichrist. As Richard Cizik, vice-president of the National Association of Evangelicals, acknowledged, "Muslims have become the modern-day equivalent of the Evil Empire."

For foreign-policy experts, George Bush's biblical rhetoric before the invasion of Iraq was the most alarming sign that Armageddon theology was shaping geopolitics. Initially dubbing the war a "crusade," he cast it as an epic confrontation between good and evil being waged on the very geography where the prophecies of the Old Testament were said to unfold. To the world, Saddam Hussein's crime was harbouring alleged weapons of mass destruction, but to dispensationalists an equally significant provocation was his grandiose scheme to rebuild the biblical kingdom of Babylon, the seat of Nebuchadnezzar, who had driven the Israelites from the Promised Land.

Bush's apologists have attempted to wave off his scriptural allusions as mere figures of speech, but such disclaimers failed to mollify former French president Jacques Chirac. In a 2007 interview, Chirac recalled listening in stunned disbelief as Bush tried to persuade him to join the Iraq invasion by characterizing it as a struggle against the Old Testament forces of Gog and Magog. So horrified was Chirac that he had his staff consult a Swiss theologian on the implications of those references to the book of Ezekiel. "This confrontation is willed by God," Bush reportedly told Chirac, "who wants to use this conflict to erase his people's enemies before a New Age begins."

Bush's defence secretary, Donald Rumsfeld, one of the chief advocates of the war, used the Bible to steel his boss's resolve in the face of mounting casualties. At the suggestion of a Pentagon major general who was a born-again Christian, Rumsfeld headlined the cover sheets for his daily intelligence briefings with bellicose quotations from the Old and New Testaments. "Therefore put on the full armor of God," read one exhortation from Ephesians 6:13 after a particularly bad setback, "so that when the day of evil comes, you may be able to stand your ground."

For most Canadians, those revelations might seem as alien as they are alarming, but some of the same influences are, in fact, gaining traction in Harper's government. They are the product of a partnership between Canadian evangelicals and conservative Jews that was forged nearly a decade ago, expressly with Middle East foreign policy in mind.

⁂

In Frank Dimant's executive suite at B'nai Brith in northwest Toronto, the decor provides a handy index of his political alliances. On one wall, his honorary doctorate from Canada Christian College hangs in a commanding frame; on another, a giant dreamcatcher commemorates his induction as an honorary chief of the Keewatin Tribal Council—a memento of the myriad overtures the Jewish community has made to the First Nations, complete with exclusive tours of Israel. But it is an impromptu photo spread on the coffee table featuring Stephen Harper when he was leader of the Canadian Alliance that provides the backdrop to the history Dimant is eager to relate. He has summoned me to B'nai Brith's headquarters to recount how the partnership between Jews and evangelicals developed in this country, thanks largely to his own efforts. That complex narrative turns on long-standing rivalries within the Canadian Jewish community and Harper's own political calculations.

Despite the fact that B'nai Brith is the country's oldest Jewish organization, known for documenting and denouncing acts of anti-Semitism for over a century, it has found itself increasingly sidelined by a band of wealthy Jewish tycoons led by Onex chairman Gerry Schwartz, once a leading fundraiser for the Liberal Party. That marginalization was no accident. Under successive Liberal governments, Dimant had been pushing for more aggressive support of Israel at the United Nations and opposed a two-state solution in the Middle East, both positions clearly at odds with the foreign policies of Jean Chrétien and Paul Martin. Schwartz's group accused Dimant of muddying the political waters by exposing the fact that the Jewish community did not speak with a single voice—a point that Dimant was only too happy to make. As the child of Holocaust survivors, he blames the pre-war Jewish establishment in the United States and Britain for being afraid to raise an unseemly fuss against Hitler. "It's dangerous for any community to have one voice," he insists. "I believe if there had been more voices in the 1930s, there would have been more Jews saved."

But the standoff was about more than strategy. While Schwartz and company represented the Jewish intellectual and corporate elite, B'nai

Brith's constituency had shrunk to the most conservative and orthodox segments of the community—what Dimant likes to call "the Jewish street." As Schwartz and his wife, Heather Reisman, were hailed as glittering jet-setters, bringing the heady scent of Hollywood to Liberal backrooms, Dimant sought out his own ideological soulmates: first, Reform Party founder Preston Manning, later Stockwell Day. "There were vicious accusations in our community that they were anti-Semitic," he says, "which was total lies." Years earlier, B'nai Brith had honoured Ernest Manning for excising the anti-Semitic elements from Alberta's Social Credit Party, and Dimant sought a similar undertaking from his son at Reform. "We got assurances from him and from Stockwell Day," Dimant says, "that if ever they found someone anti-Semitic in the party, he'd be turfed out."

Having forged those bonds with Day, Dimant was less than thrilled when Harper triumphed over him in the Alliance leadership race. Within days of that upset, he and former B'nai Brith president Rochelle Wilner arranged a meeting to take the measure of the party's new boss. According to Dimant, they never discussed Harper's spiritual views, but by the time they left his office, they had garnered a commitment to Israel from him that would outlast his arrival at 24 Sussex Drive. "We couldn't have asked for more," Wilner would later tell me.

Over the next two years, as the Conservative leader crafted a party-building strategy that would appeal to theo-conservatives across faith lines, Dimant became his chief interlocutor in the Jewish community. Not only did B'nai Brith's right-wing membership share evangelicals' concerns about such issues as same-sex marriage, he and Harper felt a kinship as outsiders. In 2004, Schwartz and his group had finally provoked a controversial shakeup of the country's main Jewish organizations for which they controlled the purse strings, forcing them under one new umbrella and a single board. But that shakeup—likened to the hostile takeovers that had won Schwartz respect on Bay Street—left B'nai Brith out in the fundraising cold. In the heyday of Paul Martin's government, Schwartz and company had unveiled their revamped lobby at an Ottawa banquet where Martin was the undisputed star and the Conservatives were given short shrift. It was a snub that Harper would not forget. At his first post-election speech to Toronto's business elite, the new prime minister made sure that Frank Dimant was at the head table as the chief representative of the Jewish community, not his better-known rivals from Schwartz's crowd.

Later, when the prime minister's office was criticized for plying Jewish Canadians with Rosh Hashanah cards—some non-religious Jews had even protested to the privacy commissioner—Dimant rushed to Harper's defence in a letter to the *Globe and Mail*. After years of receiving Christmas greetings from previous governments, he wrote, he was "delighted" to find wishes for the High Holidays in his mailbox. But such cards were not the only overtures Harper made to Dimant's community. He was pointedly photographed visiting some of the most conservative synagogues in the country, and Georganne Burke, a former Conservative staffer in charge of Jewish outreach, organized Friday Shabbat dinners, complete with kosher meals and rabbinical prayers, for Dimant, Joseph Ben-Ami and other Orthodox delegates during party conventions. His solicitude was not limited to gestures of good-will. In 2009, when the Canadian Press tallied up the funds doled out by a new federal program to provide security for groups at risk of attack from hate crimes, 84 percent of the money had gone to Jewish groups in the first year. In Winnipeg, Conservative MP Rod Bruinooge, one of the up-and-coming evangelicals in Harper's caucus, also presided over the announcement that $320,000 in economic stimulus funds had been allotted to a new Jewish Learning Centre in the city's south end planned by the Orthodox Chabad-Lubavitch sect.

Still, even some members of the Jewish community were outraged when the Conservatives attempted to convert their policies into a partisan vote grab: in late 2009, taxpayer-funded flyers suddenly appeared in the mailboxes of heavily Jewish ridings in Toronto, Montreal and

Winnipeg, accusing the Liberals of actions hostile to Israel, including Michael Ignatieff's 2006 denunciation of the country for war crimes. "Who is on the right track to represent and defend the values of Canada's Jewish community?" the leaflet demanded in a mock quiz beside the portrait of a beaming Harper. Veteran Liberal MP Irwin Cotler, a staunch supporter of Israel whose daughter had even served in its army, denounced the mailings as "scandalous" and an attempt "to associate the Liberal party with anti-Semitism," while House speaker Peter Milliken issued an official reprimand. But Jason Kenney scoffed at the notion that an apology was in order. Clearly on the same page, B'nai Brith's weekly *Jewish Tribune* offered not a word of disapproval, choosing instead to reprint the parliamentary debate, thereby offering ample space to a stinging put-down of the Liberals' record by Harper's parliamentary secretary, Pierre Poilievre.

In forging that alliance with Dimant and company, Harper has aligned himself with the wing of the Jewish community that holds the most uncompromising views on the Middle East peace process, but that gamble appears to have paid off so far. B'nai Brith's *Tribune* has been unfailingly complimentary in its coverage of Harper's government and at least two of the organization's former officials, including Rochelle Wilner, have run as Conservative candidates. It is an allegiance that Dimant himself has worked to promote, propelled in part by the demographic writing on the wall. Statisticians predict that, by 2011, Toronto will be home to at least 400,000 Muslims—more than the country's entire Jewish population. "The Jewish community is stagnating and will probably shrink, while the anti-Israel forces in this country are growing,"Dimant points out. "We need a strategic ally, and that ally is the evangelicals."

In 2003, just as Harper was crafting his theo-con strategy to include the Jewish community, Dimant himself swung into action, convening a meeting of B'nai Brith's board to table an unprecedented motion authorizing a formal partnership with the Christian right. The move was opposed by only one long-time director. To foster that alliance, Dimant hired Joseph Ben-Ami, the convert to Orthodox Judaism who had worked with evangelicals as a former strategist for Stockwell Day, and later for Harper himself. Like Dimant, Ben Ami had done the math: "The Jewish community in Canada is 380,000 strong," he notes. "The evangelical community is three and a half million. The real support base for Israel is Christians."

✢

Dimant's first contact was with a group called Christians for Israel run by John Tweedie, the pastor of a breakaway evangelical congregation in Brantford, Ontario. A Protestant from Northern Ireland, Tweedie's devotion to Israel came after a series of epiphanies, the first of which convinced him to enroll in divinity school—no mean feat for a twenty-seven-year-old high-school dropout then employed as an electrician. But Tweedie worked his way through the University of Guelph and Emmanuel College, eventually earning ordination as a minister in the United Church. As a graduation gift, a member of his congregation bankrolled a trip to Israel, which proved to be a life-changing experience. Eight years later, Tweedie had a life-changing experience of another sort: he broke with the United Church over its decision to allow the ordination of practicing homosexuals. "For me, it was a crossroads," he later told a church historian.

When most of his parishioners followed him, Tweedie began holding Sunday services in a Brantford school. Inspired by a passage from Jeremiah 31:31—"Behold I make a new covenant with the House of Israel"—he christened his congregation the New Covenant Christian Fellowship, and now regards the name as a prophetic sign. That year Tweedie led the first of many evangelical tours to Israel, and as word of his work spread over the next decade, Christians for Israel International, based in the Netherlands, approached him to start a

Canadian branch. Founded during the period when Menachem Begin was courting American evangelicals, the organization was so close to Begin's ally, Jerusalem mayor Ehud Olmert, that he often let it use his city hall boardroom. Although much of the group's focus was raising money for Israeli charities, it was also a major force in the aliyah movement that brought more than 100,000 Jews from Ethiopia and the former Soviet Union to Israel. Those activities later proved problematic for Tweedie when he sought charitable tax status for his Canadian operation. Initially, Revenue Canada refused his application, ruling that his group was engaged in political activity because it had relocated most of those Soviet Jews to disputed West Bank settlements.

But the settlement program was not the organization's only foray into the charged arena of Middle East politics. In 2004, as the International Court of Justice in The Hague contemplated the legality of the security wall Israel was constructing through the West Bank, Tweedie's organization brought the burned-out skeleton of a Jerusalem bus that had been attacked by Palestinian suicide bombers to the Dutch capital, parking it outside the court in a bold public-relations move. "We thought this would help them understand what the people of Israel are up against," Tweedie later explained in an interview. "Why they need a wall."

Those ventures onto the global stage proved a boon to Tweedie's career: he now chairs the parent organization, Christians for Israel International, which, as part of a continental coalition, lobbies the European Parliament on Israel's behalf. Meanwhile, from his modest Brantford church, he still runs the Canadian branch, which boasts a $600,000 annual budget. One of his chief contributors has been Sydney Harkema, the Dutch-born trucking tycoon who sold his fleet to American interests and has used that windfall to underwrite evangelical causes, including Charles McVety's Institute of Canadian Values. With Harkema's backing, Tweedie continued to lead evangelical tours to Israel even after the outbreak of the second intifadah. "That was remembered in Israel," he says. "I began to sense a real warming. More than once, people would come over in a restaurant and thank us for coming."

Despite that history, Dimant was wary when he met Tweedie over kosher muffins and coffee to draft plans for the first Canadian evangelical-Jewish delegation to Israel. "There was trepidation," Dimant admits. "We worried, 'Would there be continual references to Christ?'" But even in the Galilee, where Tweedie tutored the group on Jesus's early life, Dimant found his sermons couched in a context he could accept. When they visited a West Bank settlement, he was taken aback when the Orthodox residents greeted Tweedie and his evangelical members with more gusto than they did fellow Jews. As it turned out, Christians for Israel had sponsored fifty of those settlers from Ukraine. Later, in Jerusalem, Dimant caught sight of his evangelical tour mates returning from a shopping trip. "They were carrying shofars!" he marvelled. "Menorahs! I couldn't believe it: they were so respectful of our heritage."

Tweedie has since turned footage from the trip into an eight-part DVD series called *Why Israel? What Time Is It?*, which has been sold to evangelical congregations around the world. But it seems clear that at least part of the purpose of the delegation was to reassure B'nai Brith's own membership about its newfound alliance with conservative Christians—a strategy that appears to have paid off. Wilner later won Tweedie a weekly spot on one of Toronto's top Jewish radio programs, the *Zelda Young Show*, where he spent three years explaining to skeptical callers why Christian Zionists are so attached to Israel. "I've had Holocaust survivors phone in and weep," he says, "because they've never heard a Christian speak like that."

While Tweedie is careful not to make overt foreign-policy statements on behalf of Christians for Israel, his personal views match those of Dimant and the most hardline parties on Israel's right wing. He opposes calls for a Palestinian homeland. "I have a biblical worldview so I don't agree with trading land for peace," he admits. "The Bible says, 'Treat

the strangers among you with respect,' but not with their own state."
Articles on his website go so far as to question Palestinians' historical
claims. "In the Bible there never was a nation called Palestine," he
insists. "It was a concept brought in by the Roman empire."

Since his first trip with Tweedie, Dimant has forged ties with other
evangelical groups and taken part in numerous joint delegations to
Israel. In the midst of one fact-finding mission for MPs that included
Jason Kenney, he was en route to a briefing in the Palestinian town of
Ramallah when the group ran into El Fatah's security chief, the much-
feared Jibril Rajoub. Dimant was already wearing a Greek fisherman's
cap over his kippah, but Kenney suggested a quick revision of titles.
The vice president of B'nai Brith Canada suddenly found himself introduced as Kenney's parliamentary aide.

Such gestures have cemented Dimant's ties to the country's emerging Christian right and, above all, to its most vocal standard-bearer,
Charles McVety. In return, Canada Christian College has not only
awarded honorary doctorates to Dimant and John Tweedie, but McVety
has restored the college's once-controversial department of Jewish
Studies and named his B'nai Brith pal as its chair. Still, that alliance
has horrified some members of the Jewish community, notably Stephen
Scheinberg, a professor emeritus at Concordia University and former
B'nai Brith vice-president, who vociferously opposed Dimant's initia-
tive. In a scathing denunciation published in the summer of 2008 in
Canadian Jewish Outlook, Scheinberg lambasted Dimant for linking
B'nai Brith, a historic human rights organization, with "the anti-gay,
anti-feminist, pro-censorship stance of Reverend Charles McVety."

He has also warned that evangelical interest in Israel may not bode
well for the survival of Judaism. By underwriting Jewish immigration
to Israel, Scheinberg argues, Christian Zionists may be engaged in little
more than theological opportunism. While that return of Jews to biblical territory is a prerequisite for the dispensationalist scenario, Darby's
plot line provides no celestial escape hatch for them in the end times:

according to most interpretations of the Rapture, only those who have accepted Jesus Christ as their personal saviour will be summoned heavenward to escape the seven years of tribulation and the final battle unleashed by the Antichrist.

Indeed, borrowing from the book of Revelation, Hal Lindsey's *The Late Great Planet Earth* paints a horrendous portrait of Israel as a mass killing ground during the final days, awash in rivers of blood, predicting that only a remnant of 144,000 Jews will survive the Battle of Armageddon, all of them having accepted Christ as the true Messiah. Rather than repudiating that prospect, Scheinberg charged, "The pragmatic Jewish right prefers the dispensationalist money and support in the here and now."

Similar objections have been raised in Israel, where a handful of prominent rabbis have barred some charities from accepting evangelical funds, charging that their true agenda is the mass conversion of Jews. It is a message the Israeli government has taken pains to downplay, but the controversy has posed an ongoing problem for Tweedie and his Christian Zionist colleagues. Although he believes in the Rapture, he insists that he also embraces a "dual covenant theology"—the theory that God has made end-times pacts with both the Jewish people and born-again Christians—but Tweedie admits that he generally tries to avoid the issue. "It's a complicated question," he tells me. "We don't find it profitable to get too specific about end-times prophecy."

In the spring of 2007, however, another Christian Zionist organization was concerned enough to host a series of theological seminars on the subject. On a Saturday morning, three dozen evangelicals showed up at a hotel conference room in north Toronto, well-thumbed Bibles and notebooks at the ready, to listen to Reverend Malcolm Hedding, the South African–born Pentecostal who is executive director of the International Christian Embassy in Jerusalem. As quickly becomes apparent, this is no crowd of blinkered country bumpkins. Among those in the audience is a physician at a downtown hospital who has devoted her career to saving lives and now worries that she also ought to be saving her Jewish colleagues' souls by proselytizing to them. For her, it would be a great relief to learn that God had already taken care of the matter. "I look at the head of my department," she confides, "and I think, 'No way can I go into his home and talk about Jesus.'"

For three hours, Hedding winds his way through the theological maze raised by competing passages in the Old and New Testaments. Rhyming off scriptural references, he takes aim at replacement theology—the belief that God's covenant with Israel was declared null and void when the Jewish nation rejected Jesus Christ as the Messiah and Christians stepped into the role of the chosen people. "The New Testament fully affirms the Abrahamic covenant," Hedding assures his audience. "The Jews—they are the custodians of the redemptive purpose of God. Jesus said it. He has never changed his mind."

But the longer Hedding talks, the more he seems mired in a dispensational minefield. The return of the Jewish people to Israel, he concedes, is "the trigger mechanism for the return of Jesus." Then he blurts out a conviction that might have left a Jewish audience aghast. "From a theological point of view, there is only one way of salvation," he says. "Jesus said it: 'I am the way, the truth and the life.' If they believe in Jesus, they can be saved." A man in a sport shirt presses him: Does he mean that Jews must convert or perish? "Now, I am not going to play God," Hedding says, shimmying around the question. "I'm going to let God work that out."

By the end of the seminar, Hedding looks as if he wishes the entire discussion would go away, but as one attendee can testify, that possibility seems increasingly improbable. In his audience is Conservative MP James Lunney, one of the leading Christian Zionists in Harper's caucus, whose wife, at that very moment, was en route to an evangelical women's conference in Israel co-sponsored by Hedding's organization. Only days earlier, a group of Israeli rabbis had tried to cancel the event because, as Lunney puts it, "They were afraid there was a conversionary agenda." Given that threat, it's no wonder that Hedding is rushing about, trying to put out theological fires. As he well knows, if evangelicals were to get the idea that some Jews did not want their money and support, it could prove disastrous to both sides, threatening Israel's economy and putting the brakes on Christian Zionists' fast track to the Rapture.

⁜

Two nights later, James Lunney is front and centre at the Toronto Centre for the Arts—seated alongside Frank Dimant and the Israeli consul general—as the International Christian Embassy in Jerusalem presents a musical called *The Covenant*. Written and produced by evangelicals, the elaborate costume drama opens with the voice of God speaking to Abraham in the desert, then sweeps through the rest of the Old Testament at a dizzying pace. A musical number with Ruth and her mother-in-law Naomi here. A cameo by Esther pleading for her people there. Daniel being consigned to the lion's den. Then, suddenly, Jesus of Nazareth materializes onstage, trying to prevent zealots from stoning an adulteress and cautioning the restive crowd, "Let he who is without sin cast the first stone." As Christ is hustled off to an unseen fate, it is not the rabbis who persecute him as they do in Mel Gibson's controversial recapitulation of the passion play; here, Roman soldiers are the villains and the rabbis cry out in Jesus's defence: "He is one of us."

But *The Covenant* makes no further mention of the defining events at the heart of the Christian story: the Crucifixion and Resurrection, the rolling away of the tombstone and the Apostles' shock of recognition at the risen Messiah. Its script focuses on another narrative beyond the Bible's final chapter. Speeding through centuries of Jewish persecution—from the Spanish Inquisition to the Warsaw ghetto uprising and the horrors of the Holocaust—it climaxes with its own resurrection story, heralded in a blaze of lights and grainy newsreel footage: the birth of Israel as a nation. As the cast breaks into the Israeli national anthem, then a hallelujah chorus, the spotlight falls on a platoon of Israeli soldiers massed in a heroic tableau, rifles at the ready, bathed in a glorious, otherworldly light. A rabbi carries the Torah onstage and the entire company stares heavenward as a disembodied voice beseeches an unseen power to "complete what you have planned so the world will know you are God."

Despite the elaborate costumes and slickness of the production, the show has the feel of a high-school pageant with a not-so-thinly-veiled message. Hinting at some divine denouement yet to come, it is a tribute to the Israel Defense Forces, who turn out to have been one of its target audiences. Since its debut in 2001, a Hebrew version of *The Covenant* has played for more than fifty thousand of the country's soldiers, including those stationed at lonely outposts in the Negev and West Bank. Its primary purpose, like all of the work of the International Christian Embassy in Jerusalem, is to reassure Israelis that they do not stand alone; Christian Zionists around the world are on their side.

That message of solidarity dates back to the ICEJ's founding in 1980, when Menachem Begin defied international agreements to annex East Jerusalem as Israel's capital. Thirteen nations moved their embassies out of the city in protest, setting up shop in Tel Aviv, but in a counter-protest discreetly backed by his government, a group of charismatic Christians took over Chile's former building and proclaimed it their diplomatic headquarters. Now, with a staff of sixty and offices in eighty-two countries around the globe, the International Christian Embassy in Jerusalem is the largest and most influential of the country's Christian Zionist organizations.

Although run largely by Dutch and South African Pentecostals, ICEJ counts among its founders two Canadian musicians, Merv and Merla Watson, who moved to Israel in the 1970s. At that time, the Watsons had already made a name in charismatic circles, presiding over a mini-revival in a Toronto church where an Israeli-born teenager named Benny Hinn declared he had found Jesus, enlisting in their itinerant troupe as a dancer years before he emerged as a multi-millionaire televangelist and faith healer himself.

The Watsons would never attain a fraction of Benny Hinn's celebrity or his wealth, but, known for performing their own Israel-inspired compositions—Merla on violin, Merv on accordion and guitar—they came up with the idea for a celebration to mark the ICEJ's opening, which would coincide with the annual Jewish festival of Sukkot. Christened the Feast of Tabernacles, it attracted more than a thousand evangelicals from twenty-three countries to Jerusalem, where they were blessed by Israel's chief rabbi. By 1983, the Feast had become an annual event, and among those who signed up for it was James Lunney, then a chiropractor in Kitchener, Ontario, with no interest in running for office at the time. For Lunney, that visit was the first of fourteen trips to Israel and left him so moved that he returned home to take part in an Israel Awareness Rally in Toronto's Nathan Phillips Square. Later, he came involved with the Canadian branch of the International Christian Embassy in Jerusalem, originally chaired by Vancouver's gravel-voiced evangelist, Bernice Gerard.

Now, nearly three decades later, the Feast of Tabernacles has become Israel's largest single tourist draw—a ten-day extravaganza that brings more than eight thousand Christians to the country, most of them charismatics who march through the streets of Jerusalem in exuberant carnival mode, flags waving, decked out in national costumes, including the gigantic starred-and-striped top hats of Uncle Sam. To cater to that growing Christian tourist clientele, ICEJ has launched a monthly evangelical edition of the *Jerusalem Post* and, on its twenty-fifth anniversary in 2008, the Knesset held a special tribute, hailing the organization as "a central pillar in the efforts to win international support for Israel."

⁂

That tribute was organized by the Knesset Christian Allies Caucus, a committee of Israeli parliamentarians set up to foster alliances with evangelical politicians in governments around the globe. In 2006, the two-year-old caucus—then chaired by former Israeli tourism minister Benny Elon—spun off a mirror-image of itself in the United States called the Congressional Israel Allies Caucus and announced plans to follow suit in nine other countries. A year later, the Knesset delegation arrived in Ottawa, leaking the news that it was launching a chapter composed of Canadian MPs. Although the *Jerusalem Post* announced the development with fanfare, reporting that the new parliamentary lobby would be unveiled "in the presence of Canadian Prime Minister Stephen Harper," not a peep about the event appeared in government press releases or in this country's mainstream media. One reason may be that reporters' interest would hardly have been piqued by the announcement of a Canada-Israel Friendship Group; after all, some version of such a caucus had existed for years. What few understood was that after Harper's election, the Canada-Israel Friendship Group underwent a shakeup. Now, more than half of its executive is made up of evangelical Conservatives, many of whom share the Christian Zionist sentiments of its new chairman, James Lunney.

The caucus chairmanship is a job that Lunney regards as a sacred mission. He has hosted his Knesset counterparts on two cross-Canada tours, and in the spring of 2008 he joined Christian Zionist lawmakers from nine other nations in Washington for a conference of their umbrella group, the International Israel Allies Caucus Foundation. There, as head of the Canadian contingent, Lunney ratified an eight-point "Declaration of Purpose and Solidarity with the People and State of Israel" that might have given pause to voters back home. One of its principles insists that any "pre-emptive" military strike Israel might take in defending its territory is justified; another proclaims Jerusalem as "the undivided capital of Israel," and declares that "all of the nations of the world should locate their embassies in Jerusalem."

But the most astonishing clause essentially pronounces all negotiations between Israeli and Palestinian officials pointless. "While we all yearn for peace, we recognize that pressure on Israel from the international community to negotiate and make concessions with those sworn to its destruction has not led to peace," it argues. "We regard such attempts as futile."

Although the declaration does not represent official government policy, it does reflect sentiments within the Conservative caucus that have bolstered Harper's pro-Israel tilt. That tilt is at odds with a 2007 Strategic Counsel poll, which reported that 77 percent of Canadians favour a neutral foreign policy in the Middle East, but when it comes to Israel, Harper seems uncharacteristically impervious to public opinion surveys. Nor is Lunney the only Christian Zionist in his caucus who is passionately applauding such a policy. Documents on the Knesset Christian Allies Caucus' website list the co-chair of the Canada-Israel group as Lunney's friend and political mentor, Stockwell Day.

As Harper's minister of public safety, Day negotiated a controversial security agreement with the Israeli government that only came to light during the 2008 shelling of Hamas militants in the Gaza Strip. Signed on a low-profile trip to Israel months earlier—a trip that coincided with a visit by then U.S. vice president Dick Cheney—the agreement was aimed at enhancing cooperation on the vaguely worded issue of "border management and security." Since the two countries don't share any common boundaries, critics speculate that the agreement commits Canadian officials, including those from the Royal Canadian Mounted Police and intelligence agencies, to assist Israel in policing its internal barriers against Palestinians in Gaza and the West Bank. The pact also promises aid in "public order capacity-building," better known as riot control. Given the 2009 United Nations fact-finding report that deemed Israel guilty of war crimes during its military offensive in Gaza, the agreement raises a discomfiting question: were Canadians complicit in those human rights violations?

Day's security agreement is not entirely unexpected from a charismatic Christian who cemented his pro-Israel credentials when he was the Canadian Alliance foreign affairs critic and pushed to have Hamas and Hezbollah classified as terrorist groups. That move was prompted in no small measure by the man he chose as his Middle East adviser, Paul Charles Merkley, a retired history professor from Carleton University in Ottawa, who is one of the country's leading experts on Christian Zionism and an ardent Christian Zionist himself. A member of the Evangelical Lutheran Church, Merkley spent six months as a visiting professor at the Hebrew University of Jerusalem in 1981, when Begin was forging ties with foreign evangelicals, and has published three books on the subject, including *Christian Attitudes Towards The State of Israel* and *American Presidents, Religion and Israel*. He remained on Day's staff after the 2006 election when Day became the country's security czar. "Stockwell Day," Merkley now says, "is the best friend Israel has ever had."

He is less complimentary about Stephen Harper. Despite Harper's unflagging support for Israel and his tendency to brand criticism of the country as nascent anti-Semitism, he has apparently failed to prove himself hawkish enough for Merkley's taste. "He's caught in the foreign affairs mindset," Merkely says, "where you can come down on either side." As a director of the Canadian branch of the ICEJ, Merkley has waged a relentless campaign against critics of Israel and Christian Zionism, dismissing them as ill-informed hysterics and worse. In the summer of 2009, he issued a blistering attack against the United Church for agreeing to debate a controversial resolution proposing a boycott of Israel at its annual general meeting. While the resolution was widely criticized by media commentators, and even some United Church members themselves, none went as far as Merkley, who compared the church's general council with Iranian strongman Mahmoud Ahmadinejad, accusing it of coming "perilously close to resurrecting the medieval blood libel against the Jews."

Addressing a seminar at Toronto's Beth Tzedec Synagogue in the winter of 2008, Merkley seemed incapable of fathoming that some members of his audience might actually endorse a two-state solution to the Palestinian conflict. He dismissed George Bush's Roadmap to Peace as the product of "irrational" behaviour and, when asked about the prospects for a Palestinian homeland, made no attempt to mask his disdain. "The Arab population of Palestine has proved itself incompetent and unworthy of creating a state," he declared.

But the chief target of his ire appears to be anyone who dares to raise questions about Israeli policy: journalists, liberals and even secular Jews. Speaking to an audience that included doctors and scholars, he took an anti-intellectual swipe at the liberalism of most fellow academics, blaming it on "a sense people acquire in universities that they don't belong to anything—they all study sociology." Still, his most withering scorn was reserved for those evangelical theologians who have dared to attack dispensationalism, the foundational theory that underpins the Christian Zionist movement. One object of Merkley's wrath is Barbara Rossing, an associate professor of New Testament at the Lutheran School of Theology in Chicago, who argues in her 2004 book, *The Rapture Exposed*, that John Nelson Darby's prophetic timeline is the product of "a dangerous and false reading" of the Bible. Nowhere in the Old or New Testaments is there any mention of the Rapture, Rossing points out, let alone any passage that makes the Second Coming contingent on the re-establishment of a Jewish state. Instead, modern-day dispensationalists have seized on the gory metaphors of the book of Revelation to hype a shock-and-awe scenario that Rossing boils down to a one-sentence precis: "God so loved the world He sent World War III."

Rossing's debunking of dispensationalism is sufficiently persuasive that I can't help wondering if the current craze for final-days film scripts is based on theological hogwash. But, as Bush's disastrous misadventure in Iraq showed, theological hogwash can be singularly dangerous in the hands of leaders so entranced with fitting together the pieces of a prophetic puzzle that they embark on a damn-the-torpedoes foreign policy. Dispensationalists never seem to be the ones counselling diplomatic restraint. At a time when *Left Behind* followers can check the proximity of the end times on the Rapture Index at raptureready.com, the worry is that a government that has aligned itself with the most belligerent voices in Israel—and is riddled with biblical literalists certain of the inevitiability of an end-times conflagration in the Middle East—could, wittingly or not, hasten that apocalyptic scenario.

HERE TO STAY

XI

The day after Barack Obama's inauguration, Canada's leading pro-life website zapped a provocative question into the global ether: "Is Obama the Anti-Christ?" The source of that query was Michael O'Brien, an Ottawa-area writer best known for his novel, *Father Elijah: An Apocalypse*, whose protagonist receives a commission from the pope to confront the fabled personification of evil. O'Brien claimed to have received inquiries from around the world about the striking similarities between the new U.S. president and his demonic villain, concluding, "There is more here than meets the eye." Obama, he wrote, "probably is one of several key figures in the world who (knowingly or unknowingly) will be instrumental in ushering in the time of great trial for the Church under its last and worst persecution."

That inflammatory bulletin was a telling counterpoint to the celebratory hoopla surrounding Obama's arrival in power in January 2009. At the time, most voices in the continent's mainstream media were once again pronouncing the religious right in extremis and every update on the nightly news seemed to confirm that diagnosis. Even within the U.S. movement itself, disillusionment had given way to disarray as many of the titans who had fuelled its rise were fading from their electronic pulpits, some toppled by death or scandal, others like James Dobson handing over the reins to a younger, less charismatic generation. In the prelude to the 2008 presidential election, the decline of the once-feared electoral juggernaut that Jerry Falwell had founded three decades earlier seemed beyond dispute when it proved incapable of settling on a new presidential standard-bearer to challenge the disappointing candidacy of John McCain.

On both sides of the border, Obama's election was hailed as a tipping point, the moment when a majority of Americans finally revolted against years of overheated piety in favour of an appeal for spiritual tolerance. In the wake of the economic tsunami that helped sweep him into office, the preoccupations of the Christian right suddenly appeared irrelevant. "Here at last is one piece of good news in the global economic meltdown," trumpeted *New York Times* columnist Frank Rich. "Culture wars are a luxury the country can no longer afford."

As it turned out, those elegies were premature. Rather than banishing Bush's faith-based bureaucracy and rhetoric from the White House, Obama has actually outdone him in public religiosity. From the invocation by celebrity pastor Rick Warren at the inauguration to his own address to the Islamic world enunciating his belief in Jesus Christ, he has "embraced faith in a more visible way than any other president in recent memory," according to Dan Gilgoff, the religion writer for *U.S. News & World Report*. While Bush was careful, even covert, in his scriptural allusions, Obama opened major presidential rallies with prayers solicited from local pastors, and mentioned Jesus with a frequency his predecessor would never have dared. Instead of scrapping Bush's Office of Faith-Based Initiatives, he expanded its mission and named a new twenty-five-member Faith Advisory Council, prompting Gilgoff, the founder of Beliefnet's "God-o-meter," to dub him the "faithiest" president in American history.

Those gestures may be aimed at breaking the Republican monopoly on the evangelical vote, but they also confirm that religion will not be shunted to the sidelines of American politics any time soon. Two of the leading contenders for the next Republican presidential nomination are conservative Christians whose support comes primarily from the party's evangelical base: guitar-strumming ex-pastor Mike Huckabee and former Alaska governor Sarah 'Palin, who is tied to the radical charismatic renewal movement that is reshaping Pentecostalism.

Not only is the U.S. Christian right alive and kicking under Obama, but mere months after he took office, the culture wars erupted again in the ugly hysteria of the health-care debate. America seemed more polarized than ever—the right and left locked in a bitter TV advertising war, town-hall meetings seething with venom and threats of violence that suddenly materialized in an unexpected context. On a sunlit Sunday morning in May 2009, a lone gunman pumped a fatal bullet into George Tiller, one of the leading U.S. abortion providers, as he went about his weekly ushering duties at a Kansas Lutheran Church. For pro-choice advocates, it was all the more alarming that Tiller's assassination came early in Obama's presidency, right after he had reversed two of Bush's pro-life measures by executive order: when the shooting of abortion doctors began in March 1993, it was three months after the swearing in of Bill Clinton, the first openly pro-choice occupant of the White House.

Feminists were not alone in seeing Tiller's murder as an ominous sign. As corporate behemoths teetered on the brink of financial ruin and tens of thousands lost their jobs, a movement that feeds on anxieties about society's moral breakdown invoked unsettling historic parallels. It was the anguish of the Great Depression, after all, that provided fertile ground for demagogues like Father Charles Coughlin, whose radio audience in the 1930s—estimated to be one-third of the U.S. population—helped to build the fascist Christian Front.

The day after Tiller's assassination, twenty pro-life groups across the continent condemned the shooting, but the Canadian evangelical website No Apologies posted an essay by Doug Phillips, one of the most controversial figures in the U.S. Christian nationalist movement. "Tiller the Killer is dead," it began. "Who shall mourn for this man? Perhaps the bigger question is this: who will mourn for the more than 60,000 babies that Dr. George Tiller brutally murdered in the most horrific manner imaginable?" Calling Tiller the "church-going Sweeney Todd of the medical profession," who prayed on Sundays, then "chopped up babies" on Mondays, the essay made a point of deploring homicide, but much of it read like a rationale for the shooting and a veiled encouragement for others to follow suit.

Although pundits like to insist that the virulence of the U.S. political debate could never infect this country, the Internet is increasingly blurring cross-border distinctions and calling that assumption into question. No Apologies is not the product of a rogue cabal on the extremist fringe; it is the news site of the ECP Centre, an organization that is funded by some of the country's leading businessmen and now headed by Timothy Bloedow, one of the most experienced hands on Parliament Hill. As the chief aide to Saskatchewan MP Maurice Vellacott, Bloedow has helped turn his boss's office into a clearing house for Christian-right activity in the capital, and on his own website, christiangovernment.ca, he openly calls for the establishment of a "Christian theocracy." Linking environmentalism with Nazism and damning human rights tribunals as instruments of Soviet-style repression, Bloedow could hardly be accused of moderation as he insists that "Christian government is an idea whose time has come."

⁜

From the moment I began this book, I was confronted by skeptics who insist that a truly influential religious right could never take root in Canada. For some, that denial seemed like an exercise in wishful thinking, a refusal to face the possibility that the idea of the country they cherish—liberal, tolerant, and not given to extremes of action or belief—might not be in sync with the changing reality. Others argued that if a Christian right did exist here it would have burst fully formed onto the political scene, a carbon copy of that in the U.S.—raucous and confrontational, openly pulling the strings of the Conservative Party and captained by outspoken television preachers with millions of viewers ready to respond to their bidding. But the American movement has had more than three decades to take shape and flourish; by the time scholars and the mainstream media noticed, it had already infiltrated nearly every level of government from school boards to the Senate, often by stealth.

In this country, where the CRTC has kept the reins on religious broadcasting and Catholics make up a larger proportion of the faith community, the emergent Christian right may look and sound different than its American counterpart, but in the five years since the prospect of same-sex marriage propelled evangelicals into political action, it has spawned a coalition of advocacy groups, think tanks and youth lobbies that have changed the national debate. The "sleeping giant" that *Capital Xtra!* magazine had warned against in 2005 is now up and about, organizing with a vengeance that will not be easily reversed. As Faytene Kryskow told a parliamentary reception, "We are here, and we are here to stay."

With funding from a handful of conservative Christian philanthropists and a web of grassroots believers accustomed to tithing in the service of their faith, those organizations have built sophisticated databases and online networks capable of mobilizing their forces behind specific legislation with instant e-mail alerts and updates. Setting up an array of internship programs, they are also training a new generation of activists to be savvier than their secular peers in navigating the corridors of power. Already, their alumni have landed top jobs in the public service, MPs' offices and the PMO, prompting one official from the National House of Prayer to boast in an unguarded moment, "If the media knew how many Christians there are in the government, they'd go crazy."

In fact, as the movement focuses on taking over the "gateways of influence," one of the portals within its sights is the mainstream media itself. Where once social conservatives regarded the fourth estate as hostile territory from which they had been sidelined, now the heads of religious-right think tanks, such as Dave Quist and Joseph Ben-Ami, have become regular spin-meisters for the social conservative point of view, their numbers on the speed-dial of Ottawa reporters seeking an instant quip or a quote. At the same time, Faytene Kryskow is training her young activists in the art of getting letters to the editor and opinion pieces published—furnishing online examples to copy and a daily index of articles demanding commentary—none of them betraying their links to 4MYCanada. As she crowed to a gathering of MPs, "You are likely reading our words much more often than you realize."

Numerically, the Canadian religious right may still be a fraction of that in the U.S., but as Ottawa communications consultant Dennis Gruending points out, "Groups that are well-organized can punch above their weight—particularly in an era of fractured parliaments and minority governments." A former New Democratic Party MP, Gruending laments that "there is little in progressive Ottawa to rival the networks that have been created by the religious and political right."

Moreover, pundits who predicted those networks would vanish in the wake of the same-sex marriage defeat have instead seen them proliferate. Amid the stormy U.S. health-care debate of 2009, most Canadians were stunned to discover that one of their own was the star of a two-million-dollar television campaign warning Americans about the perils of this country's publicly funded medical system. Shona Holmes, the poster girl for that attack, turned out to be fronting a lawsuit against Ontario's health ministry spearheaded by a Calgary-based legal advocacy group named the Canadian Constitution Foundation. Originally created by Conservative MP John Weston, the foundation was at first not considered part of the Christian right, but one of its board members, Dr. Will Johnston, is president of Canadian

Physicians for Life, and Weston himself is an evangelical who once told Christian law students that what set his Vancouver law firm apart was "the regularity and informality of prayer practiced by the partners." Although Weston's initial focus was on pet libertarian peeves like medicare, since he stepped down to run for Parliament, the foundation has devoted many of its resources to defending evangelicals like former Alberta pastor Stephen Boissoin in freedom-of-speech cases against another perceived incursion of the state: human rights commissions.

Nor is the foundation the only new presence on the evangelical political scene. In 2008, it was joined by the Association for Reformed Political Action (ARPA) founded by Mark Penninga, a Laurentian Leadership Centre alumnus and former spokesman for Focus on the Family Canada, whose mission it is to "bring a biblical perspective to civil governments." Both ARPA and the Canadian Constitution Foundation are working with more established evangelical groups in a new push to coordinate their campaigns for greater effect. Nowhere has that joint strategizing been more evident than on the issue that has been pegged as the next flashpoint in the values wars: the decriminalization of assisted suicide, or, as the religious right prefers to call it, euthanasia.

✢

In Ottawa, the debate was reignited in the spring of 2009 by a diminutive Bloc Quebecois MP named Francine Lalonde, who introduced a private member's bill to eliminate the penalties for physician-assisted suicide. It was Lalonde's third attempt to win death-with-dignity legislation and it is unlikely to be her last. Her determination is fuelled by a poignant personal saga that began a year after she introduced the first version of her bill: on her way to a meeting with Belgium's right-to-die society, Lalonde bent over to pick up her suitcase and felt a searing pain rip through her lower back that was diagnosed as a rare form of cancer. After months of radiation and chemotherapy, she had just returned to the House when she found herself battling a new, more aggressive form of the disease. Now those health woes have steeled her resolve. When critics decry her measures as the first step down a slippery moral slope, Lalonde points to the growing numbers of Quebecers prosecuted for giving in to the pleas of loved ones to end their suffering. "That to me is the slippery slope," she says. "They put pressure on their relatives and that's really a tough situation."

A majority of Canadians appear to agree. Polls show that 76 percent of the population favours legalizing some form of physician-assisted suicide, but opponents are unmoved by the weight of public opinion. For Alex Schadenberg, head of the Euthanasia Prevention Coalition, Lalonde's bill is a direct threat to those with disabilities or chronic conditions, and as the father of an autistic son, he fears a law that could see medical authorities making life-and-death decisions based on a scale of social utility. "Once society allows one person to kill another," he says, "it becomes impossible to protect those who are made to feel like a burden."

As baby boomers confront their impending mortality and the marvels of medical science pose new ethical dilemmas for families and physicians, the debate over assisted suicide threatens to become as polarizing as those over abortion or same-sex marriage, pitting primeval fears against the proscription laid out in the Judeo-Christian rulebook handed down to Moses on the mount: "Thou shalt not kill." Still, the issue is not as clear-cut as it might seem. Conservative MP Steven Fletcher, a quadriplegic who relies on an intricately equipped wheelchair and a full-time personal aide, published a moving explanation of why he felt compelled to abstain from the vote on Lalonde's bill. Although he criticized it for lacking sufficient measures to support the severely injured and ill, Fletcher said he could not deny others the choice to end lives of intolerable pain, nor had he entirely ruled it out as an eventual option of his own. "I do not want to be forced to live in a hell because the law does not take into account my 'unique' circum-stances or because someone imposed their values on the meaning of life on me," he wrote in the *National Post*. "Given the choice of exist-ence without living or death, I would rather choose the latter and take my chances on the other side."

Calgary's Bishop Fred Henry has warned that right-to-die legislation risks eroding trust in doctors—no small concern to the medical profes-sion itself. Anticipating the looming ethical morass, Quebec's College of Physicians became the country's first medical body to adopt a set of guidelines that includes drug-induced euthanasia as a legitimate treat-ment option for patients facing "imminent and inevitable death."

Although it seems inconceivable that Harper's government would introduce assisted-suicide legislation, public pressure is building for Canada to follow Belgium, the Netherlands and Switzerland in allowing some form of the practice. That pressure increased in November 2008 when a ballot initiative made Washington the second state after Oregon to pass a death-with-dignity measure, sending shock waves through the Christian right in neighbouring B.C. "Things really have heated up," Schadenberg worries. "This is an issue that is not going to go away."

Preston Manning predicts that a debate on the subject today could make the passions unleashed by the 1993 case of Sue Rodriguez look like a polite grade school debate. Paralyzed by Lou Gehrig's disease and facing inevitable death, Rodriguez became a compelling national figure as she petitioned the Supreme Court for the constitutional right to assistance in ending her life. Although she lost in a five-to-four ruling, her fate transfixed the country and sent emotions off the charts, inspir-ing books and a film. Now, more than a decade after that decision, Schadenberg claims that lawyers for the right-to-die movement have crafted legal arguments for another Supreme Court challenge; all they need is a suitably sympathetic complainant on whom to base their case. This time around, Manning warns, the court could well reverse its stand—Chief Justice Beverley McLachlin was one of the dissenters in

the Rodriquez decision—directing Parliament to come up with legislation. "If that's the case," he says, "it makes it especially important to
stiffen the backs of parliamentarians by stiffening public opinion."

To that end, Manning assembled representatives from a half-dozen
Christian right organizations for a "Wilberforce Weekend" of concerted
strategizing in the fall of 2009. The invitation-only conference was
also an attempt to rally evangelicals to a cause that, like the anti-
abortion movement, has been largely dominated by Catholics. Although
Schadenberg insists his Euthanasia Prevention Coalition is secular, his
background and support base undercut that claim. He spent five years
running a pro-life ministry for the Catholic church in London, Ontario,
and a 2007 symposium on euthanasia that he organized with the
archdiocese of Toronto in an airport hotel wrapped up with a ritual not
usually associated with secular confabs: a solemn mass in the hotel's
basement ballroom presided over by Archbishop Thomas Collins in
full regalia.

Still, right-to-die initiatives may not be the only intractable issues in
the next generation of culture wars. From unsettling questions regarding organ transplants to prospective court challenges over reproductive
technology, a host of other explosive ethical dilemmas threaten to grab
the attention of the religious right. For Charles McVety, the polygamy
charges against the leaders of a fundamentalist Mormon sect in
Bountiful, B.C.—since dropped pending a Charter query by the provincial government—were a vindication of sorts. As he and other
religious-right spokesmen had predicted, Bountiful's patriarchs were
preparing to use the legal precedent of same-sex marriage as their main
defence. Should the charges be revived, they risk opening another
round in the tumultuous marriage debate—one that also has more than
passing interest for those Muslim immigrants who contend that the
Koran allows them up to four wives.

Meanwhile at almost every Christian right conference these days,
organizers are peddling DVDs warning of an impending "demographic

winter"—a metaphor for the declining birth rate of Christians in many Western countries with soaring Muslim populations. An inflammatory YouTube posting that scored more than eleven million hits in six months came straight to the point: "Islam will overwhelm Christendom," it warned, "unless Christians . . . begin reproducing again." Quite aside from its implicit racism, the video signals the first stirrings of a resuscitated campaign, backed by the Vatican, that is guaranteed to ignite feminist rage: yet another war against contraception.

Those new battle fronts are emerging at a time when the old conflicts have by no means lost their power to inflame. On university campuses across the country, clashes between pro-life clubs and student governments have become more frequent and explosive. Many have been sparked by the Canadian branch of the Center for Bio-Ethical Reform, an American anti-abortion lobby founded by a former member of the Reagan administration, whose "Genocide Awareness" billboards feature montages of mangled fetuses next to photos from Nazi concentration camps. That blatant attempt to raise the emotional temperature in an already volatile debate comes as two U.S. polls show that, for the first time since 1995, opposition to abortion is on the rise while support for it is slipping even more sharply. Some pro-life activists credit advances in medical technology with boosting their cause in a way that picket lines outside abortion clinics never could—an argument with which Dave Quist of Ottawa's Institute of Marriage and Family Canada concurs. "As we see ultrasounds and microscopic pictures of what goes on in the womb," he told an evangelical conference, "I think science is going to help us a great deal on that issue."

The persistence of these moral disputes means that Christian-right organizations such as Quist's will remain players in the political arena for years to come. Asked when he would consider his mission accomplished in Ottawa, he admits he cannot imagine such a time: "There's always going to be a social issue to deal with," he says.

At Saint Matthew's Anglican Church in a suburb of Abbotsford, B.C., the priest's robes glitter with gilt embroidery and the rites smack of its Church of England roots, but as Revered Mike Stewart launches into a sermon capped off with a reference to the coming end-times, a visitor could be forgiven for concluding that this is a gussied-up evangelical service. Ever since Saint Matthews joined more than a dozen other renegade Anglican congregations in a revolt against same-sex marriage blessings, the church has been part of a conservative exodus from the country's second-largest mainline Protestant denomination. Many of those defectors call themselves evangelicals, including acclaimed Anglican theologian James I. Packer, a professor emeritus at Vancouver's Regent College whom *Time* magazine named one of the twenty-five most influential evangelicals on the continent. Where once Protestants were divided by denominational loyalties, now social issues like same-sex marriage are provoking a far broader realignment along ideological lines, prompting dissident Anglicans like those at Saint Matthew's to see their natural political allies not in mainline Protestantism, but in the Christian right.

One of those who has recognized that realignment is Pope Benedict XVI, who stunned both Catholics and Protestants in 2009 by inviting disgruntled Anglicans around the world to join his flock. Some Canadian religious scholars lauded the papal overture as a strategic masterstroke while others have scorned it as crass opportunism. But it serves as a reminder that the political alliance between conservative evangelicals and Catholics forged by Brian Stiller in the 1980s remains the heart of this country's unique Christian right, and seems poised to expand. Stiller himself has plans for a new evangelical-Catholic think tank, and in the spring of 2009, Bruce Clemenger, the president of the Evangelical Fellowship, took an unprecedented high-profile role at what has been largely a Catholic event, Ottawa's annual March for Life, vowing to increase evangelical participation.

Stephen Harper has profited from the evangelical-Catholic nexus at the polls, but he now faces competition for the affections of that conservative Christian voting block from an unlikely source. Quietly and without fanfare, both the Liberals and the NDP are attempting to take a page from Obama's strategic playbook, making overtures to faith communities in an effort to cobble together a credible political counterweight—a religious left.

When news leaked out that Liberal leader Michael Ignatieff was embarking on such an outreach to evangelicals and Catholics in the spring of 2009, it seemed like a startling about-face for a party that only three years earlier had run campaign ads portraying conservative Christians as scary. The inspiration behind that initiative was the man whom Ignatieff chose as his envoy; Scarborough MP John McKay, the lanky Baptist lawyer who co-founded the Christian Legal Fellowship and had become a fixture at Christian-right conferences as the party's token evangelical. McKay's chief concern was recouping the Catholic vote that had once constituted the party's base, but for him it was also a chance to make amends to fellow Bible believers.

Before the 2004 election, the Liberals had commissioned a controversial "push poll"—a marketing tool designed to plant ideas as much as detect electoral intentions—asking voters in Ontario whether they would support the Conservative Party if they knew it had been "taken over" by evangelicals. McKay was revolted, denouncing it as "offensive" and "just plain stupid politics," but his embarrassment was compounded two years later when the party's election advertising suggested that conservative Christians harboured a sinister hidden agenda at odds with the Charter of Rights. "That was just wrong," he says.

His efforts have been bolstered by research from the Evangelical Fellowship of Canada. In a study of its members' voting patterns dating back to 1996, the EFC concluded it was not primarily issues such as same-sex marriage that had prompted evangelicals to switch their allegiance to the Conservatives; it was the Liberals' insulting election ads.

"The Liberal Party repeatedly tried to marginalize evangelicals for short-term electoral gain, mocking their beliefs and styling those beliefs as a danger to 'Canadian values,'" the report argued. "Other parties from across the political spectrum engaged evangelicals differently, picked up passengers, and continued on."

These days, McKay is trying to convince faith groups that Ignatieff is eager to welcome them back into the party. He doesn't promise radical policy shifts—"There's not much that's going to change in the Liberal Party with respect to abortion," he admits—but he has ushered more than a dozen Christian leaders into Ignatieff's office in an attempt to find common ground. One result was a speech McKay made in the House opposing Francine Lalonde's assisted suicide bill, and calling for increased palliative care funding—an initiative aimed at those Catholics in right-to-life organizations who had just met Ignatieff.

Still, McKay is wary of appearing to ape Harper's theo-con strategy, which he calls "deeply disturbing." That disdain increased in the fall of 2009 with the news that the government had abruptly cancelled $7 million in funding for KAIROS, a thirty-five-year-old foreign aid and eco-justice group made up of representatives from the leading Protestant churches as well as left-leaning Mennonites and Quakers. At first, a spokesperson for the Canadian International Development Agency had insisted that the move had nothing to do with KAIROS's criticism of the Alberta oil sands or Canadian mining companies's abuses overseas; the organization no longer met CIDA's criteria, she said. But when it turned out that KAIROS had developed its proposal with CIDA's help, Jason Kenney offered another explanation from the stage of a conference he was attending in Jerusalem, declaring that organizations such as KAIROS had been "defunded" because they had participated in boycott and divestement campaigns against Israel—a move he equated with anti-Semitism.

Suddenly, in that admission, Kenney made clear that, within the parameters of Harper's theo-con strategy, some expressions of

Christianity were acceptable and others were not. Those that fell in line with Conservative policies and values would benefit from the government's magnanimity; the rest would be left to fight for survival in a struggle that was ultimately not as much about faith as it was about political hardball. "It's offensive, it's a Bush strategy," McKay says. "If you start dividing Jews and Muslims and Christians for political purposes, you set up a dynamic that doesn't serve Canada well. The only phrase I can think of is Machiavellian."

At the same time the Liberals were romancing religious groups, the NDP relaunched its own Faith and Social Justice Commission, attempting to assure left-leaning evangelicals concerned with peace and anti-poverty issues that the Conservatives have no monopoly on the moral high ground. Originally announced in 2006, the caucus took three years to get underway, in part because of ideological schisms within the party. Those reservations may seem surprising given the NDP's roots in the Social Gospel movement of the 1930s, when a Baptist minister named Tommy Douglas stumped the drought-ravaged Prairies demanding justice for dispossessed farmers. But in recent years the party has come to be regarded as a champion of secularism and gay rights—an image reflected in the bitter internal divisions that emerged during the same-sex marriage vote. In the heat of that debate, one evangelical New Democrat left to sit as an independent MP and others, like Ontario MP Joe Comartin, a devout Catholic who opposed the legislation, felt caught between party fealty and faith: after Comartin voted for the bill, his church refused to let him continue teaching its marriage classes. But inspired by Obama's success in courting left-leaning evangelicals in the U.S., Comartin and a dozen others resurrected their foundering faith caucus at the NDP's 2009 convention, heralding its rebirth by handing out brochures that insisted, "There is a religious left!"

For moderate and left-leaning evangelicals who have seen their faith expropriated by hostile forces, such moves come as a relief. Watching the antics of Charles McVety as he demanded Beverley McLachlin's removal as chief justice of the Supreme Court, many shared the sentiments of Kitchener author James Bow. "Speaking as a Christian, I just want to say I am embarrassed that social conservatives like Charles McVety claim to represent who I am and what I believe," Bow declared on his website. "Nothing could be further from the truth." Another group of evangelicals have created Religiousrightalert.ca, a collection of investigative blogs devoted to tracking the extremism of this country's aspiring Jerry Falwells and Pat Robertsons.

Still, for many secularists, the attempt by both parties to build a religious left is an unsettling development—one that guarantees Harper will face no objections as he hands conservative Christians an increasing role in government. After all, how can Ignatieff and Jack Layton decry the growing prominence of religion in politics when they are scrambling to court the evangelical and Catholic vote themselves? Rather than creating a riposte to the religious right, they may simply have pre-empted their parties' ability to critique the increasing Christianization of the public square. If so, they are helping to ensure that religion remains an irrevocable force in Canadian politics, regardless of whether Stephen Harper is tossed out of office.

As the American experience shows, even such a change in Conservative electoral fortunes would not necessarily send the religious right into retreat. In *Kingdom Coming: The Rise of Christian Nationalism*, Michelle Goldberg notes that voting Republicans out of power in the 1990s not only failed to halt the momentum of the U.S. movement, it may have fuelled its growth. "The Christian right had some of its greatest organizing triumphs under Bill Clinton," Goldberg writes. Indeed, as British religious scholar Karen Armstrong points out, fundamentalism of every sort grows "in symbiosis" with secularization. "The more it is thwarted," Armstrong says, "the more extreme it becomes."

⚜

At a New Brunswick press conference in the midst of the 2008 election campaign, Stephen Harper staked out his political legacy, arguing that under his government, the Canadian public had already become more conservative. Although he seemed to be referring to fiscal attitudes, social conservatives like Joseph Ben-Ami did not disagree. "In the real world, you measure success not so much on whether you won or lost but where the centre of gravity is," Ben-Ami says. "And I think in this country, it has shifted somewhat to the right."

When Harper came to office, he adopted an electoral script crafted by his ideological soulmates in the Republican Party, nurturing a religious-right constituency that had never before enjoyed such attention or access to government. But unlike George W. Bush's evangelical base, Harper's theo-conservative constituency is not large enough to guarantee him a clear majority. He cannot win without it, but he cannot win with theo-cons alone. That conundrum leaves him, in some ways, a prisoner of his own electoral calculations, consigned to tread an uneasy tightrope between the social- and economic-conservative wings of his party. In scrambling to present policies that appeal to both camps, he has often ended up pleasing neither.

For those hard-core believers who expected him to roll back same-sex marriage and enshrine fetal rights, he has been a major disappointment. Even the Evangelical Fellowship has noted the "lack of policy gains" on his watch. More importantly, because those measures he did proffer seemed born of calculation, not conviction, many came across as awkward and opportunistic, executed under a veil of secrecy and withdrawn at the first sign they might exact too high a price at the voting booth.

What he has accomplished, however, may be less obvious and more lasting. Without putting forth a single piece of provocative legislation, he has used the enormous patronage powers of his office to shift the ideological leanings of key institutions, from the federal courts to federal regulatory agencies, toward a more socially conservative worldview.

At the same time, he has eliminated many of the forces that opposed such a policy drift. With the stroke of a budgetary pen, he has defunded agencies such as the Status of Women Canada and the Court Challenges Program, leaving both feminists and gay activists without resources to take on hostile government policies, while his cutbacks to scholarly granting bodies have helped silence environmental critics in academia and science. Even arm's-length agencies have not been safe from his reach. At Montreal's Rights and Democracy organization, which had okayed three grants to the Palestinian cause, two Harper appointees—chairman Aurel Braun, a militantly pro-Israel political science professor, and vice-chairman Jacques Gauthier, the lawyer for the International Christian Embassy in Jerusalem—engineered a coup that has been blamed for driving out respected international board members.

Although some Reform veterans have reproached Harper for failing to keep his campaign promises for an elected Senate, putting the chamber's fate in voters's hands might never have accomplished what his rash of appointments over recent years did: giving the Conservatives a majority in the once Liberal-dominated upper house. That shift will mean no future dissidents can block his legislation as the Senate banking committee did with its hearings on his film-tax-credit bill. Lest there be any doubt, before naming eighteen new senators in 2008, Harper extracted an agreement from them to support the government's initiatives—a move designed to ensure that he did not suffer the same humiliation Brian Mulroney did in 1991 when a handful of senators from his own party killed his attempt to bring in abortion legislation.

Ironically, the global economic crisis that has obliged Harper to undertake the sort of state spending that is anathema to fiscal conservatives appears to have an ideological upside for him. With the government's financial reserves exhausted and the deficit on the rise, he can follow the example of his heroes, Ronald Reagan and Margaret Thatcher, arguing that the country's financial straits leave no room for further spending on social programs. While that approach is sure to please fellow economic conservatives, it also plays to the convictions of many in the religious right who believe that education and social welfare ought to be administered by churches and other religious organizations—two of the foundational units of Christian government. Indeed, Christian Reconstructionists like Rousas J. Rushdoony argue that poverty and social misery are part of "God's inscrutable decree," to be solved not by the state but by penitence and prayer.

Meanwhile, buried among the Conservatives' billions in economic stimulus grants are hints of a future trend should Harper attain a majority. A number of those grants went to infrastructure improvements at churches and other religious organizations that dispense social services—one of them the home congregation of Indian and Northern Affairs minister Chuck Strahl—a sign that the government may be testing the waters of public opinion before making the faith community a larger partner in such programs.

In his 2003 Civitas speech, Harper called for a foreign policy based on morality—a criterion that he equated with unflinching support for Israel, the only democracy in the Middle East. That shift not only altered the nation's image as an even-handed power-broker on the world stage, it tied Canadian diplomacy to a less idealistic objective: sewing up both the Jewish and Christian Zionist vote for the Conservatives.

Those same domestic considerations appear to have guided Harper's belated trips to two emerging economic superpowers to which he had offered a cold shoulder, India and China, a vivid reminder that morality itself can be an elastic concept. On a visit to India aimed at selling nuclear reactors and uranium to a country that has already used Candu technology to build its own bomb—and still refuses to sign the Nuclear Non-Proliferation Treaty—Harper took pains to tour two sites representing only tiny fractions of the Indian population. Those sites, however, are sacred to key elements in his theo-conservative constituency back home: the Golden Temple in Amritsar, the holiest of shrines to Canada's nearly three hundred thousand Sikhs, and the Chabad-Lubavitch outreach centre in Mumbai, a symbol of Judaism attacked by Islamic terrorists.

For years, Harper and the Conservative Party had refused to consort with China, lambasting its human rights record. To social conservatives like Stockwell Day, who became the leading cheerleader for its island rival Taiwan, the mainland republic of Mao represented a twofold cause for concern: like the former Soviet Union, it was officially godless, and it had viciously persecuted Christians. That strategy left Canada at a marked disadvantage as China became a global powerhouse that controlled America's financial fate in the wake of the 2008 economic meltdown. When free-trade treaties with the U.S. proved no bulwark against congressional Buy America bills, a parade of Conservative heavyweights, led by Day—by then Harper's minister of international trade—began shuttling to Beijing in search of new markets. In 2009 alone, seven ministerial missions visited China, almost as many as in all of the previous four years.

As it turns out, the religious right has played a role in justifying that about-face. On one of Day's earliest China trips, he made a point of touring the scene of the 2008 Sichuan earthquake, where shoddy construction and corruption was blamed for boosting the death toll to more than eight thousand. There, a leading figure in the rebuilding effort is Dr. Zhao Xiao, a prominent economist and one of the country's rare influential Christians, who is best known for a research paper arguing that the secret to America's financial success is its churches. Setting out to train a new generation of Communist Party officials in ethics, Zhao chose an unusual partner: the Masters of Arts Leadership program at Trinity Western University set up by Don Page, the former external affairs mandarin who established the Laurentian Leadership Centre in Ottawa and specializes in teaching management techniques modeled on the example of Jesus Christ. In a country where Christians have been jailed and Bibles banned, Page found himself at a state university lecturing on Christ as the ultimate leader, even scribbling scriptural quotations on the blackboard. "They said to me, 'We want you to come here and teach ethical values and we don't care if you use the Bible,'" he recounts. "In fact, we'll supply free Bibles in Mandarin if you want."

Now, Trinity Western is overseeing the education of thousands of Chinese officials, even offering them degrees, but Page wrestled with his own ethical dilemmas before accepting the job. "I thought, 'Why do they let me teach on Christ as a leader and yet punish so many others?'" he says in an interview. "Then I realized that the people who are being persecuted are stepping out and criticizing the government. I am not doing that. In fact, Jesus did not criticize Rome. He said, 'Pay unto Caesar what is Caesar's.' It's okay as long as I don't criticize the government or proselytize."

Some in the Christian right have also been agitating for another, more contentious shift in foreign policy, which has already found a champion in a Conservative backbencher. Only a few months after Obama ended George Bush's ban on congressional funding for overseas aid groups that counsel abortion, Saskatchewan MP Brad Trost circulated a petition among religious-right groups to drum up support for a move in the opposite direction—one that may be a sign of things to come. In the letter, signed by thirty like-minded MPs, Trost demanded that the Canadian International Development Agency (CIDA) end its $18 million in annual grants to overseas programs run by the International Planned Parenthood Federation. That initiative may be useful to keep in mind in the wake of Harper's proposal to the Group of Eight to focus on maternal health care.

Harper's theo-conservative constituency applauds Trost's initiative as an example of foreign policy crafted according to biblical principles—at least those principles sacrosanct to the religious right—but his government has vigorously opposed a private member's bill by a fellow evangelical, John McKay, equally inspired by a sense of Christian morality: a measure calling for controls on Canadian mining companies whose overseas operations have been accused of egregious environmental and human rights abuses. Despite protests from international human rights groups and a critical United Nations report, Stockwell Day has consistently blocked attempts to take action against those firms whose hired guns have been accused of shooting and gang-raping local protestors.

Even Harper's supporters fault him for producing few social Conservative policy victories, but he has changed the nation in far more profound ways, aligning it increasingly with the United States. A population that once basked in its image as an international peacekeeper now glories in a more muscular militarism, and Harper has been happy to trade the diplomatic independence of a middle power to walk in loyal lockstep with Washington on almost all matters of national security. But in keeping with that increasing Americanization, Harper has also altered the terms and tone of the debate, thrusting God into the centre of the national conversation. Whether signing off his throne speeches with a blessing or lavishing invitations on the leaders of the Christian right, he has brought religion out of the closet and into the public square for the first time in recent memory. "We're talking about things in a different way than we did three years ago," says Brian Rushfeldt, Harper's old ally from the Canada Family Action Coalition.

Much of that new spiritual consciousness comes from the increasing presence of conservative Christians in the capital. As Harper has gradually unmuzzled his evangelical Christian MPs, allowing them a higher profile and letting them test public sentiments with private members' bills, he has emboldened the religious right as a whole. "They're more brazen and confident," says Joyce Arthur, director of the Abortion Rights Coalition. "That's the big change. Being in power has given them legitimacy."

On talk radio and in the pages of the *National Post*, the best source of news on the religious right, a new stridency has emerged: critics of the government's efforts to pander to its theo-conservative constituency are dismissed as god-hating secular zealots and opponents of its pro-Israel policy are routinely branded anti-Semites. In the blogosphere, the rhetoric has become even more shrill, fuelling an angry strain of faith-based intolerance. Scarcely three decades after Brian Stiller recoiled at the mix of religiosity and righteous patriotism spouted by Falwell and his fellow televangelists in the U.S., the prime minister now sends his public blessings to prayer rallies where Christian nationalists brandishing Canadian flags are calling for a Bible-based theocracy.

By opening the government to the religious right, Harper has attempted to correct an imbalance—a perception by many evangelicals that religion had been shoved off to the sidelines of public life. But in doing so, he has also given access and prominence to forces he may be unable to control. Those Christian nationalists have become influential players, feted by his government even as they hold out the prospect of Canada's singular, scripturally inspired manifest destiny: an eleventh-hour role as a healing refuge—a sort of last-ditch drop-in centre for a world in the grip of the Apocalypse.

However delighted they might seem by Harper's attentions and governance—part of their credo is to honour those in authority—they are not likely to be mollified by his plodding incrementalism or cautious tweaks of the bureaucracy. Aggressive and insistent, they are driven by a fierce imperative to reconstruct Canada in a biblical mould.

Waving their bright flags on the lawns of the Parliament Buildings, extolling the country's Christian roots to a compelling soft-rock beat, they might seem to offer a refreshing recipe for morality and national pride, but their agenda—while outwardly inclusive and multi-racial—is ultimately exclusionary. In their idealized Christian nation, non-believers—aetheists, non-Christians and even Christian secularists—have no place, and those in violation of biblical law, notably homosexuals and adulterers, would merit severe punishment and the sort of shunning that once characterized a society where suspected witches were burned. Theirs is a dark and dangerous vision, one that brooks no dissent and requires the dismantling of key democratic institutions. A preview is on display south of the border, where decades of religious-right triumphs have left a nation bitterly splintered along lines of faith and ideology, trapped in the hysteria of overcharged rhetoric and resentment.

For this new wave of Christian nationalists, united across the continent by the charismatic renewal movement, the signs and portents of the end-times are unmistakable, apparent in each new earthquake report or tremor of the global financial system, and they feel they have no time to waste. Their mission is to prepare God's dominion on earth, and they are unlikely to rest until they see their perceived scriptural prophecies fulfilled in Ottawa and Jerusalem alike. As Faytene Kryskow underlines in her book, *Marked*, she and her fellow revivalists are no longer content to agitate for policy crumbs. They have "a take-over mentality," she writes: "They are convinced that God has called them to take over the world!"

☩

On a call-in show discussing the emergence of the Christian right in Canada, an angry male voice exploded over the line. "You're nothing but one of those Christ-haters," he screamed at me. It was not the only tirade to which I was subjected. On another occasion, an interviewee asked for my bona fides before agreeing to respond to my questions: "Are you a Christian?" he demanded. Even then, I knew that my answer in the affirmative did not meet the criteria that my interlocutor had in mind. I am, to put it bluntly, not his kind of Christian, and as such, I am the Other, the enemy—an irksome reporter to whom, according to *The Tactics of Christian Resistance*, it is even justifiable to lie.

In the course of my travels through the Canadian Christian right, I would often find my beliefs tested and my opinions called into question. As on any venture into the spiritual realm, this, too, became a personal quest of sorts. I met people of profound faith and dedication for whom I have great admiration, but I also found myself listening to rants against other religions and lifestyles that left me sick with revulsion. In the end, what matters is not my faith or my assessment of others' spiritual practices and beliefs, but the questions that this book attempts to explore.

When my first study of the Canadian religious right was published in the *Walrus* magazine in the fall of 2006, one Ottawa columnist dismissed it as much ado about nothing, scorning the leaders of the movement I had profiled as "a bunch of losers." Three years later, after Harper had rushed to respond to yet another outcry from those same "losers," my colleague confessed to "second thoughts." For me, it was not so much a vindication as confirmation that many of us in the mainstream media are ill-equipped to take the measure of a movement that conforms to few political stereotypes and operates in a parallel universe.

On a visit to Canada in late 2006, Pulitzer Prize–winning journalist Chris Hedges was alarmed to discover that, in a country he had always regarded as "a bit saner" than the U.S., Harper was putting out the welcome mat for the religious right. The son of a Presbyterian minister and a graduate of Harvard Divinity School, Hedges warned Canadians against following the lead of those Americans who "stood sleepily by as Pat Robertson and other religious bigots hijacked the Republican Party and moved into the legislative and executive branches of government." As he made clear, the growth of the U.S. Christian right was a long and insidious process, but one that could only have happened because the media and political moderates watched in passive disbelief or wishful denial. In tracing the influence of that emergent force in this country, I have attempted to sound a wake-up call, but, in the end, it is up to Canadian voters to write the next chapter. Only they can decide the kind of country in which they want to live.

ACKNOWLEDGEMENTS

So many people have shared their time and thoughts so generously with me in an effort to produce this book that I hope I don't fail to give proper credit where it is due. Enormous gratitude goes to my patient editor, Anne Collins, publisher of the Knopf Random Canada Publishing Group and an award-winning writer herself, who championed the book through many revised deadlines and applied her discerning eye to the final manuscript. Joining her in the latter task was Ken Alexander, the founding publisher of the *Walrus* magazine, who first ran the story that began this journey and argued even then that it ought to be a book, later cheering me on through the darkest days of research and writing with an unflagging belief in the outcome, and contributing valued editorial advice. My thanks to the adept Random House Canada team for transforming the manuscript into the finished product with miraculous speed, and to my agents Shaun Bradley and Don Sedgwick for their wise counsel. I also owe a debt of gratitude to several colleagues and experts in the field who shared their perceptions and contacts with me, among them Ralph Thomas, whose idea this book was, and Lloyd Mackey, the dean of religious writers in this country, who laid the groundwork for it with his own 2005 work, *The Pilgrimage of Stephen Harper;* Douglas Todd, the *Vancouver Sun*'s perceptive columnist on spiritual affairs; and Ronald S. Dart, a prolific author and professor from the University of the Fraser Valley in Abbotsford, B.C., whose insights and introductions were invaluable to my understanding of the evangelical experience in general and B.C.'s Bible belt in particular. Despite their generosity, none should be blamed for any shortcomings in this work.

On a more personal note, my thanks to my cousins in Calgary who so generously offered me shelter and delightful companionship on research trips, and should in no way be held responsible for anything I have written; to writer Josh Knelman for his help on my original *Walrus* piece; and to those amazing friends who remained faithful throughout the long anti-social process of writing, tactfully refraining from mentioning how often deadlines had flown by. Last but certainly not least, my infinite gratitude to my husband, Clair, who spent part of a California holiday trooping between Robert Schuller's Crystal Cathedral and Rick Warren's Saddleback lair, gamely accompanied me to Sieges and sweltering day-long editions of TheCRY, then patiently applied his seasoned editorial skills to every version of the manuscript and hand-delivered it to the publisher. You are, as always, my rock.

SOURCE NOTES

The *Armageddon Factor* is based largely on original material gleaned from scores of interviews with more than a hundred subjects, amounting to more than 300 hours of recorded conversations, between April 2006 and December 2009. Some of the interviews were done for an article in the October 2006 issue of the *Walrus* magazine entitled "Stephen Harper and the Theo-Cons"—a few of them not used at the time because of space constraints—but the vast majority were conducted afterward, either in person or by telephone. Many subjects were interviewed multiple times over the years. Much of the other material came from attending dozens of conferences sponsored by the conservative Christian organizations on which I report. Wherever possible, I have used those organizations' own words about their activities and goals from their publications, web-sites, blogs and CDs or DVDs.

Researching the history of the American religious right, I have read dozens of books on the subject but am particularly indebted to two even-handed histories by Sara Diamond, *Roads to Dominion: Right-wing Movements and Political Power in the United States* (The Guilford Press, 1995) and *Not By Politics Alone: The Enduring Influence of the Christian*

Right (The Guilford Press, 1998), as well as a collection of early essays, *Piety & Politics: Evangelicals and Fundamentalists Confront the World*, edited by Richard John Neuhaus and Michael Cromartie and published in 1987 by the Ethics and Public Policy Center in Washington, D.C. More recent studies have also been invaluable, among them Michelle Goldberg's *Kingdom Coming: The Rise of Christian Nationalism* (W.W. Norton & Co., Inc., 2006), Chris Hedges's *American Fascists: The Christian Right and the War on America* (Free Press, 2006) and Kevin Phillips' *American Theocracy: The Peril and Politics of Radical Religion, Oil and Borrowed Money in the 21st Century* (Viking, 2006).

For historical data and an understanding of the Canadian religious right, I turned to *Pilgrims in Lotus Land: Conservative Protestantism in British Columbia, 1917–1981* by Robert K. Burkinshaw (McGill-Queen's University Press, 1995), *The Eagle and the Ox: Contemplation, the Church and Politics* by Ronald S. Dart (Freshwind Press, 2006), *More Faithful than We Think* by Lloyd Mackey (Bayridge Books, 2005) and *Politics Under God* by John H. Redekop (Herald Press, 2007). Many of the other books I consulted are cited in the notes to relevant chapters.

Although I mention only a few evangelical churches in the text, I attended many more, including Central Heights Church in Abbotsford, B.C., the People's Church in Toronto and Carruthers Creek Community Church in Ajax, Ontario.

PREFACE

In this preface, I draw on my interviews with Jerry Falwell and Pat Robertson for *Maclean's* magazine in 1985 and 1988. In describing Dominionism and Christian Reconstructionism, I have relied on Sara Diamond's two books, as well as those by Michelle Goldberg and Chris Hedges, cited above. Vancouver billionaire Jimmy Pattison admitted underwriting the advertising campaign of the Alpha program on a 2009 Global Television special called *Hip2BHoly*.

CHAPTER I: GOD'S DOMINION

My account of the August 23, 2008, edition of TheCRY is based on my attendance at the event. Despite Faytene Kryskow's assertion that it attracted a crowd of four thousand to five thousand—compared with a report of four hundred by the *Ottawa Citizen*—I have chosen to use a compromise figure of one thousand based on my crowd count during the best-attended afternoon sessions and my photographs. References to TheCall, held on August 16, 2008, in Washington, D.C., come from its website and a report by *Charisma* magazine. The origins of Lou Engle's red duct tape ritual are related in *Common Ground Christian News*, April 2005. Conservative MP Bev Shipley's distribution of bookmarks in a southwestern Ontario church was reported on the CBC's Political Bytes blog on August 7, 2008.

Comments from Preston Manning and Professor John Stackhouse, who holds the Sangwoo Youtong Chee chair of theology at Vancouver's Regent College, are from my interviews with both. I owe the reference to former prime minister Lester Pearson's prayers with Social Credit leader Robert Thompson to an anecdote recounted by Trinity Western University Professor Robert Burkinshaw, to whom Thompson related it when he retired from politics to become the university's chancellor; the political science building on the campus bears Thompson's name.

Figures on voting patterns in the 2006 and 2008 elections were provided by pollster Andrew Grenville, formerly of Ipsos Reid, now senior researcher at Angus Reid Strategies. Most of the material on the prime minister's spiritual odyssey is based on Lloyd Mackey's book *The Pilgrimage of Stephen Harper* (ECW Press, 2005) which includes Harper's December 1995 interview with Jonathan Bloedow in the defunct *Ottawa Times* (an interview Mackey also cites in his 1997 book, *Like Father, Like Son*). For other biographical details, I relied on William Johnson's biography, *Stephen Harper and the Future of Canada* (McClelland and Stewart, 2005). Harper's more recent thoughts on his faith come from a tape of *The Drew Marshall Show*, which aired

February 19, 2005. Deborah Grey's comments are drawn from my 2006 phone interview with her.

I attended a service at Calgary's RockPointe Church on November 11, 2007. The account of its merger appeared in calgarychristian.com, while insights from RockPointe's senior pastor, Brad Trask, who was absent during my visit, came from an August 18, 2007, story by Douglas Todd in the *Vancouver Sun* and previous reports by Lloyd Mackey. I sat in on a service at Ottawa's East Gate Alliance Church on May 7, 2006. The history and beliefs of the Missionary and Alliance Church appear on the denomination's website as well as in a profile of its founder, Reverend A.B. Simpson in the anthology, *Canada: Portraits of Faith*, which was written by Darrel Reid, now Harper's deputy chief of staff, whose 1994 doctoral thesis was on Simpson's early years. According to a report from the 2004 general assembly of the Christian and Missionary Alliance in Canada, more than 130 of its pastors were sent for training to the Willow Creek Association in the U.S. Information on Bill Hybels is drawn from a 2007 account in the *United Church Observer* called "Inside Big Willow" and a 2009 article in *Stanford Business* magazine, "Marketing God's Word."

The notion that Manning increasingly surrounded himself with evangelicals in the Reform Party comes from Tom Flanagan's book *Waiting for the Wave: The Reform Party and Preston Manning* (Stoddart, 1995). Biographical information on Stockwell Day is drawn from Claire Hoy's biography, *Stockwell Day: His Life and Politics* (Stoddart, 2000), Thomas Walkom's profile, "From preacher to politician," in the *Toronto Star* on October 29, 2000, and an article by Gordon Laird entitled "Bentley, Alberta: Hellfire, neo-Nazis and Stockwell Day," published in *NOW* magazine in April 2000. Day's quote on God and the provincial curriculum originally appeared in *Alberta Report* magazine (later known simply as *Report*) in 1984. Roy Beyer's role in Day's leadership campaigns was reported by *ChristianWeek* in January 2002 and confirmed by interviews with Brian Rushfeldt and Charles McVety. Tom Flanagan's reflections on hyping Day's religious ties were published in his book *Harper's Team: Behind the Scenes in the Conservative Rise to Power* (McGill-Queens University Press, 2007).

Dennis Pilon spoke with me by phone in 2009. The reference to Georganne Burke comes from an assortment of Ottawa interviews, as well as a front-page story in the October 16, 2007, edition of the *Globe and Mail* that revealed Jason Kenney's ethnic outreach efforts. (Burke later joined the staff of Science Minister Gary Goodyear, then was appointed to the office of the minister of Foreign Affairs.) The *Hill Times* of April 30, 2007, reported on Kenney's whirlwind schedule and nickname, "Curry in a Hurry," while smiling Buddha appeared in the *Globe and Mail* on January 30, 2010. Figures on ethnic voting patterns come from a study by Elisabeth Gidengil, director of the Centre for the Study of Democratic Citizenship at McGill University, as reported in the *Hill Times*, September 14, 2009.

Quotes from Janet Epp Buckingham are from several interviews with her in 2006. Harper's claims about Liberal patronage threats were made in a closed-door meeting with supporters in Sault Ste. Marie on September 2, 2009, and later aired on the CBC. Reports on the board for Assisted Human Reproduction Canada appeared in various newspapers, but the best overview was that by Laura Eggertson in the *Canadian Medical Association Journal* on February 27, 2007. Paul Weyrich's column on Harper's election appeared on the Accuracy in Media website on January 26, 2006.

Information about Guy Giorno and his devout Roman Catholic faith appeared in the *Globe and Mail* on May 23, 2008, and in the *Toronto Star* on May 27, 2008. (Harper brought Giorno with him to meet the pope at the Vatican in the summer of 2009.) I interviewed Darrel Reid in May 2006 at the Civitas conference. Some of his earlier quotes as head of Focus on the Family Canada appeared in *Report* magazine on April 13, 1998, and April 24, 2000. Paul Wilson, who knew Reid from Queen's, took over his job as director of policy for the Reform Party when Reid became Preston Manning's chief of staff. Wilson's career, including his stint as the first director of the Laurentian Leadership Centre before joining the staff of former justice minister Vic Toews, has been reported by Lloyd Mackey in his Ottawa Watch column for canadianchristianity.com. Biographical material on Mark Cameron, who was in the prime minister's office from 2006 until August 2009, comes from a column by Lloyd Mackey on canadianchristianity.com on February 22, 2007; in the spring of 2008, Cameron addressed the National Student Forum in Ottawa on how he brought his faith to bear on his job.

At least $26.2 million in federal economic stimulus funds went to private Christian universities under the $2 billion Knowledge Infrastructure Program (KIP) and were announced in a series of press conferences and news releases in 2009; the unprecedented nature of those grants was noted in the January 2010 issue of *Faith Today*, published by the Evangelical Fellowship of Canada.

Harper spoke to Preston Manning's Canada Networking Conference on March 12, 2009, arguing that "conservatism is a value system, not an ideology," and adding, "I like to summarize my idea of conservatism in three Fs—freedom, family and faith." His interview with Quebec City's magazine *Prestige* was published in its September 2009 edition. Speculation on Harper's possible successors was reported on the *Globe and Mail*'s website on December 11, 2008. David Akin's profile of Stockwell Day, "Stockwell Day's Star Shining Bright," appeared in the February 23, 2009, edition of the *National Post*. On January 18, 2009, Harper named Day to the Treasury Board, releasing a statement of fulsome praise, and the following day commentators in the *Globe and Mail* and *National Post* declared it a significant promotion, although they had never before reported on a Treasury Board appointment in that light.

CHAPTER II: COAT OF MANY COLOURS
Most of the material on Brian Stiller and the Evangelical Fellowship of Canada comes from my interview with him in 2006 at Tyndale

University College and Seminary in Toronto. Additional historical data is drawn from the EFC's website as well as that of the National Association of Evangelicals. The account of the Senate abortion vote appeared in the *Toronto Star* on February 1, 1991. Ken Campbell's hosting of Jerry Falwell in Toronto and Edmonton in 1982 is reported in a sympathetic account of Campbell's activism by Michael Wagner in *Standing on Guard for Thee*, published by Tristan Emmanuel's Freedom Press in 2008. Brian Stiller's role in the preamble to the Charter of Rights is based on a telephone interview with Senator David Smith.

In 2006, I did a series of interviews with Charles McVety about his own history and that of Canada Christian College, while information about the college's origins and subsequent problems comes from reports in the *Toronto Star* on March 8, 1976, April 27, 1977, and August 12, 1982. The college's 2008 charitable tax return recorded rental revenues of $729,642. John Wesley White's book *Reentry!* (Zondervan Books, 1970), complete with a foreword by Billy Graham, was on sale in the college bookstore.

According to Ontario property records, the college building was bought from Penlea Investments Ltd. in 1995 by the Canadian Non-Denominational Association for Education and Evangelism, a corporation that is registered to Elmer McVety's widow, Elizabeth. The former minister of education targeted by Charles McVety was David Johnson, whose riding was in north Toronto. The Canada Christian College and School of Graduate Theological Studies Act proposed by Frank Klees was introduced in the Ontario Legislature on May 3, 1999. McVety's support for Klees in the 2009 Ontario Progressive Conservative leadership race was reported in the *Globe and Mail* on May 16 and May 20, 2009.

Charles McVety told me that his degree came from California State Christian College in Los Angeles. Since then he has stated that his bachelor's and master's degrees come from Canada Christian College, but his doctorate from California State Christian University. Neither that institution nor California State Christian College appears on a list of post-secondary institutions accredited by the state of California, but the university's website lists an address in the town of Fullerton and states that it was founded in 1972 by Samuel Say-Chang Kim, the son of the founder of Tae Han Theological School and College in Seoul, Korea, to which it is tied. Vision TV's vetting of Jerry Falwell's programs was reported by *NOW* magazine, March 16–20, 2000.

All information on the Canada Family Action Coalition comes from interviews with McVety or Brian Rushfeldt, or the organization's website. Accounts of the 2005 Conservative Party policy convention are based on interviews with Charles McVety and news reports from the time. The assessment of the religious right by *Capital Xtra!* was published in its July 14, 2005, issue.

Lorne Gunter's column "Canada Needs a Ralph Reed" appeared on September 26, 2005, in the *National Post*. Tom Flanagan discussed his relationship with Gunter in a sidebar to my profile of him in the *Walrus* magazine, "The Man Behind Stephen Harper," in October 2004. Accounts of Ralph Reed's Toronto speech were reported in the *Globe and Mail* on December 1, 2005, and *The Interim* edition of January 2006.

The details of Charles McVety's discussions with Mark Holland came from my 2006 interview with Holland; his aunt Carroll Holland has written extensively about her work with Ottawa Police Services on a community outreach effort called the Barrier Elimination Project. Peter O'Neill did some of the first reporting on the Exclusive Brethren's Canadian campaign in the *Vancouver Sun* on July 15, 2005, as did Lloyd Mackey on canadianchristianity.com the same month. For background material, I relied on the brethren's own website, as well as a site by dissident former members called peebs.net, and reports in the *New Zealand Herald* on September 7, 2005, and September 30, 2006; the *Sidney Morning Herald* on September 23, 2005 (weekend edition); and the *St. Petersburg Times* on January 18, 2005.

All information on the Institute of Canadian Values and Joseph Ben-Ami came from interviews with Ben-Ami or Charles McVety, from the institute's press releases or a story in the *Ottawa Citizen* on May 26, 2005. Ben-Ami's departure from B'nai Brith in May 2005 was reported in the *Jewish Tribune* by his wife, Lynne Cohen, a lawyer and former journalist for Alberta's *Report* magazine. Ben-Ami testified on his custody battle to the Special Joint Committee on Child Custody and Access on June 3, 1998. Information on Don Feder can be found on his website, donfeder.com, and in historian Elizabeth Castelli's report on "The War on Christians and the Values Voter in 2006" conference in the fall 2007 issue of the journal *differences*.

The profile of the Institute of Marriage and Family Canada (IMFC) and its executive director, Dave Quist, is based on my interview with Quist in his Ottawa office in 2006, as well as interviews with Darrel Reid and Derek Rogusky, senior vice-president of Focus on the Family Canada. Material on James Dobson and his American organizations, including the Family Research Council, are largely based on Dan Gilgoff's book, *The Jesus Machine: How James Dobson, Focus on the Family and Evangelical America Are Winning the Culture War* (St. Martin's Press, 2007). Dobson's sentiments on homosexuality were published in newsletters on the Focus website in June 1998 ("The Christian Response to the Homosexual Agenda") and September 2003 ("Marriage on the Ropes"). Reports on the Canadian affiliate's activities in the same-sex marriage debate appeared in the *Montreal Gazette* on February 10, 2005, and in a 2003 annual report on the American organization's website. Some of Darrel Reid's comments appeared in *Report* magazine on April 13, 1998. Writers for the IMFC *Review* include Peter Shawn Taylor, a former member of the *National Post* editorial board from 1998 to 2002, and Peter Jon Mitchell, who is a graduate of the Focus on the Family Institute in Colorado.

"Evangelist takes credit for film crackdown" was the front-page headline in the *Globe and Mail* on February 29, 2008, but the story actually broke in the paper the previous day. Background on the film tax credit bill came from my interviews with David Zitzerman and others involved. The details of Charles McVety's appearance before the Senate Finance Committee on June 11, 2008, were reported by Kady O'Malley on her blog, Inside the Queensway, for macleans.ca. The Evangelical Fellowship held an Ottawa screening of *Amazing Grace* for MPs on February 7, 2007.

CHAPTER III: SERPENTS AND DOVES

The account of Frank Luntz's keynote speech to the Manning Centre for Building Democracy in May 2006 is based on my reporting of the event; Luntz repeated much the same speech to a Civitas group the next day. Additional material came from Luntz's website, George Monbiot's *Heat: How to Stop the Planet from Burning* (Doubleday Canada, 2006) and my interviews with Luntz during the 1980s in Washington.

Preston Manning discussed grappling with his faith in a profile aired on VisionTV on April 26, 2006; Lorne Gunter's profile of him appeared in the *National Post* on November 11, 2005. Other material on Manning came from two interviews with him, as well as his autobiography, *Think Big* (McClelland & Stewart, 2002), and Lloyd Mackey's book on Preston and Ernest Manning, *Like Father, Like Son* (ECW Press, 1997). Tom Flanagan wrote about Manning's faith in *Waiting for the Wave: The Reform Party and Preston Manning* (Stoddart, 1995). But Manning has also written and spoken extensively on the role of faith in politics, notably in "Navigating the Faith/Political Interface" in the Manning Centre's online journal, *C2C*. Other information on the Manning Centre comes from an interview with its director, Nicholas Gafuik.

Although Manning declines to say who staked his Centre to $10 million in funding over ten years (he has referred to his benefactors as "some folks from Calgary"), there has been speculation that they include principals of the Calgary-based real estate investment firm Walton International Group (a subsidiary of InterBorder Holdings) on whose advisory board Manning and his longtime collaborator Cliff Fryers sit. Walton's chairman, Thompson MacDonald, is a director of the Manning

Centre, and until 2009, Walton International provided the Manning Centre with office space in its Calgary headquarters, while two of its developments outside Edmonton are called the Manning Estates.

Information on Morton Blackwell's Leadership Institute in Arlington, Virginia, came from a 2009 interview with Blackwell, one of the key players in the founding of the Moral Majority. Accounts of Manning's first seminar on faith and politics in Ottawa February 23–25, 2006, co-sponsored by Trinity Western University and Brian Stiller's Tyndale University College and Seminary, come from a report in the *Ottawa Citizen* on March 18, 2006, and another in *Christian Week* by Lloyd Mackey (March 17, 2006). I attended the second faith/politics seminar in Toronto from May 11–12, 2007, co-sponsored by Tyndale, as well as one for the Jewish community on November 25, 2007, at the North York Central Library. In March 2009, the Manning Centre issued a request for proposals from third parties to take over the program.

I also attended the Manning Centre's first Canada Networking Conference and Exhibition in Ottawa from February 29–March 1, 2008. Tom Flanagan's comment on Harper's strategic miscalculations were reported in the *National Post* on June 15, 2009. Manning wrote a column on the Conservatives as the natural governing party that appeared in the *Globe and Mail* on April 11, 2007. Harper's former employer, the National Citizens Coalition, presented Manning with its 2008 Colin M. Brown Freedom Medal in a Calgary ceremony. Brown, the late founder of the NCC, was a friend of Manning's father, Ernest, who served on the coalition's first advisory board.

Industry Minister Jim Prentice announced Manning's appointment to the twelve-member board of the Council of Canadian Academies on July 11, 2008. Six of the governors are appointed by the council's three member academies (the Royal Society of Canada, the Canadian Academy of Engineering and the Canadian Academy of Health Sciences) and four of the remaining six are appointed by the Canadian government. The journal *Nature* criticized the Conservatives' science policy in a February 2008 article entitled "Science in Retreat" a month after Harper abolished the position of National Science Adviser Arthur Carty. In the *Globe and Mail*, Manning attacked Richard Dawkins and other scientists whom he accused of leading a "modern inquisition in the name of science to root out . . . the mind virus of religion."

The National Association of Evangelicals' "Urgent Call to Action" on global warming is on their website and was reported in a variety of U.S. media, as well as in Dan Gilgoff's *The Jesus Machine*. Senator James Inhofe's 2003 remarks on climate change appear in George Monbiot's *Heat*. The poll on American evangelical pastors' attitudes to global warming was reported in *Baptist Press News* on April 16, 2009.

Charles McVety's remarks on the environment come from my interviews with him, while Timothy Bloedow's book, *Environmentalism and the Death of Science: Exposing the Lie of Eco-Religion*, was published by Freedom Press in 2008. Ernest Manning's deal on the tar sands with Howard Pew was reported by Lloyd Mackey in *Like Father, Like Son*. Manning's Calgary conference on faith and the environment was held on November 17, 2008. A Rocha Canada, a registered charity in Surrey, B.C., is an offshoot of the British-based Christian conservation group, A Rocha International.

Terry O'Neill's piece "A wise new strategy for pro-lifers" ran May 21, 2009, in the *National Post*; it did not mention that Pro-Life B.C. had invited guests to a cocktail reception unveiling its new identity as Signal Hill on June 14, 2008. The citation on abortion from Andrea Mrozek appeared in her opinion piece, "Thank you, Camille Paglia," in the September 23, 2008, edition of the *National Post*. John Hof, president of Campaign Life Coalition British Columbia vented his criticism of Preston Manning on June 19, 2009, on lifesitenews.com. Thomas Clarkson's role in the abolition battle is chronicled in Adam Hochschild's *Bury the Chains: Prophets and Rebels in the Fight to Free an Empire's Slaves* (Houghton Mifflin Harcourt, 2004), which also relates efforts by William Wilberforce's heirs to omit Clarkson from histories.

CHAPTER IV: WATCHMEN ON THE WALLS

Much of the material in this chapter comes from two visits to the National House of Prayer in 2006; my interviews with Fran and Rob Parker, Stephen Sowerby and others; as well as from the NHOP blog. Rob Parker reported that he had been given a parliamentary pass "by an MP" on the Miracle Channel's New Year's Eve broadcast, December 31, 2005, declaring, "I'm now an employee on Parliament Hill."

Accounts of the Toronto Blessing come from news reports in 1994, as well as from The "Toronto Blessing": A Renewal from God? by Gary W. McHale and Michael A.G. Haykin (Canadian Christian Publications, 1995), which also contains a chapter on the Latter Rain Revival. The prophecies of Reverend David Yonggi Cho appear on a number of charismatic websites, including that of the Miracle Channel. The first was uttered on a visit to Evangel Tabernacle in Kelowna, B.C., in 1975; the one I cite was made at a church growth seminar in Sackville, Nova Scotia, in 1984. According to a 2008 article by Bruce Wilson in the Huffington Post, Sarah Palin's ceremonial anointing by Kenyan cleric Thomas Muthee, who is known for banishing witches in his country, took place on October 2005 at the Wasilla Assembly of God in Wasilla, Alaska; it can be seen on YouTube.

Much of the background on C. Peter Wagner, his leadership institute and the Third Wave movement, also known as the New Apostolic Reformation movement, comes from Sara Diamond's Not By Politics Alone, which also reports Wagner's longstanding ties to Cindy Jacobs. A catalogue from the institute's Canadian affiliate, headquartered in Red Deer, Alberta, lists thirty-four faculty members in this country, including John Arnott of Toronto Airport Christian Fellowship; Stacey and Wesley Campbell, the founders of Kelowna's New Life Church; David Demian of Watchmen for the Nations; Dick Dewert, founder of the Miracle Channel in Lethbridge, Alberta; Rob Parker of the National House of Prayer; and Bill Prankard, host of the daily television show From the River.

Accounts of the founding of the International House of Prayer in Kansas City, Missouri, appear on a number of charismatic websites and in *The "Toronto Blessing"* by McHale and Haykin. The background on Lou Engle's Justice House of Prayer in Washington, D.C., was reported in *Common Ground Christian News* (April 2005) and *Mother Jones* (September 1, 2005).

The most detailed and accurate accounts of the contribution by New Brunswick Premier Samuel Leonard Tilley to the designation of Canada as a dominion appear on the Dictionary of Canadian Biography Online as well as Richard Gwyn's biography *John A: The Man Who Made Us* (Random House Canada, 2007).

The story of Pastor Bob Birch and Watchmen for the Nations comes largely from Beth Carson's biography, *Pastor Bob: A Statesman of Prayer for Canada* (Guardian Books, 2003); an article about Birch's 100th birthday by Reverend Ed Hird in *ChristianWeek* on December 1, 2007; and the Watchmen website, where David Demian posts his periodic newsletters and reports on the organization's gatherings. Lloyd Mackey has written about Stockwell Day's ties to the organization on canadianchristianity.com on May 28, 2002, and April 15, 2004. On May 28, 2009, Immigration Minister Jason Kenney named David Demian to the government's new Jewish-Canadian Advisory Committee for the Community Historical Recognition Program, which is charged with planning a monument to commemorate the St. Louis tragedy, among other things.

The report of Cindy Jacobs' prophecy over Stockwell Day was posted on the website of her organization, Generals of Intercession, now known as Generals International, on April 12, 2005, under the heading "Canada Report: 'Seize the Moment.'" Faytene Kryskow's biography is entitled *Marked: A Generation of Dread Champions Rising to Shift Nations* (Destiny Image Publishers Inc., 2009).

CHAPTER V: ROCKING THE VOTE

I attended "Acquire the Fire" on October 27, 2007, in Hamilton's Copps Coliseum. Additional background on Ron Luce and Teen Mania Ministries came from "Teenage Holy War" by Jeff Sharlet in *Rolling Stone* on April 19, 2007, and "Evangelicals Fear the Loss of Their Teenagers" in the *New York Times* on October 6, 2006. I also interviewed Kemtal Glasgow, the director of Teen Mania Canada (which is a registered Canadian charity), board member Anthony Does and administrator Maurice Vannest. Stockwell Day's appearance with Teen Mania was reported in the *Hamilton Spectator* on November 21, 2001. Christian Smith, a professor at Notre Dame University, published "Evangelicals Behaving Badly with Statistics" in *Books & Culture: A Christian Review* (January/February 2007). Accounts of Lou Engle's 2008 edition of TheCall appeared in *Charisma* magazine on August 18, the *Washington Times* on July 27, 2008 and on rightwingwatch.org, as well as on TheCall's own website. Among those on its board are Stacey and Wesley Campbell and Mike Bickle, director of the International House of Prayer in Kansas City, Missouri.

The first edition of TheCRY in 2002 was organized by Steve Osmond, then an Edmonton youth pastor who now serves at Calgary's First Assembly Pentecostal Church. According to a November 2002 account in *Charisma* magazine, TheCRY stands for Canadian Revived Youth, and even then the organization was reported to be affiliated with TheCall. The second edition, in August 2006, was organized by Faytene Kryskow and Rob and Fran Parker of the National House of Prayer. Reports about it appeared in the *Ottawa Citizen* on July 16, 2006, and the *Globe and Mail* on September 23, 2006. TheCRY is now a registered Canadian charity whose address is 337 Lemoine Avenue in Ottawa, the headquarters of Faytene Kryskow's 4MYCanada association (which was refused charitable tax status), and its directors are Kryskow, Stacey Campbell and Rob Parker. According to its 2008 charitable tax return, TheCRY donated $21,000 to Stacey and Wes Campbell's Kelowna-based ministry, Be a Hero.

Faytene Kryskow compared herself to Joan of Arc in the biography she supplied for a Siege event in Montreal in April 2008, and she spoke extensively about the French saint at the Toronto Missionfest conference I attended in March 2008. Most of the information on Kryskow comes from a brief interview I did with her a week earlier at the first Manning Networking Conference in Ottawa, as well as from her two books, *Marked* and *Stand on Guard* (Credo Publishing, 2005), her websites (including that of her Fly High Ministries) or her CDs. The Canadian address for Lou Engle's Bound4Life is the same as that for 4MYCanada and TheCRY. For background on Kryskow, I interviewed Lisa Dewar, her former counselor; Gary Klassen, regional coordinator for World Vision Canada; and Dennis Hixson, the vice president of Pacific Life Bible College in Surrey, B.C. (who had formerly worked for Accelerated Christian Education in Texas and was an organizer in the Surrey textbook fight). Material on Aimee Semple McPherson came from two books, *Aimee Semple McPherson: Everybody's Sister* by Edith L. Blumhofer (William B. Eerdmans Publishing Co., 1993) and *Aimee Semple McPherson and the Resurrection of Christian America* by Matthew Avery Sutton (Harvard University Press, 2007), as well as my own visit to her Angelus Temple in Los Angeles.

A report on Kryskow's stint in Liberia by her friend Stephen Court of the Salvation Army appeared in the *Journal of Aggressive Christianity*; Kryskow was also interviewed about her work there by canadianchristianity.com on December 11, 2003. Patricia King's autobiographical material came from an article she wrote as Patricia Cocking that appeared on christianity.ca in 2003 under the title "The Lord of the Rings: Some Thoughts to Consider." King's original ministry was a charity named the Christian Service Association that makes annual donations to Extreme Prophetic, another registered Canadian charity, which, in turn, donated $16,000 to Hope for the Nations in 2004.

Accounts of Todd Bentley's Lakeland revival appeared in *Charisma* magazine, on ABC's *Nightline* and Fox News; actual footage of his services are on YouTube, including his apostolic commissioning service organized by C. Peter Wagner, Stacey and Wes Campbell, John Arnott and many of the Kansas City prophets. Reports on the alleged Ponzi scheme that implicated members of Kelowna's New Life Church appeared in the *Vancouver Sun* in May 2006; Wesley Campbell and Ralph Bromley negotiated a settlement with the B.C. Securities Commission that was published on the commission's website on January 27, 2007. The staff of the Kelowna Christian Center includes Associate Pastor Greg Bitgood, who appeared with Faytene Kryskow on the review board of an organization called YM4C: Young Minds for Canada, a B.C.-based precursor to 4MYCanada.

Reverend D. James Kennedy, the founder of Coral Ridge Ministries in Florida who died in 2008, was regarded as one of America's leading Dominionists; the ministry continues today under his daughter and has produced a video series on hate speech laws in which Tristan Emmanuel appears. The first edition of *Canada: Portraits of Faith*, edited by Michael D. Clarke, was published in 1998 by Reel to Real Ministries; the third edition, which I cite, was published in 2001 by the Home School Legal Defence Association of Canada, then headquartered in Medicine Hat, Alberta, under Executive Director Dallas K. Miller.

Kryskow's account of her own publishing experience appears in *Marked*: she has told the story of her organization's origins in the 2005 parliamentary vote on marriage in numerous speeches, CDs and her book, sometimes mentioning Stockwell Day and his wife, Valorie, by name, sometimes simply referring to him as "a politician" and Valorie Day as a friend. The chronicle of Kryskow's first youth mission in June 2005 draws on an account by Christina Groot, then the project coordinator, in *4MYCanada—The Magazine*. On the second Siege trip to Ottawa, Kryskow's group was the first to stay at the National House of Prayer. Megawatt PR, based in Vancouver, features a testimonial from Kryskow about its work for 4MYCanada on its website. New Brunswick MP Mike Allen commented on the group's novel approach while speaking to its

"Reverse the Curse" Siege in Saint John, N.B., in November 2007. The account of Rahim Jaffer's welcome of Kryskow's group to the House of Commons appeared on Stacey Campbell's website.

The story behind the takeover of the CBC's Great Canadian Wish List appears on 4MYCanada's website, but most sources attribute the coup to Dave Gilbert, who was then a business student at Wilfrid Laurier University in Waterloo, Ontario, and the fiancé of Theresa Matters, executive director of the National Campus Life Network. Matters (now married to Gilbert) wrote about it in the August 2007 issue of *The Interim* and I later confirmed the account in an interview with Gilbert. I was in Ottawa for the vote on Ken Epp's Unborn Victims of Crime bill in March 2008; according to Dan Gilgoff in *The Jesus Machine*, George W. Bush had signed into law the Unborn Victims of Violence Act in 2004 along with other anti-abortion measures.

CHAPTER VI: IN THE BEGINNING
The conflict between Science Minister Gary Goodyear and officials from the Canadian Association of University Teachers (CAUT) was reported by the *Globe and Mail* on March 2, 2009, and I confirmed the details in an interview with CAUT's executive director, James Turk. The follow-up story, "Science minister won't confirm belief in evolution," appeared on March 17, 2009. A report on Reginald Petersen's November 6, 2007, settlement with Elections Canada appeared in the *Canada Gazette* in January 2008 and the *Ottawa Citizen* on January 15, 2008. Petersen, who sold his nursing home business, Versa Care, for a reported $220 million in 1997, was a candidate for the Reform Party in 1993 and for the Canadian Alliance in 2000.

British Columbia MP James Lunney declared his support for Goodyear with a statement in the House of Commons on April 2, 2009. Both Lunney and Goodyear are graduates of Canadian Memorial Chiropractic College in Toronto. On June 5, 2009, Goodyear announced the college had received $350,000 in federal economic stimulus funds.

I visited the Big Valley Creation Science Museum on November 10, 2007, and interviewed Harry Nibourg and Vance Nelson several times, both in person and on the telephone. After a visit to Drumheller the same week, I interviewed David Eberth, senior research scientist at the Royal Tyrrell Museum, and Reverend Blaine McDonald of Elim Pentecostal Tabernacle by phone. The opening of Big Valley's museum was reported on the front page of the *Globe and Mail* on June 6, 2007. On June 18, 2007, Angus Reid Strategies released the contradictory results of a poll that declared three in five Canadians (59 percent) believe in evolution, but 42 percent believe dinosaurs and humans co-existed on earth—a central tenet of creationism. Karen Armstrong's thoughts on creationism and the history of biblical literalism come chiefly from *The Bible: A Biography* (Atlantic Books, 2007). The history of fundamentalism is drawn from "The Evangelical Worldview Since 1890" by James Davison Hunter in *Piety & Politics*.

Information on Clearwater Christian College in Tampa, Florida, comes almost entirely from its website. Gary E. Parker discusses his conversion to creationism in a pamphlet called "From Evolution to Creation," published by Answers in Genesis. Attacks on Carl Baugh's fossil finds and his academic degrees appear on a number of websites, some authored by Glen J. Kuban under the title "A Matter of Degree: Carl Baugh's Alleged Credentials," which was published online in November/December 1989. The split between Creation Ministries International and Ken Ham is explained on the CMI website.

The Royal Ontario Museum's difficulties in raising funds for its exhibit "Darwin: The Evolution Revolution" was reported on March 27, 2008, in the *National Post*. Reports on the Dover School Board case appeared in numerous American publications, including a PBS documentary entitled *Judgment Day: Intelligent Design on Trial*. Information on teaching creationism in Canada came from Jason R. Wiles, the manager of McGill University's Evolution Education Research Centre; Wiles's research also appears in the September 2006 edition of

Geoscience Canada. An account of the Abbotsford School Board fight over creationism appears on the website of the British Columbia Civil Liberties Association.

A history of the Intelligent Design movement and the Discovery Institute appeared in the *New York Times* on August 21, 2005: "Politicized Scholars Put Evolution on the Defensive." I interviewed Denyse O'Leary twice by phone in 2008, and she has also been profiled in the *Toronto Star* on May 29, 2004, and in *Christian Week* on June 22, 2004. Additional material comes from her Post-Darwinist and Mindful Hack blogs, as well as a series she wrote for Access Research Network (arn.org). Stories on the Smithsonian's inadvertent support for the film *Privileged Planet* appeared in the *New York Times* on May 28, 2005. The ties of the New Scholars Society to Campus Crusade for Christ were reported on canadianchristianity.com on October 23, 2003. Some of Denyse O'Leary's postings on the advance screening of *Expelled* appeared on her Post-Darwinist blog on June 15, 2008.

Walt Ruloff did not return my calls, but I have drawn on interviews he did with the *Vancouver Sun* and the *National Post* on April 26, 2008, as well as stories on canadianchristianity.com and straight.com on June 26, 2008. Also helpful were interviews with his co-producer, Logan Craft, in *The New Mexican*, based in Santa Fe, New Mexico, and the *Texan*, a publication of the Southern Baptists of Texas Convention, where Craft explains the origins of the film project and why Ben Stein was chosen to star in *Expelled*: "Craft said Stein was picked because he is Jewish, not overtly religious and an intellectual with 'pro-life' sympathies," the *New Mexican* reported. In the same interview, he declared that he hoped the film would help influence views on abortion. Craft is on the board of the Centre for Cultural Renewal, a Canadian group set up to promote the role of religion in public life. Charles McVety marched directly from a showing of *Expelled* to the Royal Ontario Museum where he staged a protest against its Darwin exhibition.

Richard Dawkins and other scientists recounted how they came to appear in *Expelled* in the *New York Times* on September 27, 2007. A 2008 exhibit at the Canadian War Museum called *Deadly Medicine: Creating the Master Race* featured a brief history of eugenics in Canada, including a thesis by Tommy Douglas, and the role of feminist icon Emily Murphy, one of the Famous Five who won Canadian women the vote, in an extensive sterilization program in Alberta.

CHAPTER VII: RAISING THE JOSHUA GENERATION

I interviewed Murray and Peter Corren in Vancouver in December 2008, a year before Peter died. At the time, the Abbotsford School Board offered Social Justice 12 for the 2008 fall semester, then, after more than ninety students had signed up, cancelled the course, claiming it had not had time to properly review the requirements; it was the only B.C. school board to do so. In the fall of 2009, after the Correns filed a lawsuit, Abbotsford finally offered the course. Many of the members of the board involved in the cancellation were re-elected two months later in the November 2008 municipal elections; during the same vote, John Sutherland, the board's chairman during the 1995 brouhaha over teaching creationism, also returned to the board for the first time in years.

In the 2008 election, Liberal MP Raymond Chan charged that his opponent Alice Wong, now the Conservative MP for Richmond, had attended fundraising dinners and spoken at rallies of the Canadian Alliance for Social Justice and Family Values Association (CASJAFVA), founded in 1997 by K-John Cheung "to awaken the silent majority." CASJAFVA had also intervened in the Surrey School Board case and collected twelve thousand signatures on a petition protesting same-sex marriage.

The quip from former senator Ron Ghitter comes from an opinion piece by University of Calgary Professor Barry Cooper in the *Globe and Mail* on June 1, 2009. (Years earlier, Ghitter had chaired a provincial inquiry into tolerance and understanding in Alberta schools that singled out teaching materials from Accelerated Christian Education for criticism.) James Dobson's allegations of a homosexual plot were contained in "Education Turned Perversion" in his June 2006 newsletter.

Statistics on suicide among gay, lesbian, bisexual or transgendered youth come from a 2003 report by Calgary's Centre for Suicide Prevention; those on bullying from *U.S. News & World Report* on December 31, 2008. Biographical material on Kari Simpson is based on a profile in *B.C. Report* magazine, November 24, 1997, "The Most Dangerous Woman in B.C." She disclosed her plan to file a human rights complaint against the B.C. Human Rights Tribunal in an October 7, 2008, article in *Faith for All of Life*, formerly the *Chalcedon Report*, the journal of the Chalcedon Foundation, founded by the late Rousas J. Rushdoony, the father of Christian Reconstructionism.

Falwell's remarks on the U.S. education system appear in Kevin Phillips' *American Theocracy*. Much of the material on Christian schools came from my 2009 interviews with Dr. Adrian Guldemond, executive director of the Ontario Association of Christian Schools, shortly before his retirement, and George Petrusma, the principal of Knox Christian School in Bowmanville, Ontario, as well as two of his teachers, who were kind enough to allow me to sit in on their classes. For background, I am indebted to Lois Sweet's *God in the Classroom: The Controversial Issue of Religion in Canada's Schools* (McClelland & Stewart, 1997) and the entry "Education in Canada" in the *Canadian Encyclopedia*.

I attended the April 2008 convention of the Ontario Christian Home Educators' Connection (OCHEC), where I interviewed Diane Geerlinks, Amy Bromilow and others, and sat in on a presentation by Paul Faris, director of the Home School Legal Defence Association of Canada (HSLDA), whom I had interviewed earlier by phone. Historical material on the homeschooling movement as well as on Horace Mann comes from *Home Schooling: The Right Choice* (first published by Loyal Publishing Inc., 1995) by Christopher J. Klicka. The history of Michael

Farris, the founder of HSLDA and Patrick Henry College, is based on *God's Harvard: A Christian College on a Mission to Save America* by Hanna Rosin (Harcourt Inc., 2007).

Information on Dallas K. Miller, the Medicine Hat lawyer who became the executive director of the Canadian organization in 1994, appeared on the HSLDA website. He wrote an article on the Newfoundland case, "CRB & SGB v. Director of Child Welfare (Nfld.)," for the online magazine of the U.S.-based Howard Center (www.profam.org). Miller represented HSLDA as part of the Coalition for Family Autonomy (which also included Focus on the Family Canada, REAL Women of Canada and the Canada Family Action Coalition) in an intervention on behalf of parents' rights to spank in a 2004 case before the Supreme Court. In December 2006, Miller was appointed to the Court of Queen's Bench of Alberta by Stephen Harper's new government (see chapter eight); the announcement made no mention of his HSLDA history.

In 2003 the HSLDA published the results of a survey on homeschooling by Deani Van Pelt, a professor of education at Redeemer University College in Ancaster, Ontario, based on questionnaires from 1,648 home-educating families whose children also wrote the Canadian Achievement Test. (Van Pelt's husband, Michael, is president of the evangelical think tank Cardus, formerly known as the Work Research Foundation.) The Fraser Institute study *Home Schooling: From the Extreme to the Mainstream* was first published in 2001 and updated in 2007. Beatrice Ekwa Ekoko discussed homeschooling with the CBC's *Viewpoint* in August 2006. Lloyd Mackey has reported the fact that Ken Boessenkool and his wife homeschooled their children in Calgary. The number of interns from Patrick Henry College in George W. Bush's White House was reported by the British daily the *Independent* on April 21, 2004.

Information on Trinity Western University is based on my 2008 trip to the campus, where I interviewed Professors Robert Burkinshaw, Bruce Guenther, John Dyck, Paul Rowe and Jack Van Dyke, the former head of the science department, as well as TWU president Jonathon

Raymond. Additional material came from *Trinity Western University: Stories of Faith and Transformation* published by TWU in 2002. The history of the Laurentian Leadership Centre is based on three interviews with its founder, Don Page, and its current director, Janet Epp Buckingham, as well as a visit to the centre in 2007, when I interviewed half a dozen students. Paul Wilson's comments on the comparison between the centre and Patrick Henry College appeared in the *Ottawa Citizen* on January 15, 2006.

CHAPTER VIII: THE ELECTRONIC PULPIT

The first section of this chapter is based on my reporting from TheCRY on August 23, 2008. References to David Mainse's previous cross-country crusades come from his 1981 self-published book, *God Keep Our Land*; I also interviewed him by telephone in 2006 and briefly in person at TheCRY. Background on Crossroads Christian Communications comes from interviews and assorted news reports. The history of religious broadcasting in the U.S. comes from "Televangelism and Politics" by Jeffrey K. Hadden in *Piety and Politics. The Tactics of Christian Resistance* is the third volume of a three-volume series published in 1983 by the Geneva Divinity School Press in Tyler, Texas, and edited by Gary North, the son-in-law of Rousas J. Rushdoony. For Canadian broadcasting history, I have relied mainly on the website of the Canadian Communications Foundation.

The history of the Miracle Channel is based on interviews with Morris Watson, senior pastor at Victory Christian Fellowship in Lethbridge, Alberta, which I visited in November 2007, as well as a scrapbook of news reports he provided me with on the fight to win CRTC approval. Equally valuable was a memoir by George and Hazel Hill entitled *Adventure, Romance & Revival: An Ordinary Couple Doing Extraordinary Exploits for God*, published by House of Victory Publishing in 1999. (Both George and Hazel Hill use the title "Dr." before their names after receiving honorary doctorates from Canada Christian

College.) In the summer of 2008, I also visited Trinity Broadcasting Network in Costa Mesa, California.

The formation of the National Christian Broadcasters Association was reported in *Christian Week*, March 17, 1992. For the CRTC's side of the story, I interviewed former chairman Keith Spicer, former senior director of television policy Nick Ketchum and other CRTC officials, and read hours of hearing transcripts and complaint files. The biography of Bob Du Broy, vice-president of CHRI, on christianmedia.ca, refers to his role with Dayna Dixon in convincing the CRTC to change its religious broadcasting policy; her testimony appears in the hearing transcripts.

Dick Dewert related his station's financial miracles in the *Lethbridge Herald* on January 19, 2002. His gold tooth claims were reported in the same paper on March 26, 1999, when his dentist, Dr. Jack Sherman, corrected the record; the incident occurred two months before Willard Thiessen, the president of Trinity Television in Winnipeg, made a similar claim only to be contradicted by his brother Elmer, a dentist in B.C. I interviewed Tim Thibault numerous times over the telephone between 2007 and 2010, and also read transcripts of his complaints to the CRTC as well as its January 3, 2006, ruling on the Miracle Channel's fundraising practices.

The history of the prosperity gospel is the subject of *God's Profits* by Sarah Posner (PoliPointPress, 2008). Stockwell Day's appearance at Dewert's first Dominion Conference was reported by the *Lethbridge Herald* on June 29, 2002. Dewert's resignation from the Miracle Channel was reported in the *Calgary Herald* on May 23, 2007. Dick and Joan Dewert staged a comeback appearance on Bill and Gwen Prankard's show *From the River* on July 1, 2008. By then, Dewert had formed Auxano Wealth Group, which he claimed, in a promotional video, was the exclusive agent for the Harvest Group of companies, a real estate syndication firm for which Roy Beyer served as senior marketing director. In August 2009, Foundation Capital Corporation, identified as one of the Harvest group of companies, reached a settlement with the

Alberta Securities Commission regarding allegedly misleading statements to investors in two of its projects. As part of the settlement, Beyer agreed to pay $20,000 plus costs to the commission. Shortly after the Miracle Channel drafted televangelist Leon Fontaine as its new CEO in late 2009, Dewert announced the formation of Dick Deweert Ministries, which held a "Unite the Dominion" conference in Calgary in January 2010.

David Mainse's letter to Queen Elizabeth II was reported by the Canadian Press on July 12, 2005. His plea to viewers on same-sex marriage was on Crossroads' website until 2008. Mainse's role in Watchmen for the Nations is documented on the Watchmen website, which includes the Covenant of Christian Broadcasters sworn in at a 1999 Watchmen conference.

Mainse's statement about the devil occurred on his *100 Huntley Street* telethon in the summer of 2009. On April 15, 2009, the Ontario Securities Commission had issued a temporary cease-trading order against Gordon Driver, a former Crossroads employee, and his company, Axcess Automation; a month later, on May 14, the U.S. Securities and Exchange Commission announced an investigation into Driver's alleged $14.1 million Ponzi scheme that involved a hundred investors in Canada and the United States. The first story on the incident did not appear until May 21, 2009, in the *Hamilton Spectator*, which reported that, according to the SEC, Ron and Reynold Mainse had not only invested in the scheme but had acted as alleged "finders," bringing in an estimated sixty friends and family members as investors. On June 4, 2009, Crossroads announced that Ron and Reynold Mainse had been removed from the air pending further investigation, but the story was not reported by *Christian Week* until December of that year and received almost no other media coverage. In December 2009, Driver reached a settlement with the SEC, but apart from a confessional interview on *100 Huntley Street* before its fall telethon, Ron Mainse had not returned to *100 Huntley Street* by early 2010.

Reports on "God's Fraud Squad"—Father Seamus Mackrell, a Catholic priest from Chilliwack, B.C., and Reverend John Haycock, a Presbyterian minister at a hospital in Abbotsford—appeared in the *Globe and Mail* on October 4, 2007.

I interviewed Tristan Emmanuel numerous times over the years, usually at Crossroads' headquarters, and attended a half-dozen of his conferences there for the ECP (Equipping Christians for the Public Square) Centre. At one ECP fundraiser in June 2005 at Ebenezer Canadian Reformed Church in Burlington, Ontario, I interviewed two of his chief backers, Rob Wildeboer, executive chairman of Martinrea International Inc., and Allan Schutten, the CEO of Janco Steel Ltd. Wildeboer's appointment to the government's Science, Technology and Innovation Council was announced on October 18, 2007. The history of *WorldNetDaily* is based on interviews with Joseph Farah and his speeches to ECP conferences.

CHAPTER IX: JUDGMENT DAY

I attended the 2006 Civitas Conference and interviewed Maurice Vellacott both at the time and later by telephone. Justice Marshall Rothstein discussed his parliamentary hearing in a speech to the Canadian Constitution Foundation. Timothy Bloedow's self-published book *State vs. Church: What Christians Can Do to Save Canada from Liberal Tyranny* is an excellent primer on Christian Reconstructionism; I have also interviewed Bloedow on several occasions.

Uganda's proposed measures against homosexuality were the subject of numerous news stories, including one in the *Globe and Mail* on November 25, 2009. Many linked the measures to a March 2009 conference in Kampala, "Exposing the Truth Behind Homosexuality and the Homosexual Agenda," which featured three American evangelicals who blamed the gay movement for a wide range of evils, including the rise of Nazism in Germany and the Rwandan genocide. One of the trio was Caleb Lee Brundidge, a self-styled "sexual reorientation coach," who is a member of Patricia King's Extreme Prophetic ministry (the ministry that mentored Faytene Kryskow).

On February 13, 2007, the *Globe and Mail* reported complaints about the Conservatives' changes to the country's sixteen Judicial Review Committees; on February 21, 2007, the Canadian Judicial Council expressed its own objections in a paper it billed as an "information document." Earlier, in November 2006, the council and the Canadian Bar Association had already protested changes to the judicial appointments process. A report on the appointment of David M. Brown to the Ontario bench appeared in the *Globe and Mail* on September 21, 2006.

I attended the Christian Legal Fellowship's 2007 convention in Toronto, and most of the material on its history comes from interviews with co-founders John McKay and Calvin Beresh. Focus on the Family Canada, a registered Canadian charity, donated $38,000 to the Christian Legal Fellowship between 2002 and 2007, most of it ($35,019) in 2006. Cindy Silver was CLF executive director between 1998 and 2000, joining the organization after serving as legal counsel for five years with Focus on the Family Canada. The history of the Alliance Defense Fund is based partly on my interview with its senior counsel, Benjamin Bull, and his speech to the CLF conference.

Gerald Chipeur's biography comes from a three-hour interview with him in November 2007; his 2006 contract with the department of public safety is on file with the U.S. Justice Department's Foreign Agents Registration database. Paul Weyrich wrote about his conversations with Chipeur before and after the January 2006 election in his column for the Free Congress Foundation. All biographical material on Stephen Boissoin comes from my three-hour interview with him in Red Deer in November 2007. The complaint against him was filed by University of Calgary Professor Darren Lund, a former Red Deer high school teacher.

Craig Chandler has been the subject of numerous stories in the *Calgary Herald* (November 18, 23 and 24, 2007) and an editorial in the

Globe and Mail on November 29, 2007, entitled "The Chandler problem." *Calgary Herald* columnist Don Braid referred to him as "a roaming rottweiler in the far-right kennels of Alberta politics" on November 20, 2007. News reports of the Gay Militia's invasion of Chandler's fundraising dinner were supplemented by my interviews with Boissoin and Tristan Emmanuel. Timothy Bloedow self-published *No Sacred Ground* in 2008.

Janet Epp Buckingham's column "Abolish human rights commissions? Not so fast" appeared in *Christian Week* on February 15, 2008. Denyse O'Leary promptly lashed out at Buckingham in interviews, declaring on her website: "I think Janet Epp Buckingham owes every independent journalist in Canada an apology, but especially the Christian ones, who have—in many cases—sacrificed much and risked much." In an article on LifeSiteNews.com—and a conversation with me later—Buckingham admitted she felt "a little beaten up" by the attacks: she had assumed O'Leary was a friend, she said, but O'Leary had declined to discuss the issue with her.

Ezra Levant's account of his appearance before the Alberta Human Rights Commission was published on his blog and in his book, *Shakedown: How Our Government Is Undermining Democracy in the Name of Human Rights* (McClelland & Stewart, 2009). Gerald Chipeur spoke about the reaction from other pastors to the Boissoin verdict at an ECP Centre conference in Burlington, Ontario, in October 2008. A key moment in the debate over Section 13 (1) of the Canadian Human Rights Act came in September 2009 when Athanasios D. Hadjis, an adjudicator of the Canadian Human Rights Tribunal, ruled that the clause was inconsistent with the Charter of Rights, and declared he would henceforth "simply refuse to apply those provisions."

The issue of abolishing the Ontario Human Rights Commission came to dominate the 2009 Progressive Conservative leadership race in the province after it was introduced by dark-horse candidate, MPP Randy Hillier, whose campaign manager was Tristan Emmanuel, the former head of the ECP Centre. Tim Hudak, the eventual winner of the contest, adopted the policy as his own.

I saw Sam Solomon speak at both the 2007 Christian Legal Fellowship conference and an ECP Centre fundraiser on October 18, 2008. Solomon is listed as an "adjunct associate" on the website of Ravi Zacharias Ministries International, as well as CEO of the British-based evangelical organization Faith for the Muslims. My conversation with CLF director Ruth Ross about obtaining a tape of his remarks occurred on December 1, 2007.

CHAPTER X: THE ARMAGEDDON FACTOR

My account of John Hagee's 2006 visit to Canada Christian College is based on my attendance at the event, as well as a brief interview with Hagee at a reception in Charles McVety's office beforehand. A version of the report appeared in my October 2006 *Walrus* article. Hagee's first convocation of Christians United for Israel in Washington, D.C., took place in the summer of 2006 during Israel's military campaign against Lebanon.

On his way to the G8 summit in St. Petersburg, Russia, on July 14, 2006, Stephen Harper defended the Israeli military action as a "measured" response to provocation. He did not alter his support even after Canadian Forces Major Paeta Hess-Von Krudener was killed on July 25 in his marked U.N. post by a 500 kilogram bomb dropped by the Israeli Defense Forces. On February 1, 2008, a Canadian Forces Board of Inquiry reported that the incident was "tragic and preventable." Two years later, when Israel launched an attack on the blockaded Gaza Strip, Harper left comments to Foreign Affairs Minister Lawrence Cannon and his junior minister Peter Kent, whose Thornhill riding has a high percentage of Jewish voters.

The history of dispensationalism is based on a number of sources, including *Piety & Politics*; *Expecting the End: Millennialism in Social and Historical Context*, edited by Kenneth G.C. Newport and Crawford

Gribben (Baylor University Press, 2006); and *Skipping Towards Armageddon: The Politics and Propaganda of the Left Behind Novels and the LaHaye Empire* by Michael Standaert (Soft Skull Press, 2006). A 2007 doctoral dissertation by Winston Terrance Sutherland, called "John Nelson Darby: His Contributions to Contemporary Theological Higher Education," discusses Darby's North American travels, including his Canadian stops. In Lloyd Mackey's book *Like Father, Like Son,* Mackey describes the impact that dispensationalism had on both William Aberhart and Ernest Manning.

The history of Christian Zionism and Israeli foreign policy is based on a number of books including the groundbreaking study by Grace Halsell, *Prophecy and Politics: Militant Evangelists on the Road to Nuclear War* (Lawrence Hill & Co., 1986). More recent analyses have been published by Timothy P. Weber, a professor of church history at Northern Baptist Theological Seminary in Illinois, who wrote "How Evangelicals Became Israel's Best Friend" for *Christianity Today* in 1998; and Stephen Sizer, an evangelical Anglican vicar in Britain who is the author of *Christian Zionism: Road-map to Armageddon?* (InterVarsity Press, 2004).

The connection between the Iraq war and Saddam Hussein's plans to resurrect Babylon are based on Paul Boyer's article on alternet. org, "When U.S. Foreign Policy Meets Biblical Prophecy," on February 20, 2003. Chirac's account of his conversation with former president George W. Bush on the Iraq invasion in early 2003 first came to light in a 2007 article by Swiss theologian Thomas Romer of the University of Lausanne whom Chirac's office had contacted for advice. Chirac later confirmed the anecdote to journalist Jean-Claude Maurice for his 2009 book, *Si Vous le Répétz, Je Démentirai,* and from there it was reported by James Haught, the editor of the *West Virginia Gazette* on July 22, 2009 under the heading "Agog over Bush's comments on Gog and Magog." Donald Rumsfeld's efforts to influence Bush with Bible verses on Pentagon reports were revealed by Robert Draper in the June 2009 issue of *GQ,* "And He Shall Be Judged."

The history of the evangelical alliance with the Jewish community in Canada comes largely from several interviews with Frank Dimant between 2004 and 2006, as well as interviews with former B'nai Brith president Rochelle Wilner, and an account by Stephen Scheinberg, a former B'nai Brith vice-president and board member, called "Partners for Imperium: B'nai Brith Canada and the Christian Right," which appeared in the July-August 2008 issue of *Canadian Jewish Outlook*. In the 2008 election, Wilner ran as the Conservative candidate in the Toronto riding of York Centre; two years earlier, the Conservative candidate in the riding was Michael Mostyn, who became B'nai Brith's representative in Ottawa. I quote from one of the Conservative Party's flyers directed toward Jewish voters in the fall of 2009; although sent to a Montreal riding, it identifies the sender as Edmonton MP Rob Anders of "CRG-Government Caucus Services," an acronym for the Conservative Research Group, the party's research arm in Ottawa.

John Tweedie of Christians for Israel provided the history of his organization in a telephone interview, while other material came from the organization's website. Tweedie, who received an honorary degree from Canada Christian College, also writes a column for Charles McVety's *Evangelical Christian* magazine. An early account of the organization's burned-out Israeli bus on display at a convention of the National Religious Broadcasters in the United States appears in Chris Hedges's *American Fascists*; Tweedie himself told me about bringing it to The Hague later. On his organization's website, c4israel.org, Tweedie's article "Why Israel?" features a section entitled "Palestine: Nation or Place?" that declares "history has no record of a nation called Palestine."

The Toronto workshop of Malcolm Hedding, executive director of the International Christian Embassy in Jerusalem, took place on May 12, 2007, and the following night, I attended the Canadian debut of *The Covenant*. The history of the ICEJ came from the organization's website and Grace Halsell's *Prophecy and Politics*. The story of Benny Hinn's conversion to evangelism at a revival held by Merv and Merla Watson, the singing duo from Abbotsford, B.C., appears on Hinn's website, and is also recounted by the Watsons in the notes to their CD *Toronto Catacombs*, recorded in 1974 at St. Paul's Cathedral. According to a 1998 article by Donald Wagner of Chicago's North Park University called "Evangelicals and Israel: Theological Roots of a Political Alliance," the ICEJ was one of several evangelical groups that worked with the Israeli government to exaggerate accounts of Christian persecution in the Middle East.

I interviewed James Lunney in Toronto in 2008, when he told me his first trip to Israel was organized by Ralph Rutledge, the former pastor of Toronto's Queensway Cathedral who is also the brother-in-law of broadcaster David Mainse. The history of the Knesset Christian Allies Caucus was pieced together from its website and various other sources, including Pat Robertson's Christian Broadcasting Network. A list of sister caucuses on the Knesset Christian Allies' website until early 2009 named Lunney's co-chair as Stockwell Day. Reports of the Canadian organization's launch appeared in the *Jerusalem Post* on February 4, 2007, which claimed that the new "pro-Israel lobby" would be announced "in the presence of Canadian Prime Minister Stephen Harper" and three Knesset members. According to the *Canadian Jewish News*, the Knesset Christian Allies caucus representative in Canada is Anna-lee Chiprout, an executive assistant at the Israeli embassy. On May 22, 2008, the *Jerusalem Post* reported on the Washington conference of pro-Israel parliamentarians from around the world, who swore a "Declaration of Purpose and Solidarity with the People and State of Israel," quoting James Lunney in its story.

I attended the speech of Professor Paul Charles Merkley at Toronto's Beth Tzedec Synagogue.

CHAPTER XI: HERE TO STAY

Doug Phillips runs a Christian Reconstructionist ministry called Vision Forum, which publishes homeschooling materials that have been praised by Timothy Bloedow on his website. Phillips is the son of Howard Phillips, one of the founders of the Moral Majority. Faytene Kryskow's comments to MPs come from a parliamentary reception that her organization threw in 2009, where she summed up her organization's history and activities, including its campaign efforts. Dennis Gruending often writes about the Christian right on his blog, Pulpit & Politics.

The Canadian Constitution Foundation, founded by John Weston, now operates out of Calgary under Executive Director John Carpay, a former Reform Party candidate. I attended its first conference in October 2007, where the keynote speaker was Justice Marshall Rothstein. As part of the new strategy of coordination among the religious right, Carpay appeared at an ECP Centre conference in the fall of 2009 along with Charles McVety of the Canada Family Action Coalition, Dave Quist of the Institute of Marriage and Family Canada and Stephanie Luck of the Christian Legal Fellowship.

I interviewed Francine Lalonde in the summer of 2009, and attended the November 2007 International Symposium on Euthanasia organized in Toronto.

The Canadian Centre for Bio-Ethical Reform is based in Calgary and run by Stephanie Grey, a former president of the pro-life club at the University of British Columbia. Its American parent, the Center for Bio-Ethical Reform based in Lake Forrest, California, was founded by Gregg Cunningham, a political appointee to the departments of education and justice in the Reagan administration. The gory video on its website AbortionNO.org leaves no doubt about the organization's motto: "graphically exposing the injustice of abortion." In Canada, the centre has been at the heart of student disputes at Toronto's York University and the University of Calgary; in the latter, the Canadian Constitution Foundation provided legal counsel to U of C's pro-life club, which had displayed the centre's graphic billboards despite a warning from the administration. Dave Quist's remarks come from a 2009 ECP Centre conference.

I attended a service at Saint Matthew's Anglican Church in Abbotsford in December 2008. Professor James I. Packer's criticisms of the official Anglican hierarchy in Canada have been reported widely; Packer also wrote the foreword to a self-published book on the Anglican schism by Reverend Ed Hird entitled *Battle for the Soul of Canada: Raising up the Emerging Generation of Leaders*.

Information on the Liberal outreach effort to evangelicals and Catholics is based on a 2009 interview with Toronto MP John McKay. Reports about the government's refusal to fund KAIROS emerged in early December 2009, when a spokesperson for Bev Oda, the international minister of cooperation, declared that KAIROS no longer fell within the priorities of the Canadian International Development Agency. Two weeks later in a speech to the Global Forum for Combating Anti-Semitism in Jerusalem, Immigration Minister Jason Kenney claimed that the Canadian government had "articulated and implemented a zero-tolerance approach to anti-Semitism. What does this mean? . . . We have defunded organizations, most recently like KAIROS, who are taking a leadership role in the boycott (of Israel)." KAIROS is made up of representatives from the United, Anglican and Presbyterian churches as well as the Evangelical Lutheran Church in Canada, the Canadian Conference of Catholic Bishops and the Mennonite Central Committee.

Accounts of the New Democrats' Faith and Social Justice Commission are based on reports on the party's website and Dennis Gruending's blog. Karen Armstrong's quotation about the symbiosis between the religious right and repression comes from *The Battle for God: A History of Fundamentalism* (Ballantine, 2001). The Evangelical Fellowship noted the "lack of policy gains" under Stephen Harper's government in its August 2009 report, "Canadian Evangelical Voting Trends by Region, 1996–2008." Lloyd Mackey has written about the grant to a seniors housing program run by Chuck Strahl's Missionary and Alliance Church in Chilliwack, B.C.

Information on Trinity Western University's leadership program in China comes from two interviews with Don Page. The Cypress Leadership Institute was established by Chinese economist Dr. Zhao Xiao, who is featured in *God Is Back: How the Global Revival of Faith Is Changing the World* by John Micklethwait and Adrian Wooldridge (Penguin Press, 2009); on a 2009 trip to the United States, Zhao's only public appearance was a speech at Patrick Henry College, where he claimed China now boasts 180 million Christians (compared to the government's estimate of 30 million).

Accounts of the government's attempts to block John McKay's private member's bill imposing regulations on Canadian mining companies doing business abroad appeared in the *Globe and Mail* in November 2009. Reports on the crisis at Rights and Democracy, the human rights agency once run by former NDP leader Ed Broadbent, appeared in the *Toronto Star* on January 24 and 28, 2010, and the *National Post* on January 23, 2010. Vice chairman Jacques Gauthier, a government appointee, is not only the lawyer for the International Christian Embassy in Jerusalem, but recently wrote his doctoral dissertation on Israel's legal right to its claimed territories.

Chris Hedges's commentary appeared in "Letter from Canada: The New Christian Right" published in the *Nation* magazine on November 27, 2006.

INDEX

MARCI McDONALD is one of Canada's most respected journalists. The winner of seven gold National Magazine Awards, she is also the recipient of the Canadian Association of Journalists' investigative feature award. A former bureau chief for *Maclean's* in Paris and Washington, she has interviewed Ronald Reagan, George Bush and Bill Clinton, and spent five more years in the United States as a senior writer for *U.S. News & World Report*. A winner of the Atkinson Fellowship in Public Policy, her study of the backstage machinations behind the Canada-U.S. free trade deal led to her book *Yankee Doodle Dandy: Brian Mulroney and the American Agenda*. Her controversial cover story in the *Walrus*, "Stephen Harper and the TheoCons," inspired this book.